OUR STORY
HISTORY

UNCHAINED AND LIBERATED FROM

FRANKIE O. FELDER, Ed.D.
FOREWORD BY ORVILLE VERNON BURTON
Author of *In My Father's House are Many Mansions: Family and Community in Edgefield, South Carolina*

Copyright © 2021 by Frankie O. Felder
Cover art by Robert Carter
Book cover and interior design by Asya Blue Design
Edited and proofread by Susan Bruck
Indexed by Meridith Murray (MLM Indexing Service)

All rights reserved. In accordance with the U.S. Copyright Act of 1976, the scanning, uploading, and electronic sharing of any part of this book without prior written permission of the author constitute unlawful theft of the author's intellectual property.

Strange Fruit
Words and Music by Lewis Allan
Copyright © 1939 (Renewed) by Music Sales Corporation
All rights outside the United States controlled by Edward B. Marks Music Company
International Copyright Secured   All Rights Reserved
Used by Permission
Reprinted by Permission of Hal Leonard LLC

"Strange Fruit"
Written by Lewis Allan
Published by Edward B. Marks Music Company
All rights administered by Round Hill Carlin, LLC

Scripture quotations noted are taken from the Holy Bible, King James Version.
Copyright ©1982 by Thomas Nelson, Inc.

All quotes from *The Negro in the Civil War* by Benjamin Quarles, copyright © 1953.
Reprinted by permission of Little, Brown and Company, an imprint of Hachette Book Group, Inc.

Published in the United States of America

ISBN hardcover: 978-1-7363779-0-1
ISBN paperback: 978-1-7363779-1-8
ISBN eBook: 978-1-7363779-2-5

African American – Family History. 2. History – Civil War. 3. South Carolina – Families. 4. Mississippi – Families. 5. Louisiana – Families. 6. Texas – Families. 7. Genealogy. 8. United States – Race relations.

Edelweiss Publishers, Anderson, South Carolina

Printed in the United States of America

DEDICATION

Written for

APRYL, my daughter, who did not know the love of her father, Robert,
and has had to manage that void in her life;

TYREE, my father, whose definition of father came from experiences with his own absent father;

MY SIBLINGS, who like myself, never knew much about our relatives;

PRESIDING ELDER S. P. FELDER, my great-grandfather, who somehow
left too few clues about his family;

SGT. ISAAC FELDER, my great-great-grand-uncle who fought for our freedom;

JOSEPH and SUSANNAH, my great-great-grandparents, who were born
into slavery somewhere, and

ALL my other ancestors who lived on American soil and whose bills of sale
I will never find, for I do not even know their names.

A SPECIAL DEDICATION TO

DR. ANNE S. BUTLER
June 23, 1948 – May 3, 2013

Former Director of CESKAA: Center of Excellence for the Study of Kentucky African Americans, Kentucky State University

With heartfelt memories of "Anne's Counter" (her kitchen counter in Kansas) that we would literally hop up on and hold lengthy discussions about motivation, persistence, goal setting, and just getting it done!

Always inspiring each other to just get it done!

CONTENTS

Acknowledgements i
Manuscript Special Notations (How to Interpret Relationships) v
Foreword vii
Preface xiii
Introduction xxiii
Chapter 1: Afraid of My Roots? 1
Chapter 2: Felders in South Carolina 7
Chapter 3: Three Sides of an Uncivil War 35
Chapter 4: Antique Trunks 75
Chapter 5: But Not Hulbert 131
Chapter 6: Patterns and Legacies 165
    Religion 166
    Education 187
    Economic Empowerment and Property Ownership 209
Recalling OURstory 219
    OURstory in Louisiana 220
    OURstory in Mississippi 222
    OURstory Profile in Courage 227
Conclusion 239
Appendices
Appendix A: Ancestry.com DNA Test Results 247
Appendix B: Land Office Records of Select Mississippi and
    Louisiana Felder Property Holders 249
Appendix C: Number and Size of Farms/Plantations, 1860,
    for Louisiana and Mississippi 251
Appendix D: Property Ownership of Martin N. Hulbert 253

Appendix E: Number of Felders in the United States by Census Year 255
Appendix F: The Significance of April 257
Appendix G: Birth and Death Chart of Select Family Members 259
Photo/Illustration Credits 269
Index 271

ACKNOWLEDGEMENTS

I want to thank so many who have assisted me with this research. This journey has been long, arduous and winding, exhilarating and frustrating, conclusive and inconclusive, and I leave it knowing that there is so much more that I do not know and many answers I have not uncovered. Nonetheless, I am grateful for the gifts of time and perseverance to have pursued this project and for all who contributed to making this a manuscript reasonably complete such that I can share what I have learned so far. My journey began at the Mississippi Department of Archives and History, and I particularly want to thank the staff there, especially Ms. Anne L. Webster, author of *African Americans: A Mississippi Source Book* (2001) and co-author of *Tracing Your Mississippi Ancestors* (1994). Ms. Webster provided me with the initial direction I needed to get started researching my family in the state of Mississippi. I am likewise grateful to the staff of the South Carolina Department of Archives and History who provided guidance in locating information about the first **Felder** family that came to America. I very much appreciate the help of Lawrence Nichols, former human resource director at Clemson University, who introduced me to his friend, Mr. Tillman Whitley, owner of the Jacqueline House Museum in Vicksburg, Mississippi. After visiting with him at his museum in Vicksburg, Mr. Whitley was so kind as to send me a completed copy of a wonderful document, *Multum in Parvo*, from which I learned much about the A.M.E. Church in Mississippi, and which to my delight, included information on my own great-grandfather. Mr. Ronny Taylor, Chancery Clerk, Amite County, Mississippi, taught me how to locate, read and interpret indexes and copies of wills, probate, and other documents contained in the courthouse in Liberty, Mississippi. I appreciate the guidance of historian, Ms. Ruth Ann Butler, founder of the Greenville Cultural Exchange Center in Greenville, South Carolina, who provided examples of digging deeper into what information is available online and uncovering more than one ever knew existed in cyberspace! Rev. Dr. Grady Butler provided excellent resources for understanding the history of the role of the black church in the evolution of the literacy and social responsibility of African Americans post-slavery and the historic relevance of the church to the black race.

My research led me to the Library of Congress where Ms. Sibyl Moses assisted in identifying what was and was not available there. In the very small community of Greensburg, Louisiana, the Chief Deputy Clerk of the Court, Ms. Denise Godfrey, and her staff, Melissa Akins and Mildred Cyprian, Clerk of Court, were extremely helpful in locating documents in the files, Xeroxing materials, and explaining the system for documenting marriages and marriage bonds in the 1800s. Mr. Wesley Blades, the tax assessor, gave me a personal tour around the town of Greensburg in 2002. Dr. Marco Giardino, historian and NASA engineer at the Infinity Science Center, Pearlington, Mississippi, provided information about research on Possum Walk Trail, Logtown, and suggested the best sources to

tive as a descendant of slaves, shines a different light on the Felders of South Carolina, Mississippi, Louisiana and Texas.

Instead of learning history from books historians write, most people learn their history from monuments and statues and from houses or parks designated as historical by governments or towns. But, for African Americans curious about their history, even some public history sites were inaccessible before the Civil Rights Act of 1964. To illustrate the point, in 1953, when Gray Line Tours ferried visitors to South Carolina's Fort Sumter National Park site from the Fort Sumter Hotel, the tour boat operator refused entry to a group of African American visitors, claiming that the boat had been chartered. While the National Park Service confirmed with the concessionaire that Fort Sumter was a federal site and that should not have happened (to which he agreed), the damage was done to those citizens, and we cannot know how many more incidents of this nature may have occurred. Moreover, it is only recently that Fort Sumter and other national parks have refocused Civil War sites to include slavery and race as a part of that history.[ii]

Historian Yael A. Sternhell warns that "historians of the United States tend to look through archives, but rarely at them." She believes archives "lie at the center of our work as historians . . . define and differentiate us from fellow humanists, give credence to our claims for knowledge, and enshroud our narratives with an aura of truth."[iii] One reason our professional historical interpretation and the general public's understanding of history was so wrongheaded about race relations for so long is that sources from African American perspectives were not available to historians. Illustrative of this point was the preservation of the inspirational history of the Penn Center located on St. Helena Island in South Carolina – the first school founded in the South by abolitionists exclusively to educate former enslaved people. The facility later served as a crucial meeting place during the Civil Rights movement, hosting the Southern Christian Leadership Conference's Citizenship Schools. It even continues today as a community center. Yet, around 1963, about the time of integration of Clemson University and the University of South Carolina (USC), the Penn Center papers were offered to USC's library with the stipulation that the collection be open to all researchers. USC rejected the papers because they did not want African Americans researching in their archives. Thus, when I was writing *Penn Center: A History Preserved*, I had to travel to North Carolina where these incredible historical records are now archived in the Southern Historical Collection at the University of North Carolina instead of in South Carolina where they should be.[iv]

In addition to the lack of primary sources on, about, or from African Americans to enable alternative interpretations and perspectives from the amply-available white-based sources, there were very few perspectives from African American historians. One reason for that lacuna was segregation in the South. Seven years after the Supreme Court had decided *Brown v. Board*, in his 1961 presidential address to the Southern Historical Association, University of Kentucky historian Clement Eaton argued for desegregation. Dr. Eaton was widely criticized in newspapers. At the Association's annual

---

ii Fort Sumter Records, 1953, Fort Sumter National Monument Archives, held at Charles Pinckney Historic Site, Mt. Pleasant, South Carolina.

iii Yael A. Sternhell, "The Afterlives of a Confederate Archive: Civil War Documents and the Marking of Sectional Reconciliation," Journal of American History, vol 102:4 (March 2016): 1025-1050; quotes page 1025.

iv Orville Vernon Burton, Penn Center: *A History Preserved* (Athens: University of Georgia Press, 2014). The librarian at the time was Alfred Rawlinson. Speculation is that the rejection of the papers came from higher up in the University of South Carolina administration.

graphic designer, transformed all of my hand-drawn charts, maps, tables, and family trees into computer illustrations. It was a pleasure to get to know them all. I am honored to have found Heather Carter and to have collaborated with the Carter Fine Art Services on this project. Robert Carter, artist extraordinaire, understood my book concept and transformed it expertly into a representation of my feelings as well as my desire to communicate our history across generations. I have expanded my family in this venture! My editor and proofreader, Susan Bruck, was invaluable as a second set of eyes, and proved the point of the necessity of this step in preparation of a book for publication! Enabling a reader to quickly locate desired information is impossible without an accurate index. The index that Meridith Murray created brought organization and accessibility to a very complicated group of ancestors, their locations, and their activities! Without Asya Blue, interior and jacket designer, I would only have a manuscript suitable for filing. Her vision and skills transformed these words and illustrations into an inspiring work of art. I am so grateful to all of these highly-skilled professionals.

The opinions of noted faculty have been invaluable. Drs. Cameron Bushnell, David Blakesley and John Morgenstern were all ears and advice steering me towards resources when I was all questions and confusion! I am honored to have the Foreword written by Dr. Orville Vernon Burton, a scholar of immense reputation in the field of southern history, a man with sensitivity to the experiences of African Americans who lived in some of the South's most notorious places, and a researcher who began his studies of race relations in the South since his days as a doctoral student at Princeton. Historian Arlin Migliazzo and Journalist Berkley Hudson have inspired me through their eagerness to hear about *OURstory* and have encouraged me by sharing their experiences of researching, writing, and teaching about the interactions of people across cultures who meet under circumstances not of their making, but who must then make life work. Historian Justin Behrend's approval to reference his conference paper on the 1876 election provided clear evidence of racism's impact on Mississippi African American's participation in the freedoms gained by the Emancipation, Constitutional amendments, and Reconstruction. The unique Pointe Coupée, Louisiana Creole culture and community became evident through my conversations with local historian, genealogist, and 11th generation Creole resident, Brian Costello. And, historian Stephen Chicoine has become a friend, cheering me on with his knowledge and advice about self-publishing, as well as his enthusiastic response to read my manuscript and provide comment. Finally, former Louisiana news anchor, George Sells, shared insight regarding race relations and the distinctive early culture of Livingston Parish, Louisiana. I am indebted to all of these eminent scholars, writers, journalists and professors.

The knowledge that Dr. Frank Smith, director of the African American Civil War Museum in Washington, D.C., has about the United States Colored Troops (USCT) and their contributions in the Civil War is astounding. I am so honored to have met this scholar who has spent an inordinate amount of time developing this museum into a national treasure. His staff member, Marquett Milton, so expertly, and proudly, tells the stories of the black soldiers and heroes of the war, detailing people and places as they pertained to black Americans. I particularly thank him for lending his image to represent those soldiers as I honor **SGT. ISAAC FELDER**, my ancestor, my Civil War hero.

There is no library like that at Clemson University. The reference staff have always been available to answer questions, locate materials, and allow me to continuously check out books even when I was living in South Africa, and even during the pandemic!

To all of my friends in South Carolina and South Africa planning book signings without even seeing one word that I had written – I thank you for your support and encouragement! You have made me keep going when I really wanted to quit!

Finally, sitting at "my table" in Cracker Barrel off I-85 in Anderson County, South Carolina, where I would often go on wintery Saturday mornings to write by the fireplace, I was so encouraged by three servers, Cherith, Melanie, and Chris, who continuously checked on my progress ... "Hurry up and finish! I can't wait to read this! How long has this been now – three years?!" I thank each of them for their enthusiastic interest. Little did they know that by then it had been a 13-year journey! Little did I know that five more years were to come.

MANUSCRIPT SPECIAL NOTATIONS

In this story, names of individuals, be they black or white, are **CAPITALIZED** and **BOLDED** to denote a direct and verified family relation. For example, the name, **ALEXANDER HULBERT**, my biological grandfather, is always bolded and capitalized. Below I have included an alphabetized listing of some key relatives identified in this text and their <u>biological relation (or relation by marriage) to me specifically</u>, from which others may identify their relationship with these same individuals.

FELDER	**RELATION TO AUTHOR**	**HULBERT**	**RELATION TO AUTHOR**
IDA	Great-great-aunt	**ALEXANDER**	Grandfather
BEATRICE	Paternal grandmother	**BYRON M. (B. M.)**	Great-grandfather
CHIQUITA	Aunt	**JAMES**	Uncle (half)
DIANAH	Great-great-great-great-great-grandmother	**JOSEPH, JR.**	Great-great-great-great-great-grandfather
EMMA	Great-grandmother	**MARTIN NATHANIEL**	Great-great-grandfather
ISAAC	Great-great-grand-uncle	**PARMELIA**	Great-great-great-grand-mother
JOHN	Great-great-uncle	**ROBBIE**	Aunt (half)
JOSEPH	Great-great-grandfather	**SINAI**	Great-great-grandmother
KORRINE	Grand-aunt	**JULIAN**	Great-grand-uncle
MARTHA	Great-great-great-great-grandmother	**CALEB**	Great-great-great-grand-father
NATHANIEL	Great-great-uncle	**MARILYN**	Cousin (half)
SARAH	Great-great-great-grand-mother		

SIMON	Great-great-uncle		
SONA	Great-grandfather		
SONNY	Great-great-great-grandfather		
SUSIE	Grand-aunt		
SUSANNAH	Great-great-grandmother		
TYREE	Father		
WILDA	Paternal great-grandmother		
ADAM	Great-great-great-great-great-grandfather		

As you read this narrative, you will find that as some individuals are introduced for the first time, a portion of their name is set aside in quotations. I have used this to identify the name by which the individual chose to be called and was thus known. For example, **Henry "David" Felder**, will be discussed using his preferred name, **David**. It was rare that Jr. (Junior) was appended to names in the 1800s, and at times even when this was done, it did not necessarily connote that the individual was indeed a "junior," sharing the name and DNA of the "Senior" (Sr.) holder of the same name. Many names in the early years repeat themselves incessantly throughout and across generations making it quite difficult to read or tell a story and keep individuals separate. For example, there was a **John "Henry" Felder**, father, and **John Henry Felder**, son. Years later, many others in their extended family would honor **Henry Felder** and his name would be added to scores of descendants' names. Fortunately, when father and son lived and moved throughout Orangeburg, South Carolina together, they became known as "**Henry**" and "**John**," respectively, and are *[thank goodness!]* identified in this narrative accordingly after their initial introductions. As demonstrated here, all names of **Felders** and other primary individuals associated with the surnames incident to this research (**Felder**, **Hulbert**, **Ellis**) are bolded but lower-cased denoting individuals with this surname from the extended families who are presumed to be associated with our story but not necessarily a documented, verified direct relative.

FOREWORD

It is with enthusiasm that I greet my friend Dr. Frankie Felder's *OURstory: Unchained and Liberated from HIStory*. I taught the American South for thirty-four years at the University of Illinois before I retired and returned to my home of South Carolina, where I met Dr. Felder, who was Senior Associate Dean of the Graduate School at Clemson University when I joined the Department of History there in 2010. I appreciate very much the effort that she has made in getting her family's history told.

When I published my study of black and white families and community in a rural southern town, *In My Father's House are Many Mansions: Family and Community in Edgefield, South Carolina* (1985), historians were unaware that there were sources and historical records that contained the narratives or the materials that allowed a different interpretation of black Americans in the American South. Recent studies of African Americans and their families parallel the circuitous and complicated history of freedom, Emancipation, and race relations in the United States. Time, and change over time, are fundamental in understanding race in America. African slavery and Jim Crow prevailed for 300 years. They have been gone for just over 50 years.[i] Counting a generation as 25 years means that 12 generations of white supremacy have flourished but barely two generations have existed trying to overcome it. This is significant in that the passage of generations means the passage of heritage – twelve times, while the efforts to effect change has happened only twice.

Although the significance of American history is seen differently by differing groups, that does not mean that all interpretations are equal! Facts need to be real. "Alternative facts," that is, those without evidence, are not historical. In what historians now call "postmodern" history, we agree that interpretations are constructed, but it matters significantly *of what* the narrative or interpretation is constructed. Dr. Felder's *OURstory: Unchained and Liberated from HIStory* expands our own thinking in this regard. Historians, genealogists, and students of family history will benefit from the innovative research and fact-laden story she presents.

To construct accurate historical narratives, we need a variety of sources, and we actually need a variety of general interpretations of historical events. Usually the definition of who is "us" and who is "they" changes the story; aptly demonstrated by Dr. Felder's explanation of the African proverb, "until the lion learns to write, the story of the hunt will always glorify the hunter." Felder looks at the Civil War through three lenses – the North, the South and the African slave and freed people of color. *OURstory: Unchained and Liberated from HIStory* demonstrates the value of making accessible a variety of interpretations of events. The story of her southern family, written from her perspec-

---

i I use the 1660s and 1968 as the marking dates. 1660s: although Africans arrived in 1619, historians generally agree that the system of hereditary slavery as opposed to bonded or indentured service arose early in the second half of the 17th century. 1968: passage of the three major modern civil rights laws, Civil Rights Act of 1964, Voting Rights Act of 1965, and Fair Housing Act of 1968. From 1968 to 2021 is 53 years.

tive as a descendent of slaves, shines a different light on the Felders of South Carolina, Mississippi, Louisiana and Texas.

Instead of learning history from books historians write, most people learn their history from monuments and statues and from houses or parks designated as historical by governments or towns. But, for African Americans curious about their history, even some public history sites were inaccessible before the Civil Rights Act of 1964. To illustrate the point, in 1953, when Gray Line Tours ferried visitors to South Carolina's Fort Sumter National Park site from the Fort Sumter Hotel, the tour boat operator refused entry to a group of African American visitors, claiming that the boat had been chartered. While the National Park Service confirmed with the concessionaire that Fort Sumter was a federal site and that should not have happened (to which he agreed), the damage was done to those citizens, and we cannot know how many more incidents of this nature may have occurred. Moreover, it is only recently that Fort Sumter and other national parks have refocused Civil War sites to include slavery and race as a part of that history.[ii]

Historian Yael A. Sternhell warns that "historians of the United States tend to look through archives, but rarely at them." She believes archives "lie at the center of our work as historians . . . define and differentiate us from fellow humanists, give credence to our claims for knowledge, and enshroud our narratives with an aura of truth."[iii] One reason our professional historical interpretation and the general public's understanding of history was so wrongheaded about race relations for so long is that sources from African American perspectives were not available to historians. Illustrative of this point was the preservation of the inspirational history of the Penn Center located on St. Helena Island in South Carolina – the first school founded in the South by abolitionists exclusively to educate former enslaved people. The facility later served as a crucial meeting place during the Civil Rights movement, hosting the Southern Christian Leadership Conference's Citizenship Schools. It even continues today as a community center. Yet, around 1963, about the time of integration of Clemson University and the University of South Carolina (USC), the Penn Center papers were offered to USC's library with the stipulation that the collection be open to all researchers. USC rejected the papers because they did not want African Americans researching in their archives. Thus, when I was writing *Penn Center: A History Preserved*, I had to travel to North Carolina where these incredible historical records are now archived in the Southern Historical Collection at the University of North Carolina instead of in South Carolina where they should be.[iv]

In addition to the lack of primary sources on, about, or from African Americans to enable alternative interpretations and perspectives from the amply-available white-based sources, there were very few perspectives from African American historians. One reason for that lacuna was segregation in the South. Seven years after the Supreme Court had decided *Brown v. Board*, in his 1961 presidential address to the Southern Historical Association, University of Kentucky historian Clement Eaton argued for desegregation. Dr. Eaton was widely criticized in newspapers. At the Association's annual

---

ii Fort Sumter Records, 1953, Fort Sumter National Monument Archives, held at Charles Pinckney Historic Site, Mt. Pleasant, South Carolina.

iii Yael A. Sternhell, "The Afterlives of a Confederate Archive: Civil War Documents and the Marking of Sectional Reconciliation," Journal of American History, vol 102:4 (March 2016): 1025-1050; quotes page 1025.

iv Orville Vernon Burton, Penn Center: *A History Preserved* (Athens: University of Georgia Press, 2014). The librarian at the time was Alfred Rawlinson. Speculation is that the rejection of the papers came from higher up in the University of South Carolina administration.

meetings, African American scholars like the great historian John Hope Franklin, even when presenting papers, could not stay at the segregated hotel where the convention met. Just like USC, southern state libraries and archives were segregated. Dr. John Hope Franklin recounts in his autobiography, that in 1939 when he arrived in Raleigh at the North Carolina State Archives to research his Harvard Ph.D. thesis, archives' director, Dr. Christopher C. Crittenden, himself a history Ph.D. from Yale, told Franklin he needed a week to make segregated accommodations. When the eager graduate student looked surprised by this, Crittenden said he would only need half a week. Dr. Crittenden provided Franklin a key to the archives and set up a desk for him inside the archives so that white archivists would not have to assist Franklin. Within a few days, when white researchers expressed jealousy of Franklin's arrangement and insisted on receiving a key to the collections also, the director moved Franklin into the regular research room.[v] Fortunately, accessibility to archives is no longer governed by antiquated rules of segregation and *OURstory: Unchained and Liberated from HIStory*, reflects the extensive use of university, state and national archives in South Carolina, Georgia, Mississippi, Virginia, Washington, D.C., and Louisiana.

Since the advent of the World Wide Web in 1989, companies like Ancestry – which offer subscribers access to their massive database of historical records – have made it easier for black families to begin researching their genealogy. The success of PBS's highly celebrated television series, *Finding Your Roots*, hosted by Harvard literary critic and filmmaker Dr. Henry Louis Gates, Jr., reveals how these online databases can help uncover lost ancestral histories. In the same spirit of *Roots* and *Finding Your Roots*, *OURstory: Unchained and Liberated from HIStory* documents the author's quest – and challenges – to discover her family's history.

Genealogists are fond of saying that when the ancestors wish to be found they will guide you in your quest. From a tiny genealogy room of the Harriette Person Memorial Library in Port Gibson, Mississippi, Dr. Felder's ancestors launched her on a pilgrimage of discovery. Felder's genealogical journey is composed of, and complicated by, multiple layers of silence: the silence of white slaveholders; the silent voices of generation upon generation of enslaved ancestors; the silence of family secrets concealing unpalatable truths, revealing half-truths, and discarding unpleasant memories.

Despite experiencing the genealogist's and historian's greatest frustration – the absence of a paper trail to connect dots – Dr. Felder crafted a microhistory that embraces standard genealogical research techniques and the science of DNA with traditional research methods to weave the Felder family's story through the complicated malaise of the historical southern African American experience in the United States. She brings to life both the frustrations and joys of genealogical research, laying out the difficulties of finding ancestors behind the 1870 Census wall, as well as sifting through documents trying to verify first names and surnames that differ from one census to the next for the same person. She also conveys the exhilaration of discovery, for example, the emotions generated upon finding a marriage notation for Joe and Suzannah Felder, connecting her past with her present in the reference book, *Mississippi-Louisiana Marriages, 1800-1900*.

OURstory: Unchained and Liberated from HIStory is more than a genealogical case study grounded in Interactive Pedigree Charts and Generational Family Tree Charts populated with the names of

---

v Clement Eaton, "Professor James Woodrow and the Freedom of Teaching in the South 28 (February 1962), 3-17; John Hope Franklin, Mirror to America, pp. 83-84.

aunts and uncles and many degrees of cousins. It is the story of an African American family navigating through slavery up to and including obstructions erected by Jim Crow America. She traces the tumultuous years of southern communities between 1800 to 1865 that her ancestral survivors of slavery (Adam and Dianah, Joe and Suzannah, Martha, Sonny and Sarah, Mary Jane and others whose names are still unknown) experienced, and opens doors of history of education of blacks in the South to the general reader through the rise of her ancestors' descendants as they passed through the doors of Rosenwald Schools and Historically Black Colleges and Universities. Felder sketches a roadmap of a family that rose from slavery, through Reconstruction, Jim Crowism and finally in the late Nineteenth Century, came to embody the concept of the "New Negro," a phrase made popular during the Harlem Renaissance by novelist Alain LeRoy Locke.

Genealogy needs history and history needs genealogy. *OURstory: Unchained and Liberated from HIStory* helps to give voice to a segment of American society that mainstream history circumvented or ignored all together. Through an artful use of illustrations, photos, maps, charts and graphs to augment, and at times, simplify the narrative, Felder places her family within the context of the African American experience, merging history and genealogy in her accounts of the trauma-laden years and southern communities in which they lived. Chloe Felder cooked on a large plantation in Magnolia, Mississippi. As a Pullman Porter on a rail line in Mississippi, Sonny Felder served as a lifeline between the segregated South and the more progressive North, bringing news of a better way of life and opportunities outside of rural Mississippi. Beatrice Ottowiess Felder, residing in a community founded exclusively by and for African Americans in 1887, built a school in the middle of the Great Depression and worked as a newspaper correspondent for the Mound Bayou, Mississippi *Southern Advocate*. And, while she does not include herself in this narrative, Frankie Ottowiess Felder became the first African American dean at Clemson University.

African American history and genealogy does not exist in isolation; thus, Felder also explores the family history and experiences of the white Felder family as their lives intersected with the African American Felder's, enslaved and free. Finally, she tells the darkest secret held in her family of the great-great-grandfather she never heard a word about – and why. During this journey of discovery, Felder addresses how the South's very dark period of American history has changed in her lifetime and she offers hope for the future in the victories of the past.

Orville Vernon Burton

Judge Matthew J. Perry Jr.
Distinguished Professor of History, Sociology and Anthropology,
Pan African Studies, and Computer Science
Clemson University

Family

biological relations . . . clan . . . parents . . . children . . . cousins . . . aunts . . . uncles . . . community support . . . siblings . . . shared responsibilities . . . kindred spirits . . . unconditional love . . . kinfolk . . . togetherness . . . adopted relations . . . blended groups . . . my people . . . my tribe . . . my lineage . . . my genealogy . . . Who is my family?

AFRICA

Uprooted from Africa – OURstory twists and turns.

F. O. Felder, May 2019, Cape Town, South Africa

PREFACE

"Without a past there is no future."

— AMITE COUNTY HISTORICAL AND GENEALOGICAL SOCIETY NEWSLETTER, FEBRUARY 2012

The Impetus

My heart pounded with excitement as I carefully retrieved the dusty 12" x 15" cardboard box from the back shelf in the moldy-smelling closet where the century-old documents had been stored out of the way decades ago. My dad thought that his grandfather had been born in Baton Rouge or Scotlandville, Louisiana, but he was not really sure. Knowing that Daddy's life was quickly ebbing away with a terminal illness stirred in me a dedication to the task of searching for this tidbit of family history in order to provide whatever joy possible and to obscure the thoughts that I assumed emmeshed my dying father's mind on an hourly basis. His prognosis was five months left to live. If correct, by April, I would be fatherless.

About a month prior to this trip to Greensburg, the extremely rural Louisiana community without even a traffic light in town, I happened to be passing through Port Gibson, Mississippi, driving back from a recruitment trip to Alcorn University, a historically black college known for its famous alumni like slain Civil Rights leader, Medgar Evers, and Alex Haley, acclaimed author of *Roots, The Saga of an American Family* (the book that motivated many African Americans to begin to search for their African ancestors). I had learned while on campus that this small but beautiful university, spread across acres of lush green hills, had been built prior to the Civil War for the sons of wealthy white Mississippians. The rules of slavery precluded blacks from formal education. In fact, it was a crime punishable by severe, brutal acts to teach a slave to read. But, after the Confederacy lost the war, the college was given over to the African American community, which, by that time, was the majority population in the state.

While in Port Gibson, out of sheer curiosity, I drove to the local library, nestled between other stores, restaurants and churches on Market Street. The building had an odd combination of historic red brick on the upper level and hauntingly dark green doors sandwiched between an off-white stucco façade on the lower level, as if trying to convince prospective patrons that a 21st century Christmas present was hidden in this clearly antiquated town reminiscent of days long gone. Other than the outrageous bursts of pinks and reds of the bougainvillea lining many of the streets, and the heavy dark wood of the library floor, everything else in downtown Port Gibson felt white. I did not have any particular research question. I had never been in Port Gibson. When I entered the tiny room reserved for genealogy and Mississippi history, I was simply curious as to what I might find there. I stood for a moment surveying the room of books, which could not have been larger than the 9' x 10' bedroom I slept in with my oldest sister as a child in Petersburg, Virginia for five of my first nine years of life. I had a choice of sitting at one of two wooden tables, each surrounded by four heavy wooden chairs. My mind raced with questions now.

Someone had left a book out on the table where I chose to sit, so I picked it up as a starting point. "What's in this book?" I wondered? The title made me shiver: *Mississippi-Louisiana Marriages, 1800-1900*. Could it be possible that I would find any clue in this book? Surely not – my ancestors were slaves. I opened the book to the index and saw some unfamiliar **Felder** names. I wrote them all down, as there were only four – **Felder** being a very uncommon surname. Sitting, staring for a bit at the information I found, I recalled a sentence from the African Methodist Episcopal (A.M.E.) Church history book that said my father's grandfather, **REV. S. P. FELDER**, was the son of **JOSUF** and **SUSAN**. That's all I knew. I looked again at the names I had recorded and realized that one listing indicated **JOE** and **SUZANNAH** were a "colored" couple that married in St. Helena Parish, Louisiana in 1869. "**JOE** and **SUZANNAH**! Oh, my goodness! That's them! *Is this them?!* Is that **JOSUF** and **SUSAN**?!" I cried out loud knowing instinctively that I was looking at the names, and marriage dates, of my father's great-grandparents – people he knew NOTHING about in a place he knew NOTHING about. I was so glad no one was in the room besides me.

I made a special trip back to Greensburg, Louisiana, where all the official records of St. Helena Parish were kept. The space in the courthouse set aside for preserving the county's vital records was so small that the staff, untrained "archivists," merely pointed visitors to the storeroom where the documents were kept. One simply browsed alone, and if lucky enough to find a relevant document, asked for instructions on how to use the somewhat outmoded Xerox machine to make copies. The assumption was that once finished, the patrons would return these historic, century-old documents back to the closet!

If I recall correctly, the box was labeled "1801-1879." The records were not in any logical order, probably the result of many researchers like me thumbing through the files. Each record was contained in a standard business envelope. Handwritten on the outside of the envelopes were the names of individuals whose records they contained. After fifteen minutes or so an envelope appeared, "**FELDER, JOSEPH** and **SUSANNAH**." I trembled. I cried even before I opened the envelope to ascertain that the correct document was contained inside. I hesitated, cupped my hands over my nose and mouth and took a deep breath. With tears already streaming down my face, I slowly opened the envelope and slid the onion-skin thin crumbling paper out and laid it on the table in front of me. I had chills. I couldn't stop my tears. I'm tearing now just remembering the overwhelming feeling.

I read each line as if I had just learned to read – very slowly, enunciating under my breath each syllable. My eyes came to rest on the most poignant piece of information contained on the document. A whole story told by the simple "X" that **JOSEPH FELDER(S)** placed where his signature should have been. He could not read. I guess intuitively I should have realized that this is what I would find, but I did not think about it. The "X" is the only mark on that document that is etched in my mind, but the experience of seeing it – recognizing the reality that my great-great-grandfather was a slave and by that time had not had the opportunity to learn something as basic as how to read or sign his own name, and there sat I, his descendant, with a doctorate from Harvard, blessed in my life beyond any semblance of possibility in his – haunts me to this day.

I knew immediately in my heart that I was a beneficiary of **JOSEPH's** life and whatever he experienced on the dusty roads of Greensburg in the 1800s. I knew then that I had to tell this story. Not just the story of finding this document (and the many others that, over the years, would mysteriously fall into my lap), but the story of the lives of my ancestors who presumably came from Africa to America, and those born here whose strong bodies, minds, and constitutions made the bricks, laid the bricks, cut the timber, hauled the logs, nursed the babies, fed the animals, planted the tobacco, shucked the corn, harvested the sugar cane, and picked the cotton that made the American South prosperous. When I was in Port Gibson in that library, I knew also that I was being led divinely to the information I needed. Silently I said a prayer: "Thank you, God, that my great-great-grandparents had the opportunity to marry! Thank you for guiding me to this place. Thank you that my great-great-grandparents survived slavery. Continue to lead me to what I am supposed to know."

I copied the document, noticing how little crumbled pieces of the edges of the fragile paper were left on the Xerox machine as I folded it to return it to its envelope. "Crumbled pieces of our story," I thought to myself, not knowing that I was beginning a long road ahead to locating traces of information here and there. I picked up the crumbs of paper and slid them into an envelope that I had brought for myself. Similar to Hansel and Gretel, I imagined that our ancestors left crumbs – clues – of where they had been, not so that they could return home but so that someone could find them by beginning at the end and working backwards to the place where this all started. I knew that I was that someone. But as I would soon discover, unlike Hansel and Gretel, others removed the crumbs and placed stones in their place – stumbling blocks for our ancestors on the "stony road" to freedom and stumbling blocks for their descendants trying to write their story. I took the cardboard box back to the storeroom and just sat at the table in the workroom for a while to collect myself and calm my emotions before heading off to the post office to mail what I knew would be a beautiful surprise for my father, who had no idea that I had even gone to Louisiana in search of his grandfather's birthplace.

The Legacy

Everyone's family has a history that, if known, I believe, would provide the pride and motivation to develop qualities of greatness, and lead those who come after to seek success and to live a life of service to mankind. Much family history is lost as young and old fail to communicate across generations with one another about life experiences and lessons learned. I never knew, for example, that my paternal grandmother, **BEATRICE OTTOWIESS FELDER**, from whom I received my middle name, **OTTOWIESS**, was as fiercely an independent, vocal, and opinionated educator as I am until I found numerous articles written by her in *The Southern Advocate*, the local newspaper of the town in which she lived. In one column she wrote in 1940, she admonished everyone she thought had *remotely* participated in the gossip around town about herself, spurring these remarks:

> ... I AM NOT HEADING AN OUSTING CAMPAIGN at all. I am not an aspirant for the post office job. When I want a political job, I will make my announcement in the proper manner. I still reserve my citizenship rights which include the right to express my opinions. I still play my game with my hands above the table, and if I sign anyone's petition I will not sneak a letter out to the appointing powers telling them to disregard my signature. Now those of you who think a change is needed at the post office come out but from behind my skirt and say so; for I refuse to be named cadir [sic] of a band of sneaking, spineless, undependable, would be politicians.[vi]

In a similar vein, I spoke my mind to the entire student body at Virginia Commonwealth University in 1972:

> ... Now to you students out there: Convocations are planned for you – but where were you when the brother walked out on the speaker? I was greatly disappointed in the turnout we had at convocation on Tuesday; in fact, I am always disappointed in the student turnout. But what is most disgusting to me are those of you who yell the loudest (complaints) and work the least. Are you aware that five people are preparing to plan all of your convocations for next year? Are you aware that three of those five people will be graduating in June? Are you aware that one of those five is an administrator? Are you aware that all of those five are black? Are you aware that on club night, Lecture-Concert Committee stood in Monroe Park begging for people to join – to help – to organize? Are you aware that your money, not ours, is being spent for convocation speakers and that we are solely responsible for that choice of speakers? Are you aware that unless YOU – the students – get on the ball, Lecture-Concert Committee is going to become a clique just as so many forces on our campus have become?   ... as chairman of the committee I am really concerned that unless you students swallow some of your apathy and run off some of your laziness, your mouthing about our choice of speakers for next year will be to no avail. Specifically, what I am asking you to do is – JOIN![vii]

Needless to say, I was quite amused when I found my grandmother's article – and equally amused when I found mine, as I certainly had forgotten about writing it! All I could think was, "Oh my goodness! Now I know where I get it from!" Sadly, I did not know until conducting this research that my grandmother's father was a highly respected and incredibly influential minister in the A.M.E. Church in Mississippi – a career, though female, I, too, considered pursuing off and on over the course of my teenage and early adult life, but never knew why I was so inclined. Nor did I ever know that my father was the president of our elementary school's PTA (Parent-Teacher Association) – a role I assumed at my daughter's high school for two of her four years there (president one year; vice president another year). What else, I wonder, is there in the history of my family that has permeated my parents' and

---

vi Beatrice Felder, *Southern Advocate*, vol. 7, no. 25, April 6, 1940, 1.

vii "Miss Felder urges students 'swallow apathy,'" *Commonwealth Times*, volume 3, no. 26, February 24, 1972, accessed May 22, 2009, http://dig.library.vcu.edu/cdm/landingpage/collection/com. Permission to print provided by VCU *Commonwealth Times*.

ancestors' life experiences and their childrearing philosophies and practices – or my genes – that has influenced me to develop into the person I have become?

Although my journey into finding my ancestors initially began in 2002 with the intent to divert my father's full attention from his diagnosis of a terminal illness, my research quickly evolved into a curiosity to know from which African country I am a descendant. An African colleague from the Democratic Republic of the Congo said he felt like Ancestry.com's analysis of my DNA sample matched me perfectly, that I indeed "looked like" someone from the Ivory Coast (4% Ancestry DNA match) or Cameroon (29% Ancestry DNA match). My Egyptian friends insisted that with my bone structure, facial features, and complexion, that surely I was their "sister," although no DNA match to Egypt was identified by Ancestry.com's analysis. Yet, I had an odd childhood affinity for reading everything about the pyramids of Egypt and Egyptian culture and religions.

It has occurred to me – what if I, an African American woman, discovered that I am descended from Cameroon ancestors as my DNA analysis – and Oprah's and Condoleezza Rice's – suggest? I'd be in good company with awesome distant cousins! Or, what if I could trace my Irish (8% Ancestry DNA match) ancestors to Oscar Wilde, infamous author (brilliant but with a checkered past) who penned among many, *The Picture of Dorian Grey*, the 1891 novel that gripped the literary world with a controversial story of good and evil that is still considered one of the best 100 novels ever published? Or, what if my purported Cherokee ancestors can be traced to Sequoyah, creator of the Cherokee alphabet and written language? Would any of these discoveries impact my self-perception, my self-esteem? Would I speak with pride as my family physician does when he tells me that he has traced his wife's ancestors to the Mayflower voyage to America? I do not know the answers to these questions because, as I write this preface, I do not have a clue about my family lineage, but my intuition and my brief foray into psychology lead me to an affirmative inclination. In a very unscientific manner – through my "gut instincts" – I conclude that young people would draw upon and continue the positive legacies of their family histories if they only knew what they were.

I remember as a child my father reading the *Bible* to my sisters and me and reading bedtime stories about Brer Rabbit and the Sly Fox. I continued Daddy's bedtime ritual with my child by reading stories to her every night, first *in utero*, then every night after she was born until she began to learn to read on her own; then she had to read bedtime stories to me. I took her to get her first library card at the local public library when she was six years old. When we took long trips (like to Virginia for Christmas), I would have my daughter read books to me while I drove. We talked about the stories. We often even made up stories along the way. And, throughout the entire 18 years that she lived at home, we spent untold hours together browsing around in libraries and bookstores engrossed in the many stories – real and fancied – that books tell. Even as adults we attended a wonderful weekend authors' conference together.

When my daughter became a mom, she and her husband read bedtime stories to **JORDAN** until he could read. At the age of eight he began to read himself to sleep. When "Grandma Frankie" read to him, I required that we take turns – I would read a page or become a character – and then he would read the next page or become the next character. Later, brother **JULIEN** at age two or so became the recipient of the night-time family reading ritual handed down through at least over

Gladys reading

half a century in the **FELDER** family – selecting his own book before hopping into bed, and sometimes asking his big brother, or any adult available, to read it to him.

My father, **TYREE PRESTON FELDER**, began a tradition in our family that left a legacy that I hope will continue as a key component of the education and socialization of extended **FELDER** family children for generations in perpetuity: he taught us to value education. However, there are more legacies – good and bad – that were passed down from ancestors, some of whom we knew, some of whom we only heard stories about, and most of whom we never even heard of until this research brought them to light. While I treasure the memories of night-time storytelling and *Bible* reading, and all the moral lessons learned from these experiences that continue to influence me even to this day, I wish to uncover and pass on other significant lessons from our family history that will help strengthen the resolve, and guide the destinies, of our descendants *ad infinitum*. I wish to contribute something to our family that has never been established before now – a documentation of who we are. I leave this to our family and hope that these discoveries will facilitate family conversations, prideful revelations, introspection, and commitment to becoming one's most excellent self.

The Search

I am a "**FELDER**" due to my paternal grandmother's decision to legally reclaim her maiden name for herself and her teenage children. Technically, my father was born a **HULBERT**. As such, this research is bifurcated, including both **FELDER**, my father's mother's paternal line, and **HULBERT**, my father's paternal line.

In searching for the origin of **FELDERs** in America and attempting to locate information on my relatives in Mississippi, the only place I ever associated with my father's family, I spent an inordinate amount of time reading the history of South Carolina because, purportedly, the first **Felder** to enter the country, **Hans Heinrich Felder**, settled his family in Orangeburg, South Carolina. His son and other descendants became very influential citizens in the South Carolina "low country" (from Columbia south and east in the state), and those who moved to Mississippi, Louisiana, and Texas, likewise, assumed roles of significance in the settling of those territories. Much is written about these individuals, among them – **John**, **Henry**, **Samuel, Sr.**, and **Abraham Felder**, all of whom remained in South Carolina; **Peter**, **John**, **Aby Jane** and **Charles**, all of whom moved to Mississippi; **Gabriel**, who first moved to Mississippi but ultimately settled in Texas, and **David**, who moved to Louisiana. These **Felders**, all members of the same extended family, contributed to the early settlements of whites in these states.

However, absent from the *hi*stories of these early southern settlements is essentially *any* mention of the contributions of the **Felders** of color; the slaves that these **Felder** men and their families "owned," or the freedmen that they later became. Thus, the more I learned about the white **Felders**, the more poignant the realization that I was learning absolutely nothing about the experience and lives of the black **Felders** – my relatives. An April 2000 Ancestry.com message board note states the following: *"Ancestry.com has an interesting slave narrative that mentions Mr. Sandel and his **Felder** son-in-law. To view it, click on the narratives index on the main page at Ancestry.com, then type SANDEL into the search field ... interesting.. .Geezz... I hope I don't get into trouble for this :o)."* The unavailable documentation on the **Felder** slaves, clearly intentionally omitted in a conspiracy of silence as this message verifies, has motivated me to persist with this research and to travel to the relevant states, cities, and towns to search for answers to enable me to begin to uncover why a more complete story is not told of what really happened on these farms and plantations as the U.S. slowly stretched its boundaries westward to the Pacific.

The quote introducing this preface, *"[w]ithout a past there is no future,"* comes from the front page of the Amite County Historical and Genealogical Society's Newsletter, (February 2012, volume 8, number 2), which ironically features in the column, "Bits and Pieces of Amite County History," the family of **Dr. Charles F. Felder**. I had known about **Dr. Charles F. Felder** for 13 years before finding this newsletter. However, it took me the entire 13 years to realize who **Dr. Felder** was in relation to my family. Only by sitting at my desk with mounds of unrelated papers, books, and notes scribbled on the backs of any little piece of paper I could find when my notebook was not handy – pre-cell phone and tablet days – did I discover a tidbit of information that seemed to relate to some other tidbit that I had previously recorded. Crumbled traces of our story most of them turned out to be. Reviewing every piece of information collected over the then 13 years of this project for a supposedly final time before bringing this daunting search to conclusion, on one exciting evening – February 10, 2015 – I spliced together two crumbs of information and realized that **Dr. Felder's** first wife, Ann O'Neal, was the daughter of the slave "owner" of my father's great-great-great-great-great-grandmother – the oldest relative found to date, whose name I still do not know, but a piece of whose story I was just getting ready to uncover! To learn that she was purchased from a slave ship in New Orleans and brought to Amite County helped me to establish that several families from South Carolina – the O'Neals, **Felders**, Vaughns, Leas, Sandels, Bonds, Everetts, and Raborns – were all a part of a close network of extended family and friends living in Amite and Pike counties, and indeed were all associated with the relatives I had been seeking. As such, the seemingly unrelated stories I found about individuals from these families were threads in the tapestry of my own search. Intuitively I knew this many years before and had said as much to my father – I just had no proof. More accurately, in hindsight, I had the proof but could not assemble the puzzle!

The plethora of family histories and genealogical societies' newsletters written extolling the virtues of cities, towns, communities and local people, biographies and novels *[some true, some not, most embellished]* weaving tales of old, reenactments of Civil War battles and Revolutionary War battles, and so on, reflect the importance in people's minds of the significance to *their* self-preservation of knowing *their* history. As such, I found this research experience to be incredibly energizing but nonetheless frustrating to believe that at one moment I had found the answer to a given question, or that I had at least uncovered a source for the answer, only to discover that my search led me only to white **Felder's** records and *his*tories, which omitted any references to the slaves or "chattel" they had bought. So, my question is simply: If one truly believes that, "*[w]ithout a past there is no future,*" then why the continued omissions about the slaves that made these families so wealthy, the slaves that were obviously extensions of these families, the slaves that all too often left the plantations with their former "owner's" surnames? Surely not to obliterate the possibility of prosperous futures for these black men and women! I thank the Lord that while my search has indeed been stifled by these secrets, it was never aborted.

"The True History of Our People"

Our history as a people was all but lost until the decade of the 1970s when an explosion of African Americans embarked on the scholarly study and documentation of black history, possibly inspired by John Hope Franklin, W. E. B. DuBois, Benjamin Quarles, and other early historians whose scholarship was excellent but read by limited audiences. The emergence in the 1970s of Afro-, African-, Black- and Pan-African studies departments in colleges and universities has contributed significantly to the scholarship that has been devoted to the unearthing of a more comprehensive and more accurate history of blacks in America. Yet even with the proliferation of recent scholarship, far too few of us black Americans have delved into our collective history, and even fewer have engaged in writing our individual family histories. Because of widely-acclaimed and televised movies and documentaries such as Alex Haley's 1976 *Roots: The Saga of an American Family*, and Dr. Henry Louis "Skip" Gates' PBS documentary series, *Finding Your Roots*, African Americans are realizing the very important task of learning our history from multiple perspectives – first by identifying who, in fact, our ancestors actually were; second, by gathering objective detail *[original source information]* about what *really* occurred historically in the lives of our ancestors; and third, most importantly, by telling these stories from our own perspectives – as Chief Michell Hicks of the Eastern Band of the Cherokee Nation termed it when we met, telling the "true history of our people"[viii] – or as I will now say, coining a phrase for fun, "telling *OURstory*" *(pronounced with a confluence of German and southern: ahh sto' ry)*!

I have come to have a newfound appreciation for historians. Without having personally engaged in the research process, it is nearly impossible to understand the tediousness with which this type of research must be conducted to not overlook critical variables or data located in original source materials or gleaned from personal interviews, and even more importantly, to not misinterpret that which is found. As I conducted historical research on several topics for presentations I made at the Conference of Southern Graduate Schools' (CSGS) annual meetings of graduate deans, I came to conclude this about history: history happened – but how it is told depends upon the storyteller. At each presentation I make now that has a historical backdrop or focus, I make this statement because I think it is crucial that we understand the biases that are *naturally* inherent in, and often *unnaturally* (consciously) inserted into, the narratives that are told about this country and the people who have made it what it is today. History vs *his*tory. Note the use of both terms throughout this book. They intentionally convey very different meanings.

My writing, likewise, understandably and unfortunately, projects biases. I abhor the idea of slavery. I hate it that some of my ancestors were slaves. And thus, in this story I tell of our **FELDER** and

---

viii Meeting with Chief Michell Hicks, Eastern Band of the Cherokee Nation, August 1, 2014.

HULBERT journey over the past 150 years, my biases will be revealed also through my choice of vocabulary, my choice of phraseology, my tone of voice, and my choice to include – or exclude – information that I discovered. But, at no time will there be an attempt to obscure facts, hide realities, or fabricate or embellish the narrative. Nonetheless, at times the reader will find that I may inject my opinion, interpretation, explanation or correction into this narrative – set aside in *[square brackets and italicized, and on a rare occasion, bolded]*. At times the reader will sense my anger; at other times, my pride. But most importantly, I hope the reader will recognize the essence of this historical narrative and will be able to imagine the emotions and experiences of these ancestors as their lives unfolded in the era of their existence.

An African proverb says that "*[u]*ntil the lion learns to write, the story of the hunt will always glorify the hunter." This story glorifies neither the hunt nor the hunter because, unfortunately, the lion could not write, and the hunter hid the truth. But as the new hunter, I feel humbled to be able to present at least a miniscule piece of *OURstory* – unchained and liberated from *his*tory.

The Documentation

Despite the very real possibility of the encroachment of bias in our writing, the very important task of beginning to help reclaim, clarify, and preserve our stories as best we can by taking the time to write down what we do know about our ancestors, our living relatives, and ourselves remains before us all, I believe, a task significant to intragroup African American pride and success. Particularly in black families is there a need to document who we are. Mississippi native author, William Alexander Percy, expressed an incredulous perspective of blacks relative to documenting *OURstory* in his 1941 book, *Lanterns on the Levee*. Humorously his comments had an unintended impact – they inspired black Americans in Greenville, Mississippi to begin a serious documentation of their lives in that city. Percy said: "This failure on their *[African Americans]* part to hold and pass on their own history is due, I think, not so much to the failure to master any form of written communication as to their obliterating genius of living in the present. The American Negro is interested neither in the past nor in the future, this side of heaven."[ix] While this is obviously a highly insulting and inaccurate exaggeration of a total falsehood, it did then and somewhat unfortunately now reflect a quasi-reality of the tradition in the black community of "oral history" and the state of our scholarly writings about who we are as a people.

Consequently, I am hopeful that you, the reader, will be inspired to begin to record the contributions that you have made and are making to your families by the traditions and practices you establish in your lives by recognizing that despite the challenges of my search, I made some progress. Little pieces of information are what weave together the stories of our lives. I encourage you to keep scrapbooks, or digital journals, of your children's activities. Save their favorite toys from their childhoods. Record their successes and note a few of their failures. Keep a journal of your own experiences as parents and employers or employees. Collect newspaper accounts of family members' involvement in political, social, religious, and educational issues. Choose someone in your family to become the family historian – store pictures and videos with dates, complete with *full* names (especially of the women who get lost in documentation after marriages) – and hopefully one day, a hundred and fifty years from now, your

---

ix Levye Chapple, Sr., *History of Blacks in Greenville, Mississippi*, 1868-1975, Hykt 4-5, 1975, Foreword.

great-great-grandchildren will not spend untold hours as I have, wondering and researching who you were, what you contributed in your community, how you came to be yourself, and the impact of your life on theirs.

I am so grateful that God led me to begin this research and guided me through not only the conclusion of the research but, more importantly, through the documentation of the discoveries. I am just sorry that my father did not live to see the completed project, initiated at the discovery of his illness and the inception of treatment in his battle with lung cancer – already at stage four – but completed only now, 18 years later. His prognosis was nearly exact. Daddy died on April 30, 2003.

INTRODUCTION

Context: State of the States and Places

I believe that it is important to understand who we are as a people and as individuals in historical and cultural context. My search for my relatives led me immediately to the recognition that knowing their names would mean absolutely nothing except that I could fill their names in a Family Tree Chart. I wanted to know more: who they were, where they lived, what they experienced. What did they stand for? What did they fight against? What was important to them? Why did they become the people they became? What circumstances did they have to manage in their lives? What lessons did they try to teach? What legacies did they leave? Am I following in their footsteps?

In attempting to research some of these questions, having initially no one to ask who knew much or who would share what they did know about the answers, I read all that I could find that provided insight into the happenings in the counties and cities of South Carolina, Mississippi, and Louisiana – the primary residences where I located **Felders** and **Hulberts** that I assumed were likely associated with my family, and I attempted to place the people I learned about in the circumstances with which they must have dealt on a daily basis. Fortuitously, I traveled on occasion to these states on business and met people who could augment what I already knew. I spent innumerable hours in state archives reading microfilm and microfiche copies of local newspapers and church minutes, plantation diaries and genealogical histories from other families, theses and dissertations and other books about virtually every aspect of life and history of the periods in the states in which I was seeking my relatives. I drew heavily on these primary and secondary sources, and of necessity, this narrative cites and references many sources in the attempt to provide the reader with a reasonably accurate sense of the social, economic, and political conditions of the state – what I will reference as the "state of the state" and the "state of the place" – as well as the people who inhabited them.

I buried myself in libraries and bookstores, reading material I would have never touched in earlier years of my life. And the more obviously interpretive the narrative was that I uncovered about the "*his*tory" of these states, particularly local *his*tories written by the family and friends of the pioneers who settled them, the more factual (original source) documents I wanted to locate. By this I mean that this research adventure has fully concretized into a belief what was once only a perception that I held previously, and that is that h-i-s-t-o-r-y happened, but how it is told depends on the storyteller, and because of this, h-i-s-t-o-r-y often becomes *his*tory. The comprehensive, honest tale of life in the South, particularly during slavery when cameras were not plentiful, continues to reverberate with romanticized recollections of life on the plantations and the bravery of the soldiers – both northern and southern – during the Civil War. Hollywood has biased our abilities to see the South as the complicated malaise of complete contradictions that it was *[and still is]*, and many family memoirs embellish accomplishments and dare not mention misdeeds.

Unfortunately, this manuscript does not provide a comprehensive, unbiased tale either, particularly because *OURstory* of the **Felder** and **Hulbert** slaves and 19th century ancestors is nowhere written nor is there even an oral version of *OURstory*. Except for a couple of slave narratives gathered during the important research on slavery contributed by the Works Progress Administration (WPA) in the 1930s, I am unable to integrate disparate experiences I have learned about into a story with which I feel comfortable to be even reasonably representative of the reality of my ancestors' lives. As such, I can only postulate on the black **Felder** and **Hulbert** ancestors' experience, extrapolated from analyzing the limited documented stories of the white **Felder** and **Hulbert** families and the histories/*his*tories of the communities in which they lived. I have chosen to do very little postulating, leaving it to the reader's imagination to discern what life might have been like in the circumstances described.

OURstory in History

This family research reaches back into the early 1800s and concentrates on providing a descriptive narrative reflecting some of the realities and routines of these people and their communities, which obviously contributes to the history of those places. An unanticipated theme that emerged from this research is that everyone is a part of history. Although scholars, journalists, and news reporters may not have determined the lives of common community members to be noteworthy for inclusion in published narratives, every person in those places played a role in shaping the social progress of their communities. Unsung heroes existed everywhere. Slaves were unsung heroes – the builders of the South. Freedmen were unsung heroes – the survivors of the South.

Having conducted this research, I feel assured in saying that residents of South Carolina, Mississippi, Louisiana, and Texas during slavery, Reconstruction, and the Jim Crow eras all have different perspectives of what happened. I am convinced that what *really* happened has never been quite told because much of the published literature, just like real life in much of America, remains intentionally segregated. This especially includes most of the family *his*tories that have been written and sit on library shelves in the genealogical rooms across the American South. Fortunately, some families have progressed to the point of truth telling and have begun to share shameful secrets. *Slaves in the Family* by Edward Ball provides a laudable attempt to tell the type of stories that I believe need to be told.

It has taken me 18 years to research and write this story of who I am ... a **FELDER**. I have discovered that mine is a story of slavery and bravery; property rights and civil rights; patterns of destruction and patterns of instruction; Jim Crowism and activism; Biblical misappropriation and prayerful supplication. It is a story that angers me and one that empowers me. It is my story, but it is your story, too, if you are American. *OURstory*, as I call this narrative, is my attempt to show the relevance of *his*tory to the present state of blacks in this country who descended from that cruel institution of American-style human bondage – slavery. Because *OURstory* was pruned from the branches of the **Felder** and **Hulbert** family trees, I invite anyone knowledgeable to add to this story, to help clarify, correct and more comprehensively write what clearly is an intermingled, although calculatedly concealed, history of **Felders** (and **Hulberts**) in the South.

Family Tree

ancestry . . . sprawling roots . . . stalwart trunks . . .
broken branches . . . scattered leaves . . .

FRANKIE FELDER'S FAMILY TREE

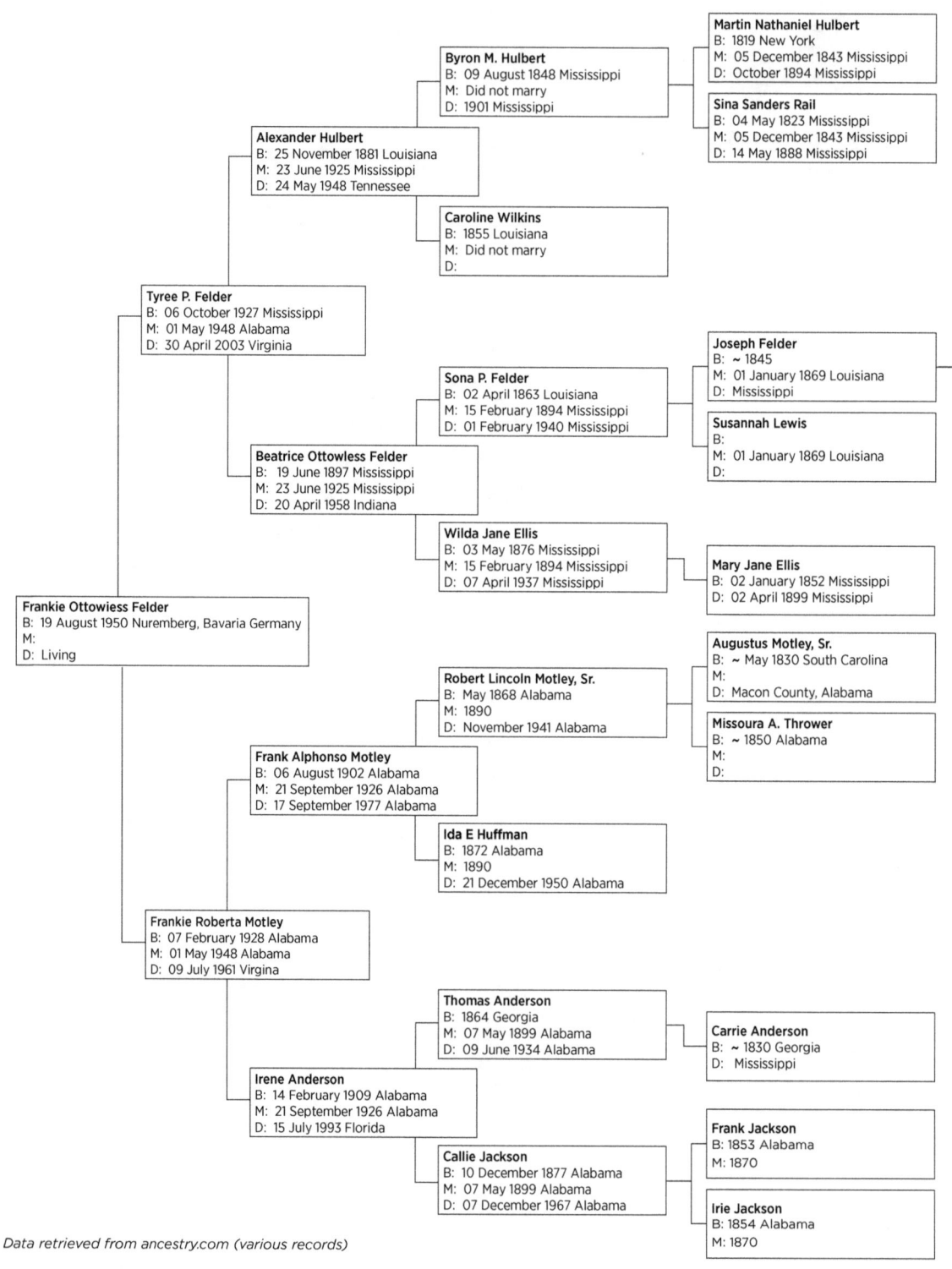

Data retrieved from ancestry.com (various records)

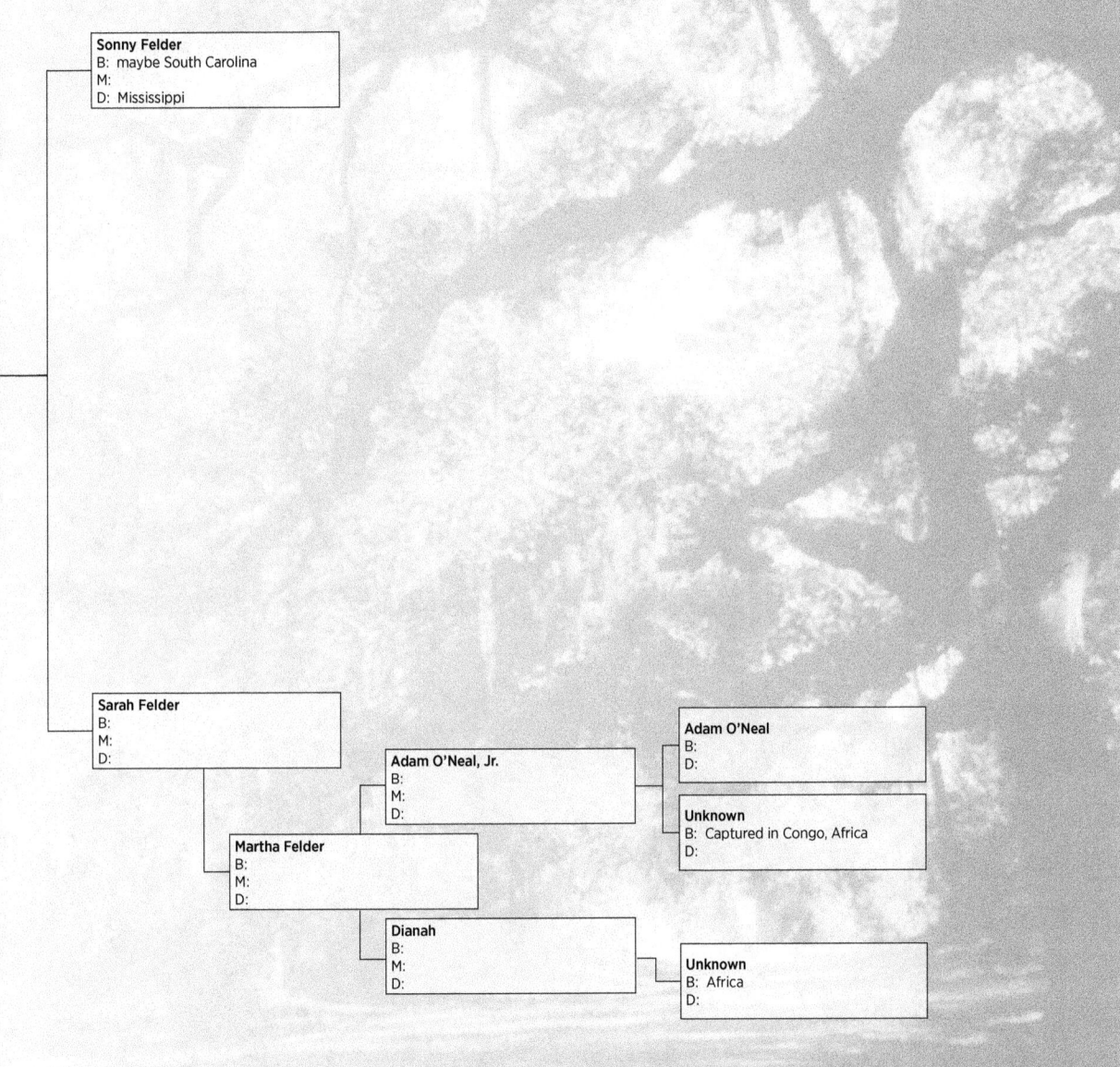

xxvii

"*Afraid of roots and depths, we have no tree, no height.*"
— **ARNOLD KENSETH**

F. O. Felder, February 2017, Greenville, South Carolina

1 | AFRAID OF MY ROOTS?

My father was born in Mississippi, my mother in Alabama, and most of my sisters in Virginia – all states with *his*tories that I, as a child growing up in the 1950s and 1960s in Petersburg, Virginia, had little interest in studying. First, what was being taught in the schools did not teach me much about myself, a black American, and second, what I experienced first-hand related to race relations left absolutely no positive impressions on my perceptions of southern *his*tory, and certainly did not encourage me to seek out the ties that bound me to localities, people, or institutions in any of these states.

My last name, **FELDER**, I have known since my childhood was of German derivation and meant "fields." I was born in Nuremberg, Germany, the second daughter of a young army soldier and his wife, and so I always felt a special kinship with my last name. My dad had a beautiful Hershey-chocolate-brown complexion, baby-fine, wavy hair and Indian features. My mother was extremely fair – "high yellow" as it was then called in the black community – with fine cottony hair and a nose so sharp that as kids we used to tease her and call it a "chicken nose." Her father's eyes were gray; her mother's eyes were blue. Her grandmother was full-blooded Cherokee, so we had always been told. I had heard that Mound Bayou, the town in which my father grew up,

Daddy

Mother

1

Granddaddy Motley

was in the poorest county in the Mississippi Delta. I had never heard anything else about this town. I had heard that my mother's father was a "root doctor" in Tuskegee, Alabama. What did that mean? I had never met another person other than my sisters, my father, and his mother who carried the same surname and was related to me. In fact, I had never met another **Felder** at all, black or white, until at the age of 28, I moved to Kansas and hired a young lady, Vickie Felder, to work on my staff at Kansas State University. Vickie was African American and from South Carolina.

I knew that the Confederate flag flew over both states of my parents' childhoods – Mississippi and Alabama. I had seen the Ku Klux Klan in Virginia where I grew up and experienced fear as an innocent nine-year-old child who did not comprehend why they would burn a cross in our churchyard or, more frighteningly, in our yard at home. I participated in the picketing of Petersburg's Woolworth's lunch counter. Our beloved pastor, Rev. Wyatt Tee Walker, left us at Gillfield Baptist Church and joined Rev. Martin Luther King and the Civil Rights Movement in Atlanta. I refused to wear the Confederate rebel mascot pin on my high school band uniform. I did not go into any of the Confederate buildings on our high school senior class trip from Suffolk to Richmond. I recognized in myself a real hesitancy – almost a fear – to speak up, initially, to white students and faculty on matters of race at the predominately white university I attended in Richmond.

At the onset of this project, I had lived for 15 years in South Carolina, where the Civil War began, where staunch segregationist Strom Thurmond died without ever publicly acknowledging his black daughter, where the Confederate flag flew over the statehouse, and the Legislature and citizens debated annually about its proper location – in a museum or "in your face."[1] The flag ended up "in your face" on the statehouse grounds, where it reminded us all of South Carolina's influence in race relations in the South. As I neared the conclusion of this project, a very sick young man, to whom I give no deference to even mention his name, in efforts to rekindle "a race war," gunned down nine innocent African Americans in Emanuel A.M.E. Church's basement in Charleston, South Carolina, after joining them on June 17, 2015 in their Bible study and prayer meeting. Ten days later, a courageous young African American, Bree Newsome, in defiance to this sick man's act, boldly climbed up the flag pole on the State Capitol grounds in Columbia and cut the Confederate flag down! I contributed to the GoFundMe campaign to pay her legal expenses. So, why not be afraid of my roots?

My complexion and features resembled my mother's. Intuitively I knew my family history was convoluted, complete with storm-tossed leaves, broken branches and decayed roots that reached from way down south on some plantation and all the way to somewhere in Africa. Something in me always embraced Africanism or Afro-Americanism, even though I knew virtually nothing about most

---

[1] "Confederate Flag Removed from S.C. Statehouse," *Los Angeles Times*, July 2, 2000, accessed July 5, 2015, http://articles.latimes.com/2000/jul/02/news/mn-47061.

of the African countries or its people, as we were not exposed to Africa in school. Although I had never been there, I bought books as a teenager about the pyramids in Egypt and often read about their construction. My first oil painting was of King Tut. I looked, some said, a bit like Angela Davis with my Afro, big earrings and Army jacket that I used to wear to class at Virginia Commonwealth University when I was among the first black students in 1969 to attend that institution in Richmond. I was not militant, *per se*, but James Brown's song, "Say it loud, I'm black and I'm proud!" energized my mind. I am not sure I was proud to be "black" – the term being relatively new and not yet "politically correct" even among us "Afro Americans" or "Negroes" or "coloreds" as we were still confusedly being categorized – and even calling ourselves – in the '60s and the '70s. My step-grandmother, "Nana," always talked about the "colored" people. I never liked that. Even so, I felt proud to be me, and I was black, so James Brown's song made perfectly good sense to me, and I embraced it and all that it appeared to mean. I filed for divorce from my first husband like a true angry African American woman, but I had actually married in ancestral "African style," in the Bahamas, invoking the wisdom of our ancestors through simile and verse, African proverbs, music, and invitations to our guests to join us in jumping the broom. I had my gown made in Kenya and shipped to me and invited everyone who attended our wedding to wear African attire – including our white and German relatives and friends – and they did.

A very strong message that permeated the black community, which was taught to us as young children, was that we had to be "twice as good as white people" to be successful. I did not know exactly what that meant because I had not met any white people except the insurance salesman and his children, but nonetheless, I spent many hours practicing and trying to perfect everything I was to do – my homework, the piano, the saxophone, the speeches I made in church and at school, and the songs I sang in the various choirs that I joined. I was taught about excellence, not for the sake of understanding the concept, but as a means of survival. "Good" work in my family was never good enough if you could do better. I received recognitions and awards and assumed leadership positions in virtually every organization of which I was a member. I was an honor student all throughout school. I was selected as "The Most Outstanding Graduating Senior" from my undergraduate institution – the first African American to receive this distinction. I earned two master's degrees. I earned my doctorate from an Ivy League institution, Harvard University. Yet, through it all, a persistent message from the white community to successful blacks like me that I heard time and time again, even from well-meaning professionals, my peers and mentors, was that I "was not like all the rest." I was "different," by which they meant "better." That

Me in college

always insulted me. I received it as an unconscious attempt at psycho-social racial genocide, and I never fully embraced white people who made this type of blundering intended compliment to me. Thank God that I came from a well-grounded family, which understood that education *[and light skin, which made a lot of the whites around me more comfortable with me than with some of my friends and colleagues]* did not make one "better." Education, we were taught, made one knowledgeable and it made one competitive. Skin complexion was irrelevant. I inherited these values.

While conducting research for this manuscript, I flipped through a book, *Southern by the Grace of God*, which had at least one statement in it to which I could personally relate. In explaining why he wrote his book, the author recalled from his childhood a verse of Scripture from the *Bible* wherein God said, "My people are destroyed for a lack of knowledge." (Hosea 4:6). I wholeheartedly agree, and it is likewise the basis for which I committed to completing this project as well.

So, what does any or all of this say about me? That I am a black person who has been afraid, or ashamed of her roots, or that I am a black person who has pretended to be proud of her roots? Actually, I have concluded that it says none of the above. Instead, after much personal reflection during the evolution of this research, I came to realize that I have been a black person who knew *absolutely nothing* about her roots. Thus, with unbridled enthusiasm, but a cautionary sense of expectation, I began digging.

UNEARTHING FELDER

The introduction of surnames in Germany occurred in the late Middle Ages to help identify families by distinguishing their places of residence. The primary professions at the time were agricultural in nature and family names translated literally into either the nature of the specific form of agriculture in which a family engaged or the specific location in which they lived. For example, Bauer and Baumann meant "farmer"; Weide as in Fullenweide identified a pasture; Baumgaertner and Gaertner recognized a "gardener" or one who worked the "orchards"; Pflug or Pflueger meant "plowman"; Schweighof identified a "cattle farm"; and Feldmann or **Felder** identified a "field man."[2]

From this general description of the use of surnames in Germany, one would logically conclude that the **Felder** name originated from a family that toiled in the fields as farmers or agriculturalists, with little to no blood connection to nobility or feudal lords and who lived far removed from the castles that perched atop the German mountains or dotted the Rhine River. Surname introduction in Germany reasonably supports the assumption that **Felders**, generally speaking, were industrious, hard-working, and productive members of their communities, unaccustomed to being handed life on a silver platter, but were inculcated, instead, with the value of earning one's way through life. If this holds true, then I expect to not find palatial plantations on which our **FELDER** ancestors lived.

According to the 1740 immigration records, there was one **Felder** in America. He lived in South Carolina. An analysis of select U.S. census data reveals other interesting facts about **Felders** in this country. In 1840, 87% of all enumerated **Felders** (whites were enumerated only) lived in three states: 55% in South Carolina, 29% in Mississippi and 3% in Louisiana. In a little over a hundred years

---

[2] George F. Jones, *German-American Names* (Baltimore: Genealogical Publishing Company, September 2006), 31.

from the arrival of the first **Felder**, the 1850 U.S. Slave Census enumerated 1192 slaves "owned" by men with the **Felder** surname (spelled exactly), but 1576 slaves "owned" by all men with surnames of slight variation (which could represent spelling errors of the census enumerators), rendering the latter the correct number of slaves "owned" by **Felder** men. By 1880, the second U.S. census that enumerated black people by name, 99.99% of all **Felders** (total of 2344) in the U.S. were farmers or associated with farm labor and more than a third (771) of all **Felders** still lived in South Carolina. At that same time, 1534 – two-thirds (65.6%) of all **Felders** enumerated in the country were black. **Felders** lived in 33 states in 1880; however, black **Felders** only lived in nine states, none further north than North Carolina nor further west than Arkansas.

Just as the Mississippi River meanders across the southern landscape, mixing the Delta's greyish brown silt with the dark brown soils of Georgia, the Louisiana pale brown loam with the black and light olive brown clays of Texas – even seeping down into the red clay of Alabama – whites from states east and north meandered across the country to Mississippi, Louisiana, and Texas, sowing seed and lightening the load, until in the 1950's, the yellowish brown loam of Virginia nourished our family tree, unintentionally exposing an entangled and expansive propagation of roots. One hundred and nine (109) **Felders** were recorded as mulatto in the 1880 U.S. census. Some of them were us, but for reasons I could never have imagined. Indeed, *OURstory* – **FELDER/HULBERT** – is truly a southern experience. And now the discovery of what that means begins ...

SOUTH CAROLINA

The fronds of the beautiful Palmetto tree foreshadowed the beginning of the end or the end of the beginning. No one could tell — they pointed in all directions.

F. O. Felder, April 2020, Columbia SC

2 | FELDERS IN SOUTH CAROLINA

Arrival in America

In 1629, Sir Robert Heath was "granted" a massive tract of land from King Charles I of England. It was called New Carolana. Later King Charles I's son, King Charles II, revoked this landgrant to Sir Heath, but he then "granted" this same land to eight of his friends – the Lords Proprietors, renaming the land Carolina. As such, South Carolina was, according to most *his*torical accounts, "owned" by these British Lord Proprietors. It was then settled by Swiss, Germans, Scotch, and Irish.[3] Included in the first influx of German-Swiss who arrived in South Carolina was **Hans Heinrich Felder** (1687-1737), who abandoned his leather tanning business in Pont-Wattwil, Switzerland[4] (four miles east of Zurich) to seek his fortunes in this new land, America. He is the first documented **Felder** in this country. Although he was born in Switzerland, some documentation suggests

King Charles II

---

3 ___, "German-Swiss and Scotch-Irish Settlements in South Carolina," *SC Scrapbook of Courtland Book Club*, 1935-36 and 1936-37, 1.

4 Julian Dantzler Kelly, "The Swiss Felder Ancestry," *Orangeburgh German-Swiss Newsletter*, Summer 1999, vol. 7, 156.

that he was of German descent from Felderin families.⁵ But, a copy of a letter in the McComb (Mississippi) public library, written in response to questions about their surname, explains that "Felderin," while used by **Hans'** wife, **Ursula Felder**, in her will, is the German practice of denoting that she was a widow, not that she was of the Felderin family. *[Ah-ha, first surprise discovery! They were Swiss, not German!!]*

The son of **Bernhardt** and **Eva (Grob) Felder**, **Hans** grew up on the outskirts of Zurich in a village called Kappel in the canton of St. Gall. At 49-years of age, he married 29-year old Ursula Zuber. Like his father (and his father's four wives), **Hans** and **Ursula** gave birth to a large family – eight children in all – but only two children (**Bernhardt** and **Johannes**) survived much beyond infancy.⁶ Both children, **Bernhardt** and **Johannes** (later Anglicized to **John**), accompanied their parents to South Carolina. Sixty-three year old **Hans** and forty-three year old **Ursula**, and their two sons (**Bernhardt**, 7 and **Johannes**, 2), were among the 250 Switzers on Captain Hugh Percy's ship, the *Samuel*, which sailed from Rotterdam, Netherlands, and landed in Charleston on July 13, 1735.⁷ They endured a treacherous 11-week voyage, sailing with passengers who died from contracting smallpox and passengers who arrived with the disease. They sailed a few days later 75 miles up the Edisto River to Orangeburgh *[original spelling]* – their final destination, a trip that took four weeks.

Jean Pierre Purry of Neufchâtel, Switzerland, was most instrumental in settling the first Swiss in the state. A bit of history about his ventures is included here for reasons later to be made apparent. In an edited and annotated publication, *Lands of True and Certain Bounty: The Geographical Theories and Colonization Strategies of Jean Pierre Purry*, Dr. Arlin Migliazzo details the succession of challenges, rebuffs, and political maneuverings which hampered, but failed to dampen, Jean Pierre Purry's enthusiastic vision and crusade to colonize South Carolina with Europeans. Rebuffed twice by the Dutch East India Trading Company, of which he was initially an employee, and then by the French, he finally persuaded the British to support his plan to settle Swiss emigrants in South Carolina in what he termed the "fifth climate zone"; regions, according to his theory, near the 33rd degree of latitude across the globe that contained the most prime soil and climate in the world, conducive to the production of crops including indigo, tobacco, corn, rice, and the silkworm. Purry quietly reasoned that not only would his colonization plan make the British Crown wealthier, it would enable him to become a part of the heretofore elusive upper elite of European society when the King would appoint him "lord" of the 600 Swiss Protestant settlers he would bring to South Carolina and then "grant" him the 48,000 acres of land he would be owed for his efforts in establishing the colony! Purry worked exhaustively to entice his countrymen to follow him to America. He wrote and distributed pamphlets extolling the riches of South Carolina awaiting those who would venture with him across the Atlantic.⁸

In 1732, Purry advertised the proposed land for his settlement being stocked full of fish, free from Indians, with capacity to grow a variety of vegetation ("vines, wheat barley, oats, peas, hemp, flax,

---

5 ___, *Felders' (Topisaw) Campmeetings: Descendants of the Founders*, 1977, 9.

6 Kelly, *Swiss Felder Ancestry*, 156.

7 Margaret G. Waters, *A Preliminary Study of the Colonial Landowners of Orangeburgh Township, SC, 1733-1749* (Savannah: self-published, 2002), 48.

8 Jean Pierre Purry, *Lands of True and Certain Bounty: The Geographical Theories and Colonization Strategies of Jean Pierre Purry*, ed. Arlin C. Migliazzo, translated by Pierette Christianne-Lovrien and 'BioDun Ogundayo, (Selinsgrove, Pa: Susquehanna University Press, 2002). For details on his colonization efforts, see 13-48.

cotton, tobacco, indigo, olives, orange, lemon and mulberry trees"),[9] easy to clear for cultivation, not requiring fertilization of the soil, on which stood stately buildings, and noble castles. He assured that "... the people of Carolina, except those who give themselves up to debauchery are all rich, either in slaves, furniture, clothes, plate, jewels, or other merchandise, but especially in cattle."[10] He re-emphasized the value of the large number of slaves: "The great number of slaves makes another part of the riches of this province. There are more than forty thousand Negroes, which are worth generally one hundred crowns each."[11] Carolina was just waiting to be settled!

Purry widely distributed his pamphlets *[propaganda]* [12] around the countryside but was quickly bombarded with questions and objections about the promises he made of Carolina. He responded immediately by rewriting his pamphlet to clarify[13] a few issues, beginning with his integrity, which had been attacked and questioned. He vowed he had only shared the solemn truth, but he agreed to respond to the many excellent questions that had been raised by the curious, but obviously interested, Swiss. In particular they wondered about the provisions that would sustain them until they became self-sufficient. They wondered about why the English were sending criminals to South Carolina if it, indeed, was such a wonderful place. Who would pay for their transport to this new land? But, forebodingly, and most importantly: would the temperatures be too hot for Europeans – particularly the Swiss? Purry, of course, provided convincing responses to each of these, and other questions, and reminded people that he could in no way have seen *everything* during his one year in Carolina! Humorously, he also mentioned a few matters that he had "been silent" on before in his first description – like the plague, crocodiles and rattlesnakes – that he thought would "frighten and discourage" those who might join him on this voyage to South Carolina![14]

Purry's persistence paid off, although he struggled for 15 years to make his dream a reality. Ultimately, he painted such vividly alluring pictures of South Carolina that they seemed almost too good to be true, but they were apparently believable enough to entice the required 600 venturers to follow him there. Jean Pierre Purry finally set sail with eager Germans and Swiss, many seeking refuge from religious persecution and poverty.[15]

Once the settlers arrived, however, indeed South Carolina *was* too good to be true! Beginning with the fact that despite his year living abroad in South Carolina prior to enlisting any settlers to accompany him, the first mistake Purry made was quite fatal. He located Purrysburg Landing near Yemassee Bluff, selected for its apparent conduciveness to trade routes,[16] unfortunately, it was also geographically sandwiched between swamps! Intolerably hot and muggy, with temperatures generally between 90° - 102°F, clearing the land was nearly impossible. In addition to the swamps, there were

---

9 Purry, *Lands of Bounty*, 137.

10 Purry, *Lands of Bounty*, 139.

11 Purry, *Lands of Bounty*, 139.

12 Purry, *Lands of Bounty*. For masterful marketing by Purry, see 137-140.

13 Purry, *Lands of Bounty*. For details on his revised descriptions of Carolina, see 147-155.

14 Purry, *Lands of Bounty*, 148.

15 Purry, *Lands of Bounty*, see 13–41 for details of recruiting efforts.

16 Josephine Shuler, "South Carolina's Other Swiss," *Orangeburgh German-Swiss Newsletter*, vol. 7, no. 4, September 1998, 85.

stagnant ponds interspersed among the useable pine lands.[17] As soon as they arrived, settlers began contracting and dying from diseases and sicknesses unknown in Europe's alpine regions – malaria, typhus, yellow fever and small pox[18] – unbeknownst to them to be caused by arthropods – mosquitoes, ticks and fleas, of which this region had an overabundance.

As it turned out, Purrysburg settlers experienced an extremely hard life. There was no minister, no books, no school, and virtually no help. It was a "wretched" community, with settlers living so far apart because of the size of their lands, like being in their "own forests," using "violent [N]egro cures" because they had no doctor. A traveling minister said every household had "the fever." Few in Carolina spoke German or Swiss-German outside of the settlers. In low country communities, because settlers who purchased slaves treated them so badly, and there were more than five times more blacks than whites, there was always an undercurrent fear that slaves were waiting for the opportue time to revolt. Settlers who had financial means left Purrysburg in droves – some to other communities in America, some trying desperately to get back home to Europe.[19]

Additionally, the British Crown reneged on its promise to provide the Purrysburg settlers with sufficient land and provisions, therefore, they had limited tools to work the land! No money as promised. Settlers were left to begging, and the Indians (who definitely were present) were *not* afraid of the settlers! The whole idea of the settlement was nearly abandoned[20] but, in fact, was not. So, despite the problems – too few provisions, challenges clearing the land, fear of the Indians, illness and death from heat and disease of most of his settlers from the first and second expeditions – Purry wove a tale that convinced even a third group of Swiss to venture to South Carolina. Interestingly, some historians describe Purry as a founding explorer; others consider him an "unscrupulous opportunist."[21] The assessment of his settlers was little different, some characterizing Purry as a liar in letters sent to friends and relatives back in Switzerland and Germany. One settler wrote to his family regarding Purrysburg, Charleston, and Carolina in general, "Let nobody hanker to come to this country! … it is a damned fraud."[22]

Jean Pierre Purry is a significant historical figure in the context of this writing for three reasons. First, although his first two settlements met with extreme failures, he was ultimately credited with furthering the concept of the township model – large numbers of people settling together around a planned community – of which Orangeburgh Township, his last settlement, became the third such community in the country.[23]

Second, the descendants of the **Felder** family that ventured to South Carolina with Captain

---

17 Robert Mills, *Statistics of South Carolina including a view of its natural, civil, and military history, general and particular* (Charleston S.C: Hurlbut and Lloyd, 1826, 1972), 658-664.

18 William Griffin, Orangeburg's Beginning, 5 and Josephine Shuler, *Orangeburg German-Swiss Newsletter*, September 1989, vol. 7, no. 4, 85.

19 Gilbert P. Voigt, "The German and German-Swiss Element in South Carolina 1732-1752," *Bulletin of the University of South Carolina*, no. 113, September 1922, 19-39.

20 Charles C. Jones, prefatory note in *Memorial Presented to His Grace My Lord the Duke of Newcastle, Chamberlain of his Majesty King George and Secretary of State: Upon the Present Condition of Carolina and the Means of its Amelioration* (Augusta, Ga: J. H. Estill, 1880), 8.

21 Purry, *Lands of Bounty*, 36.

22 Samuel Dyssli and R. W. Kelsey, "Swiss Settlers in South Carolina, December, 3, 1737," *The South Carolina Historical and Genealogical Magazine*, vol. 23, no. 3 (July 1922), 91.

23 David D. Wallace, South Carolina: *A Short History, 1520-1948* (Columbia: University of South Carolina Press, 1961), 151.

Hugh Percy were a part of the group of Swiss who settled in Orangeburg and then later migrated to Mississippi with a large contingency of their neighbors, replicating a similar settlement pattern – the township – and similar cultural expectations in that state seventy-six years later.

The third and most important reason for a discussion of Purry's ventures to South Carolina is that his story provides an instructive example of how slave trading undergirded Europeans' dreams of instant wealth and social status in America. Orangeburg was located on the 33°27' latitude, approximately one-half mile from the Edisto River and in the same climate zone as Purrysburg. The region was characterized as "subject to the fogs and deleterious vapours *[sic]* rising from swamps; and which are blown toward it by the south winds that prevail during the summer,"[24] but, in Purry's defense, this was written well after he settled his voyagers there. So unfortunately, despite the fact that the "fifth climate zone" was obviously not the best location for his settlers accustomed to the alpine air of Switzerland, he persisted with his settlement plans and pursuit of personal gain. He managed to convince prospective voyagers, including **Hans** and **Ursula Felder**, that this venture was worth the risk and that, with persistence, they would become rich. He did whatever it took to make this case.

Slavery had actually been introduced in South Carolina by the English 74 years prior to Purry's arrival; one year, in fact, after the first permanent English settlement in Jamestown, Virginia in 1670. Neither Switzerland nor Germany were countries heavily involved in the slave trade business. Three other countries – Holland, Portugal and Spain – actually monopolized the slave trade all over the world for nearly 400 years. Nonetheless, the Swiss quickly caught on.

Purry first outlined his philosophy towards slavery in 1717, in his *Memorial on the Country of Kaffraria*. Six years later, he replicated his thoughts in his *Memorial to the Duke of Newcastle* as regards settling in Carolina:

> But even if it were not possible to find some farmers, the land could in this case be farmed by slaves. ...they labor in all sorts of professions, such as tailors, shoemakers, locksmiths, carpenters, masons or others. Oboe players, violinists and musicians of other instruments used here for weddings and for other joyous festivities, are only slaves as well. Why then could we not get them used to cultivating vines, pruning trees, or other labors having to do with farming if we taught them?[25] *[As if there was no food and farming in Africa!]*

Prospective settlers boarded ships in Europe for a variety of reasons: some because they were freed from prisons and banished from their homelands; some sought freedom from religious persecution, but in the final analysis, colonizing the New World was an imperialistic, power-seeking, moneymaking venture. As did "everyone involved in the founding of South Carolina,"[26] Purry came to get rich, and, although he died in 1736,[27] only four years after his first settlers' arrival, he did gain the wealth he so desperately sought. He received the 48,000 acres of land promised, he "owned" slaves,[28] and he enthusiastically encouraged and promoted slavery as the means to sure wealth among his Swiss and German settlers.

---

24 Mills, *Statistics of South Carolina*, 662.

25 Purry, *Lands of Bounty*, 73.

26 Walter Edgar, *South Carolina: A History* (Columbia: University of South Carolina Press, 1998), 131.

27 Purry, *Lands of Bounty*, 37.

28 Purry, *Lands of Bounty*, endnote no. 70, 172.

They believed him. Disparagingly, even those seeking religious freedom to worship as their hearts desired were able to rationalize, within the context of their Christian doctrine, their schemes for claiming land that was already inhabited by more than 25 tribes of native Indians, and enslaving people – Africans and Indians *[when they could capture and subdue the Native Americans in their own homeland!]* – to do the manual labor that would enable them to become wealthy. Surprisingly, even ministers were slave "owners." Alexander Salley documented that the first minister of Orangeburgh, Rev. John Geissendanner's nephew, John, who assumed the ministerial role after the passing of his uncle, was paid "200 00 00 for slaves executed," a practice established by law to protect the investments made in this human property.[29] Even indigents, who bonded themselves as indentured servants, came to "Canaan" (as one of Purry's settlers termed it) to ultimately free themselves financially, with clear expectations of owning slaves and climbing up the landgrant ladder.

During the week (July 12-19, 1735) of the **Felder's** arrival in Charleston on the 13th, no less than five "masters" had notices in the South-Carolina *Gazette* searching for their runaway slaves, which included women and children, offering handsome rewards if returned to the "owners" and prosecution if harboring them as stowaways. Diana was still missing although she ran away June 30th. A hodgepodge of articles in the *Gazette* advertised everything from plantation estate sales, complete with land, houses, cattle, and slaves, to the arrival and departure of ships and their cargo for sale, including also anything from textiles to slaves. John Walters Esq seemed to have particular difficulty keeping his slaves content as they were "constantly running away." Tracts of land for sale, lost horses, foreign affairs, and other news of the day, like residents indicted for counterfeiting and issuing money and a wife who eloped with all her husband's goods,[30] peppered the conglomeration of articles and advertisements in the paper and provide a glimpse of life in the mid-1700s in South Carolina when the first **Felders** arrived in America.

South Carolina *Gazette*, 1735

---

29 Alexander S. Salley, Jr., *The History of Orangeburg County from Its First Settlement to the Close of the Revolutionary War, 1704-1782* (Orangeburg, S.C: R.L. Berry, 1898), 226.

30 *South-Carolina Gazette*, no. 77, July 12 – July 19, 1735, 3-4.

THE PROPRIETORS' SOUTH CAROLINA

― ― ― 1663 Charter of Carolina
───── 1665 Charter of Carolina
North Carolina split from South Carolina in 1729
South Carolina's present day boundaries established ~ 1815

© Frankie Felder, 2020

Governing South Carolina

The eight English Lords Proprietors of South Carolina governed the colony using the document known as the Fundamental Constitutions. This constitution, although never ratified in South Carolina, "granted" tracts of land to those who would risk their lives to go settle the colony. This was an economic scheme known as the "headright system" – a concept initiated by the monarchy; but ironically, it backfired on them during the American Revolutionary War when the South Carolina General Assembly promised "bounty lands" to the colonists in exchange for the risk of military service in defeating the British.[31] Nonetheless, the King's grant provided the Proprietors plenty of land to give away. The initial borders of South Carolina were unbelievably expansive, and although no Englishman had ever traveled it, they knew that more land was to the west and the British assumed that ultimately it would run into the "South Seas."[32] Consequently, they "claimed" it all! In 1665, the northern border of South Carolina – (originally from the 36°36' latitude) was extended even further north to include the rich lands of the Albemarle that the Proprietors had heard about. Nansemond, Virginia, location of Suffolk, was included in this area. South Carolina thus was comprised of all the territory south from the southern border of Virginia to the 29° latitude (near Daytona Beach, Florida) and stretched west across these latitudes from the Atlantic coast to the Pacific Ocean![33] Leading authority

---

31 Edgar, *South Carolina: A History*, 43, 231.

32 William S. Powell, *The Proprietors of Carolina* (Raleigh: State Dept. of Archives and History, 1968), 4.

33 Edgar, *South Carolina: A History*, 1.

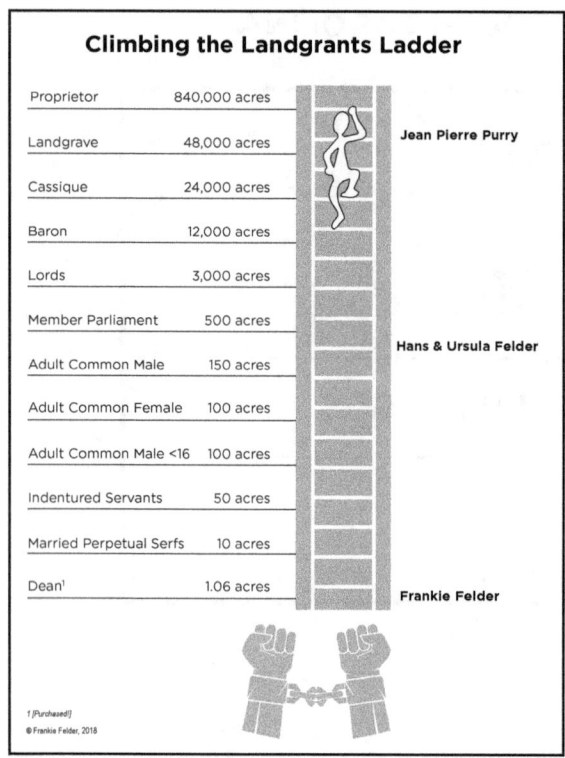

Climbing the Landgrants Ladder

Proprietor	840,000 acres
Landgrave	48,000 acres
Cassique	24,000 acres
Baron	12,000 acres
Lords	3,000 acres
Member Parliament	500 acres
Adult Common Male	150 acres
Adult Common Female	100 acres
Adult Common Male <16	100 acres
Indentured Servants	50 acres
Married Perpetual Serfs	10 acres
Dean¹	1.06 acres

1 [Purchased!]
© Frankie Felder, 2018

on South Carolina history, Dr. Walter Edgar, points out the irony of these South Carolinian boundaries encompassing virtually all of the territory which would ultimately become the Confederate states,[34] a concept South Carolina created all by herself! Hilariously, this self-assumption of ownership of this territory also "granted" to the Proprietors all the "ports, harbor, bays, rivers ... soil, lands, fields, woods, mountains, farms, lakes, rivers, bays, islets ... fish, whales, sturgeons and all other Royal fishes ... all vein, mines, quarries *[discovered and undiscovered]* of gold, silver, gems and precious stones. ..."[35] This is the territory – the colony of Carolina – that was "granted" as a gift by Charles II to his eight loyal friends and supporters, the Proprietors, for their assistance in his efforts to regain the Crown of England. *[At least the charter granting Carolina to the Proprietors did not also include the Native Americans!]*

The charter did outline, however, not only the geographical gift of the King but also his expectations for governing the colony once it was populated. The Proprietors were thus instructed specifically (through the Fundamental Constitutions) on how to establish the initial government that evolved. And, of course, it was to mirror the British structure.

Landgrants, in this quasi-feudalistic governing structure, were determined based on one's status, and one's status was determined by landholdings. As such, for loyalty to the Crown, the Proprietors were each "granted" 840,000 acres of *[Indian]* land, which they in turn "granted" to the settlers because they did not personally need it. Only two of the initial Proprietors (Sir John Colleton of Barbados and Sir William Berkeley of Virginia) ever lived outside of England.[36] Ultimately, as in England, a South Carolina constitution was framed, and a parliament was established. Also, as in England, three classes of nobility were created – "barons, cassiques and landgraves" (granted 12,000, 24,000 and 48,000 acres of land, respectively).[37] "Lords" owned "manors" of 3000 or more acres. A member of parliament would receive 500 acres. For a period of time, most common settlers received 150 acres for each adult male and 100 acres for each adult female and male under the age of sixteen in the family, although at varying times, the amount of acreage was adjusted. Indentured servants (committed as servants for

---

34 Edgar, *South Carolina: A History*, 1.

35 Cushing, *The Earliest Printed Laws of South Carolina, 1692-1734*, vol. 2 (Wilmington, Delaware: Michael Glazier, Inc., 1978), 5-6.

36 Powell, *The Proprietors*, 4.

37 David Ramsay, *History of South Carolina: From Its First Settlement in 1670 to the Year 1808, vol. 1* (Charleston: David Longworth, 1858), 17.

specified periods of time to pay the cost of their transportation to the colony), upon completion of their servitude, would receive a total of 50 acres. Perpetual serfs (committed as servants for life), upon marriage, were given 10 acres. Social mobility was thus defined by landholdings, and because it was possible to purchase more land, it was ultimately possible to buy one's way into a higher social class. Ingenuity and enterprise promised elevated social status[38] *[unless one was black]*.

When Jean Pierre Purry's and Captain Hugh Percy's settlers received their landgrants in the 1730s, the land distribution formula allotted 50 acres for each family member.[39] Although initially provided a landgrant of 200 acres by Governor Broughton, **Hans** and **Ursula Felder** acquired 150 additional acres of land. One might reasonably assume that their travels to South Carolina were not made based on poverty, and that they enjoyed a relative degree of success in Switzerland as well as in South Carolina. However, it is curious why **Hans** would leave his home country at 63 years old with no intent to return. I have found no mention of their reason for boarding the *Samuel*. Nonetheless, they had begun their climb up the land-grant ladder. Unfortunately, **Hans** and **Ursula** ultimately failed to realize their dreams to become "planters" – as they called themselves – because their property accumulation fell far short of that description. True to their German surname, they were farmers.

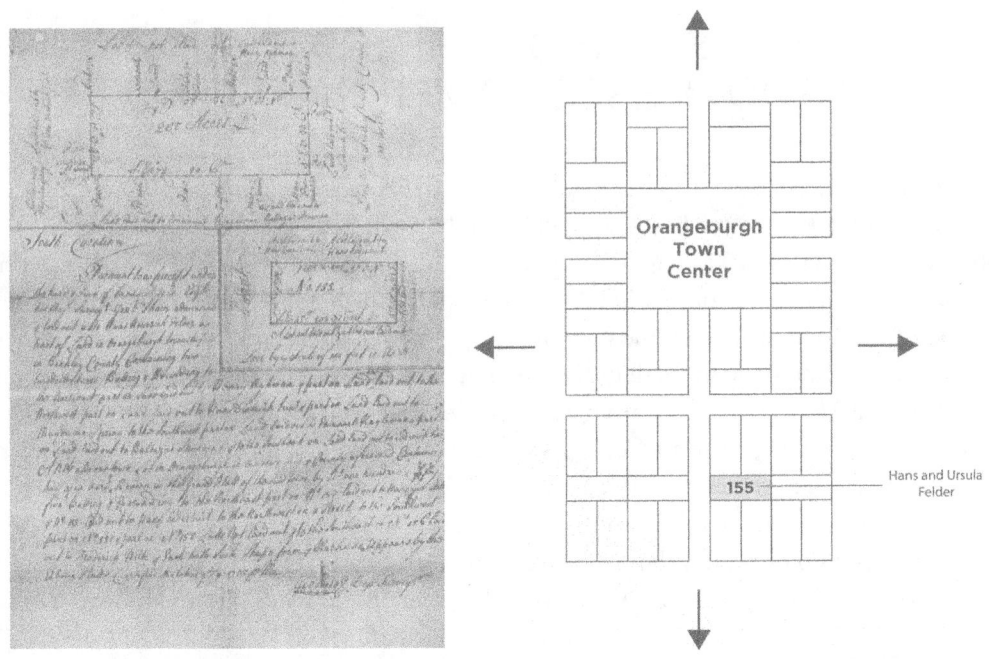

Felder landgrant in Orangeburgh

The location in Orangeburgh Township of the original landgrant to **Hans Heinrich Felder** (No. 155, near the town center), is pictured as well as a copy of the original landgrant certificate.[40]

---

38 Edgar, *South Carolina: A History*, 43.

39 Waters, *Preliminary Study*, 6.

40 Waters, *Preliminary Study*, 34.

Fortunately for Purry, personally, despite his many failures at Purrysburg and the many early deaths of the founding colonists, his settlement in Orangeburg did survive. Unfortunately for the **Felders**, however, all but one member of **Hans'** family were numbered in those early deaths. Within four years of settling in South Carolina, **Bernhardt**, named for his grandfather, and both of his parents, had died; **Hans** in 1737; **Ursula** in 1739.[41]

The only surviving family member, **Johannes Heinrich** (by then called **John Henry**), became the ward of a neighbor, Henry Wurtzer.[42] Wurtzer had also traveled from Switzerland to South Carolina as a passenger aboard the *Samuel*.[43] Apparently he was a great family friend or relative, as he assumed the legal responsibility for **John Henry** and the property left to him by his parents (land and livestock) with no financial compensation.[44] **Ursula Felder's** will does not mention that she and her husband "owned" slaves during their short duration as settlers in South Carolina; however, their son, referred forthwith as "**Henry**," and his descendants, quickly joined other South Carolinians in cultivating an economic system that simultaneously built the South into the "King of Cotton" and helped sever their loyalties to the King of England, which then engendered a distinctive form of southern patriotism that stripped more than four million Africans of basic human dignity, and ultimately brought this nation to its knees.

STATE OF THE STATE: "GOD BLESSED AMERICA FOR ME"

South Carolina, permanently settled by whites in 1670, holds the distinction of being the first state to secede from the Union, the first to fire a shot in the Civil War, and the only state in the nation in 1860 to have more than 1000 slaves living on a single plantation![45] Further, prior to the arrival of the **Felder** family in the colony in 1735, the early settlers of South Carolina had spent three quarters of a century in a "schizophrenic relationship" with the Native Americans, of which there were estimated at one time to be more than forty nations and between 17,000 and 30,000 persons prior to the Europeans' first arrival on Carolina shores.[46] At times the voyagers literally tricked the natives into bondage by inviting them to "tour" their ships and, once aboard, would sail off with them as captives to sell them into slavery in the Caribbean! Or the Europeans would incite war between the various Indian nations so that they would kill each other. But then they would also invite the natives to learn new technology ... all the while "claiming" Indian lands for the various foreign Crown that sponsored their expeditions.[47] As everyone has read in *his*tory books, treaties were established

---

41 ___, *Felders' Campmeetings*, 9.

42 .___, *Felders' Campmeetings*, 9.

43 Waters, *Preliminary Study*, 48.

44 Secretary of State recorded instruments, Wills (WPA, Works Progress Administration Transcripts), S213216, vol. 4 (Columbia: South Carolina Department of Archives and History), 205.

45 *Federal Census of 1860* U.S. Slave Schedule. (Joshua J. Ward in Georgetown had 1,130 slaves on his plantation.)

46 Edgar, *South Carolina: A History*, 12-13.

47 Revolutionary War Pension and Bounty-Land-Warrant-Application Files, Records of the *Veteran's Administration, Record Group no. 15,* National Archives Microfilm Publications Pamphlet Describing M894, 4.

between the settlers and the natives, however, most treaties, as we also know *[although not through the history books]*, were not honored. Walter Edgar expounded further on the relationship between early settlers and the natives:

> The Indian nations of South Carolina were fairly stable and were able to coexist without much difficulty until the introduction of foreign trade, technology, and disease. The incessant warfare among nations, on which Europeans almost invariably commented, was not war in the European sense. There was no attempt to eliminate a neighboring people. Rather, Indian warfare was more likely part of the natives' "eye for an eye" ethics system. Europeans frequently incited Indian warfare for their own purposes. With the arrival of Europeans, the order and harmony which were central to the world of all native America[ns] would eventually disappear. In their stead would be a European order based upon power.[48]

Sadly, illustrative of the early settlers' contemptuous disregard of the natives, and depicting the ease by which they rationalized many of their actions through religion, are the words of John Archdale, the fifteenth proprietary governor of South Carolina from 1695 to 1696, who, in a publication printed in London in 1707, had this to say:

> ... in the first settlement of Carolina, the hand of God was eminently seen in thinning the Indians to make room for the English. As for example; in Carolina in which were seated two potent nations, called the Westoes and Savannahs, which contained many thousands, who broke out into an unusual civil war; and thereby reduced themselves into a small number; and the Westoes, the more cruel of the two, were at the last forced out of that province; and the Savannahs continued good friends and useful neighbors to the English. But again it at other times pleased Almighty God to send unusual sicknesses amongst them, as the small pox ... to lessen their numbers; so that the English, in comparison to the Spaniards, have but little Indian blood to answer for.[49] *[sic]*.

From the beginning of the proprietary settlement, the early colonists spent 56 years of political infighting and experienced numerous overturns of government control, as well as a change of fundamental governing structure from proprietary, initiated in 1663, to royal, when, after many years of dissension and disharmony in the colony and anger towards the Proprietors, seven of the eight Proprietors sold their interests in South Carolina back to the Crown.[50] The colony changed governors twenty-four times during these unstable and often turbulent fifty-six years. Their relationships with the Native Americans always waxed and waned proportionate to their own needs, yet it appears that they really never acknowledged the fact that these indigenous people, if anyone, actually "owned" the land. The following proclamation in the June 14-21, 1775 edition of the South Carolina *Gazette* illustrates the point.

---

48 Edgar, *South Carolina: A History*, 20.

49 Ramsay, F*rom First Settlement* (see footnote at bottom of page 18).

50 Powell, *The Proprietors*, 5.

A PROCLAMATION

...and whereas the General Assembly of this province have taken the consequences thereof into consideration, and have agreed to allow a reward to any person whatsoever, freeman or slave, who shall kill any Tu[s]caroraw Indian, of Fifty Pounds current money, and sixty pounds like current money for every Tuscaroraw Indian who shall be taken alive, upon such persons delivering such Indians to the Publick Treasurer.
GOD SAVE THE KING!

Almost two hundred years later, surely unbeknownst to most, lyricist Woody Guthrie expressed essentially similar sentiments, originally ending the song, *This Land is Your Land*, with the phrase, "God blessed America for me!" From the very beginning of the transatlantic exploratory voyages, clearly the European's interpretation of the availability of these lands for their own coffers was evident and foremost in their minds.

FELDERS AND THE AMERICAN REVOLUTION

John Henry Felder

John "Henry" Felder, Sr. (1725-1781), the lone survivor of **Hans** and **Ursula's** family, dropped the use of his first name and as an adult was known only as "**Henry**." He married, was widowed, married a second time, and fathered a total of 13 children, some of whom later moved from South Carolina to settle new territories – Mississippi, Alabama, Louisiana, Georgia, and Texas. The challenge he faced in his late late-thirties was having to decide his loyalty to either England or to his American colony. He chose South Carolina.

For a period of twelve years, between 1763 and 1775, the British Parliament passed no less than 10 acts aimed at controlling the increasingly rebellious colonists in America. Britain passed the Proclamation of 1763, which prohibited settlements west of the Appalachian Mountains. In 1764, a series of acts – the Sugar Act, taxing colonists for commodities including sugar, indigo, coffee, textiles and wine; the Act Reorganizing the American Customs System in Support of British Trade; and the Currency Act, prohibiting the colonists from issuing legal paper money – all served to raise the ire of the colonists who believed they were unfairly being taxed without representation – a violation in their minds of their civil rights as subjects of the British Crown. Further, in 1765, Parliament passed the Stamp Act, requiring the colonies to pay England directly for maintaining its military in America as well as taxing all printed materials (newspapers, legal documents, licenses, etc.). The Quartering Act, requiring the colonists to supply room and board for British troops stationed among them, together with all earlier Parliamentary actions, inflamed mob violence – burnings and lootings – and boycotting of British goods. The incendiary reactions of the colonists motivated Britain to repeal the Stamp Act the following year, but simultaneously, on the very same day, Parliament passed the Declaratory Act, assuming total power to legislate the American colonies as they saw fit. The seeds of war had been sown.

But there was more. Other acts to regulate the colonists included the Townshend Act of 1768, which taxed, among other things, tea, and set off another boycott and initiated the circulation of a letter written by Boston activist Samuel Adams to the Assemblies of all colonies urging opposition to this act. In March of 1770, British soldiers fired into a mob of colonists and killed five of them in the incident that became known as the Boston Massacre. One by one the colonies appointed "committees of correspondence" to communicate amongst themselves about these atrocities. On December 16, 1773, unsuccessful in ending the dilemma of the new tea tax imposed in May of that year, Bostonians disguised themselves as Mohawk Indians and threw all 342 containers of tea into the harbor from three ships docked there because the British had demanded payment of the imposed import duty before the ships would be allowed to leave the port. Britain responded in March of 1774 with the Boston Port Bill, which shut down all shipping from Boston until the tax on the discarded tea was paid. Bostonians boycotted, Massachusetts was placed under British military forces, and the commander of all British forces in America came to Massachusetts and assumed governorship of the colony. Parliament took two final actions, which were the straws that broke the camel's back, so to speak. Parliament passed the Coercive Acts ending self-governing in the Massachusetts colony. The second action, the passage of the Quebec Act of May 1774, which initiated British rule in Canada and changed Canada's southern borders to include land claimed by Massachusetts, Connecticut, and Virginia,[51] exacerbated the colonists' fears that their colony would be next. These last acts fanned the flames of revolution.

While Massachusetts was the colony most frequently combating the British troops, incidents with the British also occurred in Rhode Island, Connecticut, New York. and Virginia, motivating the colonies one by one to join the Massachusetts' boycott of British goods. Most significant, however, Pennsylvania, Massachusetts, and New York urged the colonists to come together in joint session to determine a collective strategy. Fifty-six delegates from all the colonies except Georgia met in Philadelphia from September 5 to October 26, 1774 at the First Continental Congress.[52] South Carolina sent five men: Henry Middleton, Thomas Lynch, Christopher Gadsden, John Rutledge and Edward Rutledge,[53] all

---

[51] The History Place, "American Revolution, Prelude to Revolution, 1763-1775," accessed December 20, 2014, http://www.historyplace.com/United States/revolution/rev-prel.htm.

[52] The History Place, "American Revolution."

[53] William E. Hemphill, ed, *The State Records of South Carolina: Extracts from the Journals of the Provincial Congresses, 1775-1776* (Columbia: South Carolina Archives Department, 1960), 19.

extremely wealthy from low country plantations or businesses owned by their families. Christopher Gadsden, for example, inherited a fortune from his father – a plantation, an additional 1000 acres, land in Charleston and Georgetown, furniture, fine wines, and four slaves. He was 17 years old at the time.[54] Thomas Lynch was from a family of wealthy indigo planters in the Charleston area. Edward's older brother by ten years, John Rutledge, served alongside him in the Continental Congress. These brother lawyers were sons of a wealthy Charleston physician.[55] Finally, Henry Middleton inherited his father's (former acting SC governor) plantation, The Oaks.[56]

Henry Middleton briefly assumed the role of acting president of the First Continental Congress when Phillip Peyton, who had been elected president, left to assume urgent duties as Speaker of the Virginia House of Burgess. Congress began the arduous task of writing a Declaration of Rights and a 14-resolution document, the Continental Association, for consideration by the colonists. They expressed to the British Parliament the authors' sentiments that they had given "rights," which were not "forfeited, surrendered, or lost" when their ancestors chose to come to America. These "rights," they reasoned, were preserved for them, too, and thus, as descendants of the first settlers, they vowed to follow the model of their English ancestors. They would assert and "declare" what was just treatment under the British Constitution and the charters that established the American colonies.[57] The most salient concept underlying both of these documents, precursors to the American Bill of Rights, was the right to participate in legislating any laws that would be imposed on the colonies. This was in direct contrast to Parliament's recent actions and legislations, all of which were intended to nullify the colonies' assemblies, assemblies that were constituted by representatives voted into office by the people.

More than advising England of the colonies' intent to boycott, the Continental Association included instructions by which the colonists were to collectively ensure that the Association would be carried out. The Association addressed exportation, consumption, and importation of goods to and from Britain, Ireland, and the British-held West Indies. The boycott was to last until such time that every Parliamentary act against the colonies imposed since 1763 was repealed. A most interesting article of the document concerned the slave trade industry. In 1774, the authors wrote:

> Second, we will neither import, nor purchase any slave imported after the 1st day of December next, after which time, we will wholly discontinue the slave-trade, and will neither be concerned in it ourselves, nor will we hire our vessels, nor sell our commodities or manufactures to those who are concerned in it.[58]

When the Continental Congress recessed, the delegates returned to their respective colonies to solicit their constituents' consideration of the Declaration of Rights and the Continental Association. In order to discuss the matter in South Carolina, the colonists convened the Second Provincial Congress (November 1, 1775 – March 26, 1776) in Charleston to review these documents. Quite the community activist, **Henry Felder** had held numerous elected and appointed offices including Justice of the

---

54 E. Stanley Godbold, Jr. and Robert Woody, *Christopher Gadsden and the American Revolution* (Knoxville: University of Tennessee Press, 1982), 9.

55 Stan Klos, "John Rutledge," accessed November 2014, http://www.let.rug.nl/usa/biographies/john-rutledge/.

56 Stan Klos, "Henry Middleton," accessed November 2014, http://www.henrymiddleton.com/.

57 Hemphill, *State Records*, 12-13.

58 Hemphill, *State Records*, 245.

Peace, Justice of the Quorum for Orangeburg, and Grand Jury of Orangeburg District. Thus, it was not surprising that he would be one of six men elected from St. Matthews to attend this meeting in Charleston. It was at this meeting that **Henry** served on one subcommittee to determine where best to establish iron manufacturing for the production of weapons and another subcommittee to determine where to erect the gun powder mill. Obviously an influential politician, he was also one of two persons appointed to receive rice and flour for Orangeburg's public granary.[59] The subcommittee report indicated that he had volunteered to be the gun powder manufacturer and that the Provincial body approved and voted to allocate sufficient funds from the state treasury to pay him for his service.[60]

Very much a proponent of slavery, **Henry** voted against the article to discontinue the slave trade industry. In this, he was fully supporting the South Carolina delegation to the Continental Congress. Why would these men support ending slavery? Between the five delegates to the First Continental Congress, they enslaved nearly 2000 Africans on their rice, indigo, and cotton plantations in the low country. Southern membership of both the first and second Continental Congresses constituted less than one-third of the total delegates, however, these Southern delegates were vocal and powerfully instrumental in drafting the final form of two documents with which any elementary student of United States *his*tory is familiar: The Declaration of Independence and the United States Constitution. What *his*tory does not reveal without in-depth research, though, is who these men were that moved the colonies to the point of declaring war against, and independence from, their motherland, England.

One quite interesting aspect of the revolution not clearly evident was the age and economic status of these revolutionary leaders. South Carolina's Thomas Lynch owned seven plantations, 13,000 acres of land and was a mere 26 years old when he signed the Declaration of Independence.[61] Thomas Heyward, Jr., (whose father owned 25,000 acres of South Carolina land and 1000 slaves, and whose brother, Nathaniel, was the largest slave "owner" in the South, owning 45,000 acres of land, fifteen plantations, and 1648 slaves), was a 30-year-old "owner" of more than 130 slaves himself when he, too, signed the Declaration of Independence. Arthur Middleton was 34, and inherited Middleton Place, with more than 800 slaves.

Ten years later, included among the signers of the Constitution in 1787 were a couple of wealthy Virginians and South Carolinians. Thomas Jefferson ("owner" of 187 slaves and more than 7000 acres of land at age 32 when he was elected to the 2nd Continental Congress), ultimately "owned" more than 600 slaves before his death and fathered numerous children by his slave Sally Hemings. George Washington ("owner" of 317 slaves and 58,000 acres of land), actually "owned" 10 slaves at age 11. South Carolinians John Rutledge ("owner" of 60 slaves), became the first and only President of South Carolina and later Chief Justice of the US Supreme Court; and Charles Pinckney ("owner" of 250 slaves), former U.S. Senator and former South Carolina governor, was the father of numerous slave children. That these congressional representatives insisted that the article to dismantle slavery be removed from the Constitution or face withdrawal of southern support for passage, is understandable. Freedom from England without freedom to sustain their lifestyles was not freedom

---

59 _____, *Felders' Campmeetings*, 9.

60 Hemphill, *State Records*, 77.

61 Thomas Lynch, Jr., https://www.newworldencyclopedia.org/entry/Thomas_Lynch,_Jr., accessed July 20, 2018.

to them. Samuel Johnson, author of the 1755 *Dictionary of the English Language,* must have been proud of the skill of these men in capturing his view of the "perplexity" of the English language and the "entanglement" and "energetic unruliness of the English tongue" to write language in the Declaration of Independence and the United States Constitution that no one understood precisely:[62] "All men are created equal and endowed by their Creator with certain unalienable Rights ...". What exactly was that supposed to mean? Further, in the first draft of the Declaration of Independence, Jefferson even admonished the "Christian King of Great Britain" for perpetuating slavery, an "execrable commerce" – that is, a despicable and vile business venture. The Continental Congress refused to include this language.[63] *[Amazing!]*

It has been said that the twelve-year Revolutionary War (1763-1775) was in many respects "America's first civil war,"[64] as there were many battles in which no British were involved whatsoever. Families and neighbors split sides during this war, some 20% believing that remaining loyal to the Crown (Tories or "Loyalists") was appropriate; 40% (Whigs or "Federalists" or patriots) rebelling fervently to become an independent new nation; and as always, about 40% unsure of what to think. Just as today with parents and children, it was not unusual for fathers (likely "Loyalists") and sons (likely "Federalists") to be on opposing sides of the debate. In this instance, being on opposite sides tore families apart and forced relatives to "face each other across the firing line,"[65] inflaming generations of family discord and disruptions. Thus, it is quite interesting to note that all seven of **Captain John "Henry" Felder's** sons (**Henry Jr., Jacob, John, Frederick, Samuel, Abraham**, and **Peter**) served under his command in the Revolutionary army, although one publication indicates that **Peter** was a Loyalist at heart, having joined Captain Joseph Smith's Company, King's Rangers, from April 25, 1783 to June 24, 1783.[66] After the war, thousands of warring family members – Loyalists – returned to England, taking with them nearly 20,000 of their slaves who fought with them alongside the British.

The guns of Henry Felder, Orangeburg Square

Henry was said to have singlehandedly elevated the image of the low country Swiss, German,

---

62 Samuel Johnson, Dictionary of the English Language (Dublin: James Duffy, 1847), accessed July 25, 2018, www.bl.uk.

63 Paul Finkelman, "The Abolition of the Slave Trade: U.S. Constitution and Acts," accessed July 20, 2018, http://abolition.nypl.org/print/us_constitution/.

64 Eric Herschthal, "America's First Civil War," accessed July 20, 2018, http://www.slate.com/articles/arts/books/2016/09/alan_taylor_s_american_revolutions_reviewed.html.

65 South Carolina's Revolutionary Heritage, 1, accessed April 15, 2011, http://www.schistory.org/displays/RevWar/CarolinaDay/heritage.html.

66 Murtie June Clark, Loyalists in the *Southern Campaign of the Revolutionary War,* vol. II (Baltimore: Genealogical Publishing Company, 1981), 421.

and Scotch-Irish residents of Orangeburg and nearby counties from "illiterate and uneducated" into one of a thoughtful and even scholarly people. On May 20, 1776, as foreman of the Grand Jury charged with determining how to boycott British goods, **Henry** presented their report, "The Address and Declaration of the Grand Jury of Orangeburgh District," to Chief Justice William Drayton. Some compared the articulateness of the report and his eloquence of delivery to that of Thomas Jefferson's "masterpiece," (Declaration of Independence), delivered two months afterwards.[67]

Henry became one of twelve persons appointed to ensure that the residents of St. Matthews would adhere to the instructions for the boycott.[68] Not only were British goods boycotted, neighbors who did not support the boycott were severely publicly rebuffed. Rebelling colonists were often quite brutal in enforcing loyalty to this call and strategy for freedom. Tarring and feathering loyalists and publishing their names in the local gazette to identify, embarrass, and ostracize non-supporters of independence were not unusual tactics. *His*tory does not explain how **Henry** went about his role of ensuring adherence to the boycott in his part of St. Matthews, but it is clear that he made enemies in the process.

As the story is told, **Henry Felder's** family participated in one of the British-less battles that claimed his life. In 1780, when a group of Tories set fire to his house, situated on the 2,346 acres of landgrant property he had received,[69] 45-year old **Henry** tried to escape by dressing in his wife's clothing, but as he jumped a fence, his boots revealed his identity and he was shot – by his neighbors no less (who, by the way, burned his house down the year before also)! He was rescued by one of his slaves, Fry, his plantation overseer and "kind *[N]*egro"[70] who carried him to safety. He lived for a day or two afterwards but then died of his wounds.[71] His oldest son, **Henry, Jr.**, not only assumed the command of his father's regiment,[72] he continued his father's legacy of service to Orangeburg and St. Matthews, serving as a representative in the state legislature for nearly seven years (1782-86; 1792-94) and, according to the 1790 census, "owning" 21 slaves.

Prior to **Henry Sr.'s** death, his third oldest son, **John**, was killed by the British in an earlier battle. The rest of the **Felder** brothers who survived the American Revolution – **Henry Jr.**, **Frederick**, **Samuel**, **Abraham** – raised families, supported, and engaged in the slave trade, became prominent and wealthy citizens of the state, and were buried in or near Orangeburg and St. Matthews. All except **Jacob** and **Peter**.

Today, Highway 176, off 301 North headed towards Santee, leads to Felderville A.M.E. Church, where I stopped and met the men and women working in the churchyard. It was not possible for me to drive through Felderville, named for one of **Abraham's** sons, **Captain J. Hamilton Felder**, without reflecting on the lives of the many slaves held by these **Felder** families. Nor was it possible to not stop and pick from the remnants of the cotton fields that served as the primary source of

---

67 D. Graham Copeland, *Many Years After: a bit of history and recollections of Bamberg*, (University of South Carolina Digital Collection), 367, https://digital.tcl.sc.edu/digital/collection/manyyears1/id/406.

68 Clark, *Loyalists*, 23.

69 Peggy Easterling, Felders, *Orangeburgh German-Swiss Newsletter*, vol. 9, no. 3, Summer 2001, 29.

70 Mary E. Sandel and Elias W. Sandel, *The Felder Family in South Carolina, Mississippi, Texas and Louisiana* (Roseland, Louisiana: self-published, 2000), 5.

71 Daniel M. Culler, *Orangeburg District: History and Records* (Spartanburg, S.C: Reprint Company 1995), 281.

72 Culler, Orangeburg District, 281.

wealth gained by these brothers and cousins from Switzerland. Without the chapped hands, blistered feet, tormented minds, blood, sweat, tears, and toil of the **Felder** slaves and their kindred spirits in Orangeburg and St. Matthews, the low country would not have developed into the economic powerhouse that it did during the 19th century, nor would the above-named **Felders** have lived the lives they did – in relative luxury and prominence.

To truly know and tell the true h-i-s-t-o-r-y of South Carolina, the contributions of the slaves, who at one time constituted more than two-thirds of the population of the state, must be uncovered and told also. But while this project has a different focus, I will provide a brief overview of slavery in the state because South Carolina's slave history is quite instructive to understanding how slavery developed throughout the rest of the South as well as the culture in which the **Felder** slaves survived in South Carolina. Then we will follow **Henry Felder's** seventh son, **Peter**, to Mississippi, where he moved at the age of fifty-two with his wife and thirteen children, and where he and much of *OURstory* was buried.[73]

State of the State: South Carolina's Slave Culture Evolves

Between 1670 and 1690, South Carolina was heavily populated by whites from English Barbados, a small Caribbean Island that had institutionalized a Brazilian model of slavery of Africans and Indians. It was primarily South Carolina's Fundamental Constitutions which lured scores of Brits to Carolina from Barbados, which by this time was so heavily populated that it had become short on land. For example, the largest sugar "planters" in Barbados owned on average only 200 acres of land, but most Barbadian "planters" actually had less than 10 acres. Average land ownership for a "planter" in Barbados was thus equivalent to the holdings of an "indentured servant" in South Carolina and nowhere close to the thousands of acres owned by a South Carolina "planter." Always the promise of more land, and thus more wealth – which translated into elevated social status and personal power – lured Europeans to risk their lives to relocate to "new worlds" *[other people's worlds and other people's nations]*.

England dominated in the multiple foreign takeovers in South Carolina, and consequently, the English culture and political mindset most heavily influenced the emerging culture of South Carolina. As the Barbadian English settled in large numbers in South Carolina, they brought with them the culture that they had created on the tiny island in the Caribbean, including, even, the names of nine of the 11 parishes. They gained a reputation as self-absorbed and materialistic, which turned out to be the exact philosophical underpinning that led them to the belief that to cultivate the lands in South Carolina, they needed enormous slave labor. Some settlers did not anticipate the backbreaking labor required to clear and cultivate land, apparently believing Jean Pierre Purry's spin about thin-trunked trees. Some were just "pampered citizens"[74] *[spoiled and lazy]*. Barbadian English with any semblance of means, and even many without, came to South Carolina with a plan – to rely on black slave labor to become wealthy – once they realized that it was "cheaper to purchase an African for

---

[73] Peter possibly went to Mississippi from South Carolina with 13 children; numbers vary in different publications. The important information is that he had many sons who carried the Felder name to Mississippi, Louisiana and Texas and they, too, had many sons. The Felders in these four states are of the same family, originating in South Carolina with Henry Felder.

[74] Ramsay, *From First Settlement*, 20.

life than it was to contract for a white indentured servant for four or five years."[75]

Within four years of introducing slavery into South Carolina, as early as 1675, the population of South Carolina, mirroring Barbados, was estimated to be at least one-third black, and over the years of early development of the colony, the black population grew to eventually outnumber the white population. By 1717, the African and white populations were equal; by 1720, the African/African American population outnumbered the white; and by 1740, five years after the **Felders'** arrival, blacks made up two-thirds of the population of South Carolina. A further enticement to the English in Barbados to populate South Carolina was the "absolute power and authority over *[the]* negro slaves" clause in South Carolina's Fundamental Constitution, which alluded to the sustenance of the plantation system and a stronger system of personal protection to the freemen than that found in Barbados and other West Indian islands, including Antigua and Jamaica, where many insurrections had begun to put absolute fear into the minds of plantation owners who survived those slave uprisings.[76] In short, in South Carolina, the planter would have more control over his slaves.

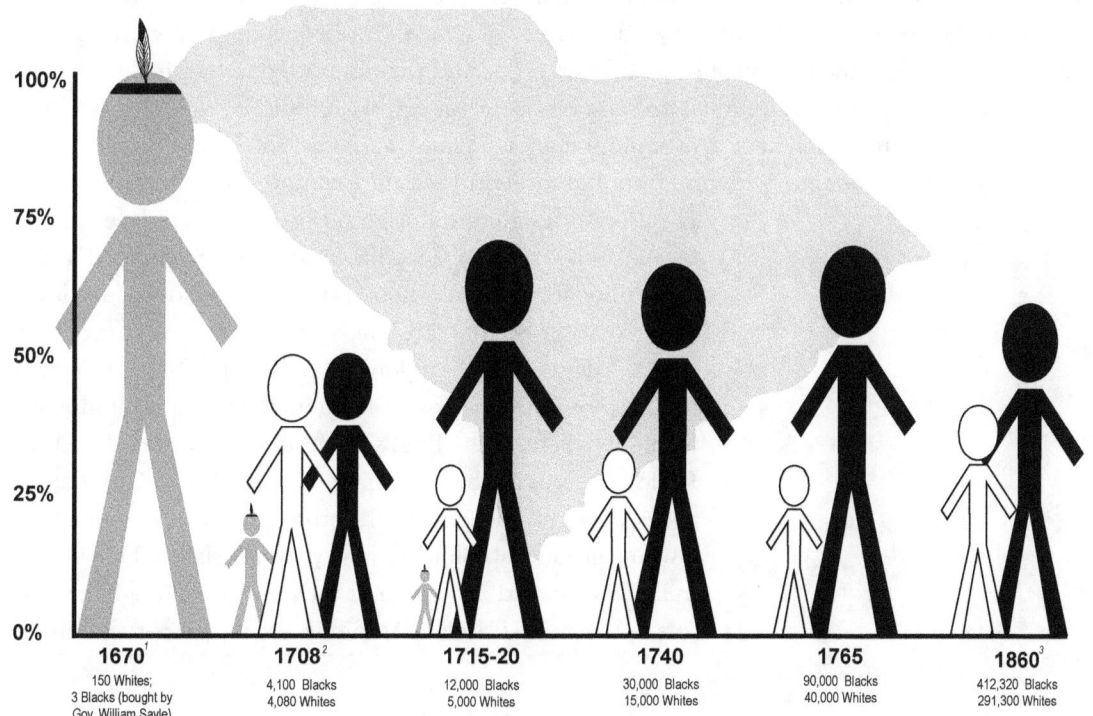

South Carolina's Population

1670[1]	150 Whites; 3 Blacks (bought by Gov. William Sayle)
1708[2]	4,100 Blacks; 4,080 Whites
1715-20	12,000 Blacks; 5,000 Whites
1740	30,000 Blacks; 15,000 Whites
1765	90,000 Blacks; 40,000 Whites
1860[3]	412,320 Blacks; 291,300 Whites

[1] "Slavery," *South Carolina Encyclopedia* (Daniel C. Littlefield) • [2] *Growth of South Carolina's Slave Population*, SCIWay.net (Michael Trinkley) • [3] *US State-level Population Estimates: Colonization to 1999* (Cousin; Joyce)

---

75 Edgar, *South Carolina: A History*, 37.

76 Thomas J. Little, "The South Carolina Slave Laws Reconsidered, 1670-1700," *The South Carolina Historical Magazine* 94.2 (1993): 86–101; 87, 90.

Jean Pierre Purry provided a perfect example of how the promise of economic prosperity drove the founding of South Carolina and the distinctive brand of U.S. slavery that evolved in this state. In Barbados, "material success, not character or honor," was the measure of an individual's worth.[77] More importantly, to further understand the settlers' attitudes towards slavery, it is instructive to note that "how a person acquired wealth was not important," just that they did accomplish this dream.[78] Much of this culture of self-indulgent greed and unrestrained attitude towards slavery was brought to South Carolina by the British from Barbados who settled the state. Included in these settlers was Edward Middleton, descendants of whom led the state from the proprietary era (Edward, himself, being the Proprietor's deputy) to the Civil War era (William, six generations later, signing the Order of Secession). The same cultural attitudes regarding slavery and wealth were brought to Orangeburg by Purry and internalized by his colonists. They were indulged in, and perpetuated and sustained by, **Felders.** They were replicated in other states as **Felders** moved westward; especially in Mississippi.

Slaves Arrive in South Carolina

Most slaves entered South Carolina through the harbor at Charleston, stopping along the way to be quarantined at Sullivan's Island – once called by historian Peter Wood the "Ellis Island of African Americans."[79] Most slaves brought to South Carolina came from the West Indies or the African countries of Madagascar, Senegal, The Gambia, Angola/Congo, Sierra Leone, the Winward Coast, and Ghana[80] and other undefined west coast African ports, and were imported to South Carolina prior to the 1808 American Constitutional prohibition of the foreign slave trade.

Sir John Yeamans, recipient of a large proprietary landgrant, and third governor of South Carolina for a two-year term, brought with him from Barbados in 1671 the first slaves that lived in the state.[81] He also was a significant importer of Barbadian slave "masters" because of fears that slave insurrections were indeed a strong possibility. This intense fear spurred the colonists to develop slave codes in South Carolina, which ultimately turned out to be, according to Winthrop Jordan, author of *White Over Black,* "the most rigorous deprivation of freedom to exist in institutionalized form anywhere in the English continental colonies."[82] Thomas Little's analysis of the development of the South Carolina slave codes, however, underscored the propensity of the South Carolina law to delegate "absolute authority" to the slaveholders to determine how to wield "power" over their slaves. Although the legislators of the South Carolina Assembly – many primary slaveholders

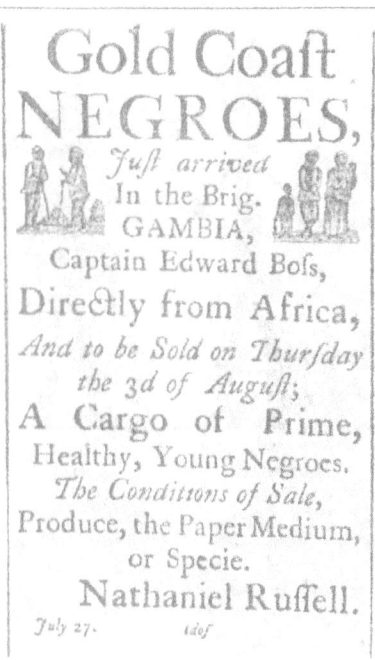

Charleston Evening Gazette, 28 July 1786

77 Edgar, *South Carolina: A History,* 37.

78 Edgar, *South Carolina: A History,* 37.

79 Alexia J. Helsley, "African American Genealogical Research in South Carolina," South Carolina Department of Archives and History, workshop handout, February 14, 2004, 1.

80 William S. Pollitzer, *The Gullah People and their African Heritage* (Athens: University of Georgia Press, 1999), 44.

81 Ramsay, *From First Settlement,* 2.

82 Little, *Slave Laws,* 101.

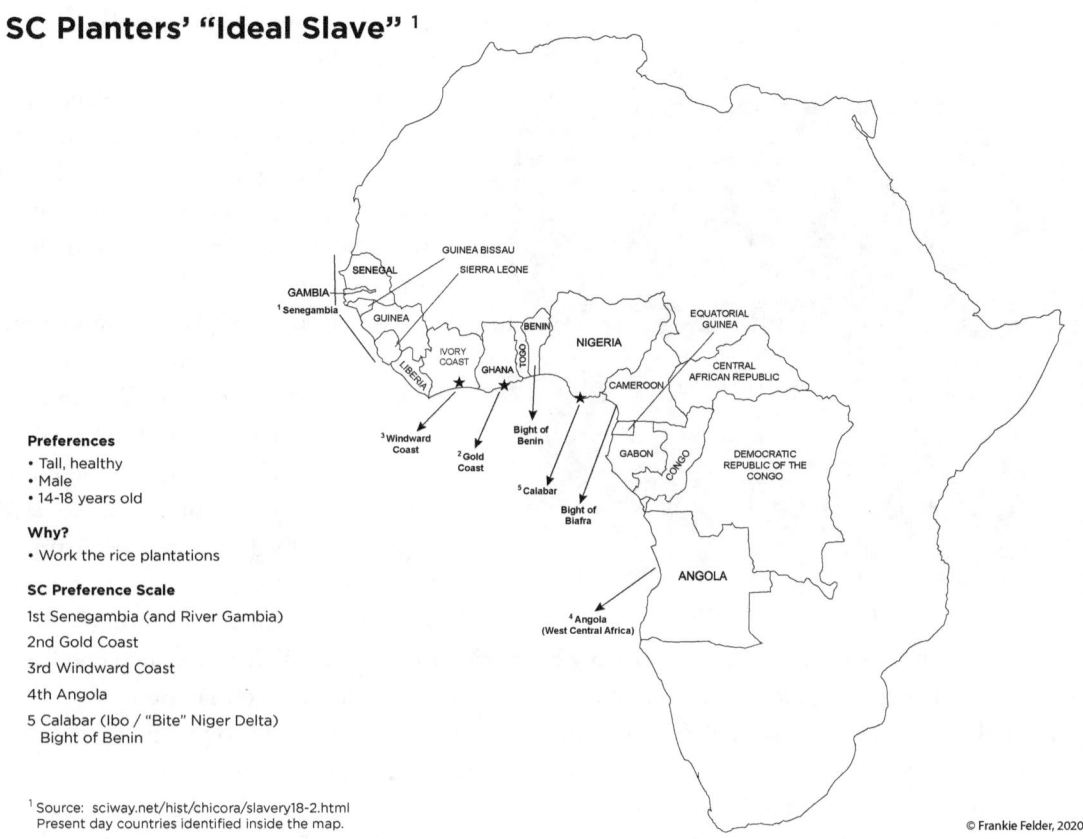

themselves – wrote the codes, the laws they passed outlined general parameters but provided discretion to the slave "owners" to define what the laws meant. Consequently, there was inconsistency in the application of the codes from plantation to plantation, adding to the peculiarness of this institution and the virtual inability of scholars to describe an accurate, comprehensive portrayal of how slavery operated in actuality in the state.

The South Carolina Slave Code's Impact

Other cultural practices from British-"owned" Barbados sailed to South Carolina in ships from the island and implanted themselves firmly upon the soil in the low-country, quickly spreading throughout the colony. As in England and Barbados, participation in the government required ownership of property. In South Carolina, by law, that required ownership of 500 or more acres of land and at least 10 slaves.[83] Political strife between pro-proprietary sentiment (English) and anti-proprietary sentiment (Barbadian) marked the early political landscape of South Carolina, although the Barbadian landholders ultimately won this political battle and were successful in enacting slaves codes that mirrored the

---

83 Charlie Tyler and Richard Young, "The South Carolina Legislature," accessed June 10, 2013, http://www.ipspr.sc.edu/grs/SCCEP/Articles/legislature.htm.

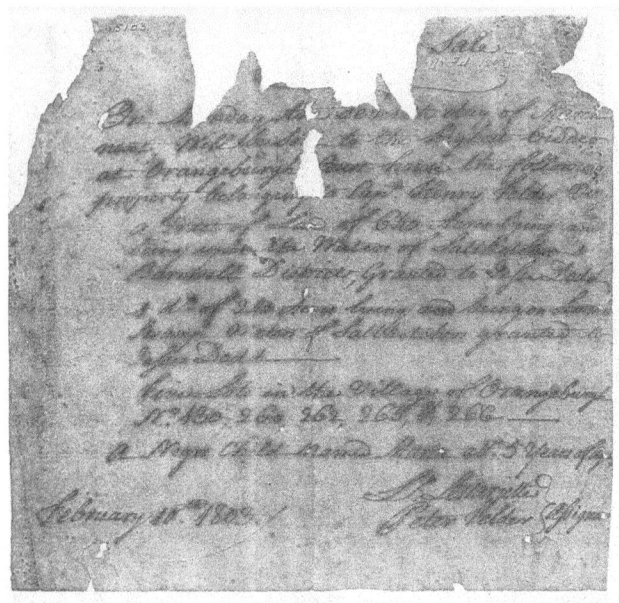
Felder sale of child, Maria, age 5

system of extreme tight control established in Barbados.[84]

Over a period of fifty-four years – from 1686 at the promulgation of the first slave code establishing slaves as "freehold property" (meaning that they belonged to the estate and not the slave holder and, therefore, could not be sold separately from the estate), to 1740, when the General Assembly passed the comprehensive slave code, "An Act for the Better Ordering and Governing of Negroes and Other Slaves in this Province" – the state passed serial legislation aimed at controlling the slave population. By 1860, slaves constituted 58% of the entire population of the state but were more than two-thirds (66%) the population of the low country, home to **Henry Felder's** descendants. Whites imagined and feared what a majority black population was capable of doing and, actually, had good reason.

Heated debates raged in the halls of the South Carolina Assembly, often concerning the writing of slave codes, or regulations, designed to protect the lives of slaveholders[85] and to secure and ensure the growth of the system that became the literal lifeblood of the South. The **Felders** were very active participants and beneficiaries of this system. **Henry Felder, Jr.**, state representative, and his nephew, **John Myers Felder**, state senator, helped to define and solidify South Carolina's slave culture. Judge **Samuel Felder**, **John Myers'** father, helped to justify and maintain that culture. **Peter Felder** assumed responsibility for auctioning off Captain **Henry Felder's** property, including his five-year-old slave child, Maria.

"Happy" and Contented Slaves?

Denmark Vesey, a Charlestonian, provided a perfect example of how the rage and seething anger, always just below the surface of the schizophrenic polite smiles and "Yes suh, boss" subservient communication style that blacks developed towards whites, coalesced slaves and free men alike together into a shared brotherhood, all fully cognizant of the pain felt by most at the degradation of stolen man- and womanhood. Vesey, in reaction to the Charleston City Council's dissolution of the African Church in that city (Emanuel A.M.E.), which he had co-founded, planned a massive insurrection to be executed in July of 1822. It was to involve thousands of slaves and free blacks. He enlisted the aid of Mozambique Gullah priest, Jack Pritchard, who lived in Charleston, as well as the aid of the President of Santo Domingo. Vesey, a former slave who had purchased his freedom and had become

---

84 Little, *Slave Laws*, 100.

85 Little, *Slave Laws*, 86-101.

a prosperous, literate businessman and leader in the African Methodist church, was hanged along with 35 other insurrection leaders for this planned rebellion, exposed by a "favorite and confidential slave" of a local plantation owner.[86]

Throughout the entire antebellum period in South Carolina, within the codified law as well as in actual practice, one can find sufficient examples of antithetical treatment of slaves that virtually any thesis one wanted to promulgate could be substantiated by documented accounts of how the institution of slavery actually functioned. There are examples of kindnesses, humane "masters," love relations between slaves and "masters," employment systems where slaves earned wages, opportunities to purchase freedom, manumissions, slaves being willed property, "masters" publicly caring for their children borne of illicit affairs with slave women, and so forth. However, there are also absolutely abhorrent, inhumane, indescribable atrocities committed upon those held in bondage. Without belaboring the point, following are a few examples that stand out in my mind from my reading, depicting the wide continuum of relations and applications of the slave code in South Carolina and challenging my capacity to comprehend how one human being could possibly, intentionally, treat another so cruelly:

Louisiana slave, Wilson Chinn, branded on his forehead by and with the initials of his "owner," Volsey B. Marmillion, sugar planter

- In the early 1600s, slaves were able to maintain "provision grounds" (about one acre provided for them to grow vegetables and to raise farm animals to feed themselves). While this appeared to be a benevolent act, underlying motives included an economic benefit to the slave "owner" who saved himself the expense of the high cost of feeding the slaves. Further, it was a means of social control – a reflection of the belief that a slave with a vested interest in the land on the "master's" plantation would not become a runaway.[87]
- Slaves' foreheads were branded, and ears cut off for committing a second petty larceny, but if a third was committed, the nose would be split. A slave who ran away more than three times had a foot or leg amputated. Burning alive was not uncommon for what was considered a "heinous crime."[88]
- Marriages between whites and mulattoes were common until 1865 when they were outlawed by slave code in South Carolina.[89]

---

86 "The Vesey Conspiracy," accessed June 10, 2013, http://www.pbs.org/wgbh/aia/part3/3p2976.htm.

87 Little, *Slave Laws*, 90.

88 David D. Wallace, *The History of South Carolina*, vol. 1 (New York: The American Historical Society, Inc., 1934), 374.

89 Wallace, *History of South Carolina*, 376.

- Slaves convicted of plotting insurrections were dealt with severely. It was not uncommon that they would be hanged or otherwise murdered and then decapitated and their heads riveted on posts lined up along a popular trail or route frequented by other slaves.

The sweeping legislation initiated in 1686 enacted slave codes that established, undeniably, the property status of the slaves and concretized an economic system that made South Carolina prosperous for the next 179 years.

The table below delineates federal census data from 1860, which reveals that South Carolina was second in the nation with extreme wealth derived from the chattel system; far exceeding all her other southern brother states, except for Louisiana, in the number of extremely wealthy slave holders. As the data reveal, most families had fewer than 10 slaves; however, the institution was an incredibly lucrative business for many. In 1860, one South Carolinian, Joshua J. Ward of Georgetown, held the largest number of slaves (1130) on any single plantation in the nation!

SLAVEHOLDERS BY STATE AND SELECT NUMBER OF SLAVES, 1860[90]

State	Number of slaveholders with ...					
	at least one slave	20-29 slaves	100-199 slaves	200-299 slaves	500-999 slaves	> 1000 slaves
SC	3763	1964	363	56	7	1
MS	4856	2322	279	28	1	
LA	4092	1241	480	63	4	
KY	9306	1093	6	1		
TX	4593	1095	52	2		
FL	863	333	45	2		
AR	2339	586	59	6		
TN	7820	1623	40	6		
VA	11,085	3017	105	8		
NC	6440	1977	118	11		
GA	6713	2910	181	23	1	
AL	5607	2323	312	24		
TOTAL	**67,477**	**20,484**	**2040**	**230**	**13**	**1**

The **Felders** who remained in South Carolina during the migration to western territories number among those who gained prosperity through the slave-trading industry, including **Captain Henry Felder, Jr.**, **Judge Samuel Felder**, **Dr. John L. Felder**, and most notably, **Senator John Myers Felder**. The **Felders** of the low country became extremely influential and economically successful,

---

90 University of Virginia Library's Historical Census Browser, accessed January 27, 2012, https://mapserver.lib.virginia.edu/Data source for select states and select number of slaves.

owing much to the slave trade industry, "owning" more property and slaves combined than any other family in the Orangeburg District, which included St. Matthews. In 1851, only one family in the Orangeburg District owned more land, and five families "owned" more slaves, than did the **Felders**. While the average number of slaves "owned" in the district by any family was fewer than 10, five of the **Felder** families in the district "owned" between 37 and 58 slaves each. In 1850, **John Myers Felder** (1782-1851), South Carolina state representative, senator, member of both the 22nd and 23rd United States General Congresses, and great-grandson of **Hans Heinrich Felder**, "owned" 285 slaves and 31,063 acres of land in Orangeburg County. He "owned" additional slaves in Lexington county.

"Planters," as distinguished from "farmers," owned substantially more property. In the 76 years between 1735, when **Hans Heinrich Felder** arrived in Orangeburg from Switzerland with his wife and sons, and 1811, when his grandson, **Peter**, moved from Orangeburg to Mississippi, **Felders** in South Carolina had:

- acquired tens of thousands of acres of land;
- vastly expanded their families and the **Felder** name through marriage and childbirth;
- helped to write South Carolina's Authority (prelude to the Declaration of Independence);
- served in the Revolutionary War;
- participated responsibly and proudly in the township, provincial, and continental government; and
- helped to legislate and perpetuate the most abusive form of slavery that evolved in America.

By the 1850's, many of the **Felders** in South Carolina had obtained the status that **Hans** and **Ursula** failed to reach – they had become "planters." Planters of cotton, corn, rice, and oats. Additionally, they had distinguished themselves as politicians, lawyers, and merchants. There were 140 **Felders** in the state according to the 1860 U.S. Census, which only identified white persons by name and included the men, women, and children of these families. These **Felders** "owned" a total of 459 slaves. Prior to the 1860 census and to the Emancipation Proclamation, some of the slaves were sold from these plantations and/or transferred to "owners" in other states (including **Felder** relatives). Some of the slaves were buried on the property of **John Myers Felder**, across the field from where he and his relatives were laid to rest in the **Felder** cemetery on what was once his property, "Midway," now a South Carolina wastewater plant. Typically buried at night after the day's work, in unmarked cemeteries,[91] many slaves believed that

"Free at Last," Boy Scouts honor slaves of John Myers Felder

---

91 SCIWAY, Grave Matters: History of African American Cemeteries, accessed August 3, 2008, https://www.sciway.net/hist/chicora/gravematters-1.html#differences.

the dead would journey back to Africa. If so, indeed, they were finally "free at last."

In the 1870 U.S. Census, the first census that called Africans and people of color by their names, 339 blacks are enumerated in South Carolina with the surname **Felder**. This number reflects several kinds of decreases – those who died of natural causes, the women who may have married by then and thus changed their surnames or remained single and adopted a different surname, the **Felder** slaves who were removed from the state or were killed during the war years, those freedmen who changed, or adopted, a surname other than **Felder** during and after the Civil War, and other forms of outmigration. As it was atypical that freedmen retained the names of their former plantation "masters,"[92] to see this many black **Felders** remaining in the low country after Emancipation is a story ready to be researched in itself.

---

92 Tom Blake, transcriber, Orangeburg County, South Carolina Largest Slaveholders from 1860 Slave Census Schedule and Surname Matches for African Americans on 1870 Census, accessed January 2, 2013, http://freepages.genealogy.rootsweb.ancestry.com/~ajac/scorangeburg.htm.

HANS HENRICH FELDER'S
FAMILY TREE OF SELECT DESCENDANTS

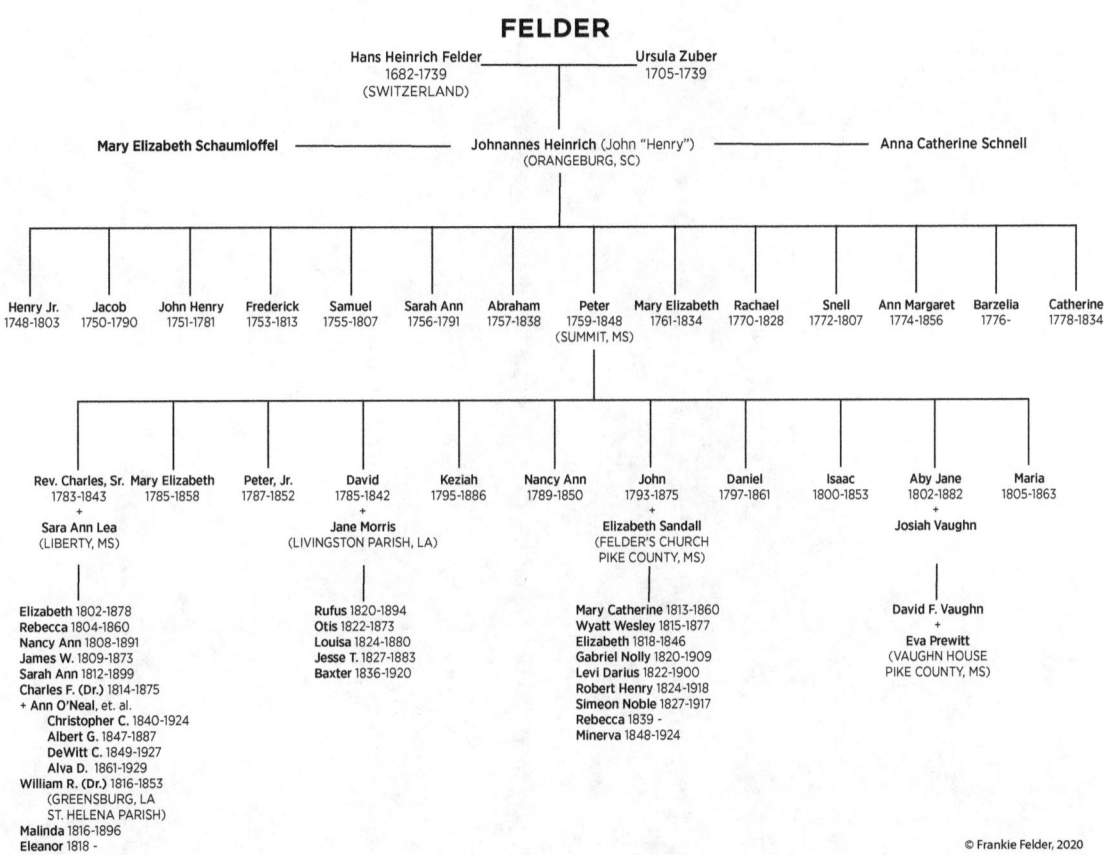

LOUISIANA

Even in swampy, alligator-infested waters, the cypress tree stands firm; roots solidly anchored despite the troubled waters.

F. O. Felder, June 2007, Nearing Angola, Louisiana

3 | THREE SIDES OF AN UNCIVIL WAR

What does Louisiana have to do with *OURstory*?

Six Louisiana parishes (counties) are significant to our family history: Livingston, Pointe Coupée, East Baton Rouge, St. Helena, Orleans, and St. Bernard.

Livingston Parish, a thriving lumber community, and home of most of the **Felders** who ever lived (and still live) in the state, was the location of the town of Gates (no longer extant), to which the first **Felder** – **David** – son of **Peter**, moved from Mississippi in 1832. Along with his family, he took the first **Felder** slaves into the state. It was a parish that participated fully in the Civil War, sending enough men and boys to war to complete a "full company" from the town of Springfield, alone,[93] although generally speaking, Livingstonians were considered "draft dodgers, desperadoes, and individual extremists,"[94] advocating for neither the Union nor Confederate position. It was a parish hardly affected by the war, and during economically depressed times nationwide, illegal stills supported the economy and provided social relief.[95]

Pointe Coupée Parish, on the contrary, bordering the Mississippi River three parishes west of Livingston, was considered as having the "South's most prosperous plantation district."[96] Pointe Coupée was the first Louisiana parish to engage in the Civil War[97] and the last to disengage – although some people accused this parish of being full of "Creoles and 'Cajuns' who heretofore had displayed not *[one]* degree of patriotism."[98] This is the parish in which **ALEXANDER HULBERT** was born.

---

93 History of Livingston Parish, "Trail Blazed," undated and author unknown; secured from Vertical File, Livingston Parish Public Library, accessed November 27, 2013, 4.

94 Kathryn McQueen Kendall, "A Study of Place Names in Livingston Parish, Louisiana" (master's thesis, University of New Orleans, 1975), 9.

95 Kendall, "Place Names," 9-10.

96 Patricia M. Smith, "Text, Context, and Identities in Pointe Coupée, Louisiana" (Ph.D. dissertation, Louisiana State University, 2004), 85.

97 Smith, "Identities in Point Coupée," 84.

98 John D. Winters, *The Civil War in Louisiana* (Baton Rouge: Louisiana State Louisiana Press, 1963), 58.

OURSTORY

OUR LOUISIANA CONNECTIONS

- Where the discovery of the first bit of documentation about our ancestors initiated this book;
- a place that introduced us to slavery in our family;
- the location of the national cemetery of our Civil War hero;
- where our roots spread and we never knew.

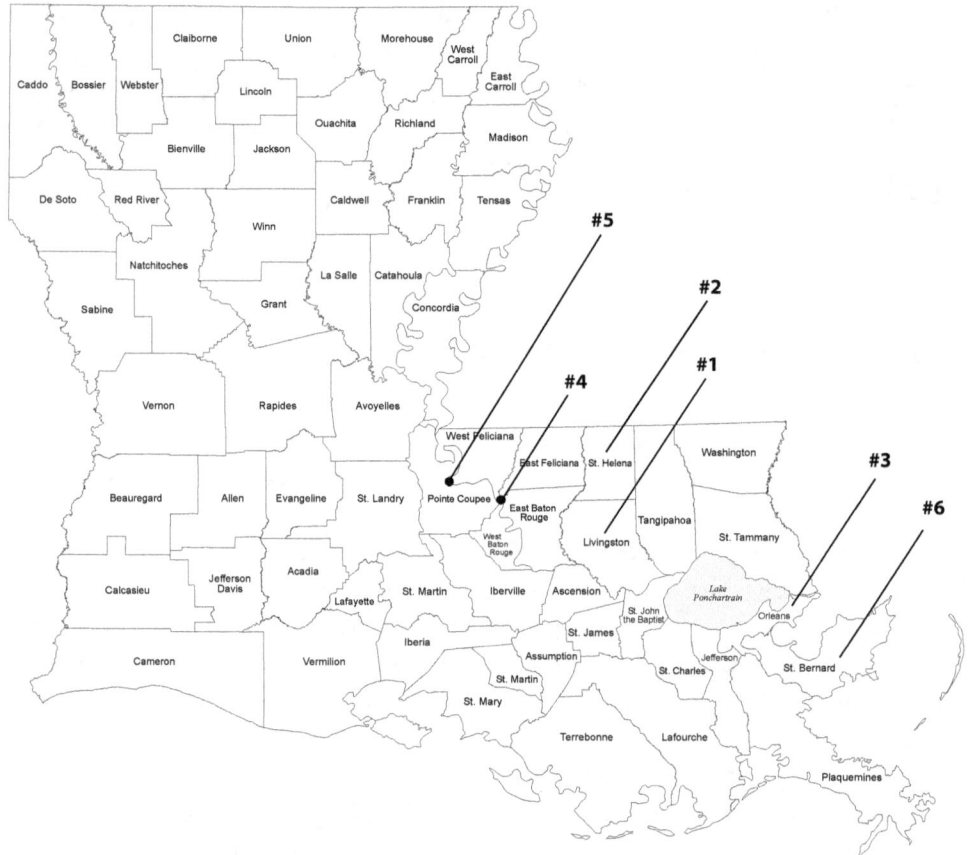

#1 Became Livington Parish in 1832; orginally southern border of St. Helena Parish

#2 Greensburg (in St. Helena Parish)

#3 New Orleans (in Orleans Parish)

#4 Port Hudson (in East Baton Rouge Parish)

#5 Batchelor/Innis (in Pointe Coupée Parish)

#6 Chalmette National Cemetery (St. Bernard Parish)

© Frankie Felder, 2020

St. Helena Parish, due north of Livingston and considered to have "the most beautiful lands in Louisiana ... rolling farm and pasture lands and ... pine-clad hills,"[99] became the parish in which **Dr. William R. Felder** established his practice. The parish seat of government, Greensburg, was likely an early childhood home of great-great-grandfather **JOSEPH FELDER**. It is from this parish's records that documentation of *OURstory* (**FELDER**) originally surfaced.

Orleans Parish became the home of the only African American Civil War veteran documented to date in *OURstory*. He fought in East Baton Rouge Parish, and St. Bernard Parish, the location of Chalmette National Cemetery, is his final resting place.

No Big Deal: It's Just Slave People

JOSEPH FELDER was 12 years old when the Democratically-controlled U.S. Supreme Court ruled on March 6, 1857 in the Dred Scott decision that the Bill of Rights and the U.S. Constitution did not apply to him, and that because he was a little African boy, enslaved in Louisiana, he could never become a citizen of the United States. In fact, this decision made clear that **JOSEPH** had no "rights" whatsoever. Seven of the nine justices were Democrats and five of them, including Chief Justice Roger Taney, were former slave-owners. Only two justices, John McLean and Benjamin Curtis, dissented – both the only Republicans on the Court.

Dred Scott

The following year, Republican Abraham Lincoln lost his bid to represent Illinois in the U.S. Senate to Stephen Douglas, a Democrat. In the famous seven-series Lincoln-Douglas debates which preceded the election, Lincoln uttered those now famous words: "A house divided against itself cannot stand." His stance on slavery was fairly evident and public years before the Supreme Court ruling. In 1855 he wrote:

> Our progress in degeneracy appears to me pretty rapid. As a nation, we began by declaring all men are created equal. We now practically read it 'All men are created equal except Negroes.' When the know nothings get control, it will read, 'All men are created equal except Negroes and foreigners and Catholics.' When it comes to this I should prefer emigrating to some country where they make no pretense of loving liberty[;] to Russia, for instance where despotism can be taken pure and without the base alloy of hypocrisy.[100]

---

99 Irene R. Morris, "St. Helena History: Greensburg Noted for Well-known School of 1880s," *Around Kentwood: It is Remembered* (Kentwood, LA: Kentwood Ledger, undated), 26.

100 "The Pre-Civil War Era Timeline," accessed May 8, 2013, (Digital History, ID2932, 2016), www.digitalhistory.uh.edu/era.cfm?eraID=5&smtID=4.

July 1, 1861, April 2, 1863 or July 1, 1863: on one of those days in Greensburg, someone possibly rang the bell or sounded the cattle horn or the bugle[101] to let folk know that **SUSANNAH**[102] **LEWIS** had given birth to a healthy baby, **SONA PAUL**[103] **LEWIS**. Since the telephone was at least 13 years from invention, this is how the neighbors communicated with each other when important news needed to be telegraphed quickly – their farms being fairly spread out, but the sounds of these instruments being capable of projecting across the distances through the thickly-wooded forestland as well as through the open spaces of the fields. A certain number of toots of the horn or bugle, or rings of the cattle bell (all of which all neighbors had at their disposal), communicated precisely the message they desired to convey; residents of the community having pre-agreed upon this code between themselves: "three long blasts" signaled to come home or come help; one long response signaled that the message was received, "I heard you." The distinctive sounds of the instruments ensured that each of the families could be identified.[104]

Slave baby

But, on second thought, maybe no one even announced this birth because the chocolate brown baby boy who could not take his father's name was only another slave baby. On moderate to large plantations, this natural increase was a significant sign of increased personal wealth, and records were maintained more precisely. But on small subsistence farms in rural communities like Greensburg, such documentation was rare given that many of the slave owners were as illiterate as the slaves themselves. Record-keeping for slave children was often scanty and inaccurate, so dates often are conflicting on documents that are unearthed. Consequently, on which of the above dates **SONA** was actually born is unclear as the *Encyclopedia of African Methodism in Mississippi* records July 1, 1861 as his birth (on which he would have been born a slave); the *Centennial Encyclopedia of the A.M.E. Church* reflects July 1, 1863, and the ***S. P. Felder Family Bible*** records April 2, 1863. The last two dates would have rendered him born technically free. Thus, the exact date of **SONA's** birth, the actual spelling of his name (Sona, Sauna, Saunie, Sonny), whether his middle name was Paul, and where exactly he was born – all of these remain suspect, but the conflicting documents and extremely limited oral family history are the best records we have. So, while we must attempt to surmise from the historical documents if **SONA** was born

---

101 "Communicating in St. Helena before Ma Bell," *St. Helena Historical Association Quarterly*, no. 54 (Winter, year not indicated), 1.

102 Susannah's name is documented with various spellings – Sussie, Susannah, Susanne, Susanna. For purposes of this paper, I will use Susannah.

103 I have yet to locate a document with Sona's middle name spelled out, however, it was suggested by oral family history that Paul was his middle name. My gut sense says it was not, as his daughter's middle initial was also "P" – Susie P. Felder, clearly getting her first name from her mother, so perhaps logically, receiving her middle name from her father; however, I have no clue what it could be!

104 "Communicating before Ma Bell," 2.

Slave auction

a slave during the Civil War or technically born free after the Emancipation Proclamation went into effect – freeing some slaves in designated locations while others remained enslaved – we know for sure from the record of Louisiana marriages that **SUSANNAH LEWIS** would wait years after his birth before she could marry, presumably, the biological father of her child, **JOSEPH FELDERs**.[105]

According to Ann P. Malone, by the 1850s, slave family life in the rural parishes of Louisiana was fairly "stable," and the early destruction of black families being separated by slave trading and selling off individual family members had somewhat subsided.[106] In Greensburg, slaves were traded and sold on the courthouse steps, right in the mid-

Greensburg Courthouse

---

105 Joseph's last name is recorded in the Greensburg Clerk of Court records as Felders with an "s," although no other subsequent records include the "s." Also, no white Felder in Mississippi or Louisiana spelled this surname with an "s" at the end so I make the assumption that this is a spelling error on the part of the parish clerk.

106 Ann Patton Malone, "The Nineteenth Century Slave Family in Rural Louisiana: Its Household and Community Structure" (PhD dissertation, Tulane University, 1985), 32.

dle of the town. All property was auctioned off from the same location – houses, cattle, horses, slaves. It was hard to escape these activities, the town being so small. Despite what historians note as the comparative relaxation of the forced separation of families and loved ones, surely no slave mother, father, or child was ignorant of the fact that a downturn in the economy, a misstep in slave protocol – like plotting to run away, resisting the advances of a white man, or yearning to learn to read – could mean that they, too, might find themselves in front of the courthouse steps, probably in chains, just like Nancy (a "mulatto," age 24) and her three children (ages 6, 4, and 1); Rhody (a "Negro woman of griffe color," age 40); Molley (a "Negro girl of black color," age 20); Judy (a "Negro girl of black color," age 16); Frances (a "Negro girl of black color," age 12); Vilet (a "black," age 11); Farry (a "black," age 7); Dick (a "Negro man," age 24) and Doctor (a "boy," age 19). These 12 slaves were seized on May 29, 1858 by Sheriff Hodges along with the 1000 acres of property being auctioned by him to satisfy the demands of plaintiffs who won a case in the local court.[107] And so, **SUSANNAH** and **JOSEPH** probably moved cautiously through Greensburg and through the parish of St. Helena, although as the teenage parents they had become, they were probably both involved in **SONA's** life in some way as they were apparently living in close proximity to each other, either somewhere in the parish or in a neighboring parish or county right across the state line in Mississippi.

THE CONFEDERATES' WAR

The Roots of War

Back east in the upstate county of Pickens, South Carolina, John C. Calhoun worked at his Fort Hill Plantation (now the home of Clemson University) sharpening more than plantation farm implements – he was sharpening his craft of persuasion. The proslavery, anti-federal government, charismatic states'-righter mentor to other southern politicians had such an influence on his peers that the lower southern states were called by some the "Calhoun states [sic] of America."[108] Although this "father of South Carolina secession" died before he had the opportunity to witness his mentorship of southern politicians on issues of slavery take roothold, his decades of teaching and mentoring his colleagues from his philosophic viewpoint that individual states should be able to nullify federal policy ultimately succeeded – essentially in less than one decade following his death in 1851. His abhorrence of the tariffs imposed by the federal government, which adversely impacted the cost of slavery for southern states, himself, and his friends, won him fame among southern legislators in Congress, but made enemies for him among the northern legislators.

Despite opposition to many of his views, Calhoun was appointed to various posts by numerous presidents, as well as reelected to Congress and to national office throughout his political life, including the post of Vice President of the United States. He served as Vice President under both John Quincy Adams and Andrew Jackson. His war hawk leanings influenced President James Monroe

---

107 *Greensburg Imperial*, vol. 2, no. 37, May 29, 1858.

108 Manisha Sinha, "The Strange Victory of the Palmetto State," February 5, 2011, accessed March 24, 2012, http://opinionator.blogs.nytimes.com/2011/02/05/the-strange-victory-of-the-palmetto-state/.

to appoint him Secretary of War in 1817, a post he held for eight years. Calhoun's ability to convince his peers to go to war against superpower Great Britain in the War of 1812, although not a slam-dunk win for the United States, left little doubt in his fellow Southerners' minds 50 years later that war against the United States federal government would be anything but successful.

And so, only nine years after Calhoun's death in 1851, it took just a brief 45 minutes for South Carolina legislators to vote unanimously – 169 to 0 – to give birth to an idea borne of his philosophy, whose spread throughout the South, however, would ultimately bring unprecedented death and destruction to the entire nation. Their unanimous vote to secede from, and thus dissolve, the union of the states of America was signed into law on December 20, 1860. Abraham Lincoln had been elected President of the United States by an Electoral College majority only six weeks before. South Carolina governor, Francis W. Pickens, father of numerous slave children,[109] by instruction of the resolution adopted in the Secession Convention on December 25, 1860, sent his colleagues in slave-holding states a unique Christmas gift – a request that they join him in forming a Southern Confederacy. Governor Pickens sent commissioners to each of these states to explain this opportunity for independence. Mississippi was the first state to join in. Florida, Alabama, and Georgia seceded next, in that order, within less than 30 days of receiving the invitation. In Louisiana, where the legislature split on seceding, and where not all representatives even signed the ordinance, the outcome remained the same – on January 26, 1861, Louisiana became the fifth state to follow South Carolina's lead in dissolving allegiance to the United States.

John C. Calhoun

Fort Hill Plantation

Aside from these five states' immediate RSVP to South Carolina's invitation, in other southern states there was hesitation, debate and deliberation, but nonetheless, in less than a year, Virginia, Texas, North Carolina, Tennessee, and Arkansas also joined their southern brothers in this "confederation." Missouri initially voted to reject secession, then went both Confederate and Union! Kentucky voted to remain neutral, but later became a Confederate state as the fighting progressed.

---

109 Orville Vernon Burton, *In My Father's House are Many Mansions: Family and Community in Edgefield, South Carolina* (Chapel Hill: University of North Carolina Press, 1985), 186.

TIMELINE OF SECESSION

December 20, 1860	South Carolina Legislature votes 169-0 to secede from the United States
December 25, 1860	Gov. Pickens invites states to join the Southern Confederacy
January 3, 1861	Delaware votes unanimously to reject secession
January 9, 1861	Mississippi votes to secede, 84-15
January 10, 1861	Florida votes to secede, 62-7
January 11, 1861	Alabama votes to secede, 61-39
January 19, 1861	Georgia votes to secede, 208-89
January 26, 1861	Louisiana votes to secede, 113-17
February 1, 1861	Texas votes to secede, 166-7
February 19, 1861	Maryland postpones vote to secede to April, and again in April to September
April 12, 1861	Confederates attack Fort Sumpter, SC
April 17, 1861	Virginia votes to secede, 88-55
May 6, 1861	Arkansas votes to secede, 69-1
May 16, 1861	Kentucky votes to remain neutral, 69-26
May 20, 1861	North Carolina votes to secede, 120-0
June 8, 1861	Tennessee votes to secede, 66-25
September 17, 1861	Federal government and Baltimore police arrive at Maryland convention to arrest pro-secessionists; no vote ever taken
October 30, 1861	Missouri votes to reject secession, 98-1
December 10, 1861	Kentucky admitted as Confederate state
December 10, 1861	Missouri votes again to reject secession (but established a fractured Confederate government as well)

The United States of America was no more.

State of the State: Louisiana

During the "high profit phase of slavery" it was, according to arguments advanced by many plantation masters, "cheaper to buy than to breed."[110] That meant, literally, that it was cheaper to work a slave to death and then replace him/her than to allow "natural increase" – children being born and reaching the age to become productive workers (somewhere around age five). Supporting natural increase meant work and expense for the slave owner who then needed to provide a reasonably healthy living space and expend cash to pay for doctors and medicine, and so forth, so that newborns and their mothers would live through childbirth. During this "high profit phase of slavery" in Louisiana and in the Caribbean on the sugar plantations, "the life of a slave from initial purchase to death was only seven years."[111]

---

[110] Antebellum Slavery, "Development of American Slavery," accessed November 15, 2014, http://www.civilwarhome.com/slavery.html. See also Edgar, *South Carolina*, 37.

[111] Antebellum Slavery, "Development of American Slavery."

In 1802, Louisiana was credited with producing 5000 hogsheads of sugar or 5 million pounds. One hogshead is equivalent to one barrel that contains approximately 1000 pounds of sugar. On the eve of the Civil War, 1300 Louisiana farms or plantations were involved in the production of sugar, which had increased ten-fold to 500 million pounds since 1802;[112] that is, the equivalent of 500,000 barrels, each containing 1000 pounds of sugar, were produced annually! Valued in 1858 at $69/hogshead, the industry had become the cash crop in the state, with the slaves of Louisiana producing 95% of all sugar in the United States; that is, slaves/workers in all other states combined only produced 5% of the sugar grown in the U.S.[113] The estimated value of Louisiana sugar was $25,000,000.[114]

Sugar scene on The Levee, New Orleans

By 1810, slaves in the South produced and picked 85,000 pounds of cotton per year, partly because Sam and his father, both slaves on the plantation of Catherine Greene in Savannah, Georgia, found a way to make this work easier. By using a comb they made, they were able to speed the process of separating the sticky seed from the cotton plant. Sam, it is said, shared this idea with Eli Whitney,[115] who as we know from *his*tory, received a patent for the invention of the cotton gin. Slaves could not apply for patents. The impact of mechanization of this step of cotton production, which is credited to Whitney, unfortunately, led to the need for more slaves on plantations to pick more cotton. Bigger cotton fields; more slaves; more backbreaking work. By 1860, more than two billion pounds of cotton were produced a year, with an increase in value from $12,495,000 in 1810 to more than $248,757,000 in 1860,[116] and nearly one-sixth of that was produced by the slave workforce on Louisiana plantations. Louisiana was home to the third, fourth, and seventh of America's ten richest slaveholding families in 1860,[117] and the state's total of 22,033 slaveholders (5.6% of all slaveholders nationwide) "owned" 331,726 (8.4%) of all slaves in the country.

---

112 Mark Schmitz, "The Transformation of the Southern Cane Sugar Sector: 1860-1930," *Agricultural History, Southern Agriculture Since the Civil War: A Symposium*, vol. 53, no. 1 (January 1979): 270.

113 "Crops in Alexandra," accessed November 15, 2014, https://www.cityofalexandriala.com/history/our-culture.

114 "Crops in Alexandra."

115 John H. Lienhard, "No. 127, Black Inventors," Engines of Our Ingenuity, accessed August 26, 2020, https://www.uh.edu/engines/epi127.htm. See also Brian L. Frye, "Invention of a Slave," University of Kentucky, *UKnowledge*, Winter 2018.

116 Antebellum Slavery, "Development of American Slavery," accessed November 15, 2014, http://www.civilwarhome.com/slavery.html.

117 Tom Blake, *The Sixteen Largest American Slaveholders from 1860 Slave Census Schedules*, accessed November 15, 2014, http://freepages.genealogy.rootsweb.ancestry.com/~ajac/biggest16.htm.

OURSTORY

AMERICA'S TEN RICHEST SLAVEHOLDING FAMILIES, 1860

Name and Number of Plantations Owned	Name of Slave "Owner" and Location of Plantations	State	Number of Slaves	Primary Crops	Notes
Brookgreen (1)	Col. Joshua Ward, Georgetown	SC	1130	rice	
Auburn (>15 in MS & LA)	Dr. Stephen Duncan, Issaquena	MS	858	cotton, sugar	(over time enslaved > 2,000 people)
Houmas (>10)	John Burnside, Ascension	LA	753	sugar	
Calhoun's Landing (4)	Meredith Calhoun, Rapides	LA	709	cotton, sugar	
Jehossee Island (entire island)	William Aiken, Colleton	SC	700	rice, sweet potatoes, corn	
Milford (SC & LA)	Gov. John L. Manning, Pinewood	SC	670	sugar	
Angola (7)	Col. Joseph Acklen, W. Feliciana	LA	659	cotton	
Chicora Wood (5)	Gov. Robert F. Allston, Georgetown	SC	631	rice	(won silver medal [1855] and gold medal [1856] for rice cultivation methods - Pans Exposition)
Bonny Hall / Plainsfield (2)	Joseph Blake, Beaufort	SC	610	rice	
The Cottage Place (5)	John Robinson, Madison	MS	550	cotton	

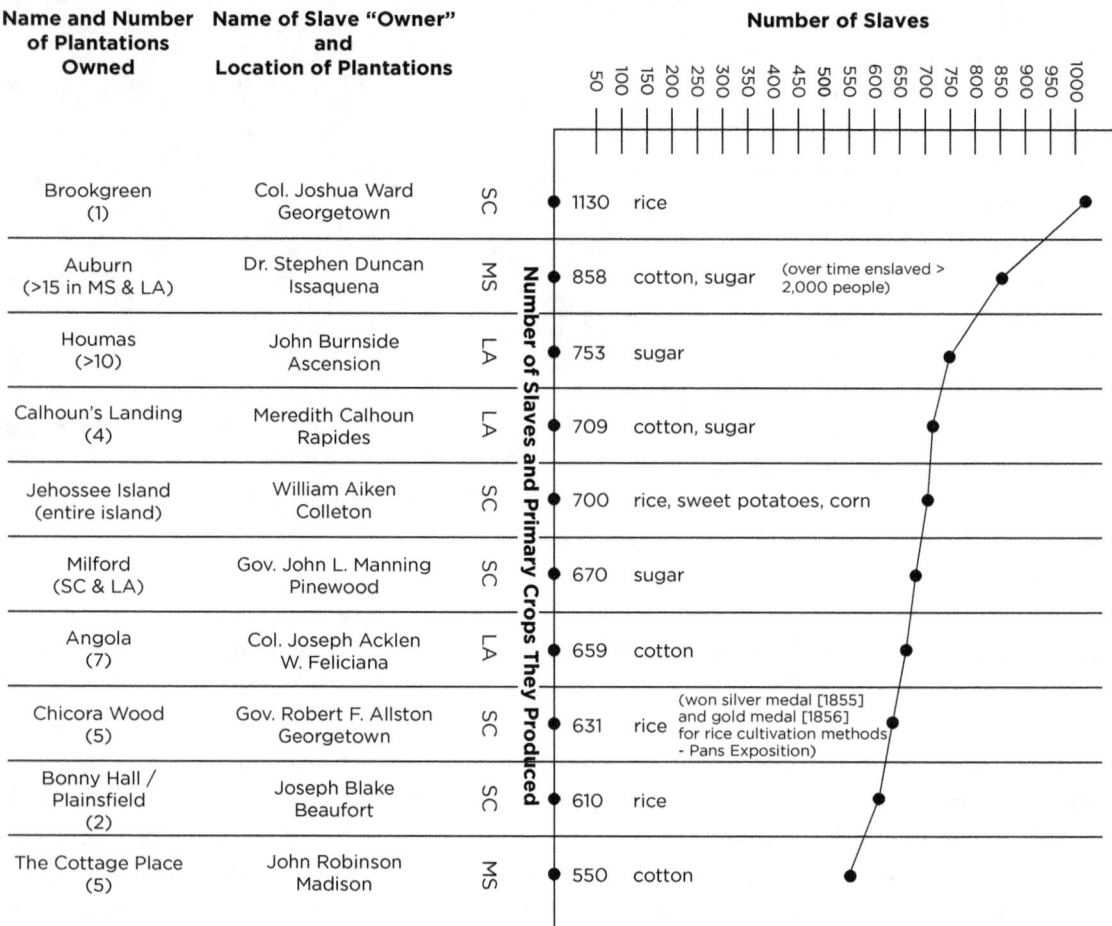

© Frankie Felder, 2020

Louisiana Goes to War

Although living in the back country of Louisiana in 1860, off the beaten path in St. Helena Parish (county) where large plantations did not exist, the eyes of little slave children on farms in Greensburg (the parish seat of government) nonetheless surely saw much fear and agony on the faces of people all around them. While they may not have been able to discern the implications of the conversations, their ears surely heard talk of a country spiraling towards seeming annihilation. The February 9, 1861 *Greensburg Imperial* ran a front-page article that predicted if the states engaged in civil war and dissolved into a number of Confederations, it would not be long before all foreign countries with prior claims to American soil would come forth to reclaim their former territories. This prediction was based on the premise that the United States had never paid France a balance of $5 million owed for the "Louisiana Purchase" and, therefore, Napoleon III would try to take back Napoleon I's earlier holdings in America if she dissolved as a nation. Surely, went the prediction, other foreign powers would follow suit: England would reclaim Oregon and other states; Spain would come for Florida, and Mexico would take back the territory of Mexico, Texas, and California. Then, as if invoking God's name in the debate would bring Southerners to their senses, the article ended, "See how Providence, having such an instrument as Louis Napoleon to work with, can bring everyone back to harmony."[118] In other words, certainly this would not be allowed to occur!

In other news from the Greensburg paper in 1861, it was learned that the State Secession Convention passed rules requiring state officers of the mint and custom house to "transfer their allegiance from the United States to the State of Louisiana"[119] – and they did. Greensburg residents who were able, read in this same edition of their local paper that "the northerners, seeing that six states have now seceded from the Union, have been roused from the imaginary security into which they had been lulled, and made to believe the fact, that secession was not at all a 'joke.'"[120] And, indeed, it was not. Despite the fact that Louisiana had only become a state 50 years earlier (April 30, 1812), its significance to the economy of the South, and the country as a whole, was undeniable. Slavery had very quickly become the staple of Louisiana's existence, with nearly half of the population of the state at the outset of the war being slaves *who, through <u>their</u> blood, sweat and tears, and in many instances, their lives*, led the nation not only in the production and exportation of sugar, but also in the production of most of the nation's cotton. In 1860, slaves constituted 47% of the population of the state

Cotton scene on The Levee, New Orleans

---

118 The Greensburg I*mperial*, no. 19, February 9, 1861, 1.

119 Greensburg *Imperial*, 1.

120 Greensburg *Imperial*, 1.

and approximately 29% of all free Louisiana households held slaves.[121] Thus, Louisiana had a vested interest in secession.

According to one source, before the war ended in 1865, Louisiana would organize 265 Confederate and 23 Union regiments, sending approximately 96,000 men into war – 86,000 of whom were Confederates and 10,000 of whom were Union soldiers.[122] Another source suggested that 82,000 total Louisiana men went to war – 77,000 of whom were Confederate and 5000 of whom were Union soldiers. And yet another source indicated that the 5000 white Louisianans who fought for the Union army did so alongside 24,000 African Americans from the state! Data from the war has wide discrepancies, especially from the South, where it was suggested that they did not have the manpower or time to keep very accurate records.[123] It is also interesting to note that a significant percentage of Louisiana's white soldiers who fought for the Confederacy were very recent immigrants, not transplanted native-born whites who had migrated from other southern states although, altogether, the Confederate army was not particularly diverse, having only 9% foreign-born soldiers. Conversely, the Union army was nearly 43% diverse, with some regiments being all foreign,[124] providing a good reason for international interest in what was happening in the war. Irrespective of wide data discrepancies, it was clear where the general constituency of Louisiana stood on the issue of slavery.

Greensburg

On April 28, 1861, the St. Helena Rifles left for the war from Greensburg, headed first to New Orleans, 87 miles southeast, and then to a myriad of locations above and below the Mason-Dixon line, to places they never dreamed they would see and certainly never dreamed that they may die. Thirty or so of the 63 men, too indigent to purchase their own uniforms, wore uniforms sewn in a two-day frenzy by the women of Greensburg who, aided by a professional tailor, used grey cloth personally selected and paid for in New Orleans by the Greensburg Clerk of the Court, James A. Williams. This former Louisiana state legislator held up the vote for secession, debating and arguing the consequences and the strategies, but ultimately voted to secede "under protest" on the very last ballot of the *[Secession]* Convention. But he then chose to personally ensure that the whole regiment, the St. Helena Rifles, would leave Greensburg for war in proper attire.[125]

This was indeed a historic moment in Greensburg. The townspeople witnessed residents ranging in age from a 14-year-old boy, too young to enlist, to a 36-year-old man, too old to enlist, stepping forward to defend their new-found country – the Confederate States. Both volunteers were ultimately discharged due to age,[126] although before the war ended, approximately 20% of the soldiers were younger than 18, and there were drummers, buglers, and other musicians as young as 10; some sources

---

121 "Selected Statistics on Slavery in the United States," accessed August 6, 2013, http://civilwarcauses.org/stat.htm.

122 Louisiana in the Civil War, http://www.historynet.com/civil-war, accessed January 7, 2014, httpss://familysearch.org/learn/wiki/en/Louisiana_in_the_Civil_War.

123 Edwin L. Ferguson, Sumner County Tennessee in the Civil War, accessed January 7, 2014, http://sites.rootsweb.com/~tnsumner/sumnfg1.htm.

124 http://rimw.xom/3940428/ciivil-war-immigrant-soldiers/, accessed January 23, 2019.

125 Amable Peltier Richards, The Saint Helena Rifles (Houston: self-published, 1968), 20.

126 http://files.usgwarchives.net/la/sthelena/military/civwsha3.txt, accessed December 27, 2013.

say some were as young as eight. They took up arms to ensure that their right to maintain and expand the system of chattel slavery would not be dissolved by the newly-elected Republican government (the "Black Republican government" as called by the Confederates) led by President Abraham Lincoln. The newly-commissioned soldiers fervently believed that they could defeat the hated president who vowed, "The Union must and shall be preserved!"[127]

With hearts filled with pride, and minds waging battle between visceral fear of defeat and prayers for victory, the parish residents cheered wildly for the St. Helena Rifles as they paraded down the street at 11 a.m. on the morning of their departure. According to Amable Peltier Richards, the 14-year old former stowaway Frenchman turned 22-year-old southern Confederate patriot who put down his carpenter tools to join

Child soldier

the fight, Greensburg hosted quite a send-off for her men and boys. As he recalled, the formal program included invited speaker Col. James Fuqua, Louisiana State Convention representative from East Feliciana. But also from the speaker's platform, Ms. Louisiana Carter, an 18-year-old local resident, presented a flag to the soldiers that the local women had made. Her speech, spoken in words that only a woman could elicit from her heart, brought tears to the eyes of men and women alike. The company commander, Capt. J. B. Taylor, handed the flag over to M. C. Williams, regiment color guard. Richards recalled the "whole town" was filled with residents from across the parish who came to this barbecue farewell celebration to bid their husbands, fathers, sons, brothers, cousins, uncles, in-laws, and himself, Godspeed before they boarded the 8 p.m. train to New Orleans.[128]

But, was the *whole* town really there? In 1860, St. Helena Parish was actually a majority black community, with slaves comprising fifty-two percent of the population. In 1861, St. Helena Parish was unique in that, although extremely rural, more than half (51.5%) of the households in the parish held slaves compared to only 29% of households in the rest of the state and 25% of most households throughout the South.[129] Eighty percent (80%) of elected officials in St. Helena owned slaves, and so these slaves likely got to observe the government up close for extended periods of time as a handful of ruling families essentially dominated the elected offices in the parish, passing the baton of local government leadership back and forth between and amongst themselves from year to year.[130]

With so many slaves in the parish – 3711 to be exact – one wonders what their role was in the preparation for this impending war. How much did they actually know about what was happening? What were they told by their slave "owners" and what else did they hear as they traveled the dusty country roads? Were they idle bystanders? Did the slaves salute the St. Helena Rifles when they boarded the train like the rest of the townspeople? Did they attend the barbeque send-off? Were they

---

127 Presidential Rhetoric, http://www.presidentialrhetoric.com/historicspeeches/lincoln/stateoftheunion1861.html, accessed December 27, 2013.

128 Richards, *St. Helena Rifles*, 20-23.

129 John Hope Franklin, *From Slavery to Freedom, a History of African Americans*, 2000, 123.

130 Samuel Hyde, *Pistols and Politics: The Dilemma of Democracy in Louisiana's Florida* (Baton Rouge: Louisiana State University Press, 1998), 65.

willing cooks, servers, and custodians? Were any of the soldier's uniforms sewn by slave women? Did they attend to the children of the townspeople during this day-long affair? Were the male slaves eager to fight for and defend their present way of life or did they lift their voices to the heavens silently praying for victory to come to the Union soldiers? Were the six free blacks that lived in the parish – two males and four females – supporters of the Union or the Confederacy, or did they have mixed allegiances among themselves? Dared any of the slaves voice their opinions, their fears, their hopes? Did they even dare to dream of freedom? Did fifteen-year old **JOSEPH FELDER** dream of freedom?

Fighting in and around Greensburg

Skirmishes occurred on May 1, 1863, on the Amite River at a location that some say was in St. Helena Parish. In 1863, Union General Benjamin Gierson's Regiment (6th Illinois) of 1700 mounted men reportedly rode from LaGrange, Tennessee to Baton Rouge, Louisiana, suffering few losses but destroying Confederate supplies, railroads, bridges, plantation homes, and soldiers ...and freeing slaves along the way. They rode through Crystal Springs and Hermanville, Mississippi into Louisiana. It was said they "occupied and camped out on the *[Greensburg]* courthouse grounds for several days."[131] Again, on October 5th and 9th in 1864, skirmishes were reported to be in St. Helena Parish, in Greensburg proper.[132]

On October 5, 1864, as Union Brigadier General Albert L. Lee marched the approximately 80 miles northeast from Baton Rouge with close to 1000 soldiers and raided the rural towns along the way for at least a second time to gather supplies for his Union regiment, they burned as much cotton[133] as possible, along with slave cabins and the barracks at Camp Moore in St. Helena Parish, only 45 miles east of Greensburg. Lee and his men returned to Baton Rouge four days later laden with quinine *[used in the treatment of malaria]*, somewhere in the neighborhood of 150 Confederate prisoners,[134] and 200 horses and mules.[135] In Greensburg,[136] they also burned the tannery and two thousand sides of leather used for making shoes and saddles, destroying the grey cloth as well as other items used in the making of Confederate uniforms.[137]

"Townspeople not engaged in the war directly," it was said, were challenged to "obtain sustenance enough to stay alive."[138] Union soldiers took chickens and other meats, as well as all the horses except one, from the Arbuthnot farm on the outskirts of Greensburg. The Arbuthnot men had joined the St. Helena Rifles or other companies, and only the women were home during this raid. Arbuthnot's granddaughter (A. P. Richards' daughter) recalled that her grandmother pleaded with the "rebel" forces to leave her one horse so that her family would have transportation – and they complied.

---

131 Edwin Schilling, Echoes from the Past (Amite, Louisiana: Saint Helena Historical Association, 1998), A. 3.

132 http://files.usgwarchives.net/la/sthelena/military/civwsha2.txt, (accessed December 27, 2013).

133 Edwin A. Davis, *Heroic Years: Louisiana in the War for Southern Independence*, Lectures in Louisiana History (Baton Rouge, Louisiana: WBRZ-TV, 1964), 62.

134 Winters, *Civil War in Louisiana*, 397.

135 Jefferson Davis Bragg, *Louisiana in the Confederacy* (Baton Rouge: Louisiana State University, 1941), 176.

136 Winters, *Civil War in Louisiana*, 397.

137 Bragg, *Louisiana in the Confederacy*, 176.

138 Davis, *Heroic Years*, 62.

The Union men also captured a young Arbuthnot son who was on his way to enlist. The story was told that they would not let his mother even see him before they marched him away and that she, in fact, never saw him again as he died of measles in the Union prison.[139] Clearly, whether engaged directly or not, the war impacted everyone, and details of events – real or imagined, exaggerated or not – certainly buzzed around Greensburg by relatives of soldiers who had gone off to fight, by those directly affected by the pilferage of the Union forces, and by those Confederate neighbors who returned home mortally wounded but who lived long enough to tell their side of the story. The slaves of Greensburg knew something. They felt something. Fear? Excitement?

Camp Moore

Camp Moore was one of only two major camps in Louisiana, and it was the largest of all of them. There, approximately 35,000 men were processed and prepared for battle; teamed up in battalions (of 300 to 1000 men), companies (of 62 to 190 men), and platoons (of 16 to 44 men). Elections were held to select the leadership of the troops (e.g., captains, majors, and generals, etc.). These men were not professional soldiers – they were volunteers – and so rank was often obtained through a popularity vote and was seldom based on military experience, skill, or merit, which was a typical Confederate practice in the beginning of the war.[140] The camp boasted a grocery store, a coffee house, refreshment and soda shops, a barber shop, photographer's salon, butcher shop, and a post sutler who operated a store with non-essential items that the soldiers desired but were not provided by the military (like sardines, chewing tobacco, candy, etc.). Camp Moore also had "old black Mary's restaurant,"[141] which I suspect every soldier thoroughly enjoyed; clearly home cooking for many.

Camp Moore was located in the St. Helena up-woods because its wide-open space was sufficient to accommodate the thousands of men who volunteered or were later drafted into service, and because it was situated on the Tangipahoa River, which provided fresh water for drinking and swimming. That Camp Moore was so situated ensured that it had few mosquitoes. This was a blessing in disguise as the doctors did not know at the time that both malaria and yellow fever were mosquito-borne diseases. These two diseases ravaged soldiers, particularly throughout the South, where the swampy grasses and high humidity supported breeding through much of the year causing the doctors at Camp Moore, and everywhere else, to work overtime. The cemetery outside the camp was inundated with soldiers, many of whom, arriving with illnesses festering in their bodies, never made it beyond the initial mustering at the camp.

Although some hospitals were more sanitary than these and were indoor facilities, most were quite unsanitary

War ambulance

---

139 Richards, *St. Helena Rifles*, iv.

140 Mary W. Schaller, Martin N. Schaller and Frank Schaller, ed., Soldiering for Glory: *The Civil War Letters of Colonel Frank Schaller, 22nd Mississippi Infantry* (Columbia, South Carolina: University of South Carolina Press, 2007), 156.

141 Members.tripod.com/j_richard/18_history_camps_forts.html, accessed January 17, 2014 (page removed).

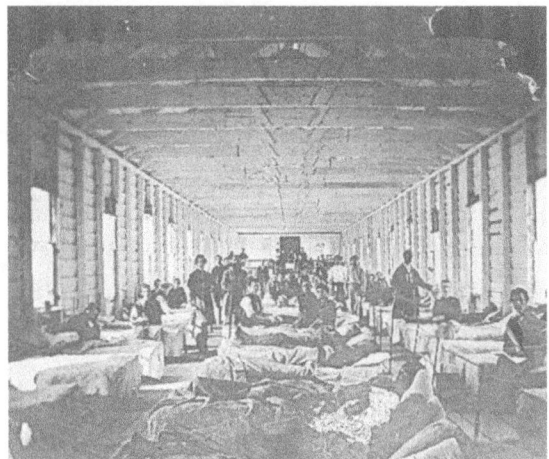
War hospital

Surgery in field hospital

City Point, Hopewell, Virginia makeshift cemetery

and outside. Many soldiers in both the Union and Confederate armies, and most in both armies in rural communities, particularly, received little more aid than such as depicted here. Imagine living through the amputation shown in the middle photo!

The southern landscape turned into makeshift graveyards of wretchedness by armies too consumed to honor the lives of their fallen men. Bodies too numerous to identify by name were often dumped into quickly carved out trenches. Finally looking eye to eye, but too late to see, dead soldiers in blue and grey would lay forever side by side, positioned by the black hands of slaves over whom they fought and died. It is estimated that more than 620,000 men died in the Civil War, but approximately two-thirds of them died from diseases, including tuberculosis, chicken pox, measles, pneumonia, scurvy, small pox, and ague *[the "shakes"]*. Dysentery and typhoid ranked at the very top of these diseases, taking the lives of more than 150,000 soldiers, almost equally divided between the Union and the Confederate armies. The primary culprit? Filthy water that bred mosquitoes.[142] One New York *Times* reporter wrote of the "clouds of mosquitoes that enveloped the soldiers *[and descended]* upon you like a hawk on a June bug, without warning of any kind...".[143]

In November 1864, Camp Moore was attacked for a second time by Union forces, this time by General John Wynn Davidson's 5000-strong army. They burned everything, effectively shutting the camp down. It was never used again. What remains today is a monument, more than 400 graves, a museum, and an annual November war enactment.

---

142 Civilwaracademy.com/civil-war-diseases.html, accessed January 18, 2013.

143 Terry L. Jones, "The Canal to Nowhere," Opinionator/Disunion: *The New York Times* (New York: Black Dog and Leventhal Publishers, 2013).

Confederate Felders Everywhere

Within a few months after Louisiana seceded on January 26, 1861, **Felder** men were beginning to experience the war all across the country. First, in Livingston Parish, **David Felder's** son, **Otis Henry** enlisted as a 1st Sergeant in Company G, 9th Louisiana Infantry. He was the first brother to serve in the war from this family, returning home once wounded. He also, however, served as a mail contractor during the war, ensuring that the mail would go through. **Jesse** and **Baxter** also enlisted, both in Corpl. Co. D. 3rd (Wingfield's) Confederate unit, on June 16, 1862, one month after **Otis** returned home. **Jesse** was captured and held as a prisoner of war. [144] In Mississippi, virtually all of **Peter Felder's** descendants enlisted as Confederate soldiers or supported the seceded states in other ways to be revealed later.

Felders from South Carolina who moved to Texas participated also. On September 12, 1861, 21-year-old Chappell Hill, Texas resident, **Private Rufus King Felder**, was itching to see action. He and his older cousin, **Miers**,[145] traveled by train from New Orleans to Richmond, Virginia to begin their service in the Confederate army. Shortly after arriving, they took a photo to send home as **Rufus'** mother, **Catherine**, had asked. In the meantime, they anxiously awaited the moment when they would join the fight. **Rufus** wrote a letter home and shared: "I had the pleasure of seeing the yankee [sic] prisoners .... They sometimes got very insulting. Several of them had to be shot by the guards ...". He ended this letter by sending greetings: "Tell all the Negroes howdy for me and tell them I am growing fast and harty [sic]. Give my love to all & tell the girls [presumably his sisters] I will expect letters from all of them ...".[146]

Around November 17, 1861, **Rufus** again wrote home after the company's march north to Quantico near Dumfries, Virginia. Although they had to leave 18 soldiers behind because of poor health, and 30 of the regiment had already died of yellow fever, the men "found some relief watching each other slide and fall in the mud."[147] **Rufus** wrote:

> ...We had a dreadful march of it over the worst road I ever saw .... There was not chance for a fight [because the Federal troops had not yet crossed the Potomac River.] The useless order was from Gen. Wigfall & has I think the fancy of an intoxicated brain [sic]. ...no telling what moment the long roll will be sounded to lead us forth to battle. Come when it may they will find brave hearts to meet them & men who not only feel the power of their arm, but know that the God of battles are [sic] with us & will sustain the cause of right and justice.[148]

In their wildest imaginations, these young **Felder** boys could not begin to fathom how this war was going to change their lives. **Rufus** and **Miers**, perhaps like the whole of the many young boys

---

144 Edward Livingston Historical Association History Book Committee, *History of Livingston Parish* (Dallas: Curtis Media Corp, 1986), 400.

145 Both Miers and Rufus were from Orangeburg, South Carolina and moved to Chappell Hill, Texas with their families in 1854 and 1855, respectively. The 17 Felder slaves of Catherine and Frank Felder, Rufus' parents, were also transported to Chappell Hill. Catherine moved there with her family after Frank died.

146 Stephen Chicoine, "Notes and Documents ... Willing Never to Go in Another Fight: The Civil War Correspondence of Rufus King Felder of Chappell Hill," *Southwestern Historical Quarterly*, vol. 106, no. 4 (April 2003): 577-78.

147 Chicoine, *"Notes and Documents,"* 578.

148 Chicoine, *"Notes and Documents,"* 578.

who volunteered to fight, did so for a myriad of reasons: they loved the South; they were going to be paid for their military service; they did not have much else to do in their rural communities, although **Miers** was enrolled in college at Soule University at the time he enlisted; they were boys, and boys thought fighting was manly. What would ultimately happen to their regiment or their beloved South, they would too soon discover.

Operating on the emboldened energy and enthusiasm of their southern kinsmen and comrades, **Miers** and **Rufus** set out to help sustain the only way of life that they had known. Not long into their adventure, **Miers** was badly wounded, ultimately discharged, and retrieved from the war by a brother-in-law who came to Virginia to take him first to South Carolina, then on to Texas.[149] But **Rufus** courageously fought on, at one point in June of 1862, helping to reinforce Stonewall Jackson's men in Staunton, Virginia, of which he was quite proud. **Rufus** was one of the fortunate Confederate Civil War soldiers. He returned to Texas unharmed after three years of service, but he found that his mother's slaves – the ones he sent "howdies" to from the front lines – had been technically freed. They were "free" because when President Lincoln signed the Emancipation Proclamation on January 1, 1863, it mandated that slavery be maintained only in those states and areas of southern states that were already under Union control; however, in areas remaining in Confederate hands, the slaves, technically, were freed.[150] Chappell Hill, nor any other place in Texas for that matter, had not been captured and was not occupied by the Union army. Thus, by the technical declaration of the Emancipation, his mother's "Negroes" were now free! *[Praise God for the beginning of the end of the beginning!]*

Many enterprising, adventurous men moved their families to Texas, considered the "frontier" during the antebellum days of slavery. Many moved in order to acquire more land – basically free land, made available through the Homestead Act of May 20, 1862, although over time some went west and actually purchased land. Even though Texas joined the Confederacy, there were not nearly the number of slaveholders in that state as in other southern locations. But, even in Texas, the **Felder** family that migrated from South Carolina assumed prominent political roles and were significantly involved in what slave trade that did exist in the state. **Gabriel** had moved from Orangeburg, South Carolina, to Mississippi near his other **Felder** relatives, and then to Washington County, Texas. In South Carolina, where he had literally hundreds of **Felder** relatives, virtually all participating in the slave trade, he had been a judge, following the career path of his father, Judge **Samuel Felder**. **Peter Felder** and **Samuel** were brothers – children of **Captain Henry Felder** – the Orangeburg Revolutionary War soldier. Thus, **Gabriel** was **Peter's** nephew.

One of **Gabriel's** half-brothers was **John Myers Felder**, a prominent South Carolina state representative and senator, U.S. representative, law school roommate and friend at Yale University of John C. Calhoun, and by 2012 standards, a multimillionaire. While **John Myers Felder** and John C. Calhoun disagreed on and debated many political issues, they agreed on nullification, on states' rights, and on maintaining slavery; both having amassed tremendous financial and political capital

---

149 Stephen Chicoine, *The Confederates of Chappell Hill, Texas: Prosperity, Civil War, and Decline* (Jefferson N.C.: McFarland, 2005), 54.

150 *The African American Experience in Louisiana*, accessed May 9, 2013, https://www.crt.state.la.us/Assets/OCD/hp/nationalregister/historic_contexts/The_African_American_Experience_in_Louisiana.pdf, 23-28. Provides an excellent explanation of what "freed" meant at that time for slaves and free people of color. While this reference specifically describes "freedom" in Louisiana, it was similar everywhere.

because of their overwhelmingly successful investments in the institution of slavery. *[Calhoun's plantation, Fort Hill, is now Clemson University.]* Upon his death in 1851, **John Myers Felder's** will divided his estate equally among his four brothers. Brother **Gabriel** inherited approximately $100,000[151] in slaves and equipment for his plantation. He had this inheritance brought to Texas by his cousin, **Jesse Young Felder**, also a Yale graduate and former politician in the SC State Legislature. **Jesse's** younger brother, **Miers**, helped in the transfer. The slaves arrived on June 20, 1854.[152] Thus 95 or so *[records differ]* of the **Felder** slaves formerly of **John Myers Felder's** South Carolina plantation became **Felder** slaves on **Gabriel's** sprawling 2418-acre Texas plantation making **Gabriel Felder** the largest slaveholder in Washington County, Texas, with 130 slaves on the eve of the Civil War. During this transfer of slaves, **Miers'** mother, **Catherine Felder**, also sent her slaves from Orangeburg to Washington County to help with clearing the land. Because her husband, **Frank**, had died, the following year **Catherine** also moved to Texas with her family, which included her son, **Rufus King Felder**.[153] Consequently, another group of South Carolina **Felder** slaves became Texas **Felder** slaves. When the time came, **Miers** and **Rufus** enlisted together as Confederate soldiers to help protect their families' investment.

---

151 $100,000 in 1851, according to the measuringworth.com calculation rendered Gabriel Felder a multimillionaire in 2012 standards. The labor value of his commodity (slaves) was approximately $21.8 million; the real price - $3.1 million; historic standard of living - $3.1 million; economic power - $593 million; and economic status - $45.5 million. This was only one-fourth of John Myers' estate.

152 Texas State Historical Association, "Gabriel Felder," accessed November 28, 2013, http://www.tshaonline.org/handbook/online/articles/ffe13.

153 Chicoine, *Confederates of Chappell Hill*, 46.

CONVERGENCE AND TRANSFER OF SLAVES BETWEEN FELDER FAMILIES AND ACROSS STATES

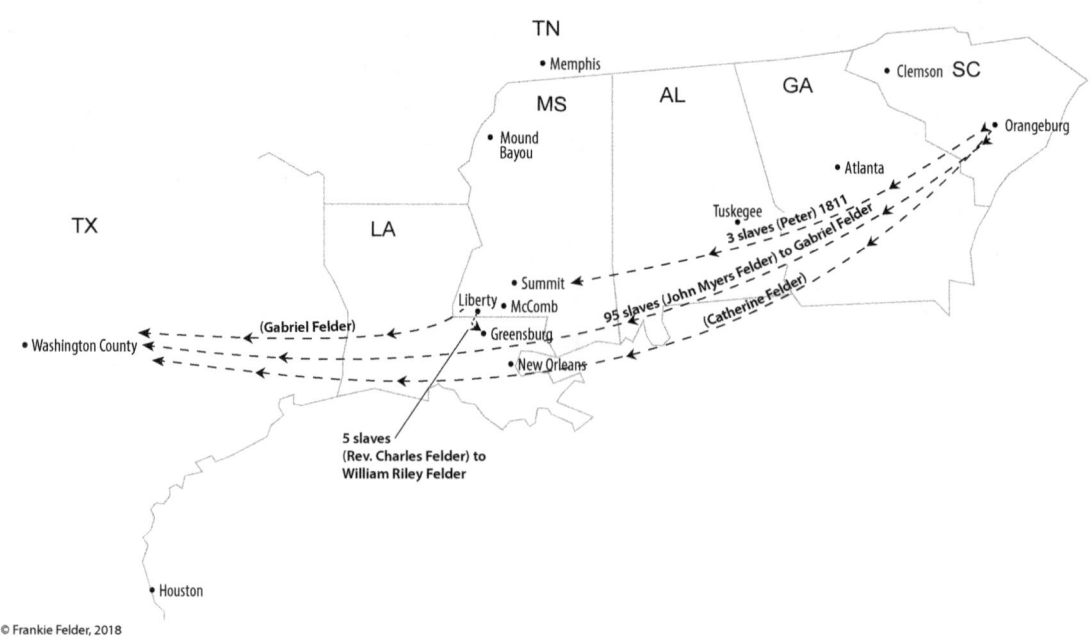

© Frankie Felder, 2018

Although **Gabriel Felder** and his Washington County friends in Texas were initially not impacted much by the war, that is, not too many soldiers left Washington County to enlist, on December 2, 1861, **Gabriel** sent notice to Major Samuel B. Davis in Galveston that he would send 50 – 75 slaves to help fortify their position, and that within a day or so would ensure a total of 100 slaves would be there at his disposal.[154] As such, the townspeople were able to keep the Emancipation edict quiet. They took "every effort to prevent the slaves from learning of the revolutionary announcement that threatened the *[very foundation of the entire]* Southern society." Texans, it was said, "discussed the matter privately."[155] Possibly for the first time, fear was beginning to creep into the conversations of once confident and defiant Confederate secessionists, and suspicions began to surface that they just might lose this war. Private conversations turned very public in Washington County, however, when

---

154 Confederate Citizens' File, Gabriel Felder, accessed May 2, 2011, https://www.fold3.com/browse/249/hchCf9X8w.

155 Chicoine, *Confederates of Chappell Hill*, 98.

the Confederacy decided to confiscate the new administration building of the Methodist Episcopal-established Soule University. Over the objections and vote of the University's first Board of Trustees, of which **Gabriel Felder** was president, the three-story education building, purportedly the largest structure "in the South,"[156] became the Confederate convalescent hospital, much also to the dismay of the Texas residents of Chappell Hill, who now realized that their efforts to ensure their slaves did not know that they actually had been emancipated would soon abruptly end![157] Indeed, despite the consternation of many of the girls on the campus who were afraid of catching the smallpox that the wounded brought with them from the war,[158] the soldiers continued to come in droves for medical attention – and the once well-kept secret spread just like the smallpox.

In October of 1864, all other avenues having failed over three years to return the building to the University, the Board of Trustees finally authorized **Gabriel Felder** to "make all arrangements necessary to place the impressments of the University Building *[sic]* by the Confederate authorities before the Confederate Congress."[159] **Gabriel**, an elder in the Methodist Church, was also owner of the Brazos River Bottomland – a sprawling 1000-acre property. Originally established as a religious Methodist campground, **Camp Felder**, as it was called, was converted into a Confederate camp near Chappell Hill. At one point, the camp took in Union prisoners relocated from another camp plagued with a "fever epidemic," but even at **Camp Felder**, the fever continued to spread. The soldiers died at such alarming rates that they were ultimately returned to the original camp.[160] This was likely a part of the smallpox epidemic spreading in both the Confederate and Union armies. Nearly 19,000 Union soldiers died from this disease despite the fact that vaccines were available.[161] Disease killed more soldiers than bullets.

Gabriel, **Rufus**, **Miers**, **Otis**, **Jesse** and **Rufus Knight Felder** are included in *OURstory* because they were associated with our ancestors. They were only a few of the Confederate **Felders** involved in the war, intending to ensure that our ancestors never experienced freedom. Before the war ended, across the country, a total of 163 **Felder** men would defend their convictions – one hundred thirty-eight (138) of them put on the Confederate grey and fought to maintain slavery; only 25 wore the Union blue to support its demise. **Gabriel's** relatives in Pike and Amite, Mississippi and in Livingston, Louisiana, assisted during the war in many ways in addition to enlisting. The Confederate Citizens' File of the National Archives shows them providing services such as loaning out wagons and drivers, and transporting food supplies to hospitals (milk, eggs, pork, mutton, butter). From February 26th to March 7, 1863, **Dr. Charles Felder** transported brigade baggage via use of his wagon and driver. These men were paid for all of these services and supplies. Indeed, **Felders** were clearly a pro-slavery group of people.

---

156 Chicoine, *Confederates of Chappell Hill*, 9.

157 Chicoine, *Confederates of Chappell Hill*, 103.

158 Chicoine, *Confederates of Chappell Hill*, 100.

159 Chicoine, *Confederates of Chappell Hill*, 103.

160 "Camp Felder," *The Handbook of Texas Online*; accessed November, 28, 2013, http://www.tsha.utexas.edu/handbook/online/articles/view/cc/quc2.html; website revised, now https://tshaonline.org/handbook/online/articles/quc02.

161 Terry Reimer, "Small Pox and Vaccination in the Civil War," National Museum of Civil War Medicine, November 9, 2004, accessed November 28, 2013, https://www.civilwarmed.org/surgeons-call/small_pox/.

THE UNION'S WAR

To change the course

Arming Slaves

Although slaves did participate from the very inception of the war in ancillary ways in the Confederate army as cooks, nurses, waiters, teamsters, musicians, burying the dead, servants, and so forth, they were not trusted to be loyal to their "masters" in this life and death situation, nor did Confederate war and political strategists think they were *["qualified"]* to be soldiers. Many slaves were hired out from plantations and farms to erect the Confederate's war infrastructure – to serve as general laborers, building and maintaining railroad lines, forts and bridges, and to provide the manpower needed to erect obstructions to retard or stop the advance of the Union army and navy. For example, 1200 slaves were hired out from local plantations in Louisiana and Mississippi and worked months in the humid and sweltering "96 degrees in the shade"[162] temperatures to clear a wooded area and dig a canal – by hand, with shovels – in an attempt to divert the Mississippi River to a different course! The objective was to enable the Confederate ships to avoid the Union cannons anchored atop the bluff overlooking the Mississippi from Vicksburg. Winters said that on this assignment, the slaves "laughed and shouted at their work, thinking they were earning their freedom."[163] *[And I say, how awesome "the power of intention".[164]]*

Other slaves remained on the plantations and became overseers in the absence of either the white

---

[162] Third World (Jamaican Reggae band), "96 degrees in the shade," released by Island Records, 1977.

[163] Winters, *Civil War in Louisiana*, 106.

[164] *The Power of Intention* is the title of a book by Dr. Wayne Dyer, 2005.

overseers who enlisted to fight or plantation owners who fled their plantations for safety. Still others provided the workforce required in the factories and mines, doing anything from extracting metals from the mines for the manufacture of war equipment – cannons, carts, bullets, guns, rifles, carriages, and so forth – to helping to manufacture shoes and boots for the army. Louisiana, for example, produced more Confederate boots than any other Southern state, farming alligators and/or catching them from the swamps, coastal marshes, wetlands, ponds, lakes, canals, bayous, and rivers for the purpose of tanning their hides for saddles and shoes.[165] Although Greensburg also established a huge tannery where leather for these purposes was stored, never were there enough shoes to outfit the Confederates. Many soldiers marched barefoot up to 40 miles a day[166] with neither boots nor shoes!

If the white residents of St. Helena Parish were within the norm, then many were as illiterate as the majority of the blacks in this rural community. By extrapolation from known data, it is estimated that somewhere between 90-95% of slaves, and 41% of white adults in slave-holding states, were illiterate prior to the war.[167] However, while many residents of the parish may not have been able to read the *St. Helena Echo* or the Greensburg *Imperial* for themselves, surely they all heard the news that on July 17, 1862, Congress passed two acts (the "Act to Suppress Insurrections, to Punish Treason and for Other Purposes," and the "Militia Act"), both of which provided President Lincoln discretion to use blacks to make the ultimate contribution to the war – *to take up arms* – in the battle to restore the Union. Hope began to spread like a raging wildfire amongst the slaves that they just might gain their freedom. Silently, they began to mentally prepare for a change.

Up North, this news caused the African and African American community to openly rejoice, for within their hearts they, too, had hope of victory, knowing that there would be no one on the battlefield more determined to win this war than those enslaved. In Washington, they praised President Lincoln and sang of his presumed victory to the tune of *Go down, Moses*: "Go down, Abraham, away down in Dixie's land, Tell Jeff Davis to let my people go."[168]

Among the benefits for the slaves, the Emancipation Proclamation, effected January 1, 1863, extended eligibility for them, now freed, to be recruited by, and enlisted in, the United States army. Before the war ended, an estimated 90,000[169] ex-slaves, then "freedmen," took up arms against the Confederacy in at least "52 military encounters."[170] These soldiers are included in the nearly 180,000 – 200,000 total black men who were able to serve in the army because of the authority granted by the Emancipation. Another 18,000 black men and 11 black women served in the navy.[171] Because it was never segregated, the navy was not impacted by the two acts that enabled enlistment. Although

---

165 "Skin Trade and Harvest History," Louisiana Department of Wildlife and Fisheries, accessed November 17, 2014, www.w/f.louisiana.gov/category/page/alligator.

166 Major, Civil War Talk, "Soldiers' Shoes," (forum), March 2, 2012, accessed November 10, 2014, https://civilwartalk.com/threads/soldiers-shoes.73013/.

167 Dan Roberts, University of Richmond, http://classroomsclips.org/video/3683 (5% of slaves were literate); *Journal of the Civil War Era* (Fall 2013), notes 2 and 3 (10% of slaves and 59% of whites were literate).

168 Benjamin Quarles, *The Negro in the Civil War* (Boston: Little, Brown and Company, 1953), 175.

169 www.history.com/topics/african-american-soldiers-in-the-civil-war, accessed April 6, 2013, cite revised.

170 Quarles, *Negro in the Civil War*, xiv.

171 Joseph P. Reidy, "Black Men in Navy Blue during the Civil War," *Prologue Magazine*, vol. 33, no. 3 (Fall 2001): 1, http://www.archives.gov/publications/prologue/2001/fall/black-sailors-1.html.

3.1 of the 4.2 million slaves in the country were freed by the Emancipation Proclamation, the war raged vigorously on for two more years with, ironically, four of President Lincoln's brothers-in-law fighting against him in the Confederate army.

President Lincoln audaciously initiated a change in the imbalance of power in race relations in America. Perhaps that was not his intent. Surely, he had no way of knowing that these courageous words, adopted by his cabinet, would earn him a unique place in presidential history and in the history of free nations everywhere; that they would be etched in stone and not just sketched on parchment:

> Now, therefore I, Abraham Lincoln, President of the United States, by virtue of the power in me vested as Commander-in-Chief, of the Army and Navy of the United States in time of actual armed rebellion against the authority and government of the United States, and as a fit and necessary war measure for suppressing said rebellion, do, on this first day of January, in the year of our Lord one thousand eight hundred and sixty-three, and in accordance with my purpose so to do publicly proclaimed for the full period of one hundred days, from the day first above mentioned, order and designate as the States and parts of States wherein the people thereof respectively, are this day in rebellion against the United States, the following, to wit:
>
> Arkansas, Texas, Louisiana, (except the Parishes of St. Bernard, Plaquemines, Jefferson, St. John, St. Charles, St. James, Ascension, Assumption, Terrebonne, Lafourche, St. Mary, St. Martin, and Orleans, including the City of New Orleans), Mississippi, Alabama, Florida, Georgia, South Carolina, North Carolina, and Virginia, (except the forty-eight counties designated as West Virginia, and also the counties of Berkley, Accomac, [sic] Northampton, Elizabeth City, York, Princess Ann, and Norfolk, including the cities of Norfolk and Portsmouth[)], and which excepted parts, are for the present, left precisely as if this proclamation were not issued.
>
> And by virtue of the power, and for the purpose aforesaid, I do order and declare that all persons held as slaves within said designated States, and parts of States, are, and henceforward shall be free; and that the Executive government of the United States, including the military and naval authorities thereof, will recognize and maintain the freedom of said persons.[172]

Louisiana and Virginia were the two states where slaves residing in "parts of [s]tates" remained enslaved after the signing of the Emancipation Proclamation. In Louisiana, for example, Orleans Parish, the location of New Orleans, was already under Union control when the Proclamation was signed, having been seized on April 25, 1862 by the federal troops, and was, therefore, a Union-occupied and controlled part of the state. As such, the status of slaves in Orleans Parish was "precisely as if [the] proclamation was not issued;"[173] they remained enslaved. However, in St. Helena Parish, the Emancipation Proclamation freed the slaves. Thus, technically speaking, **JOSEPH**

---

172 National Archives, *Featured Documents*, "Emancipation Proclamation," accessed May 9, 2013, https://www.archives.gov/exhibits/featured-documents.

173 National Archives, "Emancipation Proclamation."

FELDER, **SUSANNAH LEWIS**, and any and all of their children, were forever freed – *if* the Union won the war!

"Kum ba yah, my Lord, Kum ba yah! ...Someone's praying Lord, Kum ba yah! ..."[174]
[Come by here, my Lord, come by here! ... Someone's praying Lord, come by here!]

Supplication

---

174 African worship song from Angola.

Emancipated by Proclamation[175] shown below depicts the approximate number of slaves technically freed in the various states.

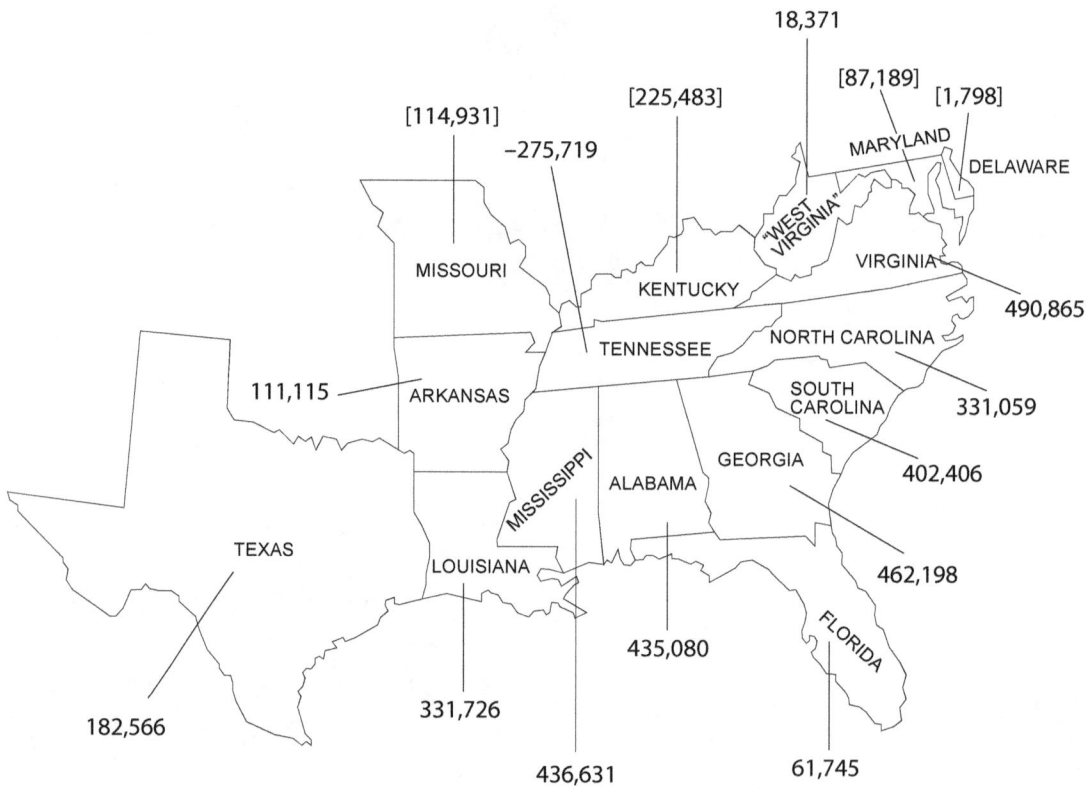

EMANCIPATED BY PROCLAMATION
(Approximate Number of Slaves/State)

1. Source on number of slaves per state: The Civil War Home Page referencing the 1860 US Census;
2. Slaves in border states [Missouri, Maryland, Delaware, Kentucky] not freed;
3. Slaves in Louisiana and Virginia freed minus those in designated counties: in Louisiana 13 parishes exempt from Proclamation including New Orleans; Virgina, 48 counties ("West Virginia") plus seven others;
4. Tennessee not included in Emancipation Proclamation.

© Frankie Felder, 2020

---

175 Concept modified from U.S. History, Pre-Columbian to the New Millennium, "Emancipation Proclamation," accessed November 21, 2012, image at http://www.ushistory.org/us/34a.asp.

FRANKIE FELDER

THE SLAVES' WAR

Despite documentation of Africans/blacks' fighting abilities on behalf of the French against various Indian nations in Louisiana in the late 1700s,[176] as well as the successful slave revolts throughout the Caribbean, a widespread perception existed in both the South and the North that black soldiers would be cowardly and would not fight.[177] Where such myths germinated is unknown. *Hi*story reveals that many such misperceptions *[or intentional fabrications]* about African Americans/blacks/Negroes/coloreds have persisted since slaves were first captured in Africa and brought to this country, and those misperceptions remain to this day, but that is another story in and of itself. Prior to the Port Hudson battle, the Confederate army did not allow the slaves to engage in battle or carry guns for fear of insurrection, such as had occurred so many times in every state where slaves were held. Joseph Holloway, Ph.D., author of *Slave Insurrections in the United States – An Overview*, stated that "John Brown's raid on Harper's Ferry in 1859 has been glamorized and Robert E. Lee's role *[in that insurrection]* magnified;"[178] meaning, basically, that this raid was one of the very few that *hi*story textbooks ever even mentioned.

And yet, from the beginning of slavery in America, and extending through the end of the Civil War, slaves engaged in insurrections, rebellions, disappearances (running away), poisonings, murders, slave ship mutinies, and plotting escapes – some little known like in New York and others highly publicized, editorialized, and well-known like Denmark Vesey's plot in Charleston, South Carolina, in 1822 and Nat Turner's rebellion in Southampton, Virginia, in 1831.

What is not told in any comprehensive fashion is that thousands of slaves participated in no fewer than 313 documented plans, plots, and rebellions, often with the aid of white men, oftentimes staunch abolitionists, but on occasion even white plantation overseers. Many slaves lost their lives, being hung or burned alive for such actions when their plots to kill their "masters," burn towns to the ground or exterminate all the white people were discovered – typically because of the snitch of a fellow slave. Decapitations and hanging the heads of rebellious slaves on posts around the town or on well-traveled roads were not uncommon judgments. Whites involved in these plots – successful or not – were also often hanged or, if lucky, banished from the state.

In Pointe Coupée Parish, Louisiana, in 1792, 1795, and 1796, slaves plotted to kill plantation owners and their whole slave-holding families and subsequently create a black state.[179] Well before the Civil War, numerous plantation owners across the South were killed by rebelling slaves. Acting alone or coalescing in numbers as small as two or as large as 7000 as they did in 1822 in Charleston, South Carolina, Africans and African Americans orchestrated plans for freedom such as that planned by the literate 24-year-old, religious blacksmith, Gabriel Prosser, in Henrico County, Virginia, in the summer of 1800, involving more than 1000 slaves right outside of Richmond.[180] Unfortunately for Gabriel and

---

176 Gwendolyn Midlo Hall, *Africans in Colonial Louisiana, The Development of Afro-Creole Culture in the Eighteenth Century* (Baton Rouge: Louisiana State University Press, 1995), 345-47.

177 Mary F. Berry, "Negro Troops in Blue and Grey: The Louisiana Native Guards, 1861-1863," in *The Louisiana Purchase Bicentennial Series in Louisiana History*, vol. V, *The Civil War in Louisiana, Part A, Military Action* (Lafayette, Louisiana, University of Louisiana at Lafayette, 2002), 630.

178 Joseph Holloway, Slaverebellion.org/index.php?page=chronology, accessed October 11, 2013 (website revised).

179 Hall, *Africans in Colonial Louisiana*, 344-380.

180 Holloway, *Slave Rebellion*.

the involved slaves, he was unsuccessful and was hanged on October 10, 1800, along with 25 other co-conspirators. Also, unfortunately for the broader slave population, Gabriel's massive insurrection ignited a barrage of legislation across the South forbidding literacy among slaves, the express purpose of which was to dismantle their ability to ever make such plans again.[181] In Louisiana alone, between 1718 and 1862, numerous massive rebellions were planned that involved an average of 852 slaves each.[182]

So, fast forward to the 1860's ... indeed the Confederates had at least one legitimate reason to fear putting weapons in the hands of their slaves in this war that seemed destined to bring freedom to the slaves and to decimate the power that whites had commanded over this population for more than 200 years – the possibility of retaliation.

Controlling the Mississippi

The Louisiana Port Hudson Campaign took place over the approximate dates of May 26 – July 9, 1863, and would become, and remain, the longest battle ever in American history. It also was a turning point in the war.

Just a few weeks after the signing of the Emancipation Proclamation, in January of 1863, the Fourth Louisiana Regiment, of which the St. Helena Rifles from Greensburg was a part, was sent to serve as post guards to secure Port Hudson, forty-five miles north of Greensburg. Port Hudson had been designated as a key Confederate defense on the lower portion of the Mississippi River and essential to feeding and supplying their troops back east. With their steamboats-turned-warships, the Fourth Louisiana Regiment captured and destroyed the "iron-clad warship," *Indianola*. The St. Helena Rifles celebrated this victory in which, according to A. P. Richards, they lost "not one man."[183]

At the same time, the Confederates' sinking of the *Indianola* further freed a slave family. Isaiah T. Montgomery, whose "owner" was Joseph Davis, witnessed the sinking of the ship, and because he was knowledgeable about where this actually occurred, Admiral David Porter of the U.S. Navy enlisted Isaiah's help to identify where the *Indianola* and its big canon lay underwater. He left Davis Bend as a serviceman, accompanying the Admiral who made arrangements for Isaiah's family's secure passage to Ohio.[184]

The escalating war brought fear to white families in Louisiana one by one as the battles came near. For white Southern belles in areas close to skirmishes and designated locations of battles – places that were their once idyllic play spaces in the open country – the activities and sounds of war now sent chills down their spines. On March 15, 1863, when the Union troops entered this area of the state through both East and West Feliciana, located, respectively, to the northwest of Livingston and due west from St. Helena, a frightened young girl from East Feliciana, Ellen Power, put her fears into words in her diary: "[W]e heard some dreadful firing last night, could see the flash from the cannon very plain," noting how the residents were terrified even before the "real fighting at Port Hudson" had even begun.[185]

---

181 *Wikipedia, The Free Encyclopedia*, "Gabriel Prosser," accessed October 10, 2013, http://en.wikipedia.org/wiki/Gabriel_Prosser.

182 Holloway, *Slave Rebellion*.

183 Richards, *St. Helena Rifles*, 7-11.

184 Isaiah T. Montgomery, Slave Narrative, accessed September 19, 2020, msgw.org/slaves/Montgomery-isaiah-xslave.htm.

185 Ann Patton Malone, *The Nineteenth Century Slave Family in Rural Louisiana: Its Household and Community Structure* (PhD dissertation, Tulane University, 1985), 318.

Port Hudson Siege

On May 23, 1863, 13,000 federal soldiers under the command of General Nathan Banks crossed the Mississippi River at Bayou Sara. His assignment was to take control of Port Hudson. Port Hudson, also crucial to the Union's victory, was the last Confederate fortification on the Mississippi that needed to be removed to clear the way for movement of the Union ships without endangerment from enemy fire.

Among the troops under Banks' command was the First Louisiana Native Guards, the first regiment of free black men from New Orleans to join the federal army in Louisiana. As war escalated in this part of the state, slaves escaped plantations and farms whenever they could, joining the Union troops as they marched toward Port Hudson. Others flocked to contraband camps at Port Hudson and Baton Rouge throughout the siege period. According to southern historian Joe Gray Taylor, the defeat of the Confederate troops at Port Hudson was "inevitable," as General Banks had the area surrounded, and either the 6000 Confederates would have to surrender because they were militarily outmaneuvered or they would run out of supplies and starve. A shortage of food came first. The "exhausted Confederate troops were reduced to eating rodents."[186]

The battle that took place in this area of Louisiana caught the attention of the entire nation as word of the fighting at Port Hudson spread quickly like a piece of juicy gossip. That the news was being sent by white soldiers to their loved ones at home, and by white commanding officers who had personally experienced the combat to their superiors at the War Department, lent credibility to what

---

[186] Joe Gray Taylor, Louisiana: *A Bicentennial History* (New York: Norton and Company, 1976), 93.

many hoped was only juicy gossip. But, gossip it was not. Indeed, the black soldiers fighting in the Union forces from the First and Third Louisiana Native Guards, which included free blacks and liberated slaves, did so with unbelievable bravery. They shocked the nation – especially the Confederacy.

The June 13, 1863, editorial in the *New York Times* lauded the bravery demonstrated by the black troops a few weeks earlier:

First Louisiana Native Guards

"They were comparatively raw troops, and were yet subjected to the most awful ordeal… The men, white or black, who will not flinch from that, will flinch from nothing. It is no longer possible to doubt the bravery and steadiness of the colored race, when rightly led."[187]

It is painfully ironic that slaves dug the three-mile-long, 15-foot-deep, 20-foot-wide canal for the Confederacy because it successfully stopped the First Louisiana Native Guards from defeating Confederates at Port Hudson on the first opportunity they had.[188] Nonetheless, it was the fierce, undeniable bravery displayed by this very regiment during the Port Hudson battle that convinced the Confederates that they had better change their philosophy regarding the use of blacks to help them fight this war. What exactly happened to change their minds?

The two and a half months of fighting that occurred at Port Hudson, from May 26 – July 9, 1863, was reported to be as brutal or more so than any that occurred in the entire war – literally blowing off black soldiers' heads with cannons and other artillery; yet, the men persisted, advancing in unbelievable fashion, never "flinch*[ing]*," never retreating, and fighting to keep their "blood-bespattered flag" above ground in this, the first combat in which the Louisiana First Native Guards participated, specifically, and in which blacks participated, generally. Under the command of Captain Andre Cailloux, a manumitted mixed-race man from New Orleans, who shouted orders in both English and French,[189] his regiment of mostly free blacks volunteered alongside enlisted runaways and technically-freed slaves to put their lives on the front line for the freedom of their brothers and sisters in captivity who, behind the lines were being forced to work against the objective of freedom. Of

Captain Andre Cailloux

---

187 *Wikipedia, The Free Encyclopedia,* "The Siege of Port Hudson: Aftermath," accessed April 24, 2014, http://en.wikipedia.org/wiki/Siege_of_Port_Hudson.

188 Quarles, *Negro in the Civil War*, 219.

189 Quarles, *Negro in the Civil War*, 217.

the 1080 men engaged in this battle, 37 were killed, 155 were wounded and 116 went "missing," yet they reportedly "marched off *[the battlefield]* as if on parade."[190] Captain Cailloux was one of those killed. On Wednesday, July 29, 1863, slaves, runaways and free people of color lined downtown New Orleans streets to pay

Military funeral and burial of Captain Andre Cailloux

respects to Captain Cailloux.[191] Cailloux was honored by a full military funeral. Sponsored by the U.S. military "and activist free people of color associated with l'Union newspaper," it was an exact replica of a funeral held a few weeks earlier in New Orleans for a white Louisiana Confederate officer, attesting to the respect the military and local community placed in the heroism and valor of this black man.[192] The pride of former slaves and freedmen to fully participate in this war was evidenced by their numbers in attendance at Cailloux's funeral and procession.

The fighting that took place at Port Hudson left no doubt in anyone's mind – including the Confederates – of the sacrifice that blacks would make in this war. When they were enlisted, "since the first hour," the black regiments were the object of disparaging talk about their "lack of soldierly qualities."[193] One might expect such remarks and attitudes to exist among the enlisted soldiers but not among the officers; but it did. General Nathaniel P. Banks, for example, former Democrat turned Republican, who served as three-term Republican governor of Massachusetts and as the first Republican Speaker of the House in Congress in 1856, was assigned to command the Department of the Gulf, but even he had little regard for black officers appointed by his predecessor, General Phelps. Consequently, early in his command, he removed all black officers and appointed white officers instead.[194] General Butler, also former Democrat turned Republican, commented that "black people ... had a 'great horror of firearms, sometimes ludicrous in the extreme.'"[195] But when the fighting at Port Hudson was over, my word, how the attitudes and the talk had changed!

General Banks reported to Major General Halleck on May 30, 1863, published June 11, 1863, in the *New York Times*:

---

190 Quarles, *Negro in the Civil War*, for detailed description of the battle, see 219-220.

191 Stephen J. Ochs, "The Rock of New Orleans," Opinionator, July 31, 2013, accessed December 10, 2014, http://opinionator.blogs.nytimes.com/2013/07/31/the-rock-of-new-orleans/.

192 Ochs, "The Rock of New Orleans."

193 Quarles, *Negro in the Civil War*, 216.

194 William Dobak, *Freedom by the Sword: The U.S. Colored Troops, 1862-1867*, accessed February 1, 2012 (Washington, D.C.: U.S. Army Center of Military History, 2011), 99-102, http://permanent.access.gpo.gov/gpo10905/CMH_Pub_30-24.pdf.

195 Dobak, *Freedom by the Sword*, 94.

The position occupied by these troops was one of importance, and called for the utmost steadiness and bravery. …It gives me pleasure to report that they answered every expectation. No troops could be more determined or more daring. …The history of this day proves conclusively that the Government will find in this class of troops effective supporters and defenders.[196]

The surgeon in charge on the battlefield said: "*[I've]* seen all kinds of soldiers, yet I have never seen any who, for courage and unflinching bravery, surpass our colored." And, a *New York Times* editorial exclaimed: "No body of troops – Western, Eastern or rebel – have fought better in the war…".[197]

Less than two weeks later, on June 7th, black soldiers once again would prove their mettle and valor. This time the Ninth Louisiana Regiment engaged the Confederate army at Milliken's Bend, just upriver from Port Hudson, and just 16 days after being mustered into service, with guns issued to them only the day before. Coupled with their unfamiliarity with the weapons, they were unable to quickly reload after firing because the guns were poorly-constructed. This necessitated that they discard their rifles for hand-to-hand combat with bayonets and musket butts. Brigadier General Lorenzo Thomas, appointed adjutant general responsible for the recruitment of black soldiers, commented on the highly unusual nature of this rare combat strategy, noting that "generally one of the party gives up before coming in contact with steel."[198] But they did not. They persisted in the "longest bayonet-charge engagement of the war,"[199] which "ranked as one of the most bitter knock-down-and-drag-out struggles during the course of a war famous for its hard-fought actions."[200] Confederate General McCulloch even reported, "More are severe *[wounds his men sustained]* and fewer slight than *[I have]* ever witnessed among the same number in *[my]* former military experience."[201]

Milliken's Bend

Commander after commander – from admirals, captains, colonels and generals – noted the bravery by which these black soldiers fought at Milliken's Bend. The Ninth Louisiana Regiment's commanding officer, Colonel Herman Lieb, stated, "There is no better material for soldiers than they." One hundred eight were killed or mortally wounded – a total reduction in force by

---

196 "Negro Soldiers The Question Settled and its Consequences," https://www.nytimes.com/1863/06/11/archives/negro-soldiers-the-question-settled-and-its-consequences.html, 4. See also Quarles, Negro in the Civil War, 220.

197 Quarles, *Negro in the Civil War*, 218-219.

198 Quarles, *Negro in the Civil War*, 222.

199 Quarles, *Negro in the Civil War*, 223.

200 Quarles, *Negro in the Civil War*, 222.

201 Quarles, *Negro in the Civil War*, 223.

45% - "the highest percent in killed and wounded suffered by any unit in a single engagement during the course of the war" ... and actually to date "in the annals of American military history"[202] no other battle was harder fought. Finally, the Assistant Secretary of War, Charles A. Dana, best summarized the general assessment of the military commanders: "The bravery of the blacks at Milliken's Bend completely revolutionized the sentiment of the army with regard to the employment of Negro troops."[203]

It was, in the opinion of the Union army strategists, one of the most important successes of the war as the control of the Mississippi River was considered absolutely crucial to an ultimate victory. The free access down the Mississippi without Confederate interference was considered worth more "than forty Richmonds."[204] Unbeknownst to anyone, destiny had been sealed. Quarles wrote this of what happened next: "The change in army sentiment produced by Port Hudson *[and]* Milliken's Bend ... did not escape the watchful eye of Abraham Lincoln. Late in August 1863 he sent a message to James C. Conkling to present at a mass meeting of 'unconditional Union men' scheduled for Springfield, Illinois. 'Read it very slowly,' cautioned Lincoln:

> I know as fully as one can know the opinions of others, that some of the commanders of our armies in the field, who have given us our most important successes, believe that the emancipation policy and the use of colored troops constitute the heaviest blow yet dealt to the rebellion, and that at least one of these important successes could not have been achieved when it was but for the aid of black soldiers. Among the commanders holding these views are some who never had any affinity with what is called Abolitionism, or with Republican party politics, but who hold them purely as military opinions.[205]

Less than a month later, on July 4, 1863, Vicksburg, 24 nautical miles upriver *[27 land miles]*, was captured by General Ulysses S. Grant, also with the aid of black troops. This defeat on such a significant national American holiday was so demoralizing to the Southerners, particularly of that town, that it took the residents 81 years before the Fourth of July was celebrated again in the city!

Promising Freedom/Restoring Manhood

As for the sentiment of the blacks who faced the enemy's fire, Private Long probably best described the deep-rooted motivation that flamed the bravery of ex-slaves everywhere, which *[so incomprehensibly]* incomprehensibly stunned the nation:

> Anoder ting is, suppose you had kept your freedom without enlisting in dis army; your chillen might have grown up free and been well cultivated so as to be equal to any business, but it would have been always flung in dere faces – "Your fader never fought for he own freedom.
> **Private Thomas Long**, First South Carolina Volunteers[206]

For Private Long, and many other black soldiers, freedom without leaving a legacy to one's family

---

202 Quarles, *Negro in the Civil War*, 224.
203 Quarles, *Negro in the Civil War*, 224.
204 Dobak, *Freedom by the Sword*, 100.
205 Quarles, *Negro in the Civil War*, 224-225.
206 Quarles, *Negro in the Civil War*, 183.

Unknown soldier

of having earned it yourself, was not worth having. The self-respect gained from knowing that freedom was not another paternalistic handout, like the two pairs of overalls many slaves were rationed yearly, meant more to these black men than the possibility that after the war they would no longer be on the face of the earth. And then there was the ability to stand up like a man to some of the people who had stripped away their manhood in front of their families and the world, like the black soldier [who] "took his former master a prisoner [and personally escorted him] into camp with great gusto."[207] These unidentified Union soldiers were but a few of the 1700 plus blacks that fought gallantly – in combat – for dignity and for their and their families' permanent release from human bondage.

Just like Private Long and many others, **ISAAC FELDER** seized upon the technical freedom that the Emancipation Proclamation of January 1863 provided to him as a 19-year-old technically-freed slave. On October 9, 1863, three months after the capture of Port Hudson and the fall of Vicksburg, the New Orleans Corps d' Afrique United States Colored Troops (USCT) 18th Regiment Infantry was organized at Port Hudson. Only 14 days later, on October 23rd, **ISAAC's** name was on the roll. It may have taken him two weeks to walk from the Carter's plantation either in St. Helena or East Feliciana parish to Baton Rouge to enlist. The 18th Regiment remained stationed at Port Hudson providing garrison duty until April 4, 1864, on which date the unit was redesignated as the 89th Regiment, USCT, but remained at Port Hudson. **CORPORAL ISAAC FELDER** and other black soldiers proudly provided garrison duty at Port Hudson through July 28, 1864. He put his life on the line for his family and his descendants. That included me.

---

207 Quarles, *Negro in the Civil War*, 223.

Rethinking Southern Strategy

By the time that **ISAAC** enlisted, the Confederate army was dwindling. Disease, lost battles, death, and desertions had reduced the southern forces to less than a third of that of the Union. In slightly over two years of the war (up to the Battle of Vicksburg), more than 158,332 Confederates lost their lives or were captured.[208] Southern dissent – those who did not support the Confederate cause or refused to go to war – was often met with death: men were often hanged or shot for such disloyalty. Yet, even with coercive recruitment tactics, only about 80% of eligible white Southern men enlisted or were drafted to fight, and many who did enlist deserted. "Official" desertions – more than 103,000[209] men over the course of the war – severely impacted strategy. The South desperately needed soldiers.

There were 476,748 free blacks in the total U.S. population of 31,118,075 in 1860, constituting 1.5% of the population. However, there were 3,950,546 slaves in slave-holding states, which comprised 12.7% of the population.[210] By early 1863, a few highly unusual proposals to arm slaves were being discussed among the Confederate military officers. Everyone had an opinion – journalists, newspaper publishers and editors, politicians, religious leaders, educators, townspeople, business owners, and, obviously, the slaves themselves, some of whom volunteered to participate. The conversation escalated among the decision-makers and influencers. Something had to be done. Quickly! But what?

On January 2, 1864, Confederate General Patrick Cleburne, commander of the 15th Arkansas division, argued at an officers' meeting in Tennessee that the South must emancipate all slaves and arm them or lose the war. The idea that blacks were inferior in every respect simply had to be discarded. This thinking, the proposal, and the man himself – General Cleburne – were all flatly rejected. Cleburne's commanding officer refused to send this proposal to Jefferson Davis; however, another general, angry at the state of the Confederate army, did. Davis ordered the proposal (The Cleburne Memorial) suppressed. Cleburne, resultantly, was passed over for promotion three times following his audacious suggestion. Cleburne's, and similar views, were truly vexing to the sensibilities of most Southerners.[211] But by late 1864, the Confederate situation was so desperate that the proposition to do something drastic was heard from all corners. Louisiana Governor Henry Allen dispatched a letter to Confederate Secretary of War, James Seddon, that was intercepted and then published by Union newspapers, in which he urged the Confederates to "put in the army every able-bodied [N]egro … immediately …"[212] and promise emancipation after the victory! Shortly afterwards, the governors of Virginia, North Carolina, Georgia, Alabama, and, *yes, even South Carolina*, coalesced in agreement, notifying the Confederate president, Jefferson Davis, that the time was nigh to change the policy of using blacks to fight, as the Union certainly was doing so. The *Richmond Enquirer*, endorsing this solution to the rapidly declining number of Confederate soldiers, urged an even more controversial

---

208 *Civil War Battles*, accessed June 24, 2015, http://iss.schoolwires.com/cms/lib4/NC01000579/Centricity/Domain/3240/Civil%20War%20Battles%20Chart.pdf.

209 Ben H. Severance, *More Damning than Slaughter: Desertion in the Confederate Army* (LSU Digital Commons, 2006), Civil War Book Review, vol. 8, no. 2, accessed July 29, 2020, https://digitalcommons.lsu.edu/cwbr/vol8/iss2/14.

210 www.bowdoin.edu/~prael/lesson/tables.htm, (accessed June 3, 2014).

211 Robert C. Kennedy, "Impetuous Charge of the First Colored Rebel Regiment," accessed January 12, 2015, https://archive.nytimes.com/www.nytimes.com/learning/general/onthisday/harp/1105.html.

212 Bruce Levine, *Confederate Emancipation: Southern Plans to Free and Arm Slaves during the Civil War* (Oxford: Oxford University Press, 2005), 31.

concept: Given the South's impending defeat, promise "emancipation and equal treatment of black soldiers"[213] in exchange for their loyalty and combat in the Confederate army! *["Equal treatment"? In the army or after the war was over? In Virginia or in all states? 150 years since and we're still fighting for "equal treatment"! Who would have imagined that black lives mattered then?]*

On January 8, 1865, former U.S. Speaker of the House and Secretary of the Treasury, turned Georgia Governor, turned provisional president of the Montgomery Convention that wrote the Confederate states' constitution, turned Civil War Confederate Major General Commander of the Georgia state troops, Howell Cobb, weighed in with his opinion regarding arming the slaves in a letter he wrote to Confederate Secretary of War, James Seddon, a short excerpt of which is below:

> The proposition to make soldiers of our slaves is the most pernicious idea that has been suggested since the war began…You cannot make soldiers of slaves, nor slaves of soldiers…. You can't keep white and black troops together, and you can't trust negroes by themselves…. If slaves make good soldiers our whole theory of slavery is wrong – but they won't make soldiers. As a class they are wanting in every qualification of a soldier. Better by far to yield to the demands of England and France and abolish slavery and thereby purchase their aid, than resort to this policy, which leads as certainly to ruin and subjugation.[214]

Behind the scenes, Jefferson Davis, while publicly rejecting the use of blacks in combat, sent Louisiana Confederate Congressman Duncan Kenner "on a secret diplomatic mission" in late January 1865 … to convince France and Britain "to issue formal recognition of a Confederate independence"[215] in exchange for emancipation of the slaves. Napoleon III of France deferred to England, whose Prime Minister, Lord Palmerston, "resolutely refused."[216] On February 10, 1865, a Mississippi Confederate Congressman introduced a bill to arm the slaves, General Order 14, which passed on March 13th; but, as one might expect, it included neither the emancipation of slaves, in general, nor emancipation, specifically, for military service for those selected for combat.

In a last minute, obviously immensely desperate move, the Confederate Congress – by a narrow margin in the House (40-37) and one vote in the Senate (9-8) – finally heeded their military officer's petitions to arm the slaves. General Robert E. Lee by now was desperate and panicking. Surely in his heart he knew the outcome of this war. His army was about to implode in Petersburg, Virginia, and he begged Jefferson Davis for immediate help. On March 23rd, Jefferson Davis issued an executive order to implement the act, which required that 1) the slave agree to enlist, 2) the "master" give written consent, and 3) the black soldier receive "equal treatment with their white comrades."[217] Emancipation for service was not a part of the deal.

The first black Confederate company of slaves formed in Richmond on March 25, 1865, but Richmond – the capitol of the Confederacy – was captured by General Grant the very next week, on April 3rd, and according to one Richmond observer: "… as the Federals rode in, the city's black residents

---

213 Kennedy, "Impetuous Charge."

214 Andy Hall, "Real Confederates Didn't Know About Black Confederates," Dead Confederates, A Civil War Era Blog, accessed March 17, 2015, http://deadconfederates.com/2015/01/08/real-confederates-didnt-know-about-black-confederates/.

215 Kennedy, "Impetuous Charge."

216 Kennedy, "Impetuous Charge."

217 David Blight, "Desperate Measures," review of Bruce Levine's, *Confederate Emancipation: Southern Plans to Free and Arm Slaves During the Civil War*, 2005, accessed March 7, 2015, https://originalpeople.org/confederate-emancipation/.

were 'completely crazed, they danced and shouted, men hugged each other, and women kissed.' Among the first forces into the capitol were the black troopers from the 5th Massachusetts Calvary."[218] President Lincoln went to Richmond the next day. Fortunately, for African Americans and for Lincoln's objectives, the Confederate Congress' passage of legislation to arm the slaves occurred far too late in the game to change the ultimate course of history. *[Thank you, Jesus!]*

Jefferson Davis and his government fled the demolished capital city on April 2nd, realizing that they were but a few hours from capture. Robert E. Lee surrendered the Confederate cause on April 9, 1865, just 27 days after the Confederate vote to arm the slaves. Lincoln would only live another six days. The battles at Port Hudson and Milliken's Bend have been identified as chiefly responsible for the estimated several hundred[219] or the 13,000[220] or so black soldiers who ultimately were recruited, volunteered, or were ordered to serve in the Confederate army. Other sources suggest an estimated 30,000[221] to 65,000[222] blacks served in the Confederate army in total, reflecting how widely the southern data varies. *[HIStory!]* The record also reflects that there were blacks who volunteered from the inception of the war to serve in the Confederate army – some free blacks from Richmond, Petersburg, and Chesterfield, Virginia "volunteered to do any work assigned," and other blacks participated in their own ways to support the Confederacy, or they were used as propaganda, such as "Blind Tom, 'the little African prodigy' *[who]* gave concerts *[in Charleston, SC]* in the summer of 1861 for the sick and wounded of the Confederate Army,"[223] and for the bank account of his "master."

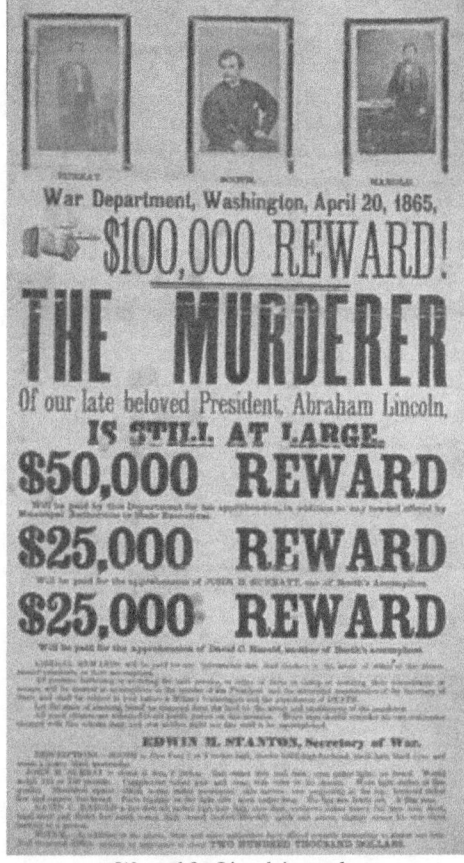

Wanted for Lincoln's murder

I wanted desperately to learn, although I did not, that all blacks who supported the Confederate cause were likely not provided a choice in the matter, like the cook who accompanied the St. Helena Rifles to Port Hudson. A. P. Richards reported that this cook "could not be trusted with the secret" (that Confederate men were deserting and returning home after the fall of Vicksburg and the capture of the Mississippi River by the Union troops). Richards found it "funny" that the deserting soldiers

---

218 "Confederate capitol of Richmond is captured," accessed June 12, 2014, www.history.com/this-day-in-history/confederate-capitol-of-richmond-is-captured.

219 Civilwargazette.wordpress.com, accessed April 22, 2014, site revised.

220 S. Williams, *Black Confederates in the Civil War*, accessed April 22, 2014, usgennet.org/usa/mo/county/stlouis/blackcs.htm.

221 Civilwargazette.wordpress.com, accessed April 22, 2014, site revised.

222 S. Williams, *Black Confederates*.

223 Quarles, *Negro in the Civil War*, 36-37.

Blind Tom

"tied the sleeping *[man]* and dragged him out of the camp, so that when he awakened he found his bundle ready for him to march, knowing nothing of his destination."[224] In contrast, however, in Point Coupée, Louisiana, many of the free blacks volunteered to serve in the Confederate army, as they were as concerned with losing their social status, their plantations and, *yes ... their slaves ...* as were their white and Creole slave-holding neighbors!

Where plantations hugged the shores of the Mississippi, or were otherwise near waterways, or in close range of the advancing federal troops, many plantation owners attempted to move their slaves to safer locations – like Texas – during the war to prevent runaways, confiscations, and general dissolution of plantation protocol and mentality. However, Providence provides. This task was more difficult than it seemed. Most of the slaves were not eager to continue their lives of servitude. Although they packed up obediently and started out on these journeys to relocate with their "masters," according to one report, as the Union forces approached, "... the slaves became very excited and hard to handle, disappearing in the night, taking carts and mules, trying to follow the Union army."[225] Winters wrote, "Many of the Negroes seemed delighted to go with their masters and set out bright and happy for Texas, but some of the slave owners soon discovered this joy was only a ruse. Each night groups of the male slaves would disappear until few were left."[226] And then many became "guides and spies" if they followed the Union army to camp, providing, according to General Abner Doubleday, "much valuable information which *[could not]* be obtained from any other source."[227] Some planters did actually reach Texas with some of their slaves and rented land to resume production. Some slave owners, however, abandoned their slaves when Union forces showed up unexpectedly – on one occasion leaving "four hundred wagonloads of *[slaves]* at Brashear City"[228] in Louisiana.

Indicative of the type of news that was traveling among the Greensburg townspeople was the account of Union General Albert Lee, officer in charge at Baton Rouge, who wrote to his commanding officer on October 9, 1864:

---

224 Richards, *St. Helena Rifles*, 15.
225 Winters, *Civil War in Louisiana*, 158.
226 Winters, *Civil War in Louisiana*, 158.
227 Quarles, *Negro in the Civil War*, xii.
228 Winters, *Civil War in Louisiana*, 158.

"General: I am just returned; captured a lieutenant colonel, captain, 2 lieutenants, and 43 enlisted men. At Greensburg burned a tannery and 2,000 sides of Confederate leather; at Osyka destroyed 4,000 pounds of bacon, 12 barrels of whisky, 100 dozen boots and shoes, and large quantity of corn and meal; also captured the telegraph operator and many important dispatches; destroyed Camp Moore and large amount of clothing and gray cloth; captured 200 head of horses and mules. Our stock is in good condition. Endless niggers have followed us in."[229]

This was a strong testament that many slaves were simply walking away from their former lives to somewhere they knew not where they would end up. Ten percent of the Union Army was comprised of freed blacks or runaway slaves. Before the war ended, 40,000 African Americans died.[230]

Slaves leaving the plantation

---

229 The War of the Rebellion: A Compilation of the Official Records of the Union and Confederate Armies, Chapter LIII, Expedition from Baton Rouge, La, 1893, 881, Google books, accessed February 27, 2013, https://books.google.com/books?id=Jr09AAAAYAAJ&pg=PA881&lpg=PA881&dq=general+albert+lee+endless+niggers+have+followed+us+in&source=bl&ots=hdrAwBCV22&sig=cuwTaF-xLKzYGUmtw-RBVtsYHLfo&hl=en&sa=X&ei=m26wU-D9J6qtsQTToIDADQ#v=onepage&q=general%20albert%20lee%20endless%20niggers%20have%20followed%20us%20in&f=false.

230 American Battlefield Trust, "Civil War Quick Facts," accessed June 24, 2015, www.civilwar.org/education/history/faq/?referrer=httisP//www.google.com/.

DOWN SOUTH

*Shouting secrets ...
Shhh ... Just listen ...*

F.O. Felder, June 9, 2020, Williamston, SC

4 | ANTIQUE TRUNKS

JOSEPH AND SUSANNAH

It is not known whether **JOSEPH FELDER**, age 19 or so at the time, was among the slaves who followed General Albert Lee and the Union army back to the fort at Baton Rouge in 1864 after the raid at Greensburg. Who knows, he could have been the unnamed sleeping black cook from St. Helena Parish disrespected by the deserting St. Helena Confederates, or he could have participated on the side of the Confederacy in other formal or informal ways – or on the side of the Union. It is not known because no records have yet been found regarding his whereabouts during the four years of the war, nor the four years immediately following the war. However, although it is unclear if he served in any capacity during the war, it is known that after the war he was safe and residing somewhere in or near Greensburg as a free black man because records do exist that inform us that **JOSEPH FELDERs**,[231] likely 24 at the time, and **SUSANNAH LEWIS**, possibly 22, married in St. Helena Parish on January 28, 1869.[232]

Article 221 of the Louisiana Slave Code, promulgated in 1825, but still in effect at the start of the Civil War, required that an "illegitimate child" not so acknowledged in the record of his birth or baptism should be acknowledged "by a declaration executed before a notary public in the presence of two witnesses." Furthermore, Article 182 of the Code stated that "... without the con-

---

[231] "S" recorded in the records at the Courthouse, St. Helena Parish; "s" not on any other documents.

[232] Marriage Certificate of Joseph Felders and Sussanna Lewis, St. Helena Courthouse, Greensburg, Louisiana. Document located by Debbie Schorlemmer on research trip, November 2013.

Marriage certificate of Joseph and Susannah

Matrimonial bond of Joseph and Susannah

sent of their 'masters,'" slaves could not marry, and even if they did, they would not be accorded "any of the civil effects which result from such contract."[233] So, by the time **JOSEPH** and **SUSANNAH** were legally able to marry, **JOSEPH** placed his mark ("**X**") to sign his name on the Matrimonial Bond,[234] and Rev. J. Reese performed the marriage rites on that same day, January 28, 1869, **SONA PAUL LEWIS**, their son, was between the ages of six and nine years old. Nonetheless, this act made a legal family union of what already was a spiritual one. **SONA PAUL LEWIS**, the little boy with a hole cut into his ear and branded as a child at the calfe [sic], hip, back and side,[235] became **SONA PAUL FELDER**, who, now "legitimate"[236] in the eyes of the Louisiana law, would begin to understand what it meant to be a free black boy in America in the

[233] A. Mary Lander, "The Law of Slavery in the State of Louisiana," *The National Era*, August 26, 1847.

[234] A bond date did not necessarily indicate the date of marriage. A marriage usually was performed a few days after the date on the bond. A "minister's return" – the report to the clerk that the marriage took place – verified the actual consummation. For more information, see Richard A. Pence, Bonds that [B]ind: *What's a Marriage Bond and Why?* Denise Godfrey, Chief Deputy Clerk of Court at Greensburg (November 2013), indicated that typically marriages occurred in St. Helena Parish within 30 days of the bond, and typically the court issued the marriage license immediately following signature on the bond. In Joseph and Susannah's case, this was precisely what occurred, and they were married by a minister on the same day that they signed the bond and received their marriage license.

[235] *S. P. Felder Family Bible*, note.

[236] Freedmen's Bureau, *Annual Narrative Reports of Operations and Conditions*, Target 1: Roll 27: New Orleans, October 1866 – October 1868.

mid- to late-1800s. In his adult life he was referred to only as **REV. S. P. FELDER**. His presumed middle name, **PAUL**, has never been found in print. He called himself "Sonny," signing his name as a newly-literate 17-year-old man: *Sonny P Felder* [Praise God!]

State of the State: Louisiana

While St. Helena Parish was originally quite expansive, covering more than 1700 square miles (more than a million acres) beginning midway the bridge of the Louisiana boot and stretching south past Baton Rouge, it was sparsely populated, inhabited by no more than 375 households in 1830, with a total population of 4028.[237] Established as a Louisiana parish in 1810, the area was, and still is, known for its lush pine trees, streams, and creeks. It is still as rural as a parish could be – very few traffic lights, parks and recreation facilities, sports or entertainment centers, mega-churches, universities, or shopping centers. In this quiet little place, however, numerous religious denominations sprang up due to the many overthrows of government that the territory experienced. The French, Spanish, and English introduced Catholicism and many sects of Protestantism into the parish as they turned over the land to one another in its early history while they fought, negotiated, and/or swindled each other over who would "own" this piece of America. Later settlers included some Scots and Irish. From the original settlers who occupied the territory – the Choctaw, Houma, Tangipahoa, and the Bayou Goula native tribes – came the indigenous religions. But today the parish is dotted by one Catholic and 15 Protestant churches,[238] remnants from the Europeans who ultimately decimated the native tribes, reducing their numbers and their religions to near extinction.

The parish was considered scenic and "exceptionally productive," with crops of all nature from corn, peas, and Irish potatoes to sorghum and sugar cane. Farmers sold pecans and berries, plums and grapes. The streams and rivers provided plentifully for those wanting fish – bass, crappie, perch – and the woods hid the bears, raccoons and opossums.[239] In the mid-1970s, St. Helena occupied approximately 268,000 acres of land (418 square miles), 198,000 of which was timber and about 35% of which was farms, with average farm sizes being about 90 acres. There remain to this day only two major communities in the parish – Montpelier, the smaller of the two, and Greensburg, the seat of government and location of the courthouse that generated and stored the parish's vital records. No more than 500 people lived in the town of Greensburg in 2000, and in 2012, the population was at an all-time high of 718.

In 1832, St. Helena Parish lost a significant portion of its southern boundary when Livingston Parish was established. Like St. Helena, Livingston was quite rural, although it absorbed the growing area that included Baton Rouge. Livingston Parish, established in 1832 as the "Free State of Livingston" – reflecting an attitude prevalent in the people as a self-reliant and independent sort[240] – apparently made a name for itself for the roughness of the men who settled there. In 2009, George Sells, Louisiana's award-winning WAFB-TV evening news anchor, shared these informed, reflective thoughts about Livingston residents of old: "It wasn't shooting to kill for independence from Spain, Britain, and Washington, D.C. that won

---

237 William Darby and Theodore Dwight, *A New Gazetteer of the United States of America* (no location: Hardpress Publishing, 2012), 469.

238 St. Helena Parish, typed history from the Clerk of Court office files, Greensburg, Louisiana, accessed November 28, 2013.

239 *St. Helena Historical Association Quarterly*, "Excerpts from Eastern Louisiana," (Winter, no. 54), 2.

240 Livingston Parish, "Culture and Traveler's Guide," accessed August 20, 2012, http://www.lapage.com/parishes/livin.htm.

Livingston Parish a reputation as the single most violent region of the United States in the early 1800s. Instead, the label was based on a brazen and widespread killing to settle personal feuds. It was suggested that if you insulted a Livingston Parish man, you should prepare to die."[241] *[If this was true for white relations with one another, imagine the white/slave, and later the white/freedman relations!]*

In addition to being an area of thick timber that needed clearing, this was also a parish with poor soil (mostly sand and clay), which did not support the Louisiana cash crop – sugar – and thus there were essentially no "plantations" in Livingston – just small "farms," which grew corn, oats, strawberries, green beans, peppers, and the like, mostly to feed the family. Small farms did not necessitate large numbers of slaves,[242] and as such, Livingston had the second least number of slaves in the entire state in 1860. Although the state of Louisiana ranked number two in the country in the number of extremely large slaveholders (four plantations had more than 500 slaves, second only to South Carolina, where nine plantations were so constituted), Livingston Parish had only two slaveholders in 1860 with more than 50 slaves: T.G. Davidson "owned" 92 slaves and Henry Womack "owned" 71 slaves.[243] It is interesting that Livingston Parish, mostly white, was sandwiched in between two parishes with some of the highest percentages of slave "ownership" per capita as well as the highest numbers of free black people in the state. George Sells continued on about Livingston: "About all the old settlers had was their home, their church, and in private, their booze."[244] The 2000-plus people of Livingston Parish were considered both proud and humble,[245] but "backwards."[246]

1860 U. S. Census in Select Louisiana Parishes[247]

County	Total Population	Male Slave	Female Slave	Free Black Male	Free Black Female	Total Slave	Total Free Black	Percent Slave	Percent Free Black
St. Helena	7130	1906	1805	2	4	3711	6	52%	.08%
Livingston	4431	659	652	0	0	1311	0	30.0%	0%
Orleans	174,491	6007	8477	4583	6356	14,484	10,939	8.3%	6.3%
Point Coupée	17,718	6753	6150	341	380	12,903	721	72.8%	4.1%

---

241 George Sells, "Louisiana: Livingston Parish Part I," November 26, 2008, accessed August 20, 2012.

242 Sells, "Livingston Parish."

243 Jeff David, "An eye-opening look at our past – The Livingston Parish," *The Livingston Parish News*, June 15, 2014, accessed January 30, 2015, http://livingstonparishnews.com/opinion/editorials/article_12a44004-e.

244 Sells, "Livingston Parish."

245 Livingston Parish, "Culture and Traveler's Guide."

246 Sells, "Livingston Parish."

247 *Wikipedia, The Free Encyclopedia*, "Demographics of Louisiana," accessed August 2, 2012, Wikipedia.org/wiki/Demographics_of_Louisiana, https://www2.census.gov/library/publications/decennial/1860/population/1860a-16.pdf.

Felder Slaves and "Masters"

Henry "David" Felder, hereafter referenced as **David**, was the second oldest child of **Peter Felder** - the progenitor of the slave-holding Swiss **Felder** family that moved to Mississippi from South Carolina in 1811, becoming one of the first to carry the **Felder** surname to the state of Mississippi. Once grown, five of **Peter's** seven sons initially settled within a few miles of him and each other in various locations in contiguous Mississippi counties: **Gabriel** and **Charles**, in Amite County; **Peter, Jr.**, **Isaac**, and **John**, in Pike County. Two sons left the state: **Daniel** went to Texas, where **Gabriel** later moved, and **David** moved to Louisiana. **Peter's** five daughters married and followed their husbands: **Aby Jane**, married Josiah Vaughn and remained in Pike County.[248] **Nancy**, with her husband, David Winborn, settled in Marion County, Mississippi, as did her sister, **Kessiah**, and her husband, Jabus Rawls. Younger daughter, **Mary**, married a Dickerson and lived in South Carolina before later moving to Mississippi. Finally, **Maria** married Isaac Carter. They moved from Marion County, Mississippi, to Pineville, Louisiana. **Peter's** sister, **Rachael**, married George Hartzog from Barnwell, South Carolina, and moved to Mississippi nine years prior to **Peter**; and finally, his brother, **Jacob**, later went to Marion County Mississippi, possibly also ahead of **Peter**.

Aside from the few **Felder** men who became ministers (**Charles [Sr.]** and his grandson, **Albert G.**), and those who became physicians (**William Riley** and his brother, **Charles F.**; and **A. D.**, **Dr. Charles F.'s** son), all of the **Felder** men who made their homes in Mississippi or Louisiana were considered "farmers" – none holding enough slaves or land to be considered "planters" or members of the wealthy, elite gentry. They each owned, on average, 408[249] acres of land, which was quite small in comparison to settlers a generation or two ahead of them, who received thousands of acres as landgrants for various reasons. Although several **Felder** men in Mississippi and Louisiana did hold more than 30 slaves at varying times, which was significant (**Gabriel** – 42, 1850; **Peter, Jr.** – 33, 1840; **James W.** – 45, 1860; **Dr. Charles F.** – 36, 1860), **Felder** men in Mississippi on average held 20 slaves per family, and **Felders** in Louisiana held on average six (6) slaves in each family. The **Felder** sisters also married men who were slave holders (Winborn, Rawls, Dickerson, Carter and Hartzog); however, as I am following the surname, "**Felder**," the daughters are not being researched at this time, with one exception, **Aby Jane**.

In 1830, **David** moved his family from Amite County, Mississippi, to become the first **Felder** in the state of Louisiana. They settled in Gates, Louisiana, a now defunct community that existed a few miles north of Port Vincent, which at that time was situated in St. Helena Parish, having yet to be divided to create Livingston Parish. He settled on the land he bought for $250 from Jesse Russell. The property was located "on the NW portion of the NE quarter ... in Township One S of Range 6 East through eight 38/100 acres."[250] On his covered wagon move to Louisiana, he was accompanied by his wife, **Jane McMorris Felder** (of Orangeburg, SC), and four children – **Rufus Knight**, age 10; **Otis Henry**, age 8; **Louisa**, age 6; and **Jesse T.**, age 3 – all of whom were born in Amite

---

248 Some records suggest that Peter Felder Jr was the only Peter Felder who left South Carolina and moved to Mississippi. Some records indicate Henry David Felder and Gabriel to not be Peter Felder's sons, as well. The discrepancies in the records I will not attempt to resolve, as the majority of records indicate the family relations as described above.

249 See Appendix B for details: Land Office Records of Mississippi and Louisiana Felder Property Holders.

250 *Direct Index to Deeds, St. Helena Parish, Louisiana*, Book 2, 197.

County, Mississippi. After establishing themselves in Louisiana, they gave birth to five more children, but only one of those five, a son named **Baxter**, survived.[251]

In the slave enumeration of the 1830 U.S. Census, 49-year old **David** is listed as having eight slaves in St. Helena Parish: one male under the age of 10; one male between the ages of 10 – 23 years; one male between the ages of 36 – 54; four females under the age of 10, and one female between the ages of 10 – 23. This could possibly have been an intact family (father, age 36 – 54; mother, age 10 – 23; children, one male under 10; one male 10 – 23 years and four females under 10). By 1840, **David's** slaves had increased to 12. The oldest male from 1830 was gone. Instead, there were now two males under age 10; one male between 10 and 23; four females under age 10; four females between 10 and 23; and one female between 36 and 54. **David** was living in the same location in 1840 as in 1830. **David** died on October 1, 1842, but in 1850, 15 "**Felder**" slaves were now living in Livingston Parish and are recorded in the U.S. Census under the name of slave "owner" **James Felder**. **James W. Felder**, however, was actually from Amite County, Mississippi, and in 1850 he "owned" 19 slaves in that county. As it turned out, **James** was **David's** nephew. Thus, it appears that **James**, then age 21, went to assist **Aunt Jane** and her family, and perhaps assumed fiduciary responsibility after his uncle's death.

By 1860, **Jane** had resumed charge of her farm, and she was enumerated in the census as still living in Livingston Parish, but owning only seven slaves. Where did the other eight slaves go? Also, by this time, **David** and **Jane's** five children had grown up. The four boys, **Rufus Knight** (then age 40), **Otis** (38), **Jesse T.** (33) and **Baxter** (24), all "owned" slaves – 3, 10, 3, and 6, respectively. With the decrease in slaves in **Jane's** holding and the small numbers held by each of her sons, it is possible that she gave each of them a slave or two from her "inventory" of 15 at some point in time to help them get started in the "business." Also, it was customary for families to give slaves to their daughters as part of the dowry they were expected to bring into a marriage, and it is likely that **Jane** gave one or more slaves to her daughter, **Louisa**, when she married William Jefferson Gates and moved with him to Chickasaw County, Mississippi. Unfortunately, no conveyance records exist which could verify **Jane's** decrease in her number of slaves. In 1850, **Louisa** and William "owned" 61 slaves in Chickasaw; in 1860, they "owned" 53 or 46 slaves, depending on the source consulted. Although the number of slaves they "owned" decreased, either amount they "owned" in 1860 still made them fairly wealthy, which was reflective of and consistent with the tremendous success of the ever-expanding cotton plantations in the northeast quadrant of the state of Mississippi. Case in point: in 1840, there were 808 slaves in Chickasaw; in 1850, there were 6,480;[252] and on the eve of the war in 1860, there were 9087 slaves and "1 free colored" person.[253] *[Wow, talk about tokenism!]*

It is not possible to verify **David Felder's** or his children's purchase of slaves in Livingston Parish, because on October 15, 1875, the courthouse fire destroyed all the vital records. My search of subsequent conveyance records in November 2013, however, revealed that **David's** family remained

---

251 Edward Livingston Historical Association History Book Committee, *History of Livingston Parish* (Dallas: Curtis Media Corp, 1986), 401.

252 http://msgw.org/chickasawcohistory.html, accessed June 8, 2014.

253 Tom Blake, transcriber, "Largest Slaveholders from 1860 Slave Census Schedules and Surname Matches for African Americans on 1870 Census, October 2001," accessed June 10, 2014, http://freepages.genealogy.rootsweb.ancestry.com/~ajac/mschickasaw.htm.

in Livingston, grew exponentially, and conducted much business. From 1835 to 1841, in addition to tending to his farm of 157.90 acres, **David Felder** was the Postmaster at Beech Hill in Livingston Parish, receiving and delivering mail to neighbors on horseback throughout his circuit route or holding the mail until residents came to pick it up. Later, all of his sons would follow in his footsteps and serve as postmasters at Port Vincent and Coelk (the same location renamed several times over the years).[254]

Once these **Felder** boys grew up, they moved within a few miles of each other in Livingston Parish, married, had small farms and large families, which included more boys (thus more **Felders** in Louisiana).[255] When **SONA FELDER** was born a few miles up the road in Greensburg in the contiguous parish of St. Helena, the **Felder** men of Livingston Parish had already become quite prominent: **Rufus** was the Commissioner of Elections, Justice of the Peace, parish treasurer, and school treasurer; **Otis Henry** was a Guardian of the Poor and a Bridge Commissioner; **George** was a tax collector and sheriff; and **George's** son, **Jesse T.**, served as sheriff on two separate occasions.[256] The Livingston **Felders** were Methodists, Democrats, members of the Farmers' Alliance, and the Confederate army. **Jesse** and **Otis** both acquired land (**Jesse T.** – 61.8 acres; **Otis H.** – 198.48) on the same day – June 1, 1860; perhaps for service in the war.

After Emancipation and the end of the war, the **Felders** continued to serve their communities in leadership positions, as responsible and engaged citizens tend to do. The problem for the freedmen is that the **Felders** gathered on July 8, 1876, at the mass meeting of the Democracy of Livingston Parish held at Palmetto Church, and pledged their full support for the redemption of Louisiana "from its political bondage" through the Democratic party. Resenting the "so-called Conservatives of the state to create a new party ... intended to divide the people of the South (who should be a unit in political matters until relieved from the tyranny which now enslaves them)," the **Felders** provided leadership to the Livingston Parish Democratic party, which vowed "undivided support" to the state Democratic party agenda. The parish elected **Rufus K. Felder** as chairman *pro tem* of the local Democratic party, and his brother, **Jesse T. Felder**, was elected to serve as one of three delegates to the upcoming State Convention in Baton Rouge. Finally, the attendees at this local parish meeting approved a resolution that the delegates to the state and district convention "exert all their influence to secure the nomination of pure and able men only, and to exclude any men "in any way, connected with robbery and corruption."[257]

Virtually all the Livingston **Felders** were buried in the **Felder Cemetery** on the east bank of Gray's Creek (at Highway 16 – "Pete's Highway"), a few miles north of Port Vincent.[258] **Rufus** lived in this community north of Port Vincent from 1849 until his death in 1894.

---

254 History Book Committee, *History of Livingston Parish*, 400.

255 For example, Rufus Knight Felder had seven children, four of whom were boys, and his brothers had boys also.

256 *Biographical and Historical Memoirs of Louisiana*, vol. 1 (Chicago: Goodspeed Publishing, 1892), 410.

257 Evening, Image 2, *New Orleans Democrat*, July 13, 1876.

258 Richard Heath, ancestry board/surnames/felder, December 19, 2001.

Greensburg Underbrush

William Riley Felder, son of **Rev. Charles Felder** and Sarah Lea of Liberty (Amite County, Mississippi), nephew of **David Felder** (Livingston Parish, Louisiana), and one of many grandsons of **Peter Felder** (Pike County, Mississippi), was one of several doctors who treated residents in St. Helena and Livingston parishes. He was the first and the only **Felder** who lived in Greensburg during slavery, surfacing initially in the St. Helena Parish census of 1850 as a twenty-five-year old "border" in the home of the Isaac H. and Catherine Wright family.[259] The Wrights had eight children and five boarders at the time. They likely knew the **Felders** in Amite and Pike counties in Mississippi as they had moved to Greensburg from Mississippi where their oldest child was born, and although Isaac Wright was originally from Vermont, his wife was from South Carolina.

Following the death of **William's** father, Rev. Thomas Bond became **William's** legal guardian, as he was not yet 21. Rev. Bond handled necessities such as paying $335 tuition for **William's** medical classes in New Orleans and $150 to A. R. Duni (or Dume) for March 1844 and 1845 board.[260] However, on April 25, 1851, **William** spent $25.00 and purchased a tract of land with a building on it on Kendrick Street in Greensburg.[261] This was the location of his medical practice and evidently his home.

Unofficial Sketch of Greensburg

On a clear day, by horse, it was about a two hour's ride to **Dr. Felder's** office in the Greensburg town center from his father's home 35 miles away in Liberty. At only 26 years of age, he was well on his way to establishing his medical practice in Greensburg. While nearby residents came to him, he also rode the circuit throughout the parish, tending to everyone stricken with the many ailments and diseases of the day. Advanced diagnostic and surgical techniques, medical instrumentation, anesthesia, and so forth, were not yet discovered, and most of the advances that had been made in medicine were unavailable anyway in the rural communities in the South. Thus, local doctors were often young people who had completed the requisite one or two years of medical school, although it was not uncommon that others in the community served as "doctors" as well – individuals who had no formal training at all. In Livingston Parish, for example, **Otis'** son, **David Watson Felder**, a carpenter, was also a Justice of the Peace and "amateur Doctor [sic]."[262] Without

---

259 St. Helena Census, 1850, family #217.

260 William R. Felder, file no. 3646, 1844, Liberty (Amite County Courthouse).

261 St. Helena Parish, *Conveyance Record*, Book J, 24 (Greensburg Courthouse November 27, 2013).

262 History Book Committee, *Livingston Parish*, 400.

formal medical training, **David Watson** probably took the local colloquialisms of the region to heart, attempting to be of service to the sick by applying the only medicine some of them knew – home remedies and superstitions – like the regional belief that to cure a child of whooping cough, one only needed to "sew a wooly worm in a small bag and hang it around his neck. When the worm die*[d]*, the whooping cough would be cured."[263] Maybe these remedies worked – **David Watson**, himself, lived to be 93! He died in 1944.

1853 was an unusually stormy summer. Elisha Andrews, one of **Dr. William Riley Felder's** patients, documented that his crops were not doing well due to the rains, but on top of that, an August storm blew timber down and scattered it all across his St. Helena plantation, destroying much of his cotton crop.[264] Louisiana, located right where the mouth of the Mississippi River emptied into the warm Gulf water, often experienced such rains and winds. During the four years of the Civil War – April 12, 1861 to April 9, 1865 – while no hurricane came ashore in the Gulf Basin, numerous strong tropical storms and winds[265] assailed the Louisiana/Mississippi terrain. At times, the soldiers on both sides had to battle the weather as much as they did their enemies. For example, on one journey headed to Camp Moore from New Orleans, it was reported that "the *[soldiers']* march was made through a heavy rain, and many of the men drowned their misfortunes in hard liquor. ... *[A]* number of the soldiers deserted, and others became so drunk they could not walk."[266] Throughout the war, soldiers battled diseases – measles, yellow fever, dysentery, body lice, "camp itch," and so forth. No one had prepared to be so occupied with fighting diseases – nor were they able to in many instances – being basically ignorant of the causes of the diseases. No one anticipated this aspect of the war, even though the weather and the Southern geography ("piney-woods" – pine trees, marshland, swamps, forests, etc.) essentially ensured that nothing short of this experience could occur.

In addition to the storms and winds, in August of 1853, yellow fever gripped the nation in an epidemic that claimed thousands of lives in Louisiana alone. The fever was so rampant in New Orleans that they struggled to complete timely and proper burials. Elisha was one of the unfortunate ones stricken with the fever, but **Dr. Felder** convinced him that he would be o.k. without constant medical care. He wrote in his journal, which he painstakingly and meticulously kept, that for 21 days he suffered so much that he could do little more than "move slowly around his house."[267]

The August 16, 1850 St. Helena Slave Schedule lists **Dr. William Riley Felder** as "owning" six slaves in Greensburg – four females (ages four, six, eight, and 18) and two males (ages one and five).[268] **JOSEPH FELDER** should have been five in 1850. It is certainly medically possible that all of these children could have belonged to the 18-year-old female slave in this household, but it is not likely. Elisha wrote in his diary that he heard that **Dr. Felder** had died so he went to Greensburg to bid his respects but arrived with his wife and "Many" *[probably the slave carriage driver]* "one day

---

263 Old Sayings and Superstitions: *St. Helena Parish Colloquialisms*, Xeroxed paper, unsigned and undated.

264 Dorothy Miller and Donna Adams, editors, *Diary of Elisha Andrews of St. Helena Parish* (Baton Rouge: Donna Adams, 1984), 11-15.

265 Craig Swain, "Earthquakes and Hurricanes: Natural Disasters and the Civil War," August 27, 2011, https://markerhunter.wordpress.com/2011/08/27/earthquakes-and-hurricanes-acw/.

266 John D. Winters, *The Civil War in Louisiana* (Baton Rouge: Louisiana State Louisiana Press, 1963), 96.

267 Miller and Adams, *Diary of Elisha Andrews*, 15.

268 St. Helena Slave Schedule, August 16, 1850, 14.

too late" for the funeral.²⁶⁹ **Dr. William R. Felder** died August 20, 1853, and was eulogized by Rev. Thomas Bond, his guardian/brother-in-law who was trained under and was assistant pastor to **William's** father, **Rev. Charles Felder**. **JOSEPH** was eight years old when **Dr. Felder** died.

The value of **William's** estate was $3227 *[$1,300,000 in 2012 economic status value, or $98,900 historic standard of living value in 2012 based on the measuringworth.com calculation]*. This estate was contested by family members at least as late as October 14, 1878.²⁷⁰ On October 3, 1857, **Dr. Felder's** property, his office, medical equipment, supplies, and personal effects, were auctioned by the St. Helena sheriff to satisfy a judgment of $3000 against his estate²⁷¹ – reason undisclosed. The auction was not consummated; with bids coming in too low, at less than two-thirds the value of the estate. As such, a second auction was advertised to be held on October 7ᵗʰ, attempting to "secure a reasonable auction price for **Dr. Felder's** property,"²⁷² which included his house, part of A Lot, his office, which was adjoining the storehouse and Mr. McKie's store. But there were no slaves listed for sale either time in his inventory. Where did they go?

Mississippi

That there was significant movement of the **Felder** relatives between the towns in which they resided in Louisiana and Mississippi has been firmly established through the records. The practice of passing slaves in this close-knit family from relative to relative, including those remaining in South Carolina and those in Texas, is also firmly established through surviving wills and stories handed down by white **Felder** relatives writing their *hi*stories. In the 1900 U.S. Census, **JOSEPH** indicated that he was born in South Carolina, but this seems unlikely. If there actually is a direct South Carolina connection, and I now believe there was, it was that one or both of his parents were born in South Carolina to African parents. Of the slaves brought to Mississippi from South Carolina with **Peter Felder**, **JOSEPH's** parent(s) could have been among them. No **Felder** seemed to have moved to Mississippi, nor is there a record of slave transfers to Mississippi during or after 1845, the recorded year of **JOSEPH's** birth. According to lore, three or four of **Peter's** slaves were brought from South Carolina in 1811, traveling overland on stagecoach through the Indian nations,²⁷³ with his son **David** and possibly another son, while **Peter** and his wife traveled to Mississippi by river. **Rev. Charles Felder** came to Mississippi in 1819, preaching and ministering in Orangeburg until that time. Consequently, by the time of **JOSEPH's** birth (~1845), one or both of his parents were likely already in Mississippi or Louisiana. Most of **JOSEPH's** records indicate that he was born in Mississippi. Other records suggest that his parents were also born in Mississippi. *[Who knows!?]*

Another possibility is that **JOSEPH** was not born exactly in 1845 but somewhere close to that;

---

269 Miller and Adams, *Diary of Elisha Andrews*, 15.

270 Ernest Russ Williams, Jr., *Genealogical and Historical Abstracts of Legal Records of St. Helena Parish, Louisiana*, 1804-1870, Successions (Probates and Wills), 1804-1854; Tax Assessment Rolls, 1823, 1824, 1826; Marriages, 1811-1870; 1995.

271 Succession of Dr. Wm R. Felder, dec'd, Application for Letter of Curatorship and for Inventory, 16th Jud. Dist Court, St. Helena Parish, La., filed August 17, 1880.

272 *Greensburg Imperial*, vol. II, no. 4, October 10, 1857.

273 Dorothy Williams Potter, Passports of Southeastern Pioneers, 1770-1823: *Indian, Spanish and Other Land Passports for Tennessee, Kentucky, Georgia, Mississippi, Virginia, North and South Carolina* (Baltimore: Gateway Press, 1982), 290. This documents that David's passport was approved on October 24, 1811 for travel through Indian lands but it does not verify that slaves, by name or number, were traveling with him.

if so, he could have been somewhere between the ages of 14-17 years old when the 1860 U.S. Slave Census was taken. Reviewing the ages of all the male slaves "owned" in 1860 by **Felders** in Louisiana and in Mississippi provides some likely locations of **JOSEPH's** "owner." In Louisiana, the only slave-holding **Felders** left living in the entire state in 1860 resided in Livingston Parish and were sons or grandsons of **David** and **Jane Felder**. **Rufus** had a 17-year-old black male slave and his brother, **Baxter**, had a 16-year-old black male slave. No other male **Felder** slave came anywhere close to the age **JOSEPH** should have been in 1860 if he was born in or around 1845. In Mississippi at the time the census was taken, the only slave-holding **Felders** recorded as living in the state were either in Pike or Amite county. During the 1860 census, **Charles F. Felder** had a 14-year-old black male slave; **James W. Felder** had two 14-year-old black male slaves; **David F. Felder** had one 17-year-old black male slave; **Christopher Columbus Felder** had one 17-year-old black male slave, and **Hansford D. Felder** had one 16-year-old black male slave. If **JOSEPH** actually lived on any **Felder** farm/plantation, it likely belonged to one of these individuals, all of whom were related to **Dr. William Riley Felder** and to each other.

The records of the Shady Grove Baptist Church in Summit, a small community located in Pike County, Mississippi (contiguous to and northeast of St. Helena, Louisiana) indicate that in 1859, **Levi Darius Felder** had a "servant" named **Joseph** who joined church and was extended the right hand of fellowship. A "servant" was a slave. **Levi Darius** was **Dr. William Riley Felder's** first cousin. **Levi's** father, **John Felder**, who co-founded Methodism in Mississippi, and **William's** father, **Rev. Charles Felder**, notable local Baptist preacher, were brothers. If this is our **JOSEPH**, he would have been 14 years old upon joining church. This seems plausible, given that **William's** slaves were not a part of his property auctioned in 1857. His six slaves clearly had either been sold prior to his death or moved somewhere after his death but before the auction. It is surely reasonable that his slaves would have ended up on one or more of his brother's or other relative's plantations or farms in Pike or Amite County, only 30 miles away. **JOSEPH** could have been the five-year-old boy in **Dr. Felder's** household in Greensburg in the 1850 Slave Schedule, who then, as an eight-year-old child, was sent to Mississippi to **Levi's** farm after **Dr. Felder** died in 1853. If so, **JOSEPH** would have found himself in a tight-knit "Christian" community filled with a host of churches and ministers – and a host of first- and second-generation **Felder** slaveholders, by then commanding the lives of more than 159 slaves in Mississippi. Neighbors, including the Sandels, Prewitts, Conerlys, and Quinns, are just a few of the others living in the community, mostly originally from South Carolina, whose "chattel" would continue to increase up to the end of the war, and whose "chattel" would have known each other in these small, contiguous communities where the residents worshipped together.

Just Short of Liberty

Summit lies nine miles north of present-day Magnolia, Mississippi, in Pike County and about 24 miles short of Liberty, where **Rev. Charles Felder**, perhaps the most notable **Felder** in Amite County, lived. Summit was the original settlement of **Levi Darius'** uncle, **Peter Felder**, and his family. When they arrived in 1811 from South Carolina, they moved in with the Elisha Vaughn family until their own home could be built. Elisha's homestead, the "Vaughn Place" or "Vaughn Home" as some later called it, spread across many acres in Summit.

Aby Jane Felder, **Peter's** daughter born between 1821 - 1823 after their arrival in Pike County, remained in this home after her parents and siblings left for their own places. It was where she lived out what was perhaps her dream life. After marrying Josiah Vaughn (Elisha's son), by 1850, this 29-year old was mother to five children, ages one to 12, and

Vaughn House

mistress to a slave population of 17, seven of whom were children ranging in age from nine months to 12 years old. The remaining 10 slaves ranged in age from 14 to 60, with most being between 28 and 30 years old; **Aby's** own age.

Hers was quite a sizeable home, with "six large rooms, a kitchen, dining room, and front and back porches." The plastered walls displayed the portraits of each child. New Orleans' artisans and artists were employed by this family, who possessed, obviously, great wealth. Fireplaces and antique furniture adorned each room in the house. Buffered at the rear by an apple orchard, to which "people from miles around came to gather fruit, as visitors were always welcome," the remainder of the plantation produced cotton. This was a home with an open door – it bustled with parties and kids' activities, with a stream of visitors staying days, weeks, and months at a time. **Aby Jane Felder Vaughn's** lifestyle was supported by the "many servants on duty at all times to serve the family and the guests" and "to do the work."[274]

Possibly Prewitt Plantation

By 1860, 39-year old **Aby Jane** was a widow. Josiah died shortly after the birth of their fifth child. Her plantation's real estate had increased in value to $25,000 *[$712,000 in 2012*

---

274 *Source Material for Mississippi History – Pike County*, vol. LVII, part I, chapter VI, "Ante-bellum Days," 107.

real price value][275] and her slave population of 63 individuals ranging in age from 1 – 60, created a "personal value" of $65,000 *[$1,850,000 real price value in 2012]* – a total historic standard of living value of $2,560,000. The 2012 unskilled labor value of her slaves was $11,600,000.

Aby's closest neighbors owned the "Prewitt Plantation." Located just east of present-day Magnolia, it was named for the beautiful magnolias blooming near Minnehaha Creek.[276] The Prewitt Plantation was contiguous to the Vaughn Place and described as among the most "impressive" and "finest" of homes in the area. Started prior to the Civil War, but not finished until afterwards, it was a house on a large cotton plantation – also the site of many parties and extended stays of visitors, relatives, and friends, who were catered to by the many slaves held on this plantation. There were "rows of slave cabins a quarter of a mile long" behind the two-story main house. The main house, which was surrounded by eight galleries *[porches]* was huge – each room measuring 20 x 24 feet. Eight-foot-high ceilings in the upstairs bedrooms stretched along the 60-foot halls from front to back. A detached, big kitchen, a dining room, and pantries completed the basic layout. The house, which sat high on a hill, was constructed of the "finest heart pine and was surrounded by tremendous *[moss-draped]* oak trees." The best hand-carved antique furnishings, much of it imported from Europe, faced huge fireplaces in each room, canopy beds, and plastered walls. This plantation house was in use until a fire destroyed it in 1910.[277] "Aunt Chloe," the cook, prepared for the many weddings, parties, and holiday feasts with foods of every imaginable type, from meats and vegetables to desserts.[278] At the Prewitt Plantation, in addition to the many slaves, there was a governess, and the house was full of many kids who came from other plantations "to school." Each daughter who married was "given a slave" as a part of her dowry, which was an accepted custom of the day.[279]

In 1850, 37-year old Ansel Prewitt and his wife, Julia, did not have slaves. However, on the eve of the Civil War, the 1860 Census reveals that he and his second wife, Lucinda (Barron) Prewitt, had 30 slaves, with a "personal" value of $46,000 *[$1,310,000 in 2012 real price value]*. His real estate value of $30,000 *[$855,000 real price value in 2012]*, resulted in a total historic standard of living value of $2,160,000. That is partly a result of Ansel's vision and strategy to bring the railroad close by. In 1854, he sold a right of way to the New Orleans, Jackson and Great Northern Railroad and established a stop for refueling and watering. He then divided much of the remainder of his plantation into town lots and sold these to investors, formally founding the town of Magnolia in 1856. Present day Magnolia was his plantation. In 1870, he became sheriff of Pike County.[280] Life could not have been better until a year later when tragedy struck this family. While Sheriff Prewitt was transporting a prisoner to jail, Ansel, his son, Elisha, and his deputy were ambushed by friends of the prisoner. Ansel was killed; the others were injured.[281] The prisoner and friends were never apprehended.

---

275 Values computed from www.measuringworth.com.

276 Lucius M. Lampton, ed., *The Magnolia Gazette*, magnoliagazette.com/magnoliahistory.

277 Mary E. Sandel and Rev. Elias Wesley Sandel, *The Felder Family of South Carolina, Mississippi, Louisiana and Texas* (Roseland, LA: self-published, 2000), 10.

278 *Source Material for Mississippi History*, 108.

279 Martha Lacy Hall, Centennial Celebration: *An Historical Sketch of Magnolia, MS*, 1856-1896, 1956, 7-9.

280 *Wikipedia, The Free Encyclopedia*, "Magnolia, Mississippi," accessed June 10, 2018, https://en.wikipedia.org/wiki/Magnolia,_Mississippi.

281 Sandel, *Felder Family*, 14.

Visits between neighbors of adjoining plantations was an accepted custom of the day. In this case, the Vaughns and the Prewitts were not only neighbors and friends; they became relatives when three of **Aby Jane Felder**/Josiah Vaughn's children married three of the Prewitt children. Clearly, there were visits back and forth from plantation to plantation! In the *Centennial Celebration of Magnolia*, the author imagines "... excursions to and from the two homes, in buggies or surreys loaded with children and perhaps a black playmate or two to help with the little ones. Narrow dirt roads which crossed shalow [sic] creek beds without benefit of a bridge surely afforded plenty of bumps, knocking bonnets askew and eliciting squeals of complaints or delight from children."[282] *[Black "playmates"? How can a "playmate" "help with the little ones"? Does not sound like play; sounds like work. Slave work.]*

Two of the children frolicking back and forth with their "black playmate[s]" from the Vaughn and Prewitt plantations were **David Vaughn** (b. 1849) and Naomi Eveline "Eva" Prewitt (b. April 24, 1853). By 1876 when they married and moved to Osyka, life had changed. Their childhood privilege of leisure while 93 black men, women, and children slaved on their parents' plantations as they matured into young adults, had been removed by the South's loss of the war. Eva's mother, Lucinda, moved with them to Osyka, possibly afraid and anxious to live without her husband's protection. Years later, **David**, Eva, and her mother returned to Magnolia to the old plantation. Once they returned, however, it is said that Eva "carr[ied] on her father's destiny in the pioneering of Magnolia, as the wife of **David Vaughn**."[283] At one point, **David** sold long leaf yellow pine lumber (the same "heart pine" that framed the Prewitt Plantation) for $6/1000 board feet. He also operated the saw mill and grist mill in the area, both of which were built years earlier by **Peter Felder, Jr.** and his cousins, **Robert Henry Felder** and **Levi Darius Felder**.

David's will reflects that until her death, Lucinda was well-loved and cared for by her daughter and son-in-law, who left in his will explicit instructions for her comfortable living. He handsomely provided for his entire family, leaving to his "loving wife," as executor of his estate, total discretion to make the decisions that she knew he would make concerning their children, her mother, and their property.[284]

Magnolia definitely provided plenty of opportunity to carry on. The town developed into a haven for the wealthy. New Orleanians caught the train north to escape their city, which was ravaged with yellow fever in the late 1870s. Although the fever was all around the local counties, the Louisiana visitors from New Orleans vacationed in Magnolia's 144-room hotel where they could bowl, skate, and dance because strangely, no deaths from yellow fever occurred in Magnolia.[285]

For nearly a decade prior to the appointment of Ansel Prewitt as sheriff, **Felders** wore the big gun in the county: both **Robert Henry Felder** and **Levi Darius Felder** preceded Sheriff Prewitt in this capacity in Pike County. **Robert** was sheriff during the Civil War from 1861 to 1865, and **Levi Darius** was installed as sheriff immediately after the war from 1865-1869.[286] During Reconstruction

---

282 Sandel, *Felder Family*, 14.

283 Hall, *Centennial Celebration*, 7.

284 Mississippi Wills and Probate Records, 1780-1982, Pike Record, vol. 1-3, D. F. Vaughn, No. 510.

285 Lucius M. Lampton, M. D., *Magnolia Gazette*: A Brief History of Magnolia, accessed October 6, 2018, http://magnoliagazette.com/magnoliahistory.

286 Sandel, Felder Family, 11.

in Pike County, a Canadian Irishman, former commander of a black regiment for the Union army, Charles B. Young, replaced **Levi Darius** as sheriff. It was later alleged that Sheriff Young absconded with "more than twelve thousand dollars in tax money."[287]

Aside from the whipping post used by the sheriffs to discipline wayward citizens and, most surely, slaves, perhaps the other most significant custom of the day in this region of Mississippi and for this community of people was attending church. Church, aside from the gatherings of select friends at large plantations, was the center of the communities' social activities, to which everyone was invited. Churches in Amite and Pike counties drew in large congregations that included **Felders**, Vaughns, Prewitts, Sandels, Leas, O'Neals, and others – as well as their slaves.

Robert (top left) and Levi Darius Felder (center)

Several names from Pike County haunted me for years, swirling in and out of my dreams like a faint spiritual whisper, summoning me to re-read closely the stories about and documents from Magnolia and Summit in Pike County. "Aunt Chloe" at the Prewitt Plantation for some reason kept coming to mind. What an odd name. A note discovered in 2002 in a vertical file in the public library in Magnolia that caught my attention revealed that "Helen and Wilma Vaughn kept family portraits and family records in the home in Magnolia." Wilma Vaugh<u>a</u>n is listed in **S. P. FELDER's** *Bible*, but was someone **TYREE** could not identify. **REV. S. P. FELDER's** *Bible* records several Vaughans' *[sic]* births and deaths among those of the **FELDER** family members. Could it be that the Vaughans *[sic]* in the family *Bible* are the Vaughn family from Magnolia?

Today, I know that our black **FELDER** family members lived in Mississippi, Louisiana, and Texas. I also know now, substantiated through court records and their written family *his*tories, that the white **Felder** family moved from South Carolina first to Mississippi, then to Louisiana and finally to Texas. However, when asked about the slaves they held and how to locate this information, Mary Sandel, author of *The Felder Family in South Carolina, Mississippi, Louisiana, and Texas*, which I purchased directly from her, encouraged me to "search the slave schedules,"[288] fully aware that the answers I was seeking were not there. I will give her credit for not being totally dismissive – making a few other suggestions, like checking church and school archives – but these records, as she well knew, also, do not tell the story of the slave "master" and his family, nor is any direct "ownership" of chattel established by those records.

Irrespective of the obvious code of silence, however, some connections have finally been made, and I can say with reasonable assurance that I found the answer. I spent many sleepless nights trying to connect the dots (or documents), literally gasping audible expressions of exasperation, staring blankly out my dining room window into the South Carolina Ansonborough Plantation neighbor-

---

287 Hall, *Centennial Celebration*, 10.

288 Letter from Mary Sandel, author of *The Felder Family in South Carolina, Mississippi, Louisiana and Texas*, February 24, 2003.

hood in which I purchased a house, trying to imagine the scenes of life on the plantations and farms in Mississippi and Louisiana where our relatives slaved. Most days ended with my head held in my hands, massaging away the headache in my temples, and wiping the tears rolling down my face. I have tried to put *OURstory* into the context of *his*tory; yet I cannot. Try as I might, I simply cannot get to a place in my mind where I understand the Southern, "Christian" relentless hatred of the Africans that they brought to America to procreate and create wealth for their families and to do the backbreaking work that they were unwilling to do for themselves. I just cannot seem to comprehend how, in this country, with founding fathers and colonists so intent on being treated with basic human dignity and fairness by the kings and queens from whose tyranny they and their ancestors rebelled during the Revolutionary War, could these same people, and an overwhelming number of their descendants, disregard the human needs of others. *[Yes, I do recognize my idealism.]*

Family lore suggests that *OURstory* occurred in Mississippi but it neither started nor ended there as I always thought. It started in South Carolina with the **Felders** and migrated to Mississippi, Louisiana, and Texas, as a part of a large slave-holding extended family that built and controlled towns as sheriffs, ministers, local politicians, farmers, and planters. In Pike County, Mississippi, and Washington County, Texas, some **Felder** plantation owners lived and entertained in the style described in the stereotypical antebellum "grand and glorious days" of *Gone with the Wind*. The overwhelming majority, however, experienced rural farm living in Amite and Pike counties, Mississippi, and in Louisiana towns in St. Helena and Livingston parishes. In actuality, most of the homes in the interior of the state, away from the mighty Mississippi River, were simple structures, typical of what one would expect to find in rural America. One-story homes with a few rooms and sparse furnishings situated on expansive landholdings were more the norm, but on occasion, a larger structure of two-stories and wrap-around porches (galleries) were owned by more affluent ministers, farmers, and doctors.

Nonetheless, local Pike County *his*torians write of the grandeur of the big houses with imported antiques and furnishings, the faithful cooks and mammies, moss-covered oak trees, meandering streams, fireplaces in every room, the gaiety of the parties and long stays of visitors who enjoyed sitting on the expansive porches at night listening to the singing of the slaves from their cabins. In the minds of the plantation owners and descendant townspeople, clearly theirs was a Christian community and theirs were happy and contented slaves. It was stated, speaking of Ansel Prewitt explicitly, although implicitly of the community in general, that "... the slaves had been so devoted to their kind, generous master that many of them refused to leave when the Emancipation Proclamation went into effect."[289] *[O.k., so exactly where would you go and with what?!]*

When the Civil War marched through Amite County, 64% of its 9500-plus residents were slaves engaged on farms and plantations producing the third largest crop of rice in the county, the sixth largest sweet potato crop, the fifth largest crop from orchards, and of course, picking cotton and shucking corn. Truly an agricultural community, fewer than 50 people were employed in industry or manufacturing,[290] so one might assume that as the war engulfed the county, the Mississippi slaves belonging to the **Felder** families, all enumerated as "black" except one, a three-year-old mulatto

---

[289] Source Material for Mississippi History, 108.

[290] *Mississippi Encyclopedia*, Amite County, accessed November 7, 2019, https://mississippiencyclopedia.org/entries/amite-county/.

male child belonging to **David F. Felder**, found themselves in the fields on a daily basis.

The Mississippi **Felder** slaves ranged in age from one to 80. An 80-year-old female and a 79-year-old male lived on **Charles F.'s** plantation among the group of 36 slaves. Only three Mississippi **Felder** men had more than 30 slaves: **Charles F.** (36); **James W.** (49); and **David F.** (44). The rest of the Mississippi **Felders** "owned" fewer than 20 slaves: **John** (15); **Simon** (7); **G.W.** (6); **Hansford D.** (4); and **Christopher Columbus** (2).[291]

In Louisiana at the beginning of the war, slaves "belonging to" the **Felder** families were all enumerated as "black" and ranged in age from one to 61 years old. No Louisiana **Felder** farmer had more than 10 slaves except **Otis Felder**, who "owned" 11. His mother, **Jane**, "owned" seven, and her sons **Rufus**, three, **Jesse**, four and **Baxter**, six.

FELDER SLAVES IN THE U.S. IN 1850 AND 1860

LOCATION	CENSUS YEAR 1850	CENSUS YEAR 1860
Mississippi	159	151
South Carolina	736	459**
Texas	2	320
Louisiana	15	30
Alabama	107	135
Georgia	173	215
Total All States	**1192**	**1310**

** Significant decline resulting from slaves transferred from Orangeburg, South Carolina, to Washington County, Texas, due to inheritance of Gabriel Felder from half-brother, John Myers Felder, and slaves of Catherine and Frank Felder being relocated to Washington County, Texas, as well.

---

291 To view a photo of Christopher Columbus, see website: http://www.angelfire.com/ms3/davidg33/biosB.htm, (accessed April 16, 2015).

SCATTERED LEAVES

JOSEPH FELDER and **SUSANNAH LEWIS** surely knew **PETER JENKINS** and **MILDRED** (**"MILLIE"**) **COFFEE**. They all lived in the tiny town of Greensburg, Louisiana, so they all probably had also known the local physician, **Dr. William R. Felder**. A year after forming into a company in 1861, the St. Helena Rifles marched back through Greensburg on their way to Baton Rouge "with firm step and manly stride, eager for the battle,"[292] but **PETER's** and **MILLIE's** children were not yet born, and **SUSANNAH** may not yet have given birth to **SONA**. The young children running through the dusty Greensburg roads at that time did not understand what it meant to be soldiers ready to sacrifice their lives in defense of their sacred homes and families; their once "boyish looks" now "bronzed and enured by a hard campaign and a winter's exposure."[293] They did not understand what it meant that of the 122 boys and men who enlisted as St. Helena Rifles throughout the duration of the war, nearly a third lost their lives either on the battlefield or from diseases or wounds of war,[294] and probably only 12 or so were "able-bodied and under arms at the last."[295] Even when the surviving but physically wounded, morally- and politically-defeated St. Helena Rifles returned home for good in 1864, **EMMA COFFEE** was but an active two-year old toddler. Her mother, **MILDRED**, was 49; **PETER**, her father, was 41. **SONA** was either one or three years old; **JOSEPH** was 19, and **SUSANNAH** was possibly 17.[296]

Very little is known about **JOSEPH** and **SUSANNAH** as a couple – whether they had more children; what they did for a living; whether they went to Shady Grove Baptist Church in Mississippi, joined Turner Chapel, the local A.M.E. Church in Greensburg established in 1868, or perhaps even attended Red Bluff Baptist Church in Greensburg where **Rev. Albert G. Felder** (son of **Dr. Charles F. Felder**) pastored after being licensed there on August 28, 1881. However, it is known that **JOSEPH** moved away from Greensburg very soon after the war concluded and went in search of employment. Given the work that he likely did in Greensburg amongst the rolling pine forests, he would already be prepared to work with timber.

In 1870, an eight[297] year old mulatto child, **EMMA (COFFEE) JENKINS**, lived on her family's farm in Greensburg with both parents – father, **PETER JENKINS**, and mother, **MILDRED COFFEE**

---

[292] Amable Peltier Richards, ed. Randall Shoemaker, *The Saint Helena Rifles* (Houston: self-published, 1968), 4.

[293] Richards, Saint Helena Rifles, 4.

[294] http://files.usgwarchives.net/la/sthelena/milarary/divwsha3.txt.

[295] Richards, *Saint Helena Rifles*, ix.

[296] To date the only records found for "Susannah Lewis" are the 1870 Census and an 1860 Census Slave Schedule. The 1870 census indicates a Susanna Lewis (mulatto, age 23, living in Township 19, Range 11, Choctaw County, Mississippi), but this is 271 miles from Greensburg, and one year after she married Joseph, so this may or may not be our Susannah; most likely not. However, in 1860 there is a 25-year-old slave woman living in St. Helena Parish, Louisiana under the ownership of "Wm Lewis." There are several men with the name William Lewis who live in nearby parishes (Orleans, Tangipahoa, East Feliciana, etc.). Lewis was and is apparently a "very common name in St. Helena Parish," according to Denise Godfrey, Greensburg Clerk of Court. It is possible that William Lewis was a large slave owner and an absentee landlord from the St. Helena Parish property. It seems more reasonable that Susannah Lewis would be a local slave as she and JOSEPH FELDER married in St. Helena in 1869 and SONA was born in Greensburg in either 1861, 1862, or 1863. If the 1860 St. Helena Parish slave is our Susannah, she was between 26 and 28 when SONA was born, was around 30 years old at the war's conclusion, and around 34 years old when she and Joseph married. Even more puzzling, however, the 1870 U.S. Census identifies a Joseph Fielder and Susan living in Choctaw County. He is 22 and she is 19. The obvious problem is that they are enumerated as white.

[297] Dates of birth and ages of Emma Jenkins are not consistent from the 1870 to the 1880 U.S. Census.

JENKINS; her siblings – twin sister, Mary; four year old twin brothers, John and William; and two others, Ripley (13) and Sarah (22), both listed as "farmhands" in the 1870 St. Helena Census, but who also were possibly siblings, as different last names are not indicated. The **JENKINS** were now a "legitimate" family in the eyes of Louisiana law, **PETER** and **MILDRED** having married in 1869 in St. Helena Parish. In the 1880 U.S. Census, **EMMA** is identified as a 14-year-old teenager living with her parents in the 3rd Ward in Greensburg. **EMMA's** date of birth is listed as 1866. She, like her parents, is enumerated as a farmer. She is single, black, and illiterate.

On February 17, 1881, when he signed his own name on the Matrimonial Bond,[298] 17 or 19-year old **SONA** was licensed to marry 19-year-old **EMMA**. It would have been one of the first documents he officially signed, perhaps three years or so after becoming a literate man. His signature on this bond initiated his life's journey as a family man, leading him from Greensburg, Louisiana, where he was either born on the heels of or in the throes of slavery, to Mound Bayou, Mississippi, where he died an educated, empowered man of God, bringing "thousands"[299] into the A.M.E. Christian family.

SONA and his wife, **EMMA COFFEE JENKINS FELDER**, had four children according to the **S. P. FELDER** *Bible*: daughter **SUSIE**, born nine months after they married, November 24, 1881; twins **ISAAC** and **JACOB**; and daughter **FROZENE**, all birthdates unknown. Little is known about these children or what happened to their mother. They are not enumerated subsequently in Greensburg or in any of the censuses of St. Helena or Livingston parishes. Oral family history indicates that they (the children and maybe their mother) died very young of "consumption" (tuberculosis). Death certificates were not required in Mississippi until 1912 and local newspapers delineating deaths from epidemics do not list them. However, several of these names appear in later U.S. censuses in Mississippi, in vicinities where **SONA** once lived, which may suggest that they did not die as children. Men with the names, **Isaac** and **Jacob**, surface in Magnolia, Mississippi (Pike County), the location of "The Vaughn Place," purportedly the original settlement of **Peter Felder** and his family when they moved from Orangeburg, South Carolina to Mississippi in 1811.

Matrimonial bond of Sona and Emma

---

298 Although unable to locate the marriage license for S. P. and Emma, the bond states that it would be issued as soon as the signatures were affixed to the bond. According to the *S. P. Felder Family Bible*, they were married on February 2, 1881. Location of the Bond – St. Helena Parish Courthouse, Greensburg, Louisiana, 2002. The bond is dated on the back side (February 17, 1881), the apparent marriage date as well.

299 Richard R. Wright, *Centennial Encyclopaedia of the African American Methodist Episcopal Church* (Philadelphia: publisher not identified, 1916), 89.

Possum Walk

Logtown was home to the largest sawmill in the world until it ceased operations in 1930,[300] contributing to making Mississippi the third largest producer of timber only behind Louisiana and the state of Washington. According to Mr. Charles Gray, executive director of the Hancock Historical Society, race relations in the early 1800s in Hancock County were "unusual for Mississippi," being "quite good" and reflecting an historic trend of intermarriage, as early settlers (mostly French) did not bring wives with them when they first settled this area. Not only did these men marry blacks, they married the Choctaw and the Acolapissa Indians in the area, as well.[301] Further, according to Etienne W. Maxson, local black author and son of former slave, Etienne Maxson, there was never a lynching in this area where the "white and colored citizens have tried to cultivate a friendly spirit and the trend of the races has been toward peace and goodwill."[302] Perhaps this was because the settlement of blacks who worked in the mills, in the forests, and on the pine plantations lived separate lives, away from the white people who also lived and worked nearby.

Possum Walk, the name given to a community of freed blacks who came to Logtown seeking work,[303] was "separated from the white area of homesteaders and workers at the Weston mill" by the bayou (the Bayou Bogue Homa) which ran "parallel to the main road leading into Logtown,"[304] and could only be reached by crossing the bridge. And so, even in this area of the state, where blacks and whites interacted in relative harmony, the loyalty shown by slaves to their owners during antebellum days did not, typically, translate into a fully-integrated coexistence for most. Etienne Maxson's father, for example, as did many slaves during the war, helped his "master" hide his possessions from the Union soldiers. With the load of cotton that he purchased on his "master's" behalf, Mr. Maxson drove a team of horses for 50

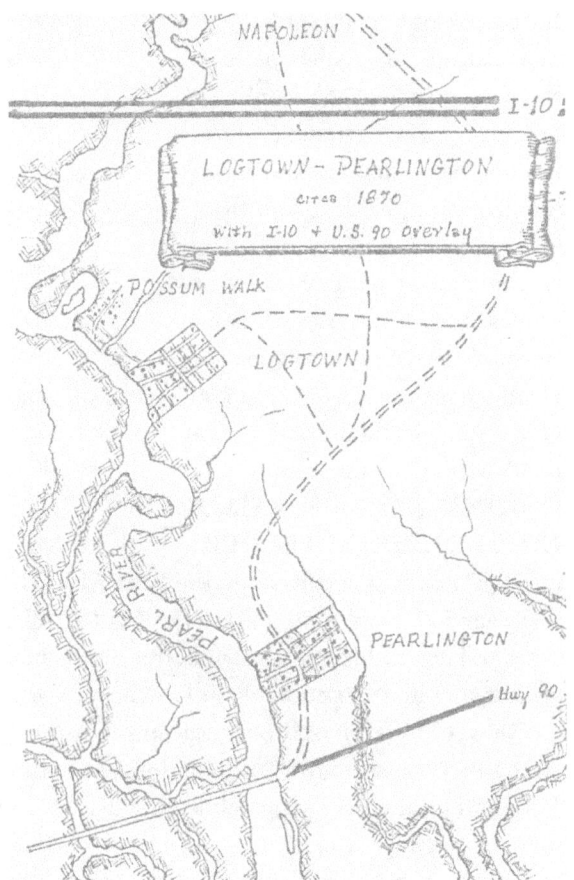

Map showing Logtown and Possum Walk

---

300 Hancock County Historical Society, Logtown Cemetery, undated online publication.

301 Phone conversation with Mr. Charles Gray, Executive Director of the Hancock Historical Society, June 17, 2014.

302 Etienne Maxson, *The Progress of the Races* (Washington, D.C.: Murray Brothers Printing Company, 1930), 20.

303 Russell Guerin, "A Slow Drift Down Pearl River," *Hancock County Historical Society Newsletter*, January 20, 2010, accessed November 16, 2014, http://www.hancockcountyhistoricalsociety.com/history/a-slow-drift-down-pearl-river.

304 Guerin, "Slow Drift."

miles during the nights, hiding out during the days, to prevent seizure by the "enemy" soldiers.[305]

Nothing remains of Logtown now except an idyllic, scenic community of trees, a cemetery, some historic markers, and directions to the Stennis Space Center now occupying the land that once was a unique country river town. In the 1840s, however, mills to saw logs were located all along the mouth of the Mississippi River in the Gulf Basin. Loggers cut the trees by ax, tied them together, and floated them downstream to the mills. The Dummy Line Railroad transported more logs for distances of one to 30 miles from deep within the forests to the mills at the river's edge. These logs were then shipped from Logtown and Pearlington to as far away as Australia and Africa.[306] The area had potential to emerge into a commercial district, and indeed, by the 1870s, it had blossomed into quite a different community, bustling with thousands of residents from nearby towns who had come to share in the economic prosperity that the logging business, over a short 30-year period, had brought to the South. Both freedmen and whites flocked here for employment after the war. With upwards of 3000 residents in its heyday,[307] the area quickly erected two churches, a commissary, post office, Masonic Lodge, its own telephone exchange, a hotel, swimming pool,[308] and practically any other amenity that the community desired – the white community.

Putting to work nearly half of the residents more than 1200 people – the Weston Lumber Company was the largest employer in the region, and its practices set the tone for the broader sociological and cultural patterns that emerged in this region of the state of Mississippi. The company paid its workers twice a month on the 1st and the 15th. All local businesses boomed on at least these two paydays, and the community swelled on those days with "Italian fruit peddlers" who came down the river from New Orleans in their luggers (fishing boats), spanning the neighborhood knocking door to door, and unloading fruit, oysters, fish and vegetables on all who would buy. Payday also brought the "floating saloon," The Blue Goose, as close to town as the barge could get. It was required that it remain at least five miles away from the local school, so technically, it was docked on a Louisiana bank and never came into Mississippi. Irrespective of its distance from town, however, the local drunks found a way to get to the saloon, hopping the water "taxis" that kept the "liquid highway" free of inebriated men, rowing them back and forth to the saloon as long as it was open.[309]

The Freedmen's Bureau Record of Deposits reflects that in 1872, **ISAAC FELDER** deposited

The Blue Goose

---

305 Maxson, *Progress*, 32. See also, Robert G. Scharff, *Louisiana's Loss, Mississippi's Gain: A History of Hancock County, Mississippi from the Stone Age to the Space Age* (Lawrenceville, Virginia: Brunswick Publishing Company, 1999), 200.

306 Mshistorynow.mdah.state.ms./us/articles/171/growth-of-the-lumber-industry-1840-to-1930.

307 Guerin, *Slow Drift*.

308 Guerin, *Slow Drift*.

309 James F. Brieger, "Logtown," *Hometown Mississippi*, 2nd edition, 1980, 158.

Isaac Felder's Freedmen's Bureau Record

money in the bank of New Orleans. He was employed as an engineer on a steamer by W. W. Carre and Company in Logtown. In 1858, W. W. Carre and his brother, Henry, and Henry Weston formed a partnership, purchasing the sawmill of Judge Wingate, where they worked. Fourteen years later, **ISAAC** was hired to work for this group of men. Six years after that, in 1878, the partnership between the Carres and Weston was dissolved by Weston,[310] who went on within a few years to become a multimillionaire, creating the largest sawmill operation in the world, right there in Logtown!

After the Civil War, blacks in Hancock County were hired in a broad array of positions at the mill, requiring advanced skills and continued trust from their white employers. It was not unusual to see black engineers, ship captains, mill foremen, carpenters, loggers, and blacksmiths.[311] Actually, this is the same as it was during slavery. The mere fact that **ISAAC** was in a coveted position as an engineer and was also a depositor in the bank in 1872 reflected that he had more than a rudimentary understanding of financial and personal responsibility.

ISAAC indicated that he was born in Pike County, Mississippi, but was raised in Louisiana, making it highly plausible that he was one of the **Felder's** slaves in Pike County who then ended up in Livingston Parish, Louisiana, with **David** and **Jane Felder's** sons. Or perhaps he was one of **Dr. William R. Felder's** slaves in Greensburg, or he may have been "hired out" as a young boy to work on another farm or plantation in Louisiana. This practice was common, and the hired-out slave would return some of his "earnings" to the "owner." Unfortunately, no work contracts or conveyance records are available to confirm any of these possibilities, as a fire destroyed the courthouse records. Another possibility was that he was sold to a Louisiana farmer or planter. According to the Freedman's Bureau Records, **ISAAC's** father's name was "**SONNY**," **ISAAC** was married to **MARGARET**, had two brothers (**JOE** and **HENRY**), three sisters (**ALIA** or **ALICE**, **CHLOE**

---

310 Hancock County Historical Society, *Logtown Booklet*, vertical files digitized, page 5, http://www.hancockcountyhistoricalsociety.com/reference/vf.php?t=subjects&vf=Logtown&i=265.

311 Maxson, *Progress*, 1930, 24-35.

Weston Mill, Logtown

and **KATIE**), and three children (**IDA, J. EZEKIEL** and **CHARLIE**). One can assume from this record that his mother, **SARAH**, had two other sons – **JOE** and **HENRY**, and three daughters. **ISAAC** was born around 1843, **JOSEPH** around 1845, and **HENRY** around 1830. Birth dates for **ISAAC's** sisters have not been found.

According to local recall, freedmen founded St. Paul Methodist Episcopal Church in 1880 in a small building on Washington Street in Logtown but then moved to a larger facility on Good Children Street by 1882.[312] And, while this is probably accurate, local residents' recollections of the beginnings of the A.M.E. religion in the area credit Rev. Robert Neville Sams with the founding of the A.M.E. religion in the area. Yet it is recorded in official A.M.E. church history that **SONA FELDER** "organized Logtown, Jordan River and Bay St. Louis, which was the beginning of the Gulf work, while he was a local preacher, and has organized many churches since."[313] All three of these towns are in Hancock County, within a 21-mile radius of each other.

Another story about the founding of the A.M.E. Church in this region is that it was not organized until 1887 in "The Point" by Rev. Brother Johnson, who served as the first pastor, and the public school for blacks was begun in this building. Mrs. Lillian Sams' husband, Rev. Robert Neville Sams, indeed served as

Weston Mill, Logtown

---

312 www.hancockcountyhistoricalsociety.com/reference/alphabetfile.htm?, 3.

313 Richard R. Wright, *Centennial Encyclopaedia*, 89.

pastor of both Big Mount Zion in Logtown and Greater Mount Zion African Methodist Episcopal Church in Pearlington for over 40 years. However, he was born July 23, 1918 or 1920 (records differ) and he died in Pearlington on August 14, 1993. Clearly, **S. P. FELDER** was well before Sams' time. What is certain is that the African Methodist Episcopal religion found its way into this community of freed slaves very soon following emancipation.

1881 was a very significant year in **S. P. FELDER's** life. It is the year that he married **EMMA JENKINS** and started a family. It is also the year that he "was converted," likely in St. Helena Parish at Turner Chapel A.M.E., which was established in 1868 in Greensburg. He was licensed as an exhorter and local preacher in 1885 and "entered the ministry" in 1887. Finally, he was ordained a deacon in 1888 and an elder in 1890.[314] **SONA's** life path led him from Louisiana shortly after he married **EMMA** in 1881 to southern Mississippi a few years later and then to other locations in the state. Most importantly, however, to *OURstory*, is the substantiation that the slave **FELDERS** from Pike and Amite counties in Mississippi and the slave **FELDERS** in St. Helena and Livingston parishes in Louisiana, are of the same family. They reunited after Emancipation, which means that they knew where each other were. *[Praise God!]*

As this type of research tends to do, other questions surface, which seem tangential at first, but then perhaps really are not, such as: Who was "Grandma Ida" that we went to visit seemingly every Sunday and who was godmother to **GLADYS**? **GRANDDADDY MOTLEY's** mother's name was also **IDA** – **IDA HUFFMAN**. Who were these women with this unusual name? Was **IDA FELDER** from Logtown in the Freedman Bureau's record any relation to Grandma Ida Carrington in Petersburg? All questions for another research project!

Entangled Roots

According to the 1900 U.S. Census, 32-year-old **SOPHIA FELDER** (b. December 1867), cooked for families during the day and spent her evenings caring for her five children, **JOHN FELDER**, age 17; **[N]ATHANIEL FELDER**, age 13; **DANIEL FELDER**, age 12; **SIMON FELDER**, age 11; **AD[E]LINE FELDER**, age 16, and a granddaughter, **ALICE RICHARDSON**, age two. Unfortunately, she was "widowed"[315] and was raising her children alone. But within 10 years, by the time of the 1910 U.S. Census, **SOPHIA** had become **SOPHIA ROUSE**. She lived in Beat 1 of Hancock County, with her children **SIMON**, then 17; **ADELINE**, then 25; and three **RICHARDSON** granddaughters, **ALICE**, then 13; **EDNA**, eight; and **OPHELIA**, two. The **FELDER** children are enumerated as "stepchildren" to **EDDIE W. ROUSE**, head of the family and laborer in the naval store. All these **FELDER** children were born in Mississippi, and by this time the whole family is fully literate (able to read and write) except for **SOPHIA**, who strangely cannot write, even though her husband, **EDDIE**, is also an African American teacher in Logtown, where it was said that the local schools "compared favorably" with any other rural schools in Mississippi. The children were required to attend school, or their parents and teachers had to be able to provide "lawful excuses for their absences" to the superintendent of schools.[316] **EDDIE** was also politically well-connected.

---

314 Wright, *Centennial Encyclopaedia*, 89.

315 1900 U.S. Census, Pearlington District 0023, Hancock County, Mississippi.

316 Maxson, *Progress*, 42.

Logtown Post Office circa 1900

President William Henry Harrison had appointed him as postmaster at Logtown, but unfortunately, he never assumed this position because he never "gave the bond."[317]

Around September 1939, **SONA**, suffering from a lengthy illness, clearly aging and ailing, asked his 12-year-old grandson, **TYREE**, to try to "locate his brother **JOHN** who lived in California" because he wanted to see him again before he died. During **JOHN's** weeklong visit in Mound Bayou, **TYREE** discovered that there were two more brothers – **SIMON** and **NATHANIEL**![318] Whether they were able to visit **SONA** before he died is not known. But what became clear in 1940, around **SONA's** deathbed, was that the **FELDER** children living in Pearlington with **SOPHIA** all knew **JOSEPH FELDER** because he was their father. Hancock County records reflect that he married their mother, **SOPHIA PARKER**, on April 5, 1875 in Hancock County.[319] This marriage was witnessed by **ISAAC FELDER**, **JOSEPH's** brother. Between the years 1885 and 1889, **JOHN**, **NATHANIEL**, **DANIEL**, **SIMON** and **ADELINE** were born to this couple in Hancock, Mississippi. One slight twist here, though, is that **SIMON's** father possibly was not **JOSEPH** unless he went by a nickname, "Dick." According to Mrs. Anna Brooks, who provided details to the coroner for **SIMON's** death certificate in 1971, his father was "**Dik**" **Felder**.[320] Possibly, also, **ADELINE's** father was not **JOSEPH** either as the 1900 census indicates "unknown" for her father's place of birth. Oddly, in 1909 when **SOPHIA** married **EDDIE ROUSE**, she married him as **SOPHIA PARKER**, not **SOPHIA FELDER**. So, once again, what happened to **JOSEPH**?

In the 1900 U.S. Census, **WILLIE FELDER**, age 7, is in Greenville (Washington County) Mississippi living with his father, **JOE FELDER**. Enumerated with **JOE** is **LUCY**, his daughter, age 14. In 1910, **JOE** is living in Washington County still, however, **LUCY**, who would have been 24, is no longer with him. **WILLIE**, now age 17, is enumerated with him and listed now as his "grandson." **SONA** and **WILDA** have been appointed to pastor in Greenville (Washington County) Mississippi at this time, and their children, **BEATRICE**, age 11, and **KORRINE**, age 10, are living with them, as well as **WINFIELD VALLEY** and **CELO**, both listed as age 16. These are two of the five children of **WILDA's** sister or cousin, **CLARA**, and her husband, **EMMIT**, who apparently went to live with their aunt and uncle (**WILDA** and **SONA**) after the death of both of their parents. Two **FELDER** young adults, **JULIA FELDER**, age 23, and **WILLIE FELDER**, age 27, later appear

---

317 Maxson, *Progress*, 52.

318 Interview with Tyree P. Felder, June 7, 2002.

319 Hancock County Historical Society, Hancock County Marriage Index (1849-1956).

320 Certificate of Death, Simon Felder, Orange County Texas Vital Statistics, Texas Department of Health, Certificate # 1701, February 11, 1971.

in Mound Bayou in the Federal Census of 1920. They are enumerated as "adopted daughter" and "adopted son" and living with Mike and Lottie Winston, who happen to live next door to Henrietta and Robert Clegg, which is a few homes away from **REV. S. P.** and **WILDA FELDER**. Who are these children? It is likely that this **WILLIE** is the same **WILLIE** from Greenville, **JOSEPH's** son or grandson, because the ages are consistent from the 1910 Census to the 1920 Census. But who is his mother? Was **JOSEPH** his father or his grandfather? It is likely that **JULIA** and **LUCY** are the same individual because their ages, too, are consistent between the 1910 census and the 1920 census. Who is her mother? Who is her father?

HENRY, **JOSEPH's** eldest brother, moved to Washington County, Texas (Brenham PO – the location of **Gabriel Felder** and Soule University), with eight children, ages three through 17, unless the 17-year-old is his wife; the 1870 census record does not delineate relationships. He was 40 years old in 1870 (b. ~1830) and was employed as a preacher, owning $600 of real estate and $250 of personal property, quite a substantial amount in 1870 for a freedman, especially just five years after the war. In 1870, **JACOB FELDER** lived in Springfield, Louisiana. He and his family (wife **MARY** and children – **JOSEPHINE**, 6; **MARTHA**, 3; and **JACOB**, 1) are the only black **FELDERs** who remained in Livingston Parish after the war. They lived next door to **Baxter Felder** and were probably working on his or **Otis'** farm as sharecroppers. **Baxter** held real estate valued at $2,000; **JACOB** had none. **Baxter** was a year older in age and was probably a childhood "playmate" in addition to being in a slave/"owner" relationship with **JACOB**. **JACOB** is not documented by **ISAAC** as a sibling, but the repetition of names – Martha, Joseph*[ine]* and Jacob – suggests possible biological kinship and a desire to sustain family ties. In 1904, **JACOB** lived in New Orleans, as did **ISAAC**.

EMMA JENKINS may have been in Natchitoches, Louisiana, living in Police Jury Ward 3 in 1900 as the census lists an **EMMA JENKINS** with the precise year of birth, 1866, as **SONA's** first wife. She is still a farmer and still unable to read or write. In the 1920 U.S. Census, there is an **EMMA JENKINS**, head of household, living in Bolivar County (Beat 1) Mississippi. She is a 31-year-old "widowed" female whose mother and father were both born in Louisiana. **EMMA COFFEE JENKINS FELDER's** mother and father were both born in Louisiana. This **EMMA** is clearly too young to be our **EMMA**, but is she related, or is there a mistake in the age listed in the census? In 1920, **SONA FELDER**, his second wife, **WILDA**, and their two children, **KORRINE** ("**AUNTIE K**") and **BEATRICE** ("**GRANDMA FELDER**"), were living in Mound Bayou, which is in Bolivar County.

In 1910, **NATHANIEL FELDER** was living with his older brother, **JOHN**, in Orange County, Texas, and they both worked as laborers at the local lumber mill. Both married young; **JOHN** at age 25 and **NATHANIEL** at age 26. **JOHN** and his wife, **MAGGIE M.** (maiden name unknown), owned their home. But, by 1930, **JOHN** and his wife had moved to Oroville, California and were living in their home valued at $1,800 *[$24,700]*. Once again, they were homeowners. **JOHN** worked at the Yellow Pine Paper Company as a "tailler." He died of acute pneumonitic atherosclerosis on February 12, 1969, at the age of 82.[321] At the time of his death, however, his surviving spouse was **CLARA ELIZABETH FOLEY**.

---

321 Certificate of Death, John Wesley Felder, Oroville, California, Vital Statistics, Certificate # 0497, February 12, 1969.

NATHANIEL married **ADA V.** (maiden name unknown) when she was just 16 years old. She was ten years his junior. By 1930, **NATHANIEL** and **ADA** had moved to Richmond, California, 12 miles north of Oakland, across the bay from San Francisco, and only a two-hour drive south from big brother, and clearly best friend, **JOHN**. There he purchased and lived in a home valued at $1,000 *[$13,700]*, became a proprietor of a notions store, and got divorced by 1940.

By 1930, **SIMON** had also moved to Orange County, Texas, owned his home there, and lived next door to his sister, **ADELINE**. He was employed as a yardman for a private family, Mrs. H. C. Lertchen. By 35 years of age, he had divorced but was raising his daughter, **ANNIE**, age 6. He died in Orange County in January 1971 at the age of 80 after a bout with cancer of the chest and spine.[322]

No further information is available on **DANIEL** after age 12.

ADELINE lived next door to her brother, **SIMON**. **ADELINE's** daughter, **ALICE RICHARDSON** (the granddaughter enumerated in Pearlington in 1900), had married and divorced by this time. At 32 years old, she was once again living with her mother, and possibly had two children – **EDDIE HURGER**, age 14, and **HENRY ALEXANDER**, who was 8 years old. Both children were enrolled in school. **ADELINE** had another daughter, **JANE MONDAY**, a 15-year old teenager not attending school. **ADELINE** owned her home, valued at $250 *[$3,440]*, and was a laundress for a private family. **ALICE** was a cook for a private family, and she and her mother supported the family on their salaries.

SOPHIA, the mother of these children, was enumerated with her daughter, **ADELINE**, in Orange, Texas, in the 1930 U.S. Census. She was 65 years old and no longer working.

These **FELDER** siblings never amassed wealth and did not earn formal degrees, but they all were extremely industrious during slavery and post-Emancipation. We can never know at this juncture for sure, without extensive DNA testing, if, in fact, they were all blood relatives or if they simply formed a family through shared experiences in bondage. We do know, however, that they were a very close-knit family, following each other from state to state and at times continuing to support each other in minimizing their expenses by living together. They believed in God, in financial stability, and in education.

Interestingly, this is the same pattern of the white **Felders** in Livingston; all having remained in this community, living close by each other. In 1870, **Baxter Felder**, then age 34, lived a few homes from his brother **Otis**, then 47. **Baxter** and **Otis** had accumulated the most wealth of the Louisiana **Felder** siblings, with real estate valued at $2000 and $4000, respectively – significantly more than any other families nearby; **Baxter** owned property worth more than twice that of any of his neighbors, and **Otis'** was four times the value of his neighbors.[323] Their brothers, **Rufus** and **Jesse**, then ages 50 and 42, respectively, owned real estate valued at $1000 each; and **Louisa (Felder) Gates**, their sister, then 48, had returned home and had an estimated real estate value in 1870 of $500. What happened to her husband, William Jefferson Gates, and their wealth is unknown. Clearly the Louisiana **Felders** were adversely impacted financially by the war. In the final analysis, at the close of the uncivil war, while the circumstances and the tasks would be different for blacks and whites,

---

322 Certificate of Death, Simon Felder.

323 1870 U.S. Census, Livingston, Louisiana. Monetary values converted to 2012 dollars: $500 = $9070; $1000 = $18,100; $2000 = $36,300; $4000 = $72,600.

everyone was left swimming upstream towards the same two boats – survival and restoration.

An interesting final note: **Rev. Albert G. Felder** (born May 22, 1847 in Amite County, Mississippi to **Dr. Charles F. Felder**) was a nephew of **Dr. William Riley Felder** of Greensburg (St. Helena Parish), Louisiana, and grandson of **Rev. Charles Felder** of Liberty (Amite County), Mississippi. On August 28th in the same year of **SONA's** conversion (1881), **Albert** was licensed to preach at Red Bluff Baptist Church in St. Helena Parish, Louisiana, and later served churches in St. Helena Parish and Amite County, Mississippi. **Rev. Charles Felder** also served multiple churches in Amite County and in Louisiana.

FELDER "MASTERS" AND SLAVE MATTERS

These 14 slaves project a likely scene on Rev. Felder's plantation

Uprooted from probate court files, Works Progress Administration (WPA) slave narratives, newspaper articles and advertisements, church minutes, and other such records are sufficient snippets of activities of slaveholding families to enable one to imagine the emotional trauma of slave families as they adjusted to the decisions made daily that impacted their lives and over which they had no control. Imagine being any one of these **Felder** slaves.

Rev. Charles Felder, slaveholder (Amite County, Mississippi)

The following distribution of slaves from a part of the **Felder** family in Mississippi demonstrates one way that slave families were separated following one of the **Felder's** deaths. **Dr. William R.**

Felder's mother, **Sarah**, preceded his father, **Rev. Charles Felder**, in death. His father, however, expressed both parents' love for all eight of their children (listed to the left) in his Last Will and Testament by equally dividing their estate in 1843 between all "*[their]* beloved" children.[324] **Rev. Felder's** will also divided his 14 slaves among his children relatively equally by "value" as indicated below in parenthesis. The "value" (real price based on the CPI [Consumer Price Index] for 2012) is provided in italicized, square brackets.[325] Children remained with their mothers. No clue is provided as to the fathers' identity.

Dr. Charles F. Felder: Jack ($700) *[$22,400]*

Dr. William Riley Felder: Easter ($500) *[$16,000]*

Sarah (Wigley): Hannah and child, Guster ($475) *[$15,200]*

Rebecca Felder (Bond): Ben ($350) *[$11,200]* and Mary ($260) *[$8,330]*

Ann Felder (Everette): Stacia and child, Anderson ($500) *[$16,000]*

Malinda Felder (Barron): Jacob ($640) *[$20,500]*

James W. Felder: Rose and child, William ($550) *[$17,600]*

Eleanor Felder (Brabham): Russell ($260) *[$8,330]*, Mariah[326] ($130) *[$4,160]* and John ($120) *[$3,840]*

To his "beloved grandchildren," the children of his deceased daughter, **Elizabeth Felder (Everette)**, he provided $150 *[$4,800]* each. **William Riley** inherited a sum of $500 *[$16,000]* in addition to the equal split of the proceeds of the sale of estate items. No reason is given why he received more than his siblings, although there is mention that other children had been previously advanced money, which was to be deducted from their total receipts.[327] An "old woman" (Mariah or Maria) was also mentioned in **Rev. Felder's** will as one of his slaves. She was "valued" at $23.00 *[$630]*. It is unclear what happened to her.

Other than Jack, these **Felder** slaves were "valued" significantly below the average $900[328] *[$24,700]* "value" that a slave brought to a seller in 1840. Typically, a premium was added to the "value" of a slave for designated skills. For example, a slave's "value" increased for blacksmithing by +55%, carpentry +45%, cooking +20%, and other domestic skills +15%. The reverse was also true – the "value" decreasing by -60% for running away or being crippled, -50% for vices, such as drinking, -30% for physical impairments. Males were more highly "valued" than females. Also, the "value" of a slave was somewhat influenced by the market for the product (tobacco, sugar, indigo, rice, cotton,

---

324 Last Will and Testament of Charles Felder, 1843, Amite County, Liberty, Mississippi, Probate Court Files, Chas Felder 1843 Estate, File 59, 3617 (Probate File #243).

325 Calculations for value of a commodity using measuring worth.com/uscompare/relativevalue.php.

326 There may be a discrepancy regarding Maria or Mariah as the disposition of property listing indicates that an "old woman," Mariah, was valued at $23.00 and there is no clear indication of who inherited the "old woman" – unless Maria noted here, as a part of Eleanor's inheritance, is the same person and there is a typo on the valuation of this woman.

327 Last Will and Testament of Rev. Charles Felder.

328 Adam Rothman, "The 'Slave Power' in the United States: 1783-1865," *Ruling America: A History of Wealth and Power in a Democracy*, edited by Steve Fraser and Gary Gerstle (Cambridge: Harvard University Press, 2005), 71.

etc.) of the plantation or farm on which he/she lived or on which he/she was being purchased to live.[329] Finally, age also impacted "value"; old Mariah not bringing much for her life. Although these slaves' "value" was appraised below market than more highly skilled artisans, they constituted the essence of worth of **Rev. Felder's** estate. Nothing in his estate was appraised to be of greater value than his slaves; his 24 head of cattle ($144) *[$3,270]* and 100 hogs ($130) *[$2,950]* being next. His large Bible was appraised at $3.00 *[$68]*.

One sees that in this instance of **Rev. Charles Felder's** probate and estate sale, slaves remained in the family following his death, being willed to his children. Although the slaves were scattered, they remained close by each other on the various farms of the siblings and they were aware of each other's whereabouts, at least initially. It would seem that after Emancipation, they would not have had too much difficulty reconnecting if this method of division and intrafamily transfer continued with other **Felder** family members as they, too, passed, although this was not always the case. Slaves were sold by **Felders** just as they were purchased. It is possible that all 14 of **Rev. Felder's** slaves were a part of the same biological family, but we have no way of knowing for certain.

Dr. William Riley Felder, slaveholder (St. Helena, Louisiana): *EASTER*

For five years, **William** kept his slave, Easter, that he inherited from his father's estate, but here is an instance where a **Felder** sold a slave. Praise God, he sold her and her two children together as a family. On March 25, 1848, Easter, Maria, age two, and a one-year old baby (sex and name unknown), were purchased by Amite county resident, Sarah Lawry, for $850 *[$23,300]*. It is interesting to note that "the old woman" mentioned in **Rev. Charles Felder's** lot of slaves and Easter's baby daughter had the same name (Maria or Mariah). Perhaps they were three generations of a family, and when **William** inherited Easter and child, they may have moved from Amite County to Greensburg in St. Helena Parish, where **William** resided. Sarah Lawry lived near other **Felders** in Amite County, but being sold back into

Advertisement for Estate Sale to be held December 8, 1843

---

[329] Samuel H. Williamson and Louis P. Cain, "Measuring Slavery in 2011 Dollars," accessed March 6, 2012, www.measuringworth.com/slavery.php. Calculated on 2012 comparison for value of a commodity.

Conveyance of Easter and children

familiar territory probably had no meaning whatsoever to her. Being transferred by inheritance from **Rev. Felder's** farm in Liberty to **Dr. Felder's** farm in Greensburg to Sarah Lawry's farm in Amite County surely felt like being moved oceans away from anything familiar.

Judge Gabriel Felder, slaveholder (Scott and Amite counties, Mississippi) and guardian for **Nathaniel F. Felder**, [330] absentee slaveholder: ***PETER*** and others

The inventory of **Nathaniel's** estate was handled by his uncle **Gabriel**, one of the largest slave holders of the **Felder** Mississippi relatives, owning 18 slaves at the time of the 1830 census. **Nathaniel** had provided power of attorney to **Gabriel** to settle his estate in Mississippi when he returned to South Carolina, actually to go to school at Yale. He was studying to become a lawyer. His rather extensive library included eight volumes of Shakespeare, Greek and Latin grammar, logic, chemistry, works by Thomas Jefferson, a collection of anecdotes, Chinese and Oriental Tales, The Digest of South Carolina Reports, novels, music books, dictionaries, a copy of the U.S. Constitution and, of course, the Holy Bible. His personal items were slim but included among them were three "common" chairs, one rocking chair, a "dressing glass" (mirror), a portable writing desk, a pair of scissors, a feather bed and pillow, five Spanish mares, one horse, one saddle horse, 23 barrels of shucked corn, some farm implements (hand saw, hatchet), a shotgun and an old wagon. His house is not described; his land is not inventoried.

In April of 1832, **Gabriel** hired out three of **Nathaniel's** oldest male slaves, now his responsibility: Ben and Sam to William Bates, Peter to Thomas McDowell; all at $10.00 *[$2,660]* per month. It is unclear how long these men were contracted to work. It is known that if Sam remained for a year at William Bates, his rate would become $100 *[$26,660]* for the year. Thirteen-year-old Jim was sent with Nathaniel from February to June, 1832, to board at Dr. Andrew Pulliam's. Two female slaves, 25-year-old Mary and Harriett, age six, were sent to the Choctaw Nation six months earlier

---

[330] Probate Records, File no. 3644, N. F. Felder, Guardianship and Final Settlement of Gabriel Felder for N. F. Felder, 1932, Liberty Mississippi Courthouse. File contains the Inventory of property and all other information pertaining to this guardianship in the subsequent three paragraphs. Values for all services based on "unskilled labor cost" as calculated by measuringworth.com for 1832 compared to 2012 value of a project and assuming all services paid in pounds.

by **Nathaniel**. What became of the other slaves (Toney, age 38; Emeline, age 2 ½; and Doll, age 90) is unclear. **Nathaniel** also had 3 other slaves still in South Carolina accounted for by **Gabriel** in the estate inventory. Prior to the inventory, records indicate that slaves were hired out to the Sandels and Lawrys in Amite County and that activity continued in South Carolina concerning the hiring of slaves to **Nathaniel's** half-brother, **John Myers Felder**, South Carolina's John Rutledge, and others.

On April 4, 1832, **Gabriel** received "$1.9 33/4 for a leg iron" for Peter and was billed $1.00 on April 17th by Charles Davis for "taking off the same." On April 20, 1832, **Gabriel** compensated Joseph Dunn $13.50 *[$3,580]* for seven days of his time and expenses to go get Peter from jail in Madison County. He also paid 15.17 pounds *[sic]* (~$1700) to Dunn for the expenses of Peter being in jail ($6.00 "taking up" slave; $2.00 "receiving and releasing"; 37_2 "commiting" *[sic]*; and $6.80 "feeding 17 days at 40¢ day.")

Gabriel was an active Mississippi democratic citizen before moving to Texas, his name appearing in newspapers often as a lawyer in Scott and Amite counties, as steward (bursar) of Centenary College at the Brandon Mineral Springs in Rankin County, and as a member of the Mississippi House of Representatives where he served a term on the Lunatic Asylum Committee. Despite all the publicity, nothing in the newspapers provides even the slightest hint of his dealings with his family or his slaves. What can be gleaned from the papers is that Peter had run away before and would run away again. Mississippi slave laws supported extreme harsh treatment of runaways – 39 lashes on one's bare back was standard for many acts. Surely, Peter received as much.

In Liberty, the records reflect that **Gabriel** executed and witnessed sales and settlements for county residents. They verify his purchase and sale of many slaves – Phill, Lydia, Elizabeth, Rogena, Tom, Adaline. There were many others – Rachael, Lucretia, Bob, Isaac, Sam, Flora, Mose, and Prince, just to name a few. He additionally hired for himself Billy, Little Jim, Sophy, Edmund, Tamarind, and so many others – too many others. They were grown men and women, and they were babies just born. They were "indentured" by **Gabriel** for life. At least, that was his plan.

Levi Darius Felder, slaveholder (Pike County, Mississippi): *JOSEPH*

November 4, 1859: "... a colored man, **JOSEPH**, a servent *[sic]*, belonging to **Levi D. Felder**, presented a written permit from his *["master"]*, related an experience of grace, read the hand of fellowship and was baptized into the fellowship of the church *[Shady Grove Baptist]*." [331] Shortly after this time, **Levi** became sheriff of Pike County.

Dr. Charles F. Felder, slaveholder (Amite County, Mississippi): *JAMES WASHINGTON*

The following is an excerpt from a slave narrative, recorded and transcribed during the two years (1936-38) of the WPA's documentation project designed to capture the nature of slavery from the slaves' perspectives before these aged freedmen died. It is this specific narrative that provides details of the relationships documented in our extended **FELDER** family as gleaned from the record of the Freedmen's Bureau Bank deposit. It is this narrative that enables us to rake the scant, scattered, and fallen leaves of our family into the pile that fertilized the roots of our family tree. New branches and new leaves owe them gratitude.

---

[331] Capitalized because I am claiming this to be our JOSEPH FELDER as only one other Joseph (Josuf) Felder is ever enumerated in the censuses and he was born in Germany in 1809. Shady Grove Baptist Church Minutes, 1854-1978; microfilm; 20.

"My names is James W. Washington. I is a Minister of de Holy Writ. I founded dis Flowery Mount Baptist Church en pastored it fur twenty years. I preached all ober de country. I wus born, so I wus tole, in July 1854, en wus a big strapping lad when freed. My mammy wus named **MARTHA FELDER**. She belong'd to **Dr. Charles Felder**, en he had a big fine house on de road frum Liberty to Magnolia. Bout 12 miles west uf Magnolia. Dat wus a big fine house but is burnt down now. It cost bout $10,000 mebby more. **Dr. Felder** had lots and lots uf slaves. I doan kno' how many. *[He had 36 slaves in 1860 per the U.S. Slave Census.]*

My mammy hed 12 chilluns – Harriet – Matilda – George – Frank – **SARAH** – Wilfred – Delia – Mary – Willie – Celia – Charlie – and me. Not all uf us hed the same pappy. My pappy wus named William Raiborn Washington. I doan kno' whut becum uf him cept he wus carried off. **Dr. Felder** cum by him through his second wife. She brung him lots uf slaves, en when her oldest boy married, she giv my pappy to him, en wus carried down en the low lands near Mobile. Yessum, I has a good memory. I ken remember a dress my mammy wore. It wus blue en had picturs uf gourds in it en mammy sed I wus 3 years old when she hed dat dress. I remember de old cow "Star" wus rattle snake bit en dey hed to kill her en mammy sed I wus only three years old when dat hap'ened. I remember ebery thing eny body tells me. I remember whut I reads in the Bible, ef I didn't I cudent preach.

I cum frum a long life stock. My mammy wus 112 years old when she died. I doan call myself old. My grand mammy on my pappy's side uf de house liv'd to be 132 years old. She died down here close ter Magnolia, near de bridge dat crosses de Tangipahoa River. Her master wus named Mr. Sandel.[332] She wus born in Madagascar, on the coast of Mozam Bisque Channel. She wus captured en put in a French vessel and landed on the coast uf Maine. Dey tole her dey wus goin' ter giv her to a Indian fer a wife, but 'stead of dat dey brung her south en sold her. She smoked a clay pipe. She wus black en she could "kunger" folks. She could put spells on 'em. She hed 13 chilluns. My great grand mammy on my Mammy's side uf de house cum from Congo Free States in Africa. She wus captur'd wid a lot uf Africans en brung to New Orleans en sold fur slaves. Mr. Abner O'Neil[333] in Amite County bought her en giv her to Adam O'Neil fur wife. Her son ernuther Adam en his wife Dinah wus my grand pappy en mammy. Den my mammy wus named Martha. **Dr. Charles [F.] Felder** bought her. *[**Dr. Charles F. Felder** was **Dr. William Riley Felder's** brother, and **Rev. Charles Felder's** son.]*

---

332 Rev. Peter Warren Sandel helped organize Muddy Springs Methodist Church in Magnolia, Mississippi and was the great-great-grandfather of Rev. Elias Wesley Sandel, Sr., co-author of *The Felder Family in South Carolina, Mississippi, Texas and Louisiana*. Peter Sandel was the brother of Elizabeth Sandell (Sandel), who was the wife of John Felder (Sandel, Felder Family, 1), thus Peter and John were brothers-in-law. Further detail on John Felder, founder of Felder's Church, is included in the chapter, "Patterns in Faith in God." It is clear that the Felders and the Sandels shared more than political and religious thought; their slaves intermingled.

333 Census records and other official documents spell O'Neil as O'Neal.

Dr. Felder wus a good man. He never 'lowed his slaves to be brutalized. He made dem wurk, but he never 'lowed the driver to strip the women folks en whip dem. En ernuther thing he never 'lowed a woman who wus breedin' to be whip'ed. He hed er overseer but he wudnt 'low him ter mistreat dem. He hed a big bell en ebery morning jes' bout daybreak dat bell wud ring callin' de slaves to cum to de field. When de crops wus pushin' en all de women wus in de field he kept two women at de house to cook for de whole force. All de slaves hed deir own gard'ns. He hed er old Colored woman named Barbara; she muster hev ben nearly 100 years old to stay at de house en keer fur de little chilluns. We played under de trees when de weather wus good en when it rained we played in de house. He give us lots uf milk en bread. Our mammys wus hoe hands en de field. When eny of de slaves got sick **Dr. Felder** doctored us. He giv us bad medicin' – Ole granny boiled herbs en giv us un be kno 'in to de Dr.

Hoeing cotton in Mississippi

Yessum, I remember de bed I slept on. It wus made uf heavy timber wid holes bored in de sides en hed en bottom, en ropes wus put through dese holes en pulled right tight, en a feather bed laid on dat. It beat springs all to pieces. We hung our close on de walls. I never seed a wardrobe till after I cum to de railroad. I slept in de quarters where all de slaves slept. Sumtimes I et en de quarters en sumtimes at de big house. Dey fixed a plate or put sumthing in a pan en set me on de steps en told me to eat. I hed plenty to eat en we all hed good homespun clothes. Sometimes he giv his slaves a holiday, eb den dey hed fine eaten's – specly Christmas when dey hed dances, en sum of de men wud git drunk. Yessum de Dr give dem whiskey to make dem feel good. Sum nigger wud call de figger en how dey wud dance. Dey played a fiddle ur de musick, dose niggers sho could shuffle deir feet. De niggers now doan kno' how to dance. ...

Dr. Felder did not go ter de war. I doan kno' why. He wus a mity busy man. I remember de Yankees when dem cum. Sum of dem wus on horses en sum uf dem wus walking. Dey all wore blue close, two uf de men hed big brass buttons on deir close. Dey talk wid de Dr. en dey took his fine horses en mules en left us deir old scrubs. Dey killed one cow en took her down de road en roasted her. Dey tuk our meal en flour. When dey left we went down de road to git whut dey left. Sum of de folks sed de meat wus not fittern to eat, but I et it en thought it wus good. Dr. had his Carriage hid in de woods en all de silver. Dey did not git dat.

One day de big bell rung jest 'fore dinner time en all de slaves cum to de big house en the Dr. sed dey wus all free now. He tole dem ef dey wud stay en finish de crop he wud pay dem for deir wurk. Dey all stayed til de end uf de year, en sum uf dem stayed a long time. My mammy left de next year en went to Mr. Sam Newmans, near Osyka ter wurk for him, en meny a time since den hev we gone hongry. We never wus hongry while we lived wid de Dr. He saw ter it dat we hed plenty ter eat.[334]

REV. JAMES WASINGTON did indeed have a good memory! Court records substantially verify the story that he told. On **Dr. Felder's** farm were numerous slaves who came from various locations. Abner O'Neal was from Amite County and was an active leader in the Mississippi Baptist Association and East Fork Baptist Church, pastored by **Rev. Charles Felder**. Abner owned 320 acres of property and 18 slaves in 1840. Upon his death in 1844, **Dr. Charles F. Felder** became administrator of his estate, auctioning off his real estate and personal property, and assuming guardianship of Abner's son, Samuel. He also assumed responsibility for dividing Abner's cash among his five children, each receiving $1,718.80. His slaves were divided among his children as well.[335] Apparently in the mix of slaves received by Abner's daughter, Ann (**Dr. Charles F. Felder's** wife), there was a hoe hand named **MARTHA**.

As detailed accurately by **REV. WASHINGTON**, **Dr. Felder** did not fight in the war. Instead, in advance of Mississippi's secession, he was intimately involved in supporting the resolutions upholding states' rights to protect their property, especially their slaves. In 1847, he was the secretary of the Democratic Meeting in Amite County. He was appointed by Governor McWillie to represent Mississippi (Amite County) at the Southern Convention held May 9, 1859, in Vicksburg, and was one of five delegates from the Tickfaw Police District appointed to attend the Southern Convention held in Jackson to nominate Mississippi delegates to go to the "Charleston Convention"[336] – the Democratic National Convention of 1860. *[Any surprise that McWillie was born in South Carolina, received his law degree from South Carolina College – now University of South Carolina, and served in the South Carolina House and Senate prior to coming to Mississippi!?]* Additionally, **Dr. Felder** was busy as a founding stockholder and member of the corporate body, the Liberty and Magnolia Railroad, created by law of the Mississippi Legislature on February 11, 1860, to erect a railroad from Liberty to Magnolia. Fellow board members included his brother, **James W. Felder**, and other prominent residents of Amite and Pike counties like Peter A. Quinn and Ansel H. Prewitt.[337]

Dr. Felder indeed lived on the road between Magnolia and Liberty, as **REV. WASHINGTON** indicated, possibly in a house similar to or larger than this six-room house built in 1840 in an "unusual dog-trot-style." It is now on the National Register of Historic Places listed as the **Felder-Richmond** home, noted for its architectural style (Greek Revival) and "rarity of the I-house form in residences in the state."[338] Ten years following the end of the Civil War, in efforts to improve his

---

334 Federal Writers' Project, Slave Narrative of James Washington, accessed November 1, 2003, http://msgw.org/slaves/washington-james-xslave.htm. Published by permission of Mississippi GenWeb. Also available via Library of Congress.

335 Parents of Lucy O'Neal, accessed November 2, 2003, http://www.rootsweb.com/~laascens/PARENTS_OF_LUCY_O'NEAL.html, site moved.

336 *The Eastern Clarion*, April 13, 1859, Image 2; The Weekly Mississippian, Jackson, September 7, 1859, Image 2.

337 Googlebooks, *Laws of the State of Mississippi*, November 1859, 426.

338 Mississippi Department of Archives and History, Historic Resources Inventory Fact Sheet, 1.

Richmond-Felder Home – near Gillsburg

deteriorating health, **Dr. Felder** left his community that held memories of a lifetime past. He left behind the prospect of future gatherings of family with neighbors and loved ones in this house with a covered walkway that protected the family from the elements as they strolled out to the dining room 200 or so feet from the main house and adjacent to the "cook house" (the kitchen – built away from the main house as a safety precaution from fires); an armoire so large it had to be built in the first-floor master bedroom; a piano and a small office in which the **Felder** owner could monitor the increase of his wealth.[339] **Felder** also left behind memories of his four wives that once lived with him in Amite County and helped oversee his slaves. In place of his vision of 36 slaves who toiled in his fields with hoes, he took with him on his journey a vision of 36 black men, women, and children still toiling in the fields, but with a hoe in one hand and freedom in the other. In 1875, he began his move to a drier climate in Texas, where he had many other **Felder** relatives, including **Gabriel**, but he died enroute. His then wife, **Lenora**, who was accompanying him, returned to Amite County where she lived out the remainder of her days.

"I Found the Answer!!"[340]

REV. **JAMES WASHINGTON** indicated that his father was not the father of each of **MARTHA's** twelve children, but that **MARTHA** was the mother of **SARAH**. The Freedmen's Bureau Record of Deposit indicates that **SARAH** was the mother of **ISAAC** who indicated in that record that he was the brother of **JOSEPH**. The A.M.E. Centennial History indicates that **JOSUF**, and his wife, **SUSANNAH**, were the parents of **SONA**. The U.S. censuses (1910-1920) indicate that **SONA** was the father of **BEATRICE**, and we know from birth and death certificates that **BEATRICE** was the mother of **TYREE** and **CHIQUITA**. **JAMES WASHINGTON's** WPA interview, corroborated by the Freedmen's Bureau Bank record, informs us that **HENRY, ALIA, CHLOE** and **KATIE** were siblings of **ISAAC** and **JOSEPH**.

Prior to the onset of the war, according to the US Census in 1860, the value of **Dr. Charles F. Felder's** real estate was $12,000 *[$342,000 real price in 2012 value]*, and his personal estate value was $40,000 *[$7,120,000 unskilled wage relative labor earnings, 2012 value]*. His brother, **James W. Felder's** real estate value was $15,000 *[$437,000, 2012 value]*, and his personal estate value was $50,000

---

339 *Amite County Historical and Genealogical Society Newsletter*, "Fifth Annual Open House: The Felder-Richmond Home, December 6, 2008."

340 "I Found the Answer," Baptist church hymn.

[$8,900,000 unskilled wage relative labor earning, 2012]. One story told by a grandchild indicated that once the war had ended, **Christopher Columbus Felder** returned home from the war with two bags of US silver dollars, which he used to relocate south of Osyka and build a home. **Christopher Columbus** was the son of **Dr. Charles F. Felder** and **Ann O'Neal Felder**. **MARTHA**, a field hoe hand on **Dr. Charles F.** and **Ann O'Neal Felder's** plantation, took her son, **JAMES WASHINGTON**, with her to Osyka the year following Emancipation to work for Sam Newman. There, according to **JAMES**, they often went hungry.

A pictorial representation of **JAMES WASHINGTON's** narrative reveals the following, which if indeed is accurate, establishes that **SONA's** paternal line can be traced back to the Congo.

JAMES WASHINGTON'S **SLAVE NARRATIVE**[341]

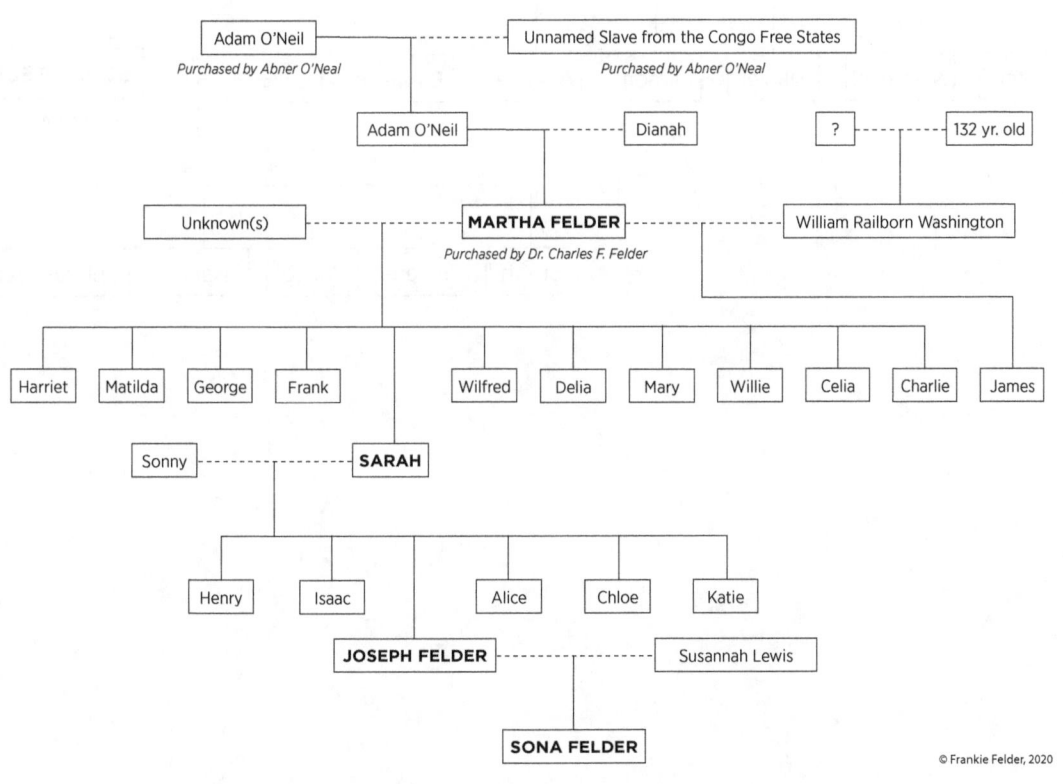

---

341 Source of relationships in family tree: WPA Slave Narrative of Rev. James W. Washington (Flowery Mount Baptist Church founder and 20-year pastor in Berglundtown, MS outside of McComb); msgw.org/slaves/washington-james-xslave.htm. Official records spell O'Neil as O'Neal.

SONA FELDER'S FAMILY TREE[342]

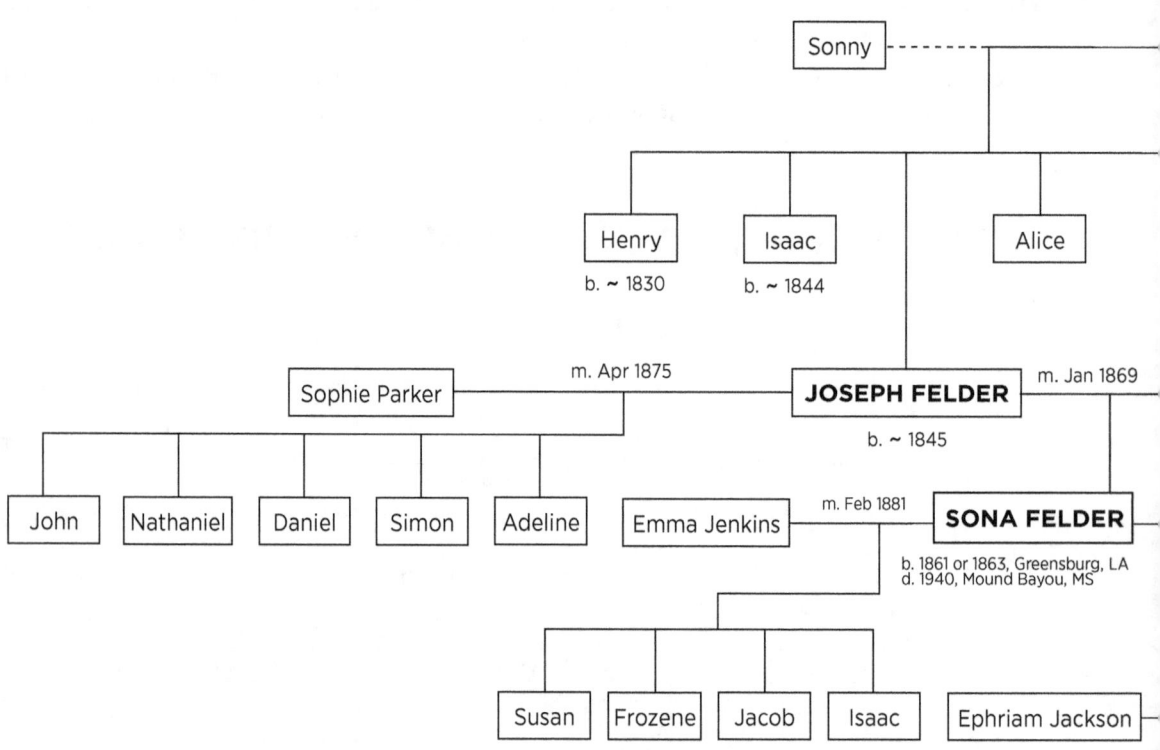

[342] The Freedman's Bank Records document the family relationship between Isaac, Henry, and Joseph as brothers, and establish Sarah and Sonny as their parents. The record is consistent with Rev. James Washington's slave narrative.

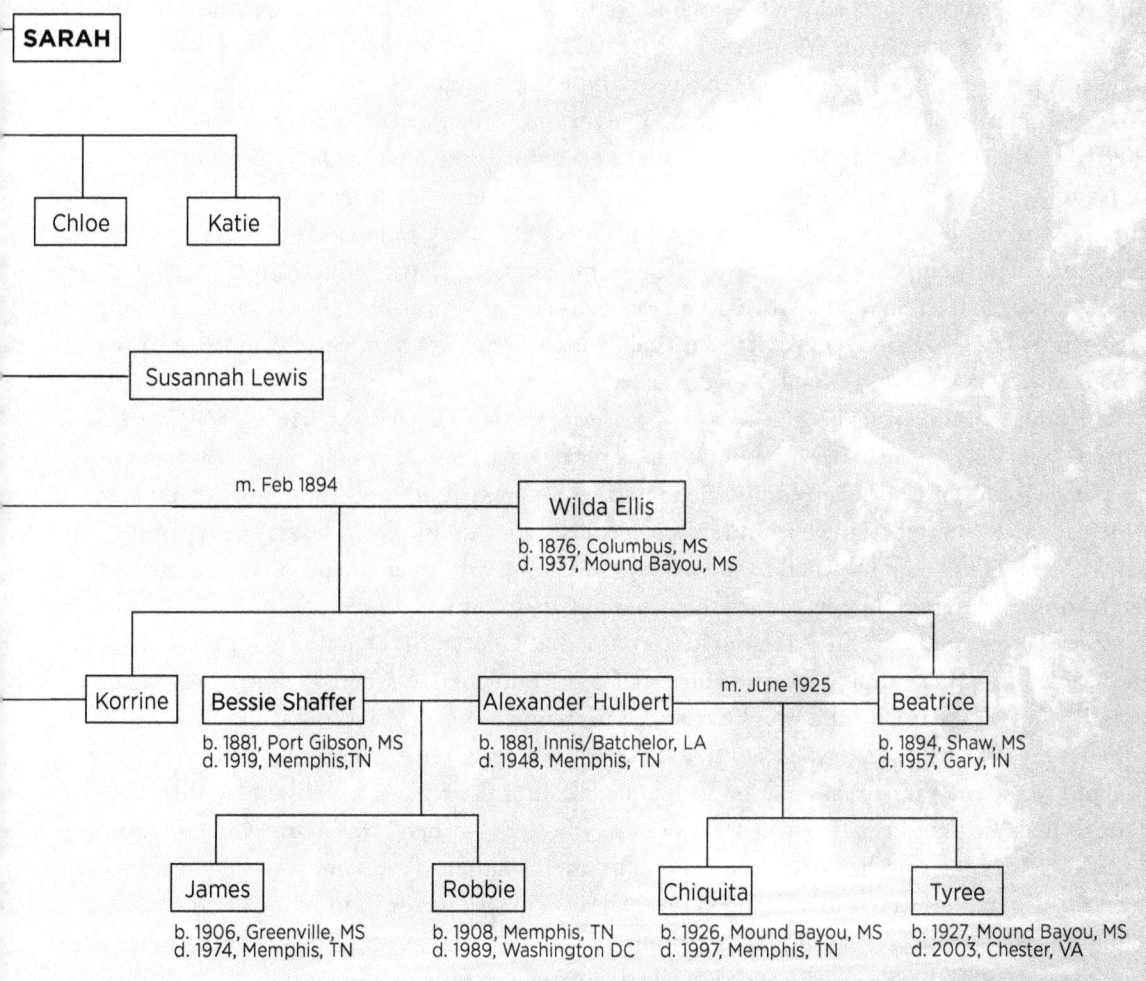

NOBODY KNOWS MY NAME

Now that we have learned the general whereabouts of our Mississippi and Louisiana ancestors, the question "How did we become members of a family called "**FELDER**?" looms large. Without any oral family history to corroborate any of the written documentation that has been found, we will never really know! So, is all this research for nothing?! Not necessarily. We are who we are, and we are called as we are called. We just do not know exactly why. Inconsistencies and surname issues abound with African Americans. The bondage imposed upon our ancestors was a painful life experience that many would never discuss again. They went to their graves with many secrets: whose children were whose; who "purchased" them; what requirements were made of them on the farms and plantations; whether they were whipped or raped or witnessed murder or were sold from place to place. Most did not know when they were born or where. They were given names that were not theirs, and often their names, and those of their ancestors, were stricken from their memories by horrors unimaginable. So many African Americans today are simply left guessing about what must have been reality, and if, indeed, what we are called today is an even remotely accurate portrayal of who our ancestors were and what they were called.

For example, John Gourdin, author of *Name Changing since the Civil War: A Case of Three USCT Regiments from South Carolina*, described numerous reasons why surnames changed. It was required that a black soldier provide a surname when enlisting for armed services. Many provided the name of their former "master." However, many also realized that to use the "master's" surname made them vulnerable to being returned to the plantation if they were ever caught by the enemy and so even before reaching the Union camps, they changed their names. *[Creative and clever and the mark of a survivor!]* For example: Bonus McDonald, so named at George McDonald's plantation, became Lewis McDonald after running away to enlist. He said, "I don't know where I come across the name Lewis."[343] But one year after the war, he changed his name to Bonus Clark.

Sometimes freedmen used a parent's first name as their surname. For example, Allen Yanney was born and raised on Yanney's plantation in Beaufort, South Carolina. He enlisted as Allen Yanney, although he knew that his father was David Cope, who was "owned" by George Cope on another plantation. After the war, he changed his name to use his father's first name and he became Allen David.[344] Also, names were often changed due to errors in spelling or in pronunciation in different sections of the country, rendering them sometimes unrecognizable, and certainly confusing, after being so decimated. I had an experience in Mississippi where I had to demand that the clerk in the courthouse print another document for me because she insisted that **BEATRICE FELDER's** name was different "because the record said so!" I told her I did not care what the record said, I knew what my grandmother's name was, and I would appreciate her correcting the document – which I was paying her for – as her court records were incorrect – likely due to an error of one of their staff. The supervisor, once engaged in this escalating debate, allowed me to receive a corrected document.

---

343 John R. Gourdin, "Name Changing Since the Civil War: A Case of Three USCT Regiments from South Carolina," *Journal of the Afro-American Historical and Genealogical Society*, vol. 21, no. 1 (2002): 50.

344 Gourdin, "Name Changing."

Sometimes a freedman would select the surname of a prominent local family or a nationally prominent individual, "living or dead," and assume their name, or they would "... adopt a name identifying them with a particular skill, trade or characteristic ... or *[choose]* the name of an 'owner' of one of their parents, grandparents or earlier forefathers; some even being able to recall a name associated with their immigrant African ancestor."[345] What they often did not do, however, was take the name of a "master" who was one of the larger slave owners![346] David Streets stated that "out of necessity many former slaves were forced to unite together for social and economic reasons into quasi-family units."[347] Consequently, a cautionary word to the wise: One should not make assumptions and one may be wrong even without making assumptions! Households with individuals of the same name may not necessarily reflect kinship through blood but kinship through bondage.

One of the important pieces of information from **REV. JAMES WASHINGTON's** slave narrative, reflective of this reality, was his indication that his father was not the biological father of all of **MARTHA's** 12 children. Unfortunately, then, without DNA documentation or oral history, we can only assume that **SONNY**, identified in the Freedmen's Bureau record of deposit by **ISAAC** as his father, was **JOSEPH's** biological father also and that **SARAH**, **ISAAC's** mother, was **JOSEPH's** mother, too. Fortunately, the Freedmen Bureau Record of Deposit states definitively that **ISAAC** had a brother named **JOSEPH**. Verification? Perhaps!

We can also assume that the continued repetition of names perhaps provides us with another clue, potentially, about relations. The name "**SONNY**" (identified in the Freedmen's Bureau record of deposit as **ISAAC's** father) was possibly passed down to **SONA**. "**SONNY**" would have been **SONA's** grandfather. **SONA** called himself "**SONNY**" as a young man. **ISAAC** was apparently **SONA's** uncle. **SONA** named his twin sons, who possibly died during childhood, **JACOB** and **ISAAC**. **SONA's** middle initial was "**P.**" His eldest daughter, **SUSIE** (by his first wife, **EMMA**), had a middle name that was likely taken from him as her middle initial was also "**P.**" I have yet to find this middle name identified for either of them, but both were **S. P. FELDER**. **TYREE's** middle initial was "**P**" for **PRESTON**. "**OTTOWIESS**" (**BEATRICE's** middle name) was passed to cousin **GWENDOLYN**, her daughter, **CHIQUITA**, and to me. "**TYREE**" was **SONA's** daughter's middle name, **KORRINE "TYREE" FELDER**, and it has been passed down four generations to **TYREE PRESTON FELDER**, to **TYREE CURTIS BEARDEN**, to **N'GAI CANUTE TYREE WASHINGTON**, and to **JORDAN TYREE CASTRO**. The practice of passing down names occurred so frequently in the white **Felder** families that I remain confused as I draw closure to this research and must constantly consult my diagrams to be certain I am reading or writing about the correct white **Felder**.

It is interesting to note that in addition to the first names of our ancestors being repeated through generations, even though it is said that many slaves did not assume their "masters'" surnames, in the 1870 U.S. Census there were 17 white **Felders** in Amite County (Mississippi) and 20 black **Felders**; in 1880, there were 20 white **Felders** and 44 black **Felders** in the county. Likewise, in Pike County

---

345 David Streets, Slave Genealogy: *A Research Guide with Case Studies* (Bowie, Maryland: Heritage Books, 1986), 9.

346 Tom Blake, transcriber, *Catahoula Parish, Louisiana, Largest Slaveholders from the 1860 Slave Census Schedules and Surname Matches for African Americans on the 1870 Census*, September 2001, accessed June 10, 2014, http://freepages.genealogy.rootsweb.ancestry.com/~ajac/lacatahoula.htm.

347 Streets, *Slave Genealogy*, 9.

(Mississippi) in 1870, there were 35 white **Felders** and 60 black **Felders**; in 1880, there were 43 white **Felders** and 20 black **Felders** in Pike. In Washington County, Texas, in 1870, there were 23 white **Felders** and 239 black **Felders**; and in 1880, there were 30 white **Felders** and 224 black **Felders** in this Texas county. The number of **Felder** slave "owners" in each of these counties was extremely small in 1860 when war broke out. In Amite, for example, only three **Felders** "owned" slaves (**Charles F.**, **Christopher Columbus**, and **James W.**); in Pike County, there were five **Felder** slave "owners" (**John**, **Simon**, **D.F.**, **F.W.**, and **H.D.**); and in Washington County, Texas, there were seven slave-"owning" **Felders** (**Gabriel**, "owning" nearly half of all slaves in the county; **C.B.**; **F.J.**; **Jesse G.**, **R.H.**, **A.F.**, and **F.**) – initials only used in the relevant censuses. All of these families were related. One can only surmise that the black **Felders** in these counties drew their surnames from these families. One could also reasonably assume that the relationships between slaves and slave "owners" were relatively palatable.

Black and white people employed at the Weston Mill worked together but lived separate lives. Possum Walk was the name given to the community of freed blacks who went to Logtown to work. This is likely the community in which **ISAAC** lived. Although in the Freedmen's Bureau record I found familiar names and correctly identified locations ... **JOSEPH**, **ISAAC**, **SONNY**, **SARAH** ... Logtown, Pearlington ... all the right people in the right place between the years 1870-1880, I found myself continuously trying to make a 2014 family unit out of them, in a style similar to that with which I have been blessed (post-Jim Crow and post-Civil Rights eras), complete with jobs and a whole new way of living; with laws that supported their freedom; with children who went to school and had plenty of clothing, food, toys, and activities to engage in after school; and with churches where they worshipped and schools in which they were educated. And then, I get brought back to reality.

The reality is that I cannot make a 21st century family out of our **FELDER** ancestors. They did not have a 2014 existence. Even in the period of Reconstruction, I cannot place them in my world of reasonable order, with the laws of America generally on my side and generally treating me pretty much like the white neighbors who live across the street and to my left and my right in my South Carolina neighborhood, named as one might guess, a "plantation." That was 1870. It was Mississippi and Louisiana. Our ancestors' lives revolved around safety and survival. In those two southern states, alone, occurred some of America's most violent crimes committed against the newly freed black race, with endorsement from local law officials, and most often with their furtive aid and/or blatant participation. Our ancestors experienced this in their everyday lives. Perhaps only in Hancock County, Mississippi where "[t]he white and colored citizens have tried to cultivate a friendly spirit and the trend of the races has been toward peace and goodwill,"[348] and where no lynchings [of blacks] ever took place,[349] were our ancestors ever handed any semblance of reprieve from fear of being black.

Despite my inability to document even one day of any of their lives, being able to retrieve from the archives of history a glimpse of the struggles, fears, and pain our forbearers musts have endured on extremely stony and bloody roads enables me to verify that in the final analysis they survived a horrendous life ordeal, were unchained and liberated from their putative "owners," and continued

---

348 Maxson, *Progress*, 20.

349 Maxson, *Progress*, 19.

to support each other until the end. This, to me, is one of the most proudful parts of *OURstory:* they were survivors.

Booker T. Washington perfectly illustrates the dilemma of the black family in America after slavery:

> No race starting in absolute poverty could be expected, in the brief period of thirty-five years, to purchase homes and build up a family life and influence that would have a very marked impression upon the life of the masses. The Negro has not had time enough to collect the broken and scattered members of his family. For the sake of illustration, and to employ a personal reference, I do not know who my father was; I have no idea who my grandmother was; I have or had uncles, aunts and cousins, but I have no knowledge as to where most of them now are. My case will illustrate that of hundreds of thousands of black people in every part of our country. Perhaps those who direct attention to the Negro's moral weakness, and *[sic]* compare his moral progress with that of the whites, do not consider the influence of the memories which cling about the old family homestead upon the character and aspirations of individuals. The very fact that the white boy is conscious that, if he fails in life, he will disgrace the whole family record, extending back through many generations, is of tremendous value in helping him to resist temptations. On the other hand, the fact that the individual has behind him and surrounding him proud family history and connections serves as a stimulus to make him overcome obstacles, when striving for success.[350]

On my last trip to Greensburg, Louisiana, I took my "research assistants," my sister, Gladys, and my friend, Dalys. We toured the town, visited the jail, talked with some of the city staff, and learned more about some of the interesting people who had lived there. I shared with them a bit of our family history in Greensburg and what I had learned about surname acquisition among the freedmen and women. A life-long resident of Greensburg and city staff member, Mrs. Elaine G. Spears, made quite an insightful comment during that discussion. I asked her permission to include it, as well as her photo, in my book. And so, I close this section on the **FELDER** family with the following quote from Ms. Spears: "You can call me what you want. I know who I am!"

Mrs. Elaine Spears

---

350 Booker T. Washington, "Will the Education of the Negro Solve the Race Problem?" in *Multum in Parvo: an authenticated history of progressive Negroes in pleasing graphic and biographic style*, compiled by I. W. Crawford and P. H. Thompson (Jackson, Mississippi: self-published, 1912), 336.

Mississippi Magnolias, Irish Blossoms, and Black Limbs

My ancestry DNA match with Ireland is 8%. Here is likely why.

The Ellises of Virginia lived for the most part, in the early 1800s, in Sussex and Surrey counties. Present day locations in these counties include Jamestown, Waverly and Wakefield, along Routes 360 and 460. A few Ellises later moved to Nansemond (location of Suffolk) and to the Norfolk region. They were cotton, tobacco, and peanut farmers. Beginning in 1830, two slave traders in particular sent 1000+ slaves from Virginia plantations by ship from Alexander, Virginia to the New Orleans and Natchez, Mississippi slave markets, the largest and second largest slave markets, respectively, in the country. Perhaps a slave named **KEZIAH** marched alongside these others shackled in chains the one-mile trek from the ship that docked in Mississippi to the Natchez market and this is how she came to be in Mississippi. **KEZIAH ELLIS** was born in Virginia in 1830. However, so was **KEZZIAH ELLIS**. Her date of birth was 1810. She would have been 20 years old, with a newborn baby, and she would have worn the chains on her legs, with the baby strapped on her back. God forbid if she actually was one of the 12,000 or so Virginia slaves who were forced to walk the 1,100-mile *Slave Trail of Tears*[351] from Chesapeake to the Mississippi River, about a four-month trek.

REV. S. P. FELDER's *Bible* documents the birthdate of **JANE ELLIS** as January 2, 1852 and indicates that other members of the **ELLIS** family are **DORA** and **CASSIR**. The 1870 U.S. Census (the first time in which blacks are identified by name), enumerates **JANE ELLIS** living in Police District 3 in the city of Columbus (Lowndes County), Mississippi. At 19 years old, she works as a farm laborer along with every one of the five others who live in this household: **KEZIAH ELLIS**, age 40; **LETETIA**[352] **ELLIS**, age 20; **CASSY**[353] **ELLIS**, age 17; **DORA**[354] **ELLIS**, age 14; and **LEWIS ELLIS**, age 12.

JANE's siblings, like herself, experienced freedom for the first time in 1863, when Lincoln signed the Emancipation Proclamation. Thirteen years later, on May 3, 1876, **JANE** gave birth to **WILDA JANE**[355] **ELLIS** in Clay County, Mississippi. The family had not moved. Clay County was created in 1872 out of the northern portion of Lowndes County. The census enumerator listed two individuals in this household as "mulatto" – **CASSY** and **DORA**. Although oral family history says that **WILDA** was one-half Irish, every census record lists her as "black." No record has yet been found that identifies **WILDA's** father. **KEZIAH ELLIS** is **JANE's** mother and likely mother to the rest of the members of this **ELLIS** family.

KEZZIAH ELLIS, at the time of the 1870 census, was 60 years old and enumerated in Memphis, Tennessee, along with **Joseph Ellis**, 23-year-old drayman, 18-year-old **Matilda Ellis**, and five other

---

351 Edward Ball, "Retracing Slavery's Trail of Tears, *Smithsonian Magazine*, November 2015, https://www.smithsonianmag.com/history/slavery-trail-of-tears-180956968/.

352 The *S. P. Felder Family* Bible lists "Loutisa" Wilson Ellis as having died on February 25, 1906. The census recording of her name is, thus, an apparent misspelling.

353 The *S. P. Felder Family Bible* lists "Cassir" as having died in December of 1894.

354 The *S. P. Felder Family Bible* lists "Dora Vaughn Ellis Dird" as having died in 1903. This last name may be significant as the Peter Felder story indicates that Peter and his family "settled the Vaughn Place" when they came originally to Mississippi. However, a Dora and Ransome Vaughan were divorced in Lowndes County on October 4, 1899 per minutes of the Chancery Court. Uhmm...

355 Per her Mississippi Death Certificate, April 7, 1937, Wilda's middle name was Jane, not Juanita, although Juanita is written in the *S.P. Felder Bible*. She was possibly named for her mother, Jane. Chiquita, years later, would receive this middle name, Jane, from her great-grandmother.

Ellis children, ages 8, 5, 3, 2, and 1 (**Stephen, Cinda, Hanny, Thomas,** and **James**, respectively). **Joseph** is the only one listed as working in this household. Except for **Kezziah**, everyone, according to this census record, was born in Tennessee. **Joseph, Matilda** and **Kezziah** are all unable to read or write. Everyone on this census page is black, which suggests that they live in a segregated, black neighborhood. **KEZZIAH** is possibly the mother of **KEZIAH**; the grandmother of **JANE**; the great-grandmother of **WILDA**; the great-great-grandmother of **BEATRICE**, and, therefore, the great-great-great-grandmother of the **FELDER** and **BEARDEN** children.

Possibly.

WILDA's sister, or perhaps cousin, **CLARA**, wed **EMMETT WHITFIELD** in Columbus, Mississippi, on August 25, 1887. **EMMETT** could have been somehow connected to the prominent Whitfield family that lived in Columbus. Between 1891 and 1899, in two-year increments, the couple gave birth to five children (**MAYMIE LOU, VALLEI EMMIT, CLARA WILLIE, VANTEE GENIA** and **CLEO LOUISE**). According to **S. P. FELDER's** *Bible*, both parents died within four years of each other – **CLARA** in January 1901 and **EMMETT** in November 1905 – leaving their children, ages 14, 13, 10, 8, and 6, parentless. Family stepped in to raise these children. By 1910, **CLEO LOUISE** and **VALLEI EMMIT** were living with **SONA** and **WILDA** in Greenville. Daughter **CLARA WILLIE** went to Mound Bayou and was enumerated as the adopted daughter of Mr. and Mrs. G. A. Lee. **MAMIE LOU** and **VANTEE GENIA** went to Memphis and lived with **DR. LEE ROY ROSS**, dentist, who later became **CLARA WILLIE's** husband.

CLARA WILLIE was born on Dec. 16, 1895, and at age 19, married **LEE ROY ROSS** in 1914 in Memphis, Tennessee.[356] Sadly, this was a short-lived marriage because **CLARA WILLIE** died on June 10, 1919 at the very tender age of 24. In 1920, 27-year old **LEE ROY** owned his home free of a mortgage, owned his own business, and was continuing to pursue his studies. Industrious and determined, he took six boarders into his home, two of whom were his sisters-in law. **LEROY** later remarried a woman named Alma.

State of the State – Mississippi

Freedom sparked a crescendo of self-esteem, which in turn ignited strong participation by freedmen in Reconstruction opportunities. Voting was at the top of the list of those opportunities. Reconstruction brought blacks to the polls; an estimated 98% – *virtually all* – eligible black males in Mississippi were registered to vote in 1868![357] The resulting elections catapulted black men into positions of responsibility and authority across the South, participating in local, state, and national offices. Intelligent, literate, thoughtful, and forgiving black men: P. B. S. Pinchback became the first black governor in America (Louisiana); Oscar J. Dunning became the nation's first Lt. Governor (Louisiana); Francis Lewis Cardozo became Secretary of State and Treasurer (South Carolina); Virginia sent Samuel P. Boling to the Virginia House of Delegates, and Mississippi voters elected the first African American U.S. Senator, Hiram R. Revels, who later led Alcorn College as president, as well as U.S. Senator Blanche Bruce who attended Oberlin College and was later appointed by President James Garfield as

---

356 *S.P. Felder Family Bible*, notes in section titled, "Marriages."

357 Berkley Hudson, "Possum Town photo-biography: culture, history and identity through the Mississippi lens of O. N. Pruitt, 1920-1955," (PhD dissertation, University of North Carolina, Chapel Hill, 2003), 5.

First black U. S. senator and representatives

Register of the U.S. Treasury. Additionally, several men were elected from their states to serve in the U.S. House of Representatives. It may come as no surprise that Hiram Revels faced discrimination when attempting to take his seat in Congress, with Democrats arguing that he had only been granted citizenship by the 14th Amendment, passed July 9, 1868, and the Civil Rights Act of 1868. They even invoked the Supreme Court's 1857 Dred Scott decision, which denied citizenship to blacks. As such, Democrat senators argued, the Mississippi Legislature should not have elected him to represent the state. But, a Senate vote of 48 to 8 enabled him to take his seat,[358] and in the one-year term that he served, he made an impact on the perspectives about how laws applied to African Americans.

But, in less than ten years, by the time **WILDA** was born in 1876, life in Mississippi had drastically changed. The 1870s were extremely frightening times, probably as much or more so than during the war years because now the uniform of the Confederate soldier no longer identified the enemy. The Civil War was a near memory, only a few years past, and still fresh on everyone's mind. White Mississippians, "80,000" of whom had fought for the Confederacy, were now coalescing to create new

---

358 Eric Foner, "There Have Been 10 Black Senators Since Emancipation," The New York Times, February 14, 2020, accessed September 24, 2020 (nytimes.com).

systems to disrupt the processes that gave citizenship, literacy, and a political voice to freedmen and women who were the beneficiaries of the war won by the aid of only "500" or so white Mississippians, but nearly "17,000"[359] Mississippi slaves and freedmen who served in the Union army. Angry and disgruntled ex-Confederate soldiers and officers formed the Ku Klux Klan in Pulaski, Tennessee, one year after the war – in 1866. The organization's ethos spread like a California brushfire throughout the South; torrid environments and political sectionalism raging out of control. Following **WILDA's** birth, Reconstruction would only survive one additional year.

The 1876 presidential election was a "hotly disputed" contest everywhere, but especially in Mississippi. Ten years of Republican federal government policies, Congressionally-imposed legislation and state Republican-revised constitutions led many Southerners to their worst persona yet. White men took to the streets, the schools, the polls, the campaign events – to anywhere they thought that blacks would gather to strategize for improved political, educational, and economic progress. Black men began carrying pistols and shotguns to a place it would never have occurred to them they would not be safe – to the church.[360] In the Natchez District of Mississippi, which included the Port Gibson area, the intent to overthrow as many duly elected black politicians as possible became the aim of the white male. In one raid on a prayer meeting, the minister was confronted: "'You have these night meetings as prayer-meetings … and then you turn them into political meetings, and we mean to break them up.'"[361] In the gunfire that was exchanged, one white agitator was killed. The following day, the whites "scoured the countryside" … and rounded up about thirty men who were accused of attending the church meeting. They took these men to the woods, conducted a "kangaroo court" where the "white club presidents" served as the judges, and executed 25-30 men that day.[362] Not only were blacks being terrorized, so were white Republican office holders and any other whites who sympathized with the black man's quest for fairness. Judges, sheriffs, and other officials were told they "must get on the Lord's side or they would be killed," so many Republican white men switched allegiance and joined the Democratic party.[363] This switch took away any remaining semblance of protection by the law and gave credence to the rapidly evolving unmitigated violence and murders perpetuated on innocent black men, women, and children.

It is uncontested that the late 1870s was the beginning of unmitigated racial attacks on African Americans. In the states that lost the war, by the 1890s, hardly a day passed[364] when at least one black person was not strung from a tree, burned alive, drowned by a vigilante group of angry, hateful, revengeful white males. More blacks were lynched in Mississippi than in any other state – a total of

---

359 John F. Marszalek and Clay Williams, "Mississippi Soldiers in the Civil War," in *Mississippi History Now*, accessed January 12, 2013 (Mississippi Department of Archives and History, http://mshistorynow.mdah.state.ms.us/articles/175/mississippi-soldiers-in.

360 Justin Behrend, "Overthrowing Local Democracies: The Political Geography of Reconstruction Violence in the Natchez District," delivered at the 13th Annual Gilder Lehrman Center for the Study of Slavery, Resistance, and Abolition International Conference at (Yale University, November 11-13, 2011), 1, Beyond Freedom: New Directions in the Study of Emancipation," accessed January 12, 2013, www.yale/edu/glc/emancipation/behrend.pdf.

361 Behrend, "Overthrowing Local Democracies," 1.

362 Behrend, "Overthrowing Local Democracies," 2.

363 Behrend, "Overthrowing Local Democracies," 6.

364 Hudson, "Possum Town," 10.

581 over 86 years (1882-1968).[365] The first lynching of an African American in Lowndes County, where **WILDA** and her family lived, occurred three months before her 13th birthday. On February 22, 1889, D. H. Smith, accused of working to colonize blacks (assisting with the return of blacks to Liberia in western Africa), was lynched. As **WILDA** matured into a young teen, six more black men would be lynched in Lowndes County; two of which occurred in the city proper (Columbus). The last lynching in her county occurred six months before she decided to get married. Farmers, businessmen, educators, ministers, women, and children – it did not matter – were lynched all across the South as Southern white Americans reeled in reaction to the loss of the war and the enfranchisement of black Americans. Mob violence raged in rural and urban areas alike.

Blacks developed a survival tactic to never look a white person in the eye for fear of being accused of insubordination or disrespect. White men of the South spoke of "honor" and "chivalry" and "protection" of their women, their mothers, wives, and daughters from the black "beasts," "monkeys," "coons," "spades," "niggers," and "boys," amongst the more palatable names they ascribed to black men, who they feared would now retaliate by raping white women as the white men had raped black women and female children, particularly during slavery. Lynching became a sport, an entertainment, a community picnic of sorts. Whites photographing these hangings included the news media as well as the local entrepreneur, who turned lynchings into parties, often advertising these murders well in advance[366] so that the white community could come celebrate the elimination of another black person from the face of the earth. I have struggled with including photographs. *[As I prepare this chapter to send to the interior designer for this book, I have made the decision to not include any photographs of lynchings, as each time I read this section, I cry, my heart hurts, and I pray for the eradication of the incredulous hate in this country. Hate borne of America's first sin. Finally, I do not want my young grandsons to see these photos in their grandmother's book.]*

The 178-plus locations of lynchings in the state of Mississippi included Amite County, Cleveland, Coahoma, Columbus, Greenville, Jackson, Port Gibson, and Shaw. All of these locations are where our ancestors lived significant portions of their lives as children and/or worked as adults. Surely the news traveled quickly from home to home; the fear from heart to heart.

The chart below shows the locations and number of lynchings that took place in Mississippi towns in which our relatives lived and worked. It also delineates which relatives were in these areas of the state during the 86-year lynching history in Mississippi.

---

365 See: http://nationalhumanitiescenter.org/pds/maai3/segregation/text2/lynchingcrime.pdf. See also, "Lynchings by State and Race, 1882-1968," accessed August 14, 2020, http://law2.umkc.edu/faculty/projects/ftrials/shipp/lynchingsstate.html. Numbers vary depending on source consulted, but all sources reveal that Mississippi led the nation in the number of murders by lynching of African Americans, with Georgia, Texas, and Louisiana following in that order. Surprisingly, South Carolina, while in the top 10, ranked number seven. Perhaps the lynching that most stunned the nation occurred on August 28, 1955, in Money, Mississippi, when Emmett Till, a 14-year-old, was murdered by a mob that accused him of whistling at and, therefore, disrespecting a white woman.

366 "The Murder of Emmett Till," Lynching in America, PBS, American Experience, accessed January 12, 2017, http://www.pbs.org/wgbh/amex/till/peopleevents/e_lynch.html.

LYNCHINGS IN OUR FAMILY'S HOMETOWNS

LYNCHING LOCATION[367]	NUMBER OF LYNCHINGS	THE WHITE CONNECTION	THE BLACK CONNECTION	RELATION
Amite County	5	Plantations of Rev. Charles Felder (Liberty), and Dr. Charles F. Felder.	Sarah Felder and children lived here as slaves to Dr. Charles F. Felder.	Sarah – Joseph's mother and Sona's grandmother
Cleveland	3		Alexander Hulbert and Beatrice Felder married here.	Alexander and Beatrice – biological father and mother of Tyree and Chiquita
Coahoma County	1		Robbie Hulbert lived here. Sona Felder pastored Friar's Point A.M.E. Church here.	Robbie - half-sister to Tyree and Chiquita, daughter of Alexander Hulbert and Bessie Shaffer; Sona – Tyree's and Chiquita's grandfather
Columbus	9	Ellis Plantation	Keziah, Jane, and Wilda Ellis lived here.	Wilda – Sona's wife and mother of Beatrice; Jane – Beatrice's grandmother; Keziah – Beatrice's great-grandmother
Greenville	6		Sona, Wilda, Beatrice, and Korrine Felder lived here. Korrine was born here. Sona pastored here. Joseph lived here.	Tyree and Chiquita's immediate family: Beatrice – mother; Korrine – aunt; Sona and Wilda – parents; Joseph – paternal grandfather
Jackson	16		Tyree Felder attended high school while working at Topps Cleaners here. Campbell College relocated to here.	Tyree – father of Gladys, Frankie, Debbie, Marva, and Tyrelle; Chiquita's brother; Bearden cousins' (Gwen, Harold, Howard and Ronald) uncle
Port Gibson	3	B. M. Hulbert was born here; Martin Nathaniel Hulbert's plantation was here.	Alexander Hulbert and Bessie Shaffer married here. Bessie lived here.	Alexander Hulbert – father of Tyree and Chiquita; B. M. Hulbert – father of Alexander; Martin Nathaniel Hulbert – great-grandfather of Tyree and Chiquita
Shaw	1		Beatrice Felder was born here.	Beatrice – grandmother of Felder and Bearden cousins

---

367 Data retrieved from GeoCities, accessed March 2, 2014, oocities.org/colosseum/base/8507/NLPlaces2.htm, now defunct.

In general *his*tory narratives, the brutality of these crimes has been so sterilized that thinking of lynching conjures up a sanitized hanging, requiring only a rope and a tree limb. But in Mississippi, particularly, where the bestiality of the brutality stunned the entire nation, the horror and the terror instilled in the black community by these lynchings produced exactly the effect that the mobs desired. Famed African American, Richard Wright, author of *Black Boy*, born in 1908 and raised in the Natchez District of the state, wrote: "The things that influenced my conduct as a Negro did not have to happen to me directly; I needed but to hear of them to feel the full effects in the deepest layers of my consciousness. Indeed, the white brutality that I had not seen was a more effective control of my behavior than that which I knew."[368]

Strange Fruit [369]

Southern trees bear a strange fruit; blood on the leaves and blood at the root;
Black bodies swinging in the southern breeze; strange fruit hanging from the poplar trees.
Pastoral scene of the gallant south; the bulging eyes and the twisted mouths;
Scent of magnolias, sweet and fresh; then the sudden smell of burning flesh.
Here is a fruit for the crows to pluck, for the rain to gather, for the wind to suck,
For the sun to rot, for the trees to drop,
Here is a strange and bitter crop.

These lyrics and tune, written by a Northern, white Jewish high school teacher, Abel Meeropol, and Billy Holliday's heart-wrenching rendition of "Strange Fruit," stirred the soul of white America in ways that apparently nothing else could. It was said that in those places where she determined it "safe" to sing it, the impact was lasting. "Whether they (white Americans) protested in Selma or took part in the March on Washington or devoted their lives to social activism, many say that it was hearing 'Strange Fruit' that triggered the process."[370] The 3446 blacks lynched in every state in America except seven[371] included women and children. As if dismembering a black male, distributing his body parts and publicly displaying them was not atrocious enough, it appeared as if the objective of lynch mobs was to outdo each other.

One of the most heinous lynchings in the South was the 1918 lynching of Mary Turner in Lowndes, Georgia. Mary, eight months pregnant, was hanged by her feet, doused with gasoline, set afire, her baby falling out with a cry after she was sliced open. The baby was stomped to death by the crowd.[372] One lynching occurred, however, that the country just could not ignore – a murder

---

368 Amy Louise Wood, Lynching and Spectacle: *Witnessing Racial Violence in America*, 1890-1940, (Google eBook, 2009), xi.

369 Abel Meeropol under the pseudonym, Lewis Allen, lyricist, 1937; first published as "Bitter Fruit" in *The New York Teacher*. Used by permission.

370 David Margolick, *Strange Fruit: Billy Holliday, Café Society and an Early Cry for Civil Rights*, 2000, accessed November 3, 2013, http://www.nytimes.com/books/first/m/margolick-fruit.html,

371 Only in the following states did no lynchings of African Americans ever occur: Arizona, Idaho, Maine, Nevada, South Dakota, Vermont, and Wisconsin.

372 Henrietta Venton Davis, "Black Women who were Lynched in America," posted August 2, 2008, accessed September 1, 2009, http://henriettavintondavis.wordpress.com/2008/08/01/black-women-who-were-lynched-in-america/.

that made America begin to crack the hardened shell of evil that encrusted her soul. On August 31, 1955, Emmett Till's body, swollen and mutilated, was recovered from the Tallahatchie River, three days after this 14-year old was lynched by two grown men, tortured and beaten unmercifully for three hours, shot in the head, tied with barbed wire to a large metal fan, and then thrown into the river.[373] The whitewashed version of the story even garnered front page headlines in mainstream newspapers like the *New York Times* and the *Chicago Tribune* during an era when "black news" typically was printed on the last page of mainstream papers, if at all. Twenty-seven-year-old Carolyn Bryant, store clerk and wife of the store owner, said that this child had flirted with and disrespected her after making his purchase. Her husband, Roy, and his half-brother, J. W. Milam, who committed the crime, were acquitted of this murder by an all-white, male jury of their neighbors.

Emmett's mother allowed an open casket funeral to force America to look at her own brutality. The black press, as well as mainstream white newspapers, ran stories and published photos about this lynching. Despite the differences in the message they portrayed – white papers being mostly sympathetic towards the murderers – publishing family photos of the men and pictures of them in their military uniforms – and black papers depicting handsome young Emmett in his middle-class neighborhood alongside his unrecognizable body at his funeral[374] – the conscience of America had finally been bared. This time, the country would not sit by and watch.

Unfortunately, unfathomable stories like these lynchings serve only as a minute backdrop to the realities of our ancestors' lives. Suffice it to say that thousands of African Americans lost their lives from the sterns of the slave ships to the limbs of the southern trees while this nation struggled with righting its many wrongs as it tried to heal itself. It is sad to note that this is a task – healing – yet to be completed in our country.[375]

One might imagine the absolute terror that young black men and women felt realizing that at any moment, they, too, could become the object of some hate-filled soul's torturous imagination. Young girls probably looked to find strong black men on whom they could depend for protection. It probably generated a sense of comfort in the mothers of girls who left home to make their lives with what hopefully would be a marriage based on love above all, but which also came with the added benefit of male power. At the age of 18, on February 15, 1894, **WILDA ELLIS** married such a man. He was 15 years her senior. First Baptist Church in Columbus, Mississippi, was the site of the wedding of **REVEREND** and **MRS. S. P. FELDER**, and later that day, at **WILDA's** mother's home, a reception was held in their honor.[376] By this marriage, she became a housewife, and within five years, she had become the mother of two daughters, **BERTHA BEATRICE OTTOWIESS FELDER** and **KORRINE TYREE FELDER**. **SONA** and **WILDA** were married in Mississippi in the same month – February – that he married his first wife, **EMMA JENKINS**, and only two days and 13 years separated the wedding dates, February 15, 1894 and February 17, 1881, respectively.

---

373 Biography, Emmett Till, January 22, 2015, accessed March 8, 2015, updated June 23, 2020, www.biography.com/people/emmett-till-507515.

374 Oby, Michael, "Black Press Coverage of the Emmett Till Lynching as a Catalyst to the Civil Rights Movement," (Master's thesis, Georgia State University, 2007), accessed March 8, 2014, http://scholarworks.gsu.edu/communication_thesis/20.

375 In 2007, at 82 years old, Carolyn Bryant admitted that she had lied. For more information on this story, read: www.nytimes.com/2017/01/27/us/emmett-till-lynching-carolyn-bryant-donham.html.

376 *S. P. Felder Family Bible* in section, "Marriages."

In the 13 intervening years between these marriages, three of the four **FELDER** children born of the first marriage, **ISAAC**, **JACOB**, and **FROZENE**, are not found in discernable documentation in any **FELDER** household.

Not only do these children essentially disappear from records by 1894, so do the men who heretofore had gone to the polls to vote. The reign of terror was at its peak throughout the South, and particularly in Mississippi. Columbus' population was majority black in 1876 when **WILDA** was born, and African Americans began exercising their newfound rights. But as the Klan escalated its presence and as whites' general hatred of blacks manifested itself as focused tyranny in the county, the involvement of African Americans in the political and economic arena declined. Lowndes County became known as "one of the most violent places in the post-Civil War South,"[377] where "Klansmen would ride up and down the roads at night, stopping at plantations along the way to 'straighten out the niggers,' by which they meant whipping everybody, men, women, and children, twenty-five or thirty people at a time. The people were so terrified that many took to sleeping in the woods."[378]

In Columbus, "the Chamber of Commerce boasted in an undated tourism brochure entitled, 'Columbus, The Friendly City,' – "We have few major crimes in the county and 95 percent of the petty offenses are committed by our colored population.'"[379] Berkley Hudson noted that the undated brochure "provided no details about the at least eighteen African Americans who were lynched in the county"[380] beginning in 1889 – clearly not "petty offenses" and clearly not committed by the "colored population." By far, the most damaging impact on the black community *en masse* was that by 1892, less than 6% of eligible black men were registered to vote, and consequently, "*[w]*ithout the ability to protect elected leaders, to hold political meetings, or to ensure an honest election, the local democracy that African Americans ha*[d]* fashioned from the ashes of slavery had now been demolished."[381] In other words, 92% of all black men who had heretofore participated in the democratic process, who had defined freedom as encompassing the opportunity to exercise their rights and responsibilities to vote, had been terrorized away from the polls and the political processes established to ensure a voice and representation in the government designed to address their needs and interests just like those of every other citizen. The A.M.E. *Christian Recorder*, the first and official voice of the A.M.E. Church, received and communicated religious and secular news from all over the country on the state of affairs for black Americans. News received by the publisher from and about Mississippi led the *Recorder* to give a clear warning to African Americans: 'Don't come to Mississippi!'[382]

Amid the escalating madness of racial crimes being perpetrated on African Americans, young black college students tried to understand the senseless killings happening all around them. At one point, there was hope that the embers from the Civil War of intense hatred of black people, still flickering in the night in both rural and urban communities, would soon be extinguished. Instead, however, the progress gained by blacks because of Emancipation and during Reconstruction only

---

377 Behrend, "Overthrowing Local Democracies," 18.

378 Behrend, "Overthrowing Local Democracies," 18.

379 Hudson, "Possum Town," 24.

380 Hudson, "Possum Town," 24.

381 Behrend, "Overthrowing Local Democracies," 16.

382 Behrend, Overthrowing Local Democracies, 8.

served to reignite those embers into a raging wildfire that spread across the South from plantation to plantation, farm to farm, and city to city. Yet, as God moves in His mysterious ways, simultaneously and unknowingly, these lynchings and demonstrations of total disdain for the black race sparked the flames of the Civil Rights movement, which would soon be led by the youth of the nation.

After being expelled from Shaw College (now Rust College) for disrespecting the president, and then taking a teaching job to help support her siblings following the death of both parents and baby brother to yellow fever, Ida B. Wells, known to most Americans as an activist in the women's suffrage movement, noticed at the age of 16 that she earned $50 a month less than white teachers. In 1886, at the age of 24, she experienced first-hand being forcefully removed, and then thrown off, a train, when she refused to move from the first-class seat that she had purchased to the back car for blacks; however, not before she sank her teeth deep into the arm of the conductor who had to get two other men to help him pull her off the train! It was obviously a traumatic experience for her, but she lived with it as a sign of the times. In 1892, however, at the age of 30, when her three friends were lynched for protecting their store from white vandals who had entered, she decided to respond. It was then that Ida B. Wells stepped forward out of the shadows of her secure job as a newspaper co-owner and journalist and completely threw herself into the fight for racial justice. Believing that knowledge was power, and that history could be used as a weapon in this fight, she created and disseminated posters like this one on the history of lynching. [383] She was of the opinion that disseminating facts about lynching would end this tragic culture of mob violence and vigilante terrorism that she, too, had by then personally witnessed firsthand. Her friends and step-uncle were lynched by a mob.[384] In 1909, she co-founded the NAACP (National Association for the Advancement of Colored People). Ida Wells was a visionary who turned history into a weapon of mass destruction. She used her skills and connections as a journalist to influence the thinking and stir the emotions of the youth of the nation. They decided to take action. Although she did not formally teach for any extended period, she master-minded a pedagogy that utilized history as the center of the curriculum. That curriculum became the weapon by which she waged, and won, psychological warfare.

Mississippi, in particular the cities of Port Gibson (home of **ALEXANDER HULBERT** and **BESSIE SHAFFER** – parents of **JAMES** and **ROBBIE HULBERT**, and father of **CHIQUITA BEARDEN** and **TYREE FELDER**) and location of the Medgar Evers 1960s civil rights saga, and Columbus (home of

Ida Wells

---

383 Ida B. Wells, *"History is a Weapon: Lynch Law,"* 1893, accessed December 8, 2013, http://www.historyisaweapon.com/defcon1/wellslynchlaw.html.

384 Wikipedia, The Free Encyclopedia, "Ida B. Wells," accessed December 8, 2013, http://en.wikipedia.org/wiki/Ida_B._Wells.

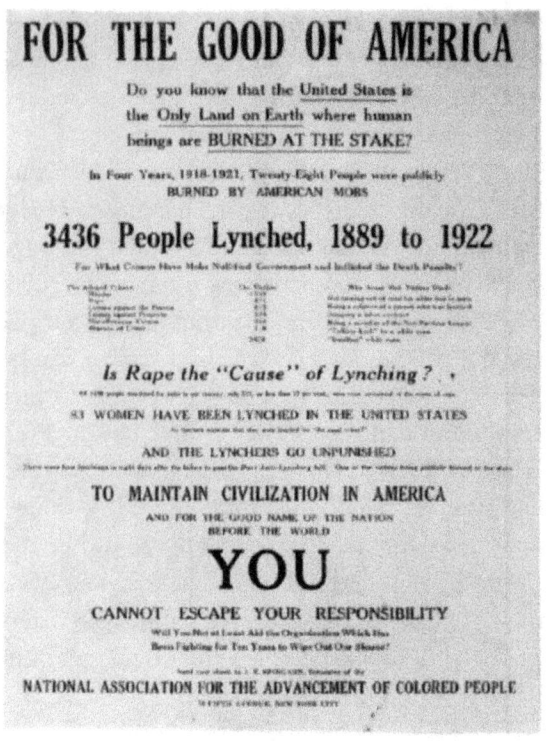

Ida Wells poster

WILDA, **JANE**, and **KEZIAH ELLIS** – three generations of grandmothers to the **FELDER** and **BEARDEN** cousins) and location of some of Mississippi's most heinous lynchings, unknowingly germinated the highly successful massive resistance, student non-violence movement in the United States. The movement culminated in the March on Washington in 1963, demanding the return of voting rights and protection of citizens to exercise those rights.

In 1957, Martin Luther King was but 28 years old when he assumed leadership of the Southern Christian Leadership Conference (SCLC), the conduit by which the "Civil Rights Movement" became a national force that garnered international attention. I was seven. Before Wyatt Tee Walker, our pastor at Gillfield Baptist Church, left Petersburg, Virginia, in 1960 at age 31 to become the first executive director of the SCLC and chief strategist for King and the Conference, he led us in picketing Woolworth's lunch counter in downtown Petersburg. The KKK burned a cross in our churchyard. I was 10. When I began school on the army base in Giessen, Germany, all of my homeroom classmates were black. At the end of the first week of placement testing, I was moved to section 9-1, where all of my homeroom classmates were white, making it evident that the school had placed all black children, on the basis of race, in section 9-4, the lowest academic section. In my new homeroom, I met a girl who became my very best friend. She was the first white person I personally knew – Mary Jane Ford. I was 14, and we both began to discover what racism meant.

What is evident in the lives of our ancestors is that they witnessed and lived in a very violent South, but they stuck together, supporting close and extended family and neighbors through frightening and painful times. One could easily fathom their daily existence and the conversations held in their homes, churches, schools, and communities. Be still and listen and hear their voices. One can hear the instructions given to school children before they left home to walk often five to six miles to school, "Make sure you do not look a white person in the face." "Never look in the eyes of a white man." "Always be polite – say, 'Yes, sir or Yes, ma'am.'" "Make sure that you come straight home from school." "Do not be loud walking down the street. Do not draw attention to yourself."

Look intently into the black community of the late 1800s through the mid-1900s and you will see evidence of the expectations that parents had regarding education: "You must always do your best." "You must be twice as good as white people to get half as far." "Good is not good enough if you can do better." "Your report card will follow you for the rest of your life." "Do not disrespect your teachers." "Your teachers have my permission to whip you if you misbehave in school." "Get your education because no one can ever take that from you."

Listen to the messages about religion (unfortunately represented in the black community of our ancestors by the Western depiction of Jesus as a white man with straight hair and fair skin from a *Bible* whose maps did not clarify that many of the stories occurred on African soil): "Just give it to Jesus. He'll solve all your problems." "Soon I will be done with the troubles of this world."

Finally, despite the sweet summer breeze, listen and you, too, will hear the prophetic admonition, borne of a life based on survival, echoing turbulently from the mouth of a Mississippi-reared father warning of the whipping about to occur: "If I've told you once, I've told you a thousand times! ..."; astutely translated: "You better listen to and follow my instructions. They can save your life!"

5 | BUT NOT HULBERT

"Maybe I never had sons to carry on the Felder name because of the sins of the father."

— T. P. FELDER

The development and expansion of the slave trade in Louisiana created a distinctive social, familial, and political environment, replicated nowhere else in slave-holding states. According to Pointe Coupée (pronounced Ku pee) Parish local historian, Brian Costello, the research of Dr. Gwendolyn Midlo Hall suggests that while very few slaves came to Louisiana from the French West Indies, the social structure that evolved in Louisiana was very similar in nature to that of the slave-holding islands in the Caribbean.[385] Helping to fuel the U.S. Civil War, between 1719-1743, the French slave-trade industry brought into the port of New Orleans more than 5,900 slaves, primarily

---

385 Brian J. Costello, Creole Pointe Coupée: A Sociological Analysis (New Roads, LA: Ewing, 2002), 9.

from Senegambia, the Congo/Angola, and the Bight of Benin.[386] Pointe Coupée records delineate more than 50 African nations as the point of origin of slaves who lived in the parish.[387] Under Spanish rule, the "peculiar institution"[388] of slavery began to change throughout the South in large part because of social practices in Louisiana. The Spanish enslaved millions of men and women around the world, especially in Caribbean countries, but during their rule of the Louisiana territory (~1762-1802), they outlawed slavery and made it a practice to allow slaves to purchase their freedom and that of others through a system they devised and termed "coartación."[389] In New Orleans alone, more than 1,400 slaves used this way to freedom, such as this calas merchant, who earned her money attracting buyers as she walked the streets shouting, "Belle Calas. Tout chauds!" (Beautiful calas! Very hot!)[390]

Calas merchant

While the Spaniards settled all throughout Louisiana, including temporarily in Pointe Coupée, they did not remain in this parish. According to Mr. Costello, only one Spanish family – the Aguiars – resided in Pointe Coupée in 2013. This area of Louisiana, about an hour's drive northwest from New Orleans, was primarily a French community, settled by Frenchmen from virtually "every province of mainland France, plus Switzerland, Quebec, Montreal, the Illinois country, New Orleans, Natchitoches, Mobile and the German Coast between Baton Rouge and New Orleans."[391] They were the LeJeunes, Lemoines, Gremillions, Guehos, Robillards, Richard de Rieutords, Tounoirs, Beauvaises, Bosseron dit Majors, and they were even of the noble houses of Du Lignon de La Mirande, De Gerlais de St. Amand, and Tetard de Folleville families,[392] but not **Hulberts**. They were not Acadian exiles (banished by the British from the Canadian uplands now known as Nova Scotia).[393] The name **Hulbert** is a French surname, but it is also an Acadian surname, a Creole surname, and a surname of refugee families from St. Dominique.[394] So an interesting question becomes, what is the origin of our **HULBERT** relatives?

Purportedly, the first **Hurlbut** who emigrated to America landed in Boston in 1635 and was a soldier serving with Lion Gardiner, an Englishman, assigned to command Fort Saybrook in Connecticut.

---

386 Costello, Creole Pointe Coupée, 9.

387 Costello, Creole Pointe Coupée, 10.

388 "Peculiar institution": a euphemism for the institution of slavery and the benefits the South derived from this unjustifiable economic strategy to gain wealth. It is also the title of an excellent book on the subject of slavery by Kenneth M. Stampp. Coined by John C. Calhoun, the term and its outcome morphed significantly from his intended meaning. "Peculiar" was the least of the appropriate descriptors for the institution of slavery.

389 Maria Godoy, Meet the Calas, A New Orleans Tradition that Helped Free the Slaves, February 12, 2013, accessed March 23, 2014, http://www.npr.org/blogs/thesalt/2013/02/10/171663336/meet-the-calas-a-new-orleans-treat-that-helped-free-slaves.

390 Maria Godoy, Meet the Calas.

391 Costello, Creole Pointe Coupe, 5-6.

392 Costello, Creole Pointe Coupe, 6.

393 Costello, Creole Pointe Coupe, 7.

394 Ensemble Encore, Together Again, The Acadian Memorial Archive, "Tracing Your Family Roots," accessed April 10, 2014, www.acadianmemorial.org/ensemble_encore2/cajunroots.htm.

Sailing from London on the *Bachilor* with a total of only 13 passengers, **Thomas Hurlbut** survived that trip, which began on August 11th but did not end until November 28th. Ancestry.com's Immigration Collection indicates that of the first 53 **Hulbert** families in the country, 31 families came from England, six from Bohemia, six from Germany, five from Ireland, three from Prussia and two from France. Henry Higgins Hurlbut, author of *The Hurlbut Genealogy*, somehow believed **Thomas Hurlbut** to be from Scotland. Why is unclear, as he had no proof whatsoever. Ancestry.com's analysis associates 23% of my DNA with Great Britain, 8% with Ireland, Scotland and Wales, and 0% with France.

Ninety-nine percent of all **Hulberts** (and others with variations on the spelling of this surname) lived in the northeast in the early history of this country. In 1790, 62% of Hulberts lived in Connecticut, 19% in Massachusetts, 10% in Pennsylvania, 8% in Vermont, and 1% in New York. By 1840, however, 57% lived in New York, and an additional 15% lived in Ohio. They remain in the northeast region of the country even today. But, in October 1773, **William Hurlbut** likely became the first **Hurlburt** (Hulburt/Hulburd/Hurlburt/Hubbard/Hulbert) to move south, arriving not in Louisiana, but in Mississippi as a part of the travelers who came to the Natchez region of the state anticipating grants of land from the British government. He and Elijah Leonard were from Springfield, Connecticut, and brought with them several slaves. A 20,000-acre landgrant was provided to Thaddeus Lyman, whose father, General Phineas Lyman, originally secured promise of Mississippi land from the British government for himself and his family and for the other men and women of the Lyman Colony. Significant parcels of Mississippi land were settled by these travelers. Some individuals received up to 1400 acres – Lyman received 1050 acres on Bayou Pierre, but not **Hurlburt/Hulburd/Hubbard**. On November 10, 1779, **William Hulburd** received his landgrant of only 100 acres on Bayou Pierre.[395]

The Cut

Designated Pointe Coupée (literal translation, "the Cut Point"), the name of this parish takes on unintentional multiple meanings even to the casual outside observer. The actual intended meaning deals with the creation of the beautiful la Fausse Riviere ("False River"), which surrounds the land that was cut away from the mainland by an "oxbow" lake created when the Mississippi River rerouted itself in the 1600's.[396] Along the lake, and in the southern part of Pointe Coupée, sprawling antebellum plantations dominated the sugar cane and cotton market in the early- to mid-1800s. Thousands of slaves worked on plantations such as those glorified in Southern writers' literature of the Old South like Evergreen in St. Francisville, and thus, the "Cut Point" unintentionally illustrates something additional – a dividing line between the life of the slave "owned" by the small farmers spread throughout most of Louisiana – even in this parish – and the life of the slave "owned" by the insidiously wealthy planter. (Evergreen is the only remaining operative plantation in the United States, still producing its staple crop of old – sugar cane.)

---

395 Katy Headley, compiler, Claiborne County, Mississippi: The Promised Land (Port Gibson: Claiborne County Historical Society, 1976, 17). See also Encyclopedia of Mississippi History: Comprising Sketches of Counties, Towns, Events, Institutions and Persons (Memphis: General Books, 2012), 150.

396 Costello, Creole Pointe Coupée, 2.

Evergreen Plantation

The "Cut Point" projects yet another unintended meaning, and in the 1800s, Pointe Coupée more than adequately reflected this sociological phenomenon. It was a place cut off from the brutal realities of the laws and customs of the Deep South. Unique to the slave industry in Louisiana, and especially prevalent in Pointe Coupée, was the perpetuation and acceptance of miscegenation. The outgrowth of this practice created a large class of free blacks – and a caste system that supported it. White Europeans from France and Spain fought with and manipulated each other for control of lands outside their continental borders throughout the 16th, 17th and 18th centuries. During the time of their initial expansion into the Florida territories – including first, the "Louisiana Territory," and finally the state of Louisiana itself, particularly in the southwest Louisiana parishes (Orleans, Pointe Coupée, etc.) –Europeans freely intermingled with slave women as they left their white women behind in their countries of origin when they embarked on these discovery voyages. Despite the introduction by the French of the Code Noir (Black Codes) in Louisiana in 1724, the 1796 ban on the importation of slaves[397] by the Spanish Louisiana governor, Baron de Carondelet, and the passage of Article 95 of the 1825 Civil Code of Louisiana making interracial marriages illegal, the practice continued.

This practice spurred a huge growth of a class of free blacks, the byproduct of which was a distinctive Louisiana cultural change – the emergence of a caste and color classification system – responsible for creating a psychological and sociological divide among black Americans based on complexion that remains to this day, not only in Louisiana but in other states where this indoctrination and attitude evolved during slavery. It was presumed and projected that the lighter the skin (meaning the greater the amount of "white blood"), the better and worthier the individual. In the "Creole" culture in New Orleans, for example, marriage between a light skinned black and a darker complex-

---

[397] Costello, Creole Pointe Coupée, 9.

ioned black was discouraged.[398] Eight stratified color distinctions were created by these unions.[399] That this social stratification system was operative in St. Coupée Parish is well-documented. Brian Costello writes of this culture:

> Occupying a unique place in the fabric of Creole Pointe Coupée were the Creoles de Couleur, or "colored Creoles," free descendants of French men and Franco-American women. Through the years, a myriad of designations have [sic] been applied to this elite group including gens de couleur libre (free people of color), free mulattos and free Negroes. The last two connotations are hardly descriptive of the subject population, however, as most of the colored Creoles had only one-fourth (quadroon) or one-eighth (octoroon) Negro "blood." Many of the mulattos (persons of one-half Negro ancestry) and most of the grifees (persons of three-fourths Negro ancestry), were slaves in antebellum Pointe Coupée.[400]

Slaves in Pointe Coupée who were unable to gain their freedom through coartacion were understandably displeased. An example of the dissension between slaves partly due to this practice, is the massive insurrection planned in April of 1795, involving slaves from numerous plantations. It was to include murder of plantation owners as well as Creole slaves who would not participate. This plot was foiled by Tunica informants. A trial was held on May 4th in which fifty-seven slaves and three whites were tried. Twenty-three of those involved were executed, decapitated, and their heads were posted along the Mississippi River.[401] Others involved were deported to Havana, Cuba, and sentenced to forced hard labor for a period of six years.

There were slaves in Pointe Coupée, however, whose French "owners" (that is, their fathers or lovers) emancipated them and their offspring. It was this common French practice to free the black women they had sexual relations with that contributed to the emergence of the large class of *Creoles de Couleur* (Creoles of Color) in Pointe Coupée and other French-established parishes in lower Louisiana. The 1860 Pointe Coupée and U.S. slave censuses revealed Pointe Coupée to be a predominantly black community comprised of 73% slaves and 4% free blacks. The population was comprised of a total of 77% "colored" people, including slave and free. Among the total population of 17,718 in the parish, 12,903 were slaves, and 721 were "free colored," clearly establishing division among the black population.

Although the practice was later discontinued, in the 1800s, a Creole of Color was referenced in such a way as to communicate if he/she was an offspring of a Frenchman. For example, Joseph Jonjon would have been known as "Joseph *dit* Jonjon"; Mary would have been Mary *dite* Jonjon. Surnames of Creoles of Color living in Pointe Coupée, and later their descendants, include Porche, DeCuir, Poydras, Honore-Destrehan, LeDuff, St. Amants, Britto, Bouligny, Colombo, Harlaut, Macias, and

---

398 Mary Genman, The Free People of New Orleans – An Introduction (New Orleans: Louis. Margaret Media, 1994), 106.

399 S-260-264, Negro Studies Project Contemporary Culture, "Negroes," once housed at Hampton Institute, identified the following classifications: Sactra (griffe and Negro); Griffe (Negro and mulatto); Marabou (mulatto and griffe); Mulatto (white and Negro); OQurteron (Quadroon – white and mulatto); Metif (white and Indian); Meameleon (white and metif); San-mele (Octaroon – white and Quarteron); and Os Rouge (Red Bone).

400 Costello, Creole Pointe Coupée, 28.

401 Lo Faber, "Slave Insurrections in Louisiana," 64 Parishes, https://64parishes.org/entry/slave-insurrections-in-louisiana.

Bonnefoi, among others, but not **Hulbert**. The story of our **HULBERT** family, thus, becomes indeed quite an interesting one, full of mystery and intrigue.

Cut Throat?

ALEXANDER HULBERT, son of "**B. M. HULBERT** and **CAROLINE WILKENS**,"[402] was born, according to several sources amalgamated, around November 25, 1881[403] in Batchelor[404] or Innis,[405] Louisiana, 20 or so years after the Civil War. **B. M. HULBERT** and **CAROLINE WILKENS** are never listed together in any federal or state census for Louisiana. **B. M.** is not enumerated in the censuses living anywhere in Louisiana at any time for that matter. However, one does find in the 1860 census a child by the name of **BRYON M. HULBURT**, born October 1847. He is the 14-year-old, second oldest child in a very wealthy family, later characterized as part of the "old elite"[406] of Port Gibson (Claiborne County), Mississippi. On the eve of the Civil War, **BYRON's** father, 41 (or 46) year old **M N HULBERT**,[407] owned more than 1700 acres of property and 77 slaves in Police District 4 (Port Gibson, Claiborne County) and 31 other slaves in Police District 2 (in Grand Gulf, Claiborne County were "owned" by **M N HURLBURT**), making him one of the largest slave holders in the state.[408] In 1860, Port Gibson, the county seat for Claiborne County, Mississippi, mirrored the South inside out. It was a black city – demographically – with a total of 12,296 slaves and 44 free blacks; and a white city – politically – powered by a total population of only 3339 whites, and that census number included women and children.

Batchelor and Innis businesses

Both Innis and Batchelor, Louisiana, were *extremely* rural communities, less than three miles apart in Pointe Coupée Parish, and remain unincorporated communities today. According to Brian Costello, it was not until the railroad came through this most northern area of Pointe Coupée in 1899, approximately 18 years after **ALEXANDER's** birth, that these areas developed into small communities with a post office and a couple of businesses. Present day Batchelor only has a convenience store and a grain elevator for the farmers. Innis, named for James Innis, the Irishman who immigrated to Louisiana to escape the potato famine in his country, has a small medical clinic, tiny post office and a branch of the Pointe Coupée library. Prior to the railroad, there simply was

---

402 Negro Yearbook and Directory of Memphis and Shelby County (Memphis: Memphis Negro Chamber of Commerce, 1943), 128.

403 AncestryLibrary.com – U.S., World War I Draft Registration Cards, 1917-1918 indicates his birth as November 25, 1881. The 1910 U.S. Census indicates his birth to be "around 1883." The 1880 U.S. Census indicates a C. Wilkins had a one-year old son in Pointe Coupée.

404 Negro Chamber, Negro Yearbook, 128.

405 Ancestry.com., Tennessee Death and Burial Index, 1874-1955.

406 Michael Wayne, The Reshaping of Plantation Society: The Natchez District, 1860-80 (Urbana: University of Illinois Press, 1990), 93.

407 The 1860 U.S. Federal Census spells M. N.'s last name as Hurlburt, with a "u," but the 1860 Slave Census spells M. N.'s last name with an "e" – Hulbert. His name and year of birth change across numerous records and, therefore, his age may not seem consistent in this narrative. He was reportedly born between 1814 and 1819. Throughout this narrative, I use the age, date of birth and name spelling in the document being referenced at the time.

408 1860 U.S. Slave Census.

nothing in either of these locations except a couple of plantations owned by the Innis and Batchelor families, which produced cotton and soybeans. These two families, plus the Steward family, owned most of the upper part of Pointe Coupée. There was virtually nothing to do in this section of the parish except work on these plantations.

West Feliciana Parish, Louisiana, contiguous to Pointe Coupée, was no different, with a total population of 11,671; 82% (9571) of whom were slaves, and an additional 64 were free people of color.[409] **CAROLINE HULBERT**, age 25 (date of birth ~1855), is listed in the 1880 U.S. Census as residing in the 3rd Ward, West Felicia Parish, Louisiana, with her husband, **ALBERT HULBERT**, age 27, and three children – **PETER**, age 11; **HENRY**, age six; and **ALBERT**, age two (born about 1878). All are enumerated as black.

Unfortunately, the 1890 U.S. Census was destroyed in a fire that occurred at the Library of Congress, and although a few counties in a few states have some censuses or partial censuses from 1890, no official census records exist for 1890 for the entire United States, therefore, it is not possible to systematically move across the decades 1880-1890 researching individuals. Skipping to the 1900 U.S. Census, however, **CAROLINE WILKINS**, age 48 (born March 1852) is listed as living in Police Jury Ward 3, Pointe Coupée, Louisiana, as a widowed, head-of-household mother of eight children, six of whom are still living. She can read and write and is a farmer. Of her children, living with her are **ALBERT ALEX**, age 20 (born May 1880); daughter, **ELISKA**, age 18; and **FREDERICK**, age 10. All are enumerated as black.

CAROLINE HULBERT of the 1880 U.S. Census (living in West Feliciana) and **CAROLINE WILKINS** of the 1900 U.S. Census (living in Pointe Coupée) are surely the same individual and is **ALEXANDER HULBERT's** mother. I believe that 20-year-old **ALBERT ALEX WILKINS** of the 1900 U.S. Census (living in Pointe Coupée) and two-year-old **ALBERT HULBERT** of the 1880 U.S. Census (living in West Feliciana) are the same individual – our **ALEXANDER HULBERT**.

So, how did **B. M. HULBERT** become **ALEXANDER's** father if **CAROLINE WILKINS** was married to **ALBERT HULBERT** at the time that **ALBERT ALEXANDER HULBERT** was born in Louisiana? The 1870 U.S. Census, taken five years following Emancipation and seven years following the end of the war, identifies, by name, for the first time in the history of American census-taking, ex-slaves – now "freedmen" – Native Americans not living on a reservation, and women. There are no black or mulatto men or women with the surname, **Hulbert**, or any reasonably-similar spelling, listed in the 1870 U.S. Census residing in Pointe Coupée. In fact, there are only 10 individuals in the entire state of Louisiana with the surname of **Hulbert** in 1870, and all of them are enumerated as black. These 10 individuals live either in Ward 4 of West Feliciana or Ward 8 of Franklin, Louisiana. One family in 1870 lives in Ward 8 of Claiborne County (LA) and is mixed race (that is, the husband is listed as black and the wife and children are listed as mulatto); however, their name is Hulbard. They are a young family; the wife being 23 years old and the husband 21; clearly not **ALEXANDER's** parents. There are no other **Hulberts** or any individuals with surnames of any reasonable resemblance of *any race or ethnicity* in the state of Louisiana at all in any census from 1860 back to 1790 when the first U. S. Census was taken.

---

409 Demographics of Louisiana parishes in Wikipedia.org/wiki/Demographics_of_Louisiana, accessed January 3, 2014.

B. M. HULBERT is not listed in the 1870 census. In the 1880 Census, however, there is a D. M. Halbart enumerated in Pointe Coupée Parish and there is also a female, C. Wilkin, enumerated on the same page (which means their homes are close by each other and possibly on the same street or rural route). She is living with five children, ages 10, 7, 6, 4 and 1, and is listed as "married" and "Chinese"! D. M. Halbart is listed as a 35-year-old, single "planter" born in Mississippi, but his mother and father are indicated as also having been born in Mississippi, which is consistent for the birthplace of **B. M.'s** mother but inconsistent with the purported N.Y. birthplace for his father. It is also interesting that this D. M. Halbart is enumerated as "mulatto" in this census. This is the only census, or any other document, that enumerates a D. M. Halbert. I believe the "D" to be an error and the last name misspelled as there is never a D. M. Halbert or anything close to this spelling ever listed again in the U.S. Census. As is evident already, **HULBERT** is often misspelled and/or spelled in numerous ways, sometimes in the same document. This 1880 Census entry is likely **B. M. HULBERT**, which would be consistent with information located in the *Negro Yearbook and Directory of Memphis and Shelby County* (Tennessee) where we learn that **B. M. HULBERT**, **ALEXANDER's** father, was a "prominent farmer," a phrase that could suggest sufficient landholdings to be considered reasonably affluent, or it could denote that he was the manager of someone else's farm/plantation – as stories do get embellished over time. However, the census denotation of D. M. Halbert's employment as a "planter" suggests that he owns significant acreage. The *Negro Yearbook* indicated as well that **B. M. HULBERT** spent time with P. B. S. Pinchback – Louisiana's first black governor (who was also mulatto; the son of a white Mississippi planter and black slave) – involved in local political issues of the day,[410] suggesting also that **B. M. HULBERT** lived in Louisiana. Perhaps **B. M.** may have been associated politically with the governor – either prior to or after his term in office – but documentation has not been found yet to this effect. However, even more of the **HULBERT** story is told by other extant records found.

Brian Costello, who is also a genealogist specializing in Pointe Coupée families, explains that the meaning of the term, "Creole," has evolved over the years and its use is still confusing, even in Louisiana. Although originally used to reference slaves who were born in Pointe Coupée, it did not mean initially that there was "mixed European-African ancestry." Creole came to be applied to describe "anything produced in the Louisiana colony, like creole ponies, creole lilies, creole onions, et. cetera."[411] Finally, it came to represent a dialect spoken by both slaves and colonists – a mixture of French and African dialects.[412] According to the *Negro Yearbook and Directory of Memphis and Shelby County*, **ALEXANDER HULBERT** was "of old French Creole stock."[413] Exactly what this means is uncertain from the record, and oral history is silent. **ALEXANDER** was not "Alexander *dit* Hulbert" in any documents seen to date.

In 1830 in Franklin (St. Mary Parish), Louisiana, there is a J. de Wilkins enumerated who "owned" 129 slaves. Hanier Whilkins is also enumerated in the 1830 U.S. Census in Natchitoches, Louisiana, "owning" three slaves. In 1840, there is a John D. Wilkins in St. Mary Parish, Louisiana, who had no

---

410 Negro Chamber, Negro Yearbook, 128.

411 Costello, Creole Pointe Coupée, 10.

412 Costello, Creole Pointe Coupée, 10.

413 Negro Chamber, Negro Yearbook, 128.

slaves at all and J. de Wilkins does not appear again in any subsequent censuses after 1830. These are French surnames; thus, it is possible that the "old French Creole stock" claimed by **ALEXANDER HULBERT** may be through his mother's family line: **WILKINS**, but not **HULBERT**. The only thing that is clear about **ALEXANDER** is that he was of mixed ancestry. I have yet to be able to document how it could be "French Creole," nor have I found any documentation that describes **B. M. HULBERT** as mulatto.

Broken Branches: Hulberts in the Civil War

On April 16, 1862, the Confederacy initiated a draft by passing the Conscription Act requiring all men between the ages of 18 and 35 to serve a three-year term of service in the army. Within 10 months of passage, the law was amended twice to increase the age of eligibility because of the severe shortage of Confederate soldiers. Ultimately, men as old as 50 and as young as 17 were ordered into service to the Confederacy. Although at its initial passage, the law provided an exemption from the draft for all men who "owned" 20 or more slaves,[414] in May 1862, two weeks after passage, **MARTIN NATHANIEL HULBERT** added his name alongside the other 122,000 Mississippians who ultimately joined the Confederate army in the life or death fight over their perceived right to own slaves. Only 663 Mississippians with *any* surname fought in the Union Army.[415] **MARTIN** enlisted as a private in Company A, 2nd Battalion State Troops Infantry Regiment of the Mississippi Infantry. This unit was not "mustered into service"; that is, they never saw action, and enlistment time required was only six months.[416] **MARTIN** did lend support in other ways, however, providing supplies and one or more of his horses to the soldiers.

MARTIN's sons, seventeen-year-old **JULIAN**[417] **M. HULBERT** and his younger brother, fifteen-year-old **BYRON (B. M.) HULBERT**, both enlisted as privates. Before the draft, **JULIAN** enlisted in the Thirty-sixth Infantry in Mississippi (in L. B. Harris' company) and was mustered into service perhaps as early as March 11, 1862. **B. M.** enlisted on April 23, 1864, in Dubecq's Company (Cavalry) and Captain Greenleaf's Company (Orleans Light Horse) Cavalry, not in Mississippi, but in Louisiana. He was mustered into service, although little information exists about the service of his unit. That **B. M.** enlisted in Louisiana documents that he had moved from Mississippi to Louisiana by the age of 15 or 16. When he enlisted, he recorded his place of residence as New Orleans, and as did many young men who wanted to fight, he fabricated his date of birth and age; some records indicating he was 15 at enlistment; others say 17.

Shortly after the enlistment of **MARTIN** and his oldest son, **JULIAN**, the war came close enough to them that there was no way they could not see the sky light up by the explosions of the cannons, could not hear the cries of the wounded, or smell the stench of the dead. General Ulysses S. Grant's capture of Vicksburg was unanticipated. It occurred by his sneaking essentially unnoticed from

---

414 American Battlefield Trust, "Civil War Facts," accessed January 23, 2014, www.civilwar.org/education/history/faq/.

415 Regimental Roster Completion Project, "American Civil War Research Database," accessed January 23, 2014, www.civilwardata.com/dbstatus.html.

416 2nd Battalion, Mississippi Infantry, State Troops, accessed January 23, 2014, https://familysearch.org/learn/wiki/en/2nd_Battalion,_Mississippi_Infantry_(State_Troops).

417 The Confederate Soldiers Service Record correctly spells Julian's name with an "a."

behind the city through the outskirts of Port Gibson, bombarding Grand Gulf on April 29, 1863, and leaving a contingency of about 1,000 soldiers there. When this occurred, the slaves in Grand Gulf started preparing for freedom, much to the chagrin of the plantation owners. The Union army then proceeded on towards Port Gibson, crossing the Mississippi at Bruinsburg on April 30th.

Only eight miles west of **MARTIN's** plantation, the day-long battle at Port Gibson preceded, and paved a clear path to, the capture of Vicksburg, which was only 30 miles away. Shortly after midnight on May 1, 1863, three hours of gunfire and fighting occurred mainly at the property line of A. K. Shaifer, who was a former Board of Police commissioner nominee along with **MARTIN**. Led by Union Brigadier General George F. McGinnis, the federal brigade was comprised of infantries from Indiana (11th, 24th, 34th and 46th), Wisconsin (29th), and the Ohio Light Artillery (2nd and 16th). These 2,839 Union soldiers ultimately were victorious, taking 200 prisoners and much needed ammunition,[418] but casualties on both sides were significant: 131 Union and 68 Confederates killed; 719 Union and 380 Confederates wounded; and 25 Union and 384 Confederates missing.[419]

On May 27th, **MARTIN** and his son, **BYRON**, along with 24 others of their Grand Gulf and Port Gibson neighbors, sent a desperate plea to General Joseph Johnston, one of Jefferson Davis' top commanders, asking that he send "immediate aid" to *[their]* families *[who were]* "in great peril," given that the "rebellious negroes" were no longer adhering to the "authority of *[their]* overseers and masters." Not only that, but the "negroes," about a thousand of them, were "drilling" to become soldiers and the citizens of Port Gibson were in "such terror" that they would not even resist the "lawless negroes."[420] On these family's plantations, they enslaved nearly 1,000 people. While they awaited a reply, which likely did not come, Union General McGinnis and his soldiers continued on towards Vicksburg.

Grant's forces overtook Vicksburg in what was considered a relatively uncontested fight where more than 31,000 (or perhaps 33,000) men engaged in battle, surrounding the city on all three land sides. Amazingly, only 200 died.[421] Following this successful siege, Grant then moved into Grand Gulf, the location of the first **Hulbert's** landgrant, and 31 of **MARTIN's** slaves. Grant's initial objective was to use Grand Gulf as a base of operation to receive supplies but decided against doing so even though the Confederates had evacuated Grand Gulf after losing the Battle of Port Gibson. Against a Confederate army of 60,000 troops,[422] or maybe only 30,000,[423] on July 4, 1863, Grant marched 70,000 or so men into Vicksburg from several directions, surrounding Confederate General John Pemberton, forcing him to surrender his troops. *[Attempting to provide definitive or nearly correct information is mostly impossible. Search 12 trusted sites or books, get 12 answers as to number of soldiers engaged in battle! Geezz! Who is correct?]*

Described in military documentation as 5'10", fair complexion, light hair, and blue eyes, **JULIAN's**

---

418 General George F. McGinnis' Brigade at the Battle of Port Gibson, by Mark, April 30, 2016, accessed December 1, 2018.

419 Civilwarwiki.net, Battle of Port Gibson, accessed December 1, 2018.

420 Fold3, Ancestry.com, Confederate Papers Relating to Citizens and Business Firms, 1861-1865, M346, NARA, Record Group 109, Roll 0021, Richard T. Archer.

421 http://www.nps.gov/vick/learn/historyculture/battleportgibson.htm (accessed March 29, 2015).

422 John S. Bowman, ed., The Civil War: The Definitive Reference Including a Chronology of Events, and Encyclopedia, and the Memoirs of Grant and Lee, Chapter III, Vicksburg (North Dighton, MA: JG Press, 2006), 476-505.

423 Civil War Biography, "Ulysses S. Grant," civilwar.org/education/history/biographies/Ulysses-s-grant.html (accessed January 23, 2014).

> VICKSBURG, MISSISSIPPI, JULY 7 1863.
>
> To All whom it may Concern, Know Ye That:
>
> I, J. M. Hulburt, a Private of Co. G, Reg't 36 Miss. Vols., C. S. A., being a prisoner of War, in the hands of the United States Forces, in virtue of the capitulation of the City of Vicksburg and its Garrison, by Lieut. Gen. John C. Pemberton, C. S. A., Commanding, on the 4th day of July, 1863, do in pursuance of the terms of said capitulation, give this my solemn parole under oath—
>
> That I will not take up arms again against the United States, nor serve in any military police or constabulary force in any Fort, garrison or field work, held by the Confederate States of America, against the United States of America, nor as guard of prisons, depots or stores, nor discharge any duties usually performed by Officers or soldiers, against the United States of America, until duly exchanged by the proper authorities.
>
> J. M. Hulburt
>
> Sworn to and subscribed before me at Vicksburg, Miss., this 7 day of July, 1863.
>
> Jno. Dunn Capt. 4th Reg't ___ Vols, AND PAROLLING OFFICER.

Julian's parole oath

name is recorded as **HULBERT** and **HULBURT** in the same document. He served in the war as a musician, playing in the regiment band, perhaps a fife and drum corps, intended to impact morale of the troops. As a prisoner of war, captured with his regiment at Vicksburg on July 4th, 1863, his July 7, 1863 parole demanded that he swear to not serve in any capacity in the C.S.A. (Confederate States of America) against the United States "until duly exchanged."[424] It is unclear exactly when this exchange occurred, but it is clear that from August 23 to October 31, 1863, and again from November 6 to December 30, 1863, he was AWOL – absent without leave. Desertion, as this clearly was, later in the war could have meant death, but in 1863, men were typically either imprisoned or re-absorbed into their units once they returned.

Although little else is known about the military service of either of the **HULBERT** brothers, and what is recorded is sketchy and somewhat inconsistent, it is known that they both were captured and held as prisoners of war by the Union forces: **BYRON M.**, a

> Confederate.
> 36 Miss.
> J M Hulbert
> Pri, Co. G, 36 Reg't Mississippi Infantry.
> Appears on a
> **Roll of Prisoners of War**
> paroled at Vicksburg, Miss., according to the terms of capitulation entered into by the commanding Generals of the United States and Confederate forces July 4, 1863.
> Roll dated Not dated.
> Paroled Not stated.
> Where captured Vicksburg Miss
> When captured July 4, 1863
> Remarks:

Julian's prison roll card

---

424 Ancestry.com, Fold3.com – Military Records, Civil War, Julian M. Hulbert, 21.

prisoner in "Private Stewart's Escort," was paroled in May 1865 in Jackson, Mississippi. One record indicates **JULIAN's** parole date was November 6, 1863; another indicated that **JULIAN** was released on January 9, 1865 and a third indicates he was held for 30 days in Citronelle, Alabama, and was paroled on May 4, 1865. Obviously, **JULIAN** was captured, or surrendered, more than once. What an irony to be later made apparent: a freed slave named I. T. Montgomery from Davis Bend, upriver, observed the battle at Grand Gulf, watched General Grant march through Port Gibson and surround Vicksburg in a surprise maneuver. He was present on the day that **JULIAN's** freedom was surrendered. July 4, 1863.

Only twenty-seven (27)[425] other **Hulberts**, aside from **MARTIN** and his sons, fought with the Confederacy. They were from Texas, Missouri, Mississippi, South Carolina, Georgia, Florida, Tennessee, Arkansas, and Louisiana. However, 243[426] **Hulberts** nationwide fought with the Union Army. They were from New York, Illinois, Ohio, Michigan, Pennsylvania, Wisconsin, Missouri, Connecticut, Iowa, New Jersey, Mississippi, Indiana, Kentucky, Kansas, Vermont, Maine, and the District of Columbia (Washington, D.C.). In June of 1863, four **HULBERT's** joined the Union army from their home state of Indiana. **HIRAM**, **JEREMIAH**, **WARD**, and **RICHARD**. They were **MARTIN's** brothers. **BENONI HULBERT**, a Union soldier in the 182nd Regiment, Ohio Infantry, was **MARTIN's** great uncle.

According to one researcher on Ancestry.com (**KATHLEEN**), **BENONI's** son, **WARD**, a cousin to either **MARTIN** or his sons, was the individual who, after discovering on a visit to **MARTIN's** plantation that **JULIEN** and **BYRON** had both been captured by Union forces, was somehow responsible for facilitating their release, and in gratitude, **JULIAN**, it was said, then named a son after **WARD**.[427] No documentation has been found to support this assertion of assistance with prison release, although **JULIAN** did name a son **WARD**, and in the 1834 Claiborne County Tax Assessment, **BENONI HURBURT** was listed as a taxpaying county resident.

Slave "Masters" in the Closet

The above notes an interesting fact: the **Hulberts** in the country very much disagreed on the issue of slavery, clearly very few fighting with the Confederacy, and even fewer ever deciding to move south. Only a handful of **Hulberts** ever participated in the slave trade, and together they "owned" a total of 42 slaves in 1840. There were only five **Hulberts** in the country "owning" slaves at that time – the number of which is indicated in square brackets: (A.G. – KY [26]; James – GA [8]; James – FL [2]; Jno – MO [1]; and Thomas – KY [5]).[428] Twenty-one (or 26) year old **MARTIN** did not "own" slaves in 1840.

The economic circumstances of **MARTIN's** life as a child, likely in New York County, New York, and other places his family lived are not known; however, it is certain that his second marriage to **SINAI (SANDERS) RAIL** catapulted him into the "upper society" of Port Gibson and surrounding communities. In 1840, **SINAI's** first husband, John Rail, was a wealthy owner of the 1,400-plus acre

---

[425] Ancestry.com, All U.S., Confederate Soldiers Compiled Service Records, 1861-1865.

[426] Ancestry.com, All U.S., Confederate Soldiers Compiled Service Records, 1861-1865.

[427] Ancestry.com, message board, Kathleen's post, 2002.

[428] Ancestry.com, 1840 U.S. Census.

Tannehill Farm that operated by the labor of his 43, 44, or 47 slaves (records differ). Some land on the plantation had passed to John through a couple of upper crust families, including Elias Bridgers and George Tannehill and wife. John apparently dearly loved his 17-year-old wife of three years, willing land and 23 slaves to her to share with their daughters, **CHRISTINA MARILLA**, and the daughter then born but yet to be named. The balance of his slaves (and 510 acres of land) he willed to another daughter apparently from an earlier marriage, **Mary (Rail) Hume**, and any children she might have. John had previously provided his then deceased son-in-law, Ezekiel Calhoun, an equal amount of inheritance. John's provisions in his will of land for his daughter, **Mary**, was protected from her husband's "interference or control" by the appointment of a friend as trustee to manage the property on her behalf. He also, however, protected the inheritance of his other two daughters, **CHRISTINA MARILLA** and the baby unnamed at the time of the writing of his will, from what he feared could become an encroaching stepfather by requiring that the 23 unnamed slaves (minus four he identified by name[429]) be distributed to his two daughters instead of being left to his wife, **SIENA** *[sic]*, should she remarry.[430] She did remarry. Newspapers and court records shed some light on what occurred.

Will of John Rail

The eight slaves that Richard Sheffield of Claiborne County "owned" in 1830 had dwindled significantly by the time his daughter, **Martha**, became executrix of her father's estate in 1839. As a matter of fact, only one slave, a child "valued" at $300, was inventoried in his estate at his death. Three years later, on January 19, 1842, **Martha** became **MARTIN HULBERT's** wife, but in less than a year of their marriage, on Christmas Day in 1842, **Martha** died. John Rail died a few months later in 1843. No details have been discovered about either of these deaths, although somewhere in the closets of our **HULBERT** family is a purported murder. Twenty-five-year old **MARTIN NATHANIEL HULBERT** and 21-year-old **SINAI (SANDERS) RAIL** were then married on December 5, 1843.

The decade of the 1850's witnessed an increase to 59 of **Hulbert** slaves in the country, "owned" by three individuals, 44 of them, however, were "owned" by **MARTIN**, with the balance being

---

[429] Old Millie, Matilda, Jacob, and Mariah were identified as the only slaves that Sinai could have should she remarry. The remaining 19 slaves were to be distributed to his and Sinai's two children, equally divided by "value."

[430] John Rail's Will, Port Gibson, Mississippi Probate Court Record, Will Book B, pages 52 and 53, recorded April 26, 1843.

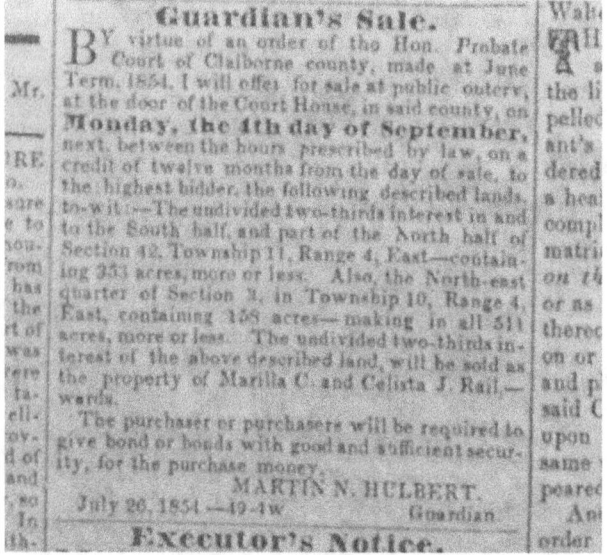
Court orders Martin to sell

"owned" by James – GA [13] and Henry – AR [4]).[431] This means that the 44 slaves that **SINAI** and her former husband, John Rail, "owned" in 1840 became the property of **SINAI** and her new husband, **MARTIN**, very much against the express wishes of John's will.

Finally, in 1854, the probate court intervened on behalf of **MARILLA** and **CELISTA**. After much maneuvering, **MARTIN** was forced by the courts to sell some of the property belonging to **MARILLA** and **CELISTA**. But, what happened to the slaves? On the eve of the war, according to the 1860 U.S. Slave Census, still only three **Hulberts** in the country "owned" slaves: Henry – AR [4]; James – GA [2]; and **MARTIN** – MS [108]. Did **MARTIN** and **SINAI** wrangle the slaves from the inheritance of John's two daughters? Did they purchased more? They had slaves in two different police districts, as shown on the following pages.

---

431 U.S. Slave Schedules 1850, Ancestry.com.

THE 77 SLAVES OF "M N HULBERT"
(1860 U.S. SLAVE CENSUS)
Police District 4, Claiborne County, 1860

NUMBER OF SLAVES	AGE	GENDER	RACE	NUMBER OF SLAVES	AGE	GENDER	RACE	NUMBER OF SLAVES	AGE	GENDER	RACE
1	61	MALE	BLACK	1	19	MALE	BLACK	2	6	MALE	BLACK
2	60	MALE	BLACK	2	18	MALE	BLACK	2	6	FEMALE	BLACK
2	50	MALE	BLACK	1	17	FEMALE	BLACK	2	5	MALE	BLACK
1	46	FEMALE	BLACK	1	17	MALE	BLACK	1	4	FEMALE	BLACK
1	45	MALE	BLACK	2	16	FEMALE	BLACK	1	4	MALE	MULATTO
2	40	MALE	BLACK	1	16	MALE	MULATTO	1	4	MALE	BLACK
2	35	MALE	BLACK	1	15	MALE	BLACK	2	3	FEMALE	BLACK
1	35	FEMALE	BLACK	2	14	FEMALE	BLACK	1	3	MALE	BLACK
1	30	MALE	BLACK	1	14	MALE	BLACK	3	2	FEMALE	BLACK
3	30	FEMALE	BLACK	1	12	MALE	BLACK	1	2	MALE	BLACK
1	28	MALE	MULATTO	2	11	MALE	BLACK	3	1	FEMALE	BLACK
2	28	FEMALE	BLACK	1	10	MALE	BLACK	1	1	MALE	BLACK
1	28	MALE	BLACK	1	10	FEMALE	BLACK				
1	24	MALE	BLACK	2	9	FEMALE	BLACK				
1	24	FEMALE	BLACK	2	9	MALE	BLACK				
1	23	FEMALE	MULATTO	2	8	FEMALE	BLACK				
1	22	MALE	BLACK	1	8	MALE	BLACK				
2	21	MALE	BLACK	1	7	FEMALE	BLACK				
3	20	FEMALE	BLACK	2	7	MALE	BLACK				
1	20	MALE	BLACK								

THE 31 SLAVES OF MARTIN NATHANIEL HULBERT ("M N HURLBURT")
(1860 U.S. SLAVE CENSUS)
Police District 2, Grand Gulf, Claiborne County, 1860

NUMBER OF SLAVES	AGE	GENDER	RACE	NUMBER OF SLAVES	AGE	GENDER	RACE
1	1	FEMALE	BLACK	1	10	FEMALE	BLACK
1	40	MALE	BLACK	1	9	FEMALE	BLACK
1	32	FEMALE	BLACK	1	8	FEMALE	BLACK
1	30	MALE	BLACK	2	8	MALE	BLACK
1	25	FEMALE	BLACK	1	7	FEMALE	BLACK
1	22	MALE	BLACK	1	6	MALE	MULATTO
1	22	FEMALE	BLACK	1	6	FEMALE	BLACK
1	20	FEMALE	BLACK	2	5	MALE	BLACK
1	18	MALE	BLACK	1	4	MALE	BLACK
2	16	MALE	BLACK	1	3	FEMALE	BLACK
1	15	FEMALE	MULATTO	1	2	MALE	BLACK
1	14	MALE	BLACK	1	1	MALE	BLACK
1	14	FEMALE	BLACK				
1	12	MALE	BLACK				
1	11	FEMALE	BLACK				
1	11	MALE	MULATTO				

    The 1860 U.S. Slave Census also lists M. N. Hurlburt in Police District 2 (Claiborne County at Grand Gulf) as "owning" 31 slaves. Different name; same guy.
    B. M. HULBERT is listed in the U.S. Census only three times. He is first enumerated in the U.S. 1850 Census as three-year old **BYRON** (born August 9, 1848) living in Port Gibson with his father, **MARTIN N. HULBERT**; his 25-year-old mother, **SINAI HULBERT**; his older brother, **JULIEN** (age 5); his younger brother, **HERMAN** (age 2); and an infant not identified by name but is likely **CLIFTON** (age 1). Also living with this family are **MARILA RAIL** (age 9) and **CALISTA RAIL** (age 7), **SINAI's** two children by her first husband, John Rail. **B. M.** is again listed in the 1860 U.S. Census as **BYRON HULBURT**, a 14-year-old living with his family, which now includes a brother, **CLIFTON** (age 11); brother, **ADRIAN** (age 8); sister, **IRENE** (age 6); brother, **CLARENCE** (age 4); and half-sisters, **CALISTA** (age 17) and **MARILA** (age 19). The third time **B. M** is listed in the census is in 1900 where he is identified as **B. M. HULBERT**, a 52-year-old white male head of household born October 1847, who has been married for one year since 1899. The Census but does not identify his spouse's name nor any other member of the household. However, the publication, *Claiborne County [Mississippi] Marriages*, indexes a **BYRON M. HULHURT** who married Maria Hulhurt on May 24, 1888. *[Initially I was wondering if this could have been Marila, his half-sister. I later*

discovered that she was, in fact, the widow of his brother, Adrian, who had died in 1867.] No children are ever enumerated or associated with **B. M.**

There are thousands of frustrated African Americans who cannot identify their ancestors for obvious reasons but there are also frustrated Caucasians who cannot identify theirs either. To date, few **Hulberts** conducting their family history research have found out much more about **MARTIN NATHANIEL HULBERT's** identity other than essentially what is listed in the census records – that he was either born in, or was from, somewhere in New York (perhaps Chatham or New York County). Frustrated with researching his background, one family's historian, **KATHLEEN**, posted this on the Ancestry.com Message Board in October 2004[432] about **MARTIN N. HULBERT**:

> I am looking for Martin Nathaniel's father and mother. Clarence's sisters *[sic]* daughter searched long for Martin Nathaniel. To my knowledge she never found his identity. Like I she felt it would be closely related to Caleb or Benoni. …I have another email that I sent Ona that explains more. If you want a copy, I will post it to this message board to you. Hopefully others will see it and help me find the illusive Martin Nathaniel Hurlburt, Hurlbert, Hulbert's father… *[sic]*

This same researcher indicated that **BENONI HULBERT** and his brother, **CALEB**, were very close. They apparently spent a lot of time together, as **KATHLEEN** often found them together in the various records she discovered. **KATHLEEN** noted that these brothers traveled together to New York to visit **WILLIAM**. In another post two years after the above, she indicated that **MARTIN's** father's name was **CALEB**. All three of these individuals were born, per the census records, in different states: **CALEB** (Pennsylvania); **BENONI** (Ohio), and **MARTIN** (New York). At one point, **CALEB** lived in Connecticut, then later in Vermont. Very interesting to our verified **HULBERT** story, however, is that **CALEB's** middle name was **ALEXANDER**. Be reminded of our known relatives: **ALEXANDER HULBERT** and his son, **JAMES ALEXANDER HULBERT**. Another **Hulbert** family researcher indicated, without sharing source information, that **MARTIN's** father was **John C. Hurlburt** and his mother was Phebe Smith.

A part of the difficulty in identifying relatives among the white **Hulberts** (**Hurlburts**, etc.) is that over time, the spelling of the name changed because a relative decided simply to change the spelling. Once he or she did so, other family members did likewise. Then, years later, a family member would decide to change back to an original spelling and, likewise, his/her relatives did the same. The spelling has fluctuated for all of those presently included in **KATHLEEN's** description. Surprisingly, **KATHLEEN**, who died in 2015, spelled her name **HURLBURT**, but her grandfather, **CLARENCE**, (**MARTIN's** son) left Port Gibson spelling his name **HULBERT**. With so little being written about the **Hulberts** in Mississippi, doubt about the accuracy of my analysis of our relationship to them was constant throughout this research. However, Ancestry.com's DNA analysis recently provided proof for *OURstory*. **SINAI HULBERT** is our great-great-grandmother.

Finally, on July 22, 2020, as I was preparing to return the **HULBERT** family tree to the printer for minor corrections, a news article came to light for the first time that provided the information needed by so many family researchers trying to identify **MARTIN's** background, his siblings, and

---

432 Kathleen Casper, Ancestry.com Message Board, posted October 20, 2004.

Sheriff's Sale.

BY virtue of an order of the Jefferson Circuit Court in chancery, in a case wherein Richard S. Canby and Samuel G. Jeffries are complainants and Harris M. Hulbert, Martin N. Hulbert, Celiste Hulbert, Hiram Hulbert, Jeremiah Hulbert Ward Hulbert and Amanda Hulbert, heirs of Caleb Hulbert dec'd. are defendants, I shall expose to public sale, on Monday the 11th day of Nov. next between the hours prescribed by law, on the premises, Lot Number seventy-seven in the addition to the town of Madison on the West, to satisfy said order of sale.

W. G. WHATON, Sheriff.
Oct. 7, 1833.

Sheriff's sale

his ancestors. As of this publication, family researchers can rest assured that **MARTIN's** father was indeed **CALEB** and his mother was **PERMELIA HULBERT**. **CALEB's** estate was insolvent.

THE MAKING OF A PLANTATION

It is ironic that this incredible 32-room, four-level, "fireproof"[433] structure, the Windsor House, the largest antebellum plantation house ever built in Mississippi (a bit over 3500 square feet), burned to the ground by a guest's carelessness with his cigar! The irony is that during Grant's march through Port Gibson, the soldiers wanted to burn the house down, however, a special guard was placed at the property to keep it standing![434] Nothing remains today but the columns. The house, completed in 1861 by 34-year-old Smith Daniell, situated on a 2,600-plus acre property right outside of Port Gibson, represented just a small part of his landholdings. Across the state line, and in other locations in Mississippi, he owned more than 31,000 additional acres of land. Smith Daniell probably did not go into each room more than a couple of times because he died a few weeks after he moved in![435] *[What a waste of his $175,000 ($4.7 million in 2012 dollars)!]* It was this home, along with other

Illustrated by unknown Civil War soldier

Windsor House ruins

---

433 Headley, Claiborne County, 196.

434 Sketched during the Civil War by Henry Otis Wright (20th Ohio Infantry). Location – Claiborne County on the outskirts of Port Gibson, http://mdah.state.ms.us/timeline/zone/1890/.https://www.google.com/?gws_rd=ssl#q=windsor+plantation+mississippi; http://www.nps.gov/vick/forteachers/upload/Windsor-2.pdf. http://www.nps.gov/vick/forteachers/upload/Windsor-2.pdf.

435 Headley, Claiborne County, 196.

grand homes and structures in Port Gibson, which rendered the city, according to local lore, "too beautiful to burn" – the sentiment purportedly expressed by General Ulysses Grant on his march through Port Gibson to Vicksburg in 1863. That the Union army used the house as a hospital during the Battle of Port Gibson probably was the real reason it was left standing.

Believe it or not, another young man attempted to outbuild Smith Danielle's Windsor House, but his plan did not materialize.[436] The opulence that surrounded **MARTIN** and his family in Port Gibson, Grand Gulf, and the Natchez region of the state no doubt added to his incessant desire to own more and more.

MARTIN's original plantation house burned down but it is said that he rebuilt in relatively the same location.[437] While he was not the richest of his immediate neighbors – the wealthiest having real estate valued at $35,000 *[$997,000 in 2012 currency]* and a personal estate of $80,000 *[$2,280,000]* – he was living a similar lifestyle. John Rail's slaves and land clearly were assumed by **MARTIN** and **SINAI**. In the January 22, 1846 edition of the Port Gibson *Herald*, one finds the State of Mississippi demanding that the sheriff of Claiborne County require **SINAI** and **MARTIN**, and others associated with the probate of John's property, to appear in court on February 23rd to explain why specifically-identified "lands and tenements" belonging to John Rail should not be sold," and especially "why said land should not be sold in preference *[sic]* of the negro slaves" in order to satisfy debts of the estate. [438] This was not the first request. At least as early as December 1845, such notices had been appearing in the newspapers.

For a period of 19 years, **MARTIN** amassed significant landholdings by purchasing the property of his neighbor, Robert Patton, when he was unable to pay his taxes. Essentially, the concept of tax lien sales was operative even then. His first purchase in 1847 was for 79 acres, for which he paid $5.45 *[$157.00 in 2012 monetary value]* when Patton did not pay his taxes in 1846. The following year he purchased 841 acres of Mr. Patton's property for a purchase price of $23.24 *[$703.00 in 2012 monetary value]* due to Patton's 1847 delinquent taxes. And finally, at a deceased estate sale, **MARTIN** purchased the balance of Robert Patton's entire estate at a price of $3000 *[$90,000 in 2012 monetary value]*, putting $1000 *[30,000]* down and signing two promissory notes for $1000 *[$30,000]* to be paid on January 1st, 1848 and 1849, respectively. By the time of the 1860 U.S. Census enumeration, **MARTIN** owned 1772.75 acres of land. Appendix D details the acreage that **MARTIN** amassed and the timeframes over which he acquired land, from the early stages of his marriage to **SINAI** to the beginning of the Civil War.

Notwithstanding all that remains unclear, *[most of which does]*, one thing is certain – 41 (or 46) year old **MARTIN NATHANIEL HULBERT** was rich on the eve of the Civil War. In 1860, the "real price" value of his real estate in Police District 2 (Grand Gulf) was $15,000 *[$427,000 in 2012 currency]* and the "real price" value of his personal estate, which included his slaves, was listed as $25,000 *[$712,000 in 2012]*[439] rendering a total "real price" estate valued at an estimated $1,139,000 in 2012 currency. His "economic status" in 2012 currency was $14,800,000, boosting his "economic

---

436 Carol Miller, Lost Mansions of Mississippi (Jackson: University Press of Mississippi, 1996), 27.

437 Notes from ancestry.com message board post by Kathleen Casper, October 19, 2004. Per her conversation with and tour provided by Mr. Mullins, former forester for Claiborne County, she was taken to the Hulburt/Hulbert Cemetery, Martin's rebuilt plantation home, and the Sanders Plantation land ("Tannyhill") [sic]. She located photos of Sinai and Clarence from Martin's daughter, Irene.

438 Port Gibson Herald, 22 January 1846, 2.

439 Estate valuations for Martin Hulbert and neighbors obtained from the 1860 U.S. Census.

power" in 2012 currency to $147,000,000 – reflecting the significant weight that his wealth had on the control of the production output in the Mississippi economy.[440] He had doubled his wealth in ten years (between 1850 and 1860) and now owned land in two contiguous counties, Claiborne and Copiah. If this valuation only included the slaves and property in Police District 2, as appears to be indicated by the census, he was really far wealthier, as the number of slaves (77) he held in District 4 was more than twice the number (31) in District 2.

The **HULBERT** plantation probably was similar to the typical rural plantation outside the city proper of Port Gibson and not on the water – a 1.5 story white clapboard house with a wide hallway spanning the entire length of the house separating large rooms on both sides, a separate kitchen and pantry out back, wide porches (galleries) on the front and back with square columns supporting the porch on the second level. As the family grew, rooms would have been added to the main structure. There would have been a horse stable, a shed for the farm implements, and a storage building for the food and cotton produced by the slaves. **MARTIN's** plantation had 10 slave houses situated in a row some distance from the main house, rendering, on average, eight slaves per slave house. Despite his wealth, however, nothing written about Port Gibson/Claiborne County indicates the **HULBERT's** involvement in high society.

Irrespective of their circumstances before secession, the war, and emancipation, the outcome of the war changed life for virtually everyone in the South. For the first time in their lives, **MARTIN HULBERT** and his family experienced what it meant to be disenfranchised. They experienced what it felt like to be destitute. They understood what it meant to not know what the future would bring, and they knew fear of what a victorious Republican government might do to their communities, now devoid of the social, political, and educational structures that they had created to undergird their own success as elite plantation owners. Reconstruction in Claiborne County put in place black mayors, sheriffs, postmasters, a president of the county governing board and, in 1870, America's first elected black U.S. senator, Hiram Revels.[441] The campus of Oakland College, 10 miles south of Port Gibson, established by the Presbyterian church for the sons of elite Mississippi planters, was turned into the first state-supported black college in Mississippi and was renamed Alcorn College.[442] Among its matriculates in 1929, only 63 years after slavery, was **BEATRICE OTTOWIESS HULBERT**, who attended the 12-week summer teacher education program[443] in preparation for opening her own school, which at that time, she probably did not know, but perhaps dreamed, she would do. On occasion, her children, **CHIQUITA** and **TYREE**, ages 3 and 4, accompanied her to school during the summer. Summer school was designed for black teachers to "do accredited work that *[would]* eventually earn for them a certificate, and probably a degree."[444]

---

440 "Real price" is what an item would cost in today's market (for purposes of this manuscript, 2012); "economic status" reflects prestige; and "economic power" reflects influence in the total production of an economy.

441 Emilye Crosby, A Little Taste of Freedom, The Black Freedom Struggle in Claiborne County, Mississippi (Chapel Hill: University of North Carolina Press, 2005), 1.

442 Crosby, Little Taste of Freedom, 3.

443 Yearbook Collection, The Alcornite, 1929, (Lorman MS: Alcorn Agricultural and Mechanical College,1929), 78, http://collections.msdiglib.org/digital/collection/p17313coll1/id/87.

444 Alcorn A and M, The Alcornite, 75.

Decayed Roots?

That the war devastated **MARTIN** financially is documented by the Dun Agency credit field agents who reported him "badly in debt."[445] Aside from noting his financial destitution, however, they observed something else about **MARTIN**. They cautioned others to "*[l]*ook out for him *[for]* he has a vy honest face," but they found him putting his "considerable estate" in his wife's name, *[or someone else's]*. The field agents said that this "*[i]*nsolvent and tricky" former slave owner used this tactic and others for years after the war in an attempt to reestablish himself. The Dun agents indicated: "*[His]* *[p]*rospects are so mixed up and impaired *[sic]* divided between his wife & children that you could not tell to who *[sic]* it belonged."[446] Michael Wayne (author of *The Reshaping of the Plantation Society*) suggested that it was not only those of "doubtful reputation" like **MARTIN HULBERT**, however, who utilized these tactics, as evidenced by the Dun Agency's records that identified well-respected, upstanding Claiborne County resident, Samuel Bridgers, "in every way reliable & responsible," dodging creditors in the same way.[447] Bridgers was an original owner of Tannehill Plantation, having sold this property years before to John Rail. The Dun agents reported six years later that nothing had changed regarding **MARTIN's** financial integrity.

The Claiborne County property records support the Dun Agency's assessment of **MARTIN's** financial maneuverings following the war. Seven months after the war ended, on November 7, 1865, **MARTIN** put everything he owned into a deed of trust in his wife's name, claiming that he owed her $21,200 from funds borrowed from her inheritance from her first husband as well as for the

Martin's Deed of Trust

---

445 Wayne, Reshaping Plantation Society, 93.

446 Wayne, Reshaping Plantation Society, 93.

447 Wayne, Reshaping the Plantation, 93.

use of her "negroes" *[sic]* that she held in a separate estate upon their marriage. Perhaps this was the additional 31 slaves recorded living at Grand Gulf in the 1860 US Slave Census belonging to **M. N. HURLBURT** (spelled so differently from the **HULBERT** owning 77 slaves in the same census that I only in 2020 realized it was also **MARTIN's** record!)

His entire 1772.75 acres of land known as Dunbarton Plantation, plus "all mules, horses, cattle, sheep, hogs, wagons, carriages, work oxen, milch cows, household and kitchen furniture, and 3000 bushels of corn" were to be held in trust for his wife.[448] Subsequent to this action, proving the Dun Agency's point, the following September, **MARTIN**, **SINAI** and **ROBERT SANDERS** (**SINAI's** brother who lived next door to them and was an "overseer"), sold **JULIAN** and **BYRON** 730.75 acres of this property for $1662 *[$24,800 in 2012 monetary value]*. The involvement of **SINAI's** brother in this transaction is unclear, and no records were found of any transfers of property to either **CHRISTINA MARILLA** or to **CALISTA**. In 1876, the State of Mississippi seized 129.50 acres of **MARTIN** and **SINAI's** property; the following year, **JULIA E*[LIZA SIMS]* HULBURT**, **JULIAN's** wife, purchased it back from the state for $30.00. This was another tactic being used by former wealthy planters in attempts to reconstruct their landholdings – asking relatives to repurchase seized property. The records do not reflect why the state seized his property; perhaps he had not paid his taxes?

Did **MARTIN** find yet another way to make money after the war? According to the military records of the Confederate Citizens' File,[449] on September 25, 1863, Lt. John Harine, Jr. "impressed of **MARTIN** one large grey horse" valued and appraised at $600. Two months later, the Confederate States paid **MARTIN** $400 (no explanation documented as to why). On August 1, 1864, the Confederate States paid **MARTIN** $3400 for "two horses." On September 14, 1864, **MARTIN** presented to the Commissioner for the 4th Congressional District of Mississippi a claim for $600 for "one grey horse" and swore that he had never been paid for use of his horse. The only documentation in the record for use of any horse is for the $600-appraised grey horse. Perhaps records are missing and there was another transaction?

In **MARTIN's** Confederate application for a special pardon from the United States, attested on August 5, 1865, and ultimately approved by President Andrew Johnson on October 19, 1865, he indicates that he was never in the Confederate service, but "that under excitement and a feeling of sympathy for *friends* who were in that service *[like his sons?]*, he *may have* done or said things that may be construed to exclude him from the benefits of the amnesty proclaimed by your excellency."[450]

MARTIN's and his family's life stories are rather sketchy, but court documentation, Ancestry.com, military records, and newspaper accounts provide tidbits about some of the family members.

---

448 Deed of Trust, M. N. Hulbert to Sinai Hulbert, Book FF 43, Port Gibson Courthouse.

449 NARA, M346, "The Citizens File," Confederate Papers Relating to Individuals or Business Firms, 1861-1865, Publication No. M346, Record Group 109, Roll 0480, accessed August 8, 2017, https://www.fold3.com/title/60.

450 Ancestry.com, Case Files of Applications from Former Confederates for Presidential Pardons ("Amnesty Papers") 1865-1867; (National Archives Microfilm Publication M1003, 73 rolls); Records of the Adjutant General's Office, 1780's-1917, Record Group 94.

Martin required to apply for "special pardon"

The Legacy

In 1870, none of **MARTIN HULBERT's** children are enumerated in the U.S. Census except his son, **CLARENCE**, who is then age 13. Why he is living in Pattona, Mississippi (which has a Port Gibson post office) in the home of 27-year-old carriage maker and farmer, M. C. Wylie (whose birthplace is Ireland) is not stated. Also enumerated in this household are James Wylie, a 37-year-old farmer; Luella Wylie, age 3; and Mary Wylie (birthplace also Ireland), age 44, who is "keeping house." This enumeration is likely another example of how information was misconstrued to minimize liability for taxes, etc. More than likely, Mary and James were married, and these were their children, with the exception, of course, of **CLARENCE**; or Mary was the mother in this household and the husband was not enumerated.

After the war, eldest son **JULIAN M.** began raising his family of three children in Hermanville where, unfortunately on October 18, 1880, he died at the young age of 38. His son, **WARD MARTIN HULBERT**, lived to be 80 years of age and died in NY City on October 2, 1951.[451]

CLARENCE EVERETT HULBERT (b. December 25, 1854) rented a house in Red Lick, Mississippi (Jefferson County), and was farming in 1900. He later moved with his wife, Nancy, and children (one of which he named **SENAI** [sic] after his mother) to Waveland near Gulfport. Ironically, this is only 17 miles from our **FELDER** family members who lived in Pearlington and Logtown following emancipation. **CLARENCE** subsequently moved to Biloxi where he resided for nearly 20 years. He died there at the age of 68 on December 3, 1923.

True to the apparent nature of the **HULBERTS**, **CLARENCE's** son, **CLARENCE JR.**, and his wife, Bell Brown Hulbert, disputed property lines with their neighbor in Biloxi, Mississippi. During the dispute, Mrs. Hulbert removed stones marking the edge of the neighbor's property and proceeded to use what they claimed to be their property as a portion of their driveway. After a surveyor placed stakes along the property lines, the **HULBERTS** also removed the stakes, which identified where the neighbors were intending to erect a fence. The case (92 So.2d 247; *HULBERT v. FAYARD*), wound its way to the Mississippi Supreme Court and ended on January 28, 1957 with a judgement for the neighbors.

HERMAN C. HULBERT was buried at the age of four in the Wintergreen Cemetery in Port Gibson, Mississippi.

IRENE was married on two occasions; first to Harrison Eddins, and after his death, to Edward B. Chapman. She and Harrison had two children, and she and Edward had three. She lived with her daughter for a short time before marrying Edward and then moved to Memphis, Tennessee following his death. Her death certificate reveals that in 1944, at age 87, she died in Memphis of a "cerebral accident." She is buried in Memphis at the famous, beautifully-appointed Memorial Cemetery, with lush landscape, fountains, stone sculptures, reflecting pond, and crystal shrine grotto, just 16 miles from her nephew, **ALEXANDER HULBERT**, who is buried in New Park Cemetery.

B. M. HULBERT appeared to show signs of financial responsibility and trust, or perhaps he was used by **MARTIN** to keep tax collectors at bay, or **SINAI's** brother finally forced **MARTIN's** hand and disallowed him to serve as administrator of her estate when she died intestate in 1888. Five

---

451 Ancestry.com public tree of Luke Letlow, accessed April 2, 2015.

months following her death, **MARTIN**, **B. M.**, and **Robert Sanders**, **SINAI's** brother, jointly executed a promissory note (administrator's bond) agreeing to designate **B. M.** as administrator of his mother's estate, which by this time included all of **MARTIN's** property and all the personal marital assets, signed over in trust to **SINAI** by **MARTIN** immediately following the war in 1865.

Once again entrusted by the courts, on November 19, 1892, **B. M.** was appointed by the Port Gibson court to serve as substitute trustee for J. B. McMurchy, who defaulted on the payment of an indebtedness owed to Laura L. and D. D. Davenport by J. W. and Mary L. Dungan. **B. M.** had no difficulty in executing the mandates of the trust, and in his capacity as substitute trustee, on December 23, 1892, **B. M.** advertised the sale of the Dungan's land in the Port Gibson *Reveille*, and ultimately sold this property for $600 to the highest bidders – the Davenports.[452] It may be safe to assume that he executed the mandates of his mother's trust properly as well.

In a 542-page book on the people and history of Port Gibson, *Claiborne County, Mississippi: The Promised Land*, names of prominent and involved citizens of the community, the schools, churches, political parties, businesses, social and civic clubs are highlighted for their contributions to Port Gibson and surrounding towns. They were lawyers, ministers, politicians, business owners, newspaper editors and journalists, teachers, authors, painters, and even a few plantation owners. Thousands of people are lauded – but not **Hulbert**. **MARTIN's** name, and two of his family members, are mentioned only once in the 27 chapters addressing social, religious, economic, political, and educational life in Port Gibson and surrounding communities. On page 398, we learn that **JULIAN** was enlisted in the Thirty-Sixth Mississippi Army of Mississippi and Tennessee, and on page 284 it is revealed that **SINAI** is buried on the property of the John Trim family on the Claiborne/Copiah county lines, which appears to be the location of **MARTIN HULBERT's** Dunbarton Plantation, just west of the Copiah/Claiborne boundary and south of International Road. In one of the unmarked graves, according to this publication, is **SINAI's** husband, **MARTIN**. In October 1894, 75-year-old **MARTIN** died in Hermanville leaving a legacy that did not even result in his name on a headstone. Six years prior, on May 15, 1888, **SINAI** died, and on her tombstone is this inscription: "One by one He robs us of our treasures, Nothing [sic] is our own except our dead." At this gravesite, **SINAI's** surname is spelled two different ways. On her tombstone, designed with an encircled cross, her name is spelled "Hulburt." A recently-placed sign, posted to mark the location of these **HULBERT** graves, reads, "Hurlburt Cemetary" [sic]. There is another cemetery nearby with "a long row of depressions, with only a few marked as graves and believed to be colored burial grounds."[453]

Lastly, **B. M. HULBERT** is listed in one final record, the Military Grave Registrations, which indicates that he died in Natchez, Mississippi, a "pauper."[454] *[What poignant lessons these lives teach!]*

---

452 LL and DD Davenport to B. M. Hulbert, Appointment of Trustee, December 27, 1892, 3-E, 587-591.

453 William L. Sanders, Carved in Stone: Cemeteries of Claiborne County, Mississippi (Pittsburg: Dorrance Publishing Company, 2014),

454 Military Grave Registrations, 1936-1941, Box 11090, Digital Folder 004813442, Image 00171; https://familysearch.org/pal:/MM9.1.1/QJB7-6VVV (accessed July 30, 2014); Mississippi State Archives, various records, 1820-1951.

Freedom is the Answer to Slavery: Storm-tossed Leaves

Despite the end of the war on April 9, 1865, a year later, in 1866, there were still 77 ex-slaves enumerated at **MARTIN's** plantation home in Port Gibson – 34 were males and 43 were females.[455] This means that none of the 77 slaves "owned" by **MARTIN** in 1860 on the eve of the war left the plantation immediately after Emancipation in 1863, or if a couple left, the exact same number were born. It is possible that they were not even told they were free. Particularly on large plantations, it was easy to isolate the slaves and withhold information. Believe it or not, this actually happened in many places. *[On one plantation in Spartanburg, South Carolina, the slaves were not told until two years after the war that they had been freed!]*

Nonetheless, four years later, by the U.S. Census of 1870, no black **Hulberts** are enumerated as living in Port Gibson, and only three black **Hulberts** are enumerated anywhere in the entire state of Mississippi! In fact, of the 63 black **Hulberts** enumerated in the entire United States in 1870, only three indicated that they were born in Mississippi, although 30 of **MARTIN HULBERT's** slaves were between the ages of one and nine in 1860, and 15 of his slaves were between the ages of one and nine in 1850. There is no doubt that slaves on **MARTIN N. HULBERT's** plantation disassociated themselves from him and his family once they gained their freedom. As the law required of freedmen, they took surnames; but not **Hulbert**. This may suggest that not only was **MARTIN HULBERT** a "tricky" businessman, he may have also been an abusive slave owner. Mundy certainly was intent on getting as far away as possible, and probably with all he owned in the world draped on his body – two shirts, a pair of pants and a pair of shoes – he tried to escape. He tried to find freedom! Freedom was the answer!

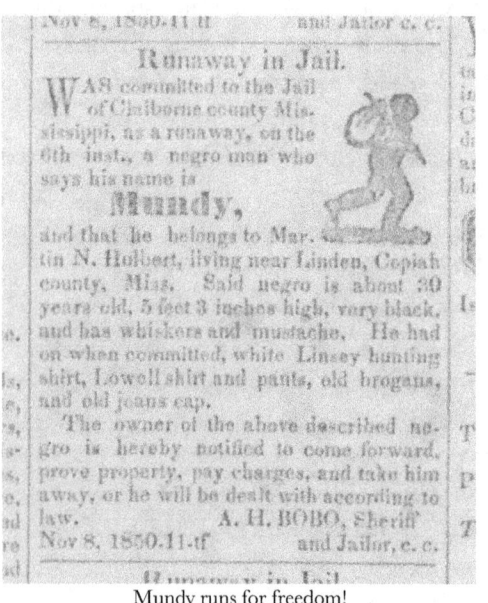
Mundy runs for freedom!

It is entirely understandable why black "**Hulberts**" either selected alternate surnames or left Mississippi as quickly as they could, especially from the Natchez District, which encompassed Port Gibson (Claiborne County) and the plantation home of **MARTIN N. HULBERT**. Citizens of Claiborne County did not respond civilly to the era of Reconstruction. The violence of the early 1870s set the tone for 100 years of senseless intimidation, fraud, murder, and lynchings in Mississippi. Moderate and liberal whites were targets as well as African Americans. Whites with any inclination to support efforts to aid the black population were intimidated and forced to pledge allegiance to the rebel Democrats' "clubs" that roamed the Natchez communities – day and night – hell-bent on eradicating any perceived impediment to the return of absolute white judicial rule, white economic and political power and racial authority. White supremacy stampeded

---

455 Mississippi State and Territorial Census Collection, 1792-1866.

out every hope for even a "taste of freedom."⁴⁵⁶ The "extensive violence and lawlessness"⁴⁵⁷ in the Natchez region was virtually unmatched anywhere else in the country. The 1876 election was the most contentious election the country had witnessed to date, as whites availed themselves of every conceivable means to eliminate the black man's participation in national, state, and local government.

In 1877, newly-elected President Rutherford B. Hayes withdrew the federal troops from the South as a concession to the Democrats who insisted that the election outcome was rigged. Hayes, like Lincoln, did not win the popular vote but was elected, instead, by the Electoral College. Termed the "Compromise of 1877" by white America, it was considered the "Great Betrayal" by black America.⁴⁵⁸ Despite the unbridled violence in the former Confederate states, the preceding U. S. President who served from 1869-1877 – Ulysses S. Grant – *[yes, the general who won the war!]* – refused to send in federal troops to restore order. Only thirteen years after Emancipation, blacks were run out of political office, church meetings were interrupted by violence and murders, black and white sheriffs were run out of town, white judges were corrupted, and all duly elected Republican Reconstruction officeholders were replaced by Democratic white supremacists.⁴⁵⁹ Emilye Crosby states, "By 1877, Reconstruction and the promise of racial equality had been destroyed nationwide."⁴⁶⁰ The country continued to reel from instability of political and personal opinion, and visions of freedom and equality anticipated by freedmen quickly died throughout the South as both "black*[s]* and white*[s]* continued to fight for conflicting interpretations of freedom."⁴⁶¹ The war had not ended at Appomattox – it had only changed form.

Case in point: nearly 100 years later, in 1966-67, the **Hulbert** name continued to resonate negatively in Port Gibson. "Klan supporter" **Ronnie Hulbert's** bullying and intimidation tactics, demonstrated throughout the famed Port Gibson merchant boycott, inflamed Charles Evers to harsh confrontational abdication of the nonviolent protest strategy of the NAACP.⁴⁶² Charles assumed the position of field secretary after the KKK murdered

Mural in town square, Port Gibson

---

456 Crosby, Little Taste of Freedom, 3.

457 Crosby, Little Taste of Freedom, 3.

458 Millercenter.org/president/hayes/key-events, (accessed December 12, 2014).

459 Jason Phillips, "Reconstruction in Mississippi, 1865-1876," accessed December 12, 2014, mshistorynow.mdah.state.ms.us/articles/204/reconstruction-in-mississippi-1865-1876.

460 Crosby, Little Taste of Freedom, 3.

461 William Iverson Horne, "Negotiating Freedom: Reactions to Emancipation in West Feliciana Parish, Louisiana" (master's thesis, George Washington University, August 31, 2013), 45.

462 Crosby, Little Taste of Freedom, 160.

the first ever NAACP field secretary in the South – Charles' younger brother, Medgar. Using rhetoric that would ultimately implicate the NAACP for inciting violence during the boycott, Charles expressed his anger and frustration with the Klan and associated Port Gibson merchants:

> Ain't nobody scared of Ronnie [Hulbert]. Tell Ronnie he ain't nothing but a coward. He needs to become a man. ...Tell Ronnie don't be picking up no more Negroes. If he picks us up, we are going to pick him up. ...We aren't going to take any more, white folks. We have taken all we are going to take. ...We will remain nonviolent as long as you let us remain nonviolent. But when you put your hands on us, we are coming back at you. ...We are going to turn our other cheek no more. If you slap one of us, we will knock [the] hell out of you.[463]

Ronnie Hulbert owned a radio repair shop in Port Gibson and used his ham radio to encourage the white merchants to fire any black person who supported or participated in the boycott. Most of the blacks to which he referred were domestics cleaning either the stores or homes of the white shop owners. Fire them and hire whites, he advised. Ultimately, the white merchants won a Mississippi State Supreme Court judgement against the NAACP, holding participants individually and personally liable for merchants' loss of income from the beginning of the boycott in 1966 through the end in 1972. However, on July 2, 1982, the United States Supreme Court reversed the decision. *[Charles Evers went on many years later to become the first black elected mayor in Mississippi since Reconstruction and the first black to run for governor of the state. He just passed on July 22, 2020.]*

The Sins of Which Father?

When **Thomas Hurlbut** left England and arrived in America in 1635, he became one of the first Puritans in the country. While considered a good man, serving often as a juror, he was fined by the court in 1642, possibly associated with an unscrupulous appraisal. He was said to be the brother of William at Windsor. He was the father of many sons in Litchfield County, Connecticut. **HULBERTS** of *OURstory* are purportedly relatives of this man. They moved frequently and settled widely across the northeast and mid-west, including in New York, Ohio, Indiana, Illinois, and Vermont. Assuming reasonable accuracy of the *his*tories of the **Hulberts/Hurlbuts/Hurlburts/Hulbuts**, etc., the fathers had illegitimate children, had children when they were but children themselves – one boy/father as young as 13. They fought in the Revolutionary War and the French and Indian War as privates and officers, and one father, Caleb, as a surgeon. They gravitated towards business ownership and the building industry – contractors and plasterers. The middle name, Alexander, which interestingly *is* a French Creole name, surfaced early in the naming of both white and black family members and has continued through the years.

ALBERT ALEXANDER HULBERT ("**ALEX**"), was enumerated as "black" as an infant and young man in Innis, Louisiana. It is well-documented that **ALEXANDER** was born either in Innis or Batchelor, Louisiana (contiguous communities) and later went to Port Gibson, Mississippi, as a young man. It is documented that he attended Tuskegee Institute (now Tuskegee University), studied in the carpentry department, and became a noted building contractor in Memphis, Tennessee,

---

463 Crosby, Little Taste of Freedom, 177-178.

"building homes in the black and white communities."⁴⁶⁴ He married in Port Gibson prior to moving to Memphis in 1906, where, in the 1910 U. S. Census, he was enumerated for the first time as "mulatto." According to the Louisiana color chart, the definition of mulatto meant that **ALEXANDER** was one-half white, one-half black.⁴⁶⁵ **BESSIE SHAFFER**,⁴⁶⁶ his wife, born 1881 in Port Gibson, was also enumerated as "mulatto" in the 1910 U.S. Census as were the children she bore, **JAMES ALEXANDER**, born in Port Gibson, and **ROBBIE**, born in Memphis. Sadly, when these children were barely teenagers, their mother died. At ages 13 and 11, **JAMES** and **ROBBIE**, respectively, were motherless *[bizarrely interestingly, the same ages of **GLADYS** and **FRANKIE**, respectively, when our mother died!]* They were sent to Phoenix and Chicago at some point where they were able to finish their elementary and secondary schooling.⁴⁶⁷ It is unclear if they lived with relatives or friends of the family or if they attended boarding schools, as they do not surface in the censuses in either of those cities.

Alexander Hulbert

In 1930, **ALEXANDER** was still living in Memphis, Tennessee, as head of his household, and his son, **JAMES ALEXANDER** ("**UNCLE JAMES**"), then 24, was living with him along with boarders, Methodist minister, Rev. Frank Brown and his wife, Mamie. His daughter, **ROBBIE HULBERT**, and son-in-law, **AUTRY THOMPSON**, both of whom were age 22, had married and were living in Beat 2 of Coahoma County, Mississippi (location of Friar's Point where **S. P. FELDER** had been appointed Presiding Elder on December 22, 1899). **AUTRY JR.**, their only child, was four months old. **ALEXANDER** claimed himself to be "widowed" in the 1930 U.S. Census, and indeed, his wife, **BESSIE**, had died 11 years earlier. However, six years following her death, on June 23, 1925, "**ALEX HULBERT**" had married "**OTTOWIESS FELDER**"⁴⁶⁸ (**BERTHA BEATRICE OTTOWIESS FELDER**) at the courthouse in Cleveland (Bolivar County), Mississippi, 10 miles east of Mound Bayou. They were married by

Certificate of Marriage of Beatrice and Alexander Hulbert

---

464 Negro Chamber, Negro Yearbook, 128.

465 Costello, Creole Pointe Coupée, 58.

466 Bessie's name was possibly Shaifer (slaves associated with A. K. Shaifer and his family in Port Gibson). The 1900 U.S. Census lists Bessie as a child of Henrietta and John Shaifer, born in January 1881, in Port Gibson. She has seven siblings and is 19 years old at the enumeration. The Negro Yearbook spells her name as Shaffer.

467 Funeral programs of James Hulbert, July 31, 1974 and Robbie (Hulbert) Thompson, June 11, 1989.

468 Certificate of Marriage, Bolivar County, Book 29, 229.

Justice of the Peace, A. H. Doyle, on the same day of the application for their marriage license. **ALEX** was 45; **BEATRICE**, 28. The next year, on September 11, 1926, **CHIQUITA JANE HULBERT** was born, and the year following that, on October 6, 1927, **TYREE PRESTON HULBERT** was born. From 1912 through 1924, **ALEXANDER** lived at four residences in Memphis. Between 1925 and 1929, he does not have a Memphis address. Not only does census documentation never show **BEATRICE** and **ALEXANDER** living as husband and wife, they are not ever documented as living in the same town.

For nine years, between 1930 and 1939, **ALEX** resided on Mississippi Boulevard in Memphis, but in 1940 was a boarder in James Williams' household on Mississippi Boulevard. He moved to his last residence in that city, 2381 Cable Avenue, in 1943. In that same year, 1943, three years after **BEATRICE's** father, **REV. S. P. FELDER**, passed, **ALEXANDER** publicly, through omission, dismissed having ever fathered his last two children when he proclaimed in an article published in the *Negro Year Book* in Memphis in 1943: "Once I enjoyed slaving for my children; now *[that]* they are grown, married and established, I hope to find my future happiness in living for my grandchildren – two of them belonging to **JAMES** and one to **ROBBIE**."[469] The article continues to inform that at the time, **JAMES** was the librarian at Virginia State College in Petersburg, Virginia, and that **ROBBIE** was working at the Treasury Department in Washington, D.C. *["Slaving" for his children. What a choice of words!]*

Tyree, Beatrice, and Chiquita Felder

What the article does not mention is that **CHIQUITA** was a 20-year-old sophomore at Tougaloo College in Jackson, Mississippi, studying music, and that **TYREE**, in 1945, would become a freshman at Tuskegee Institute and begin to study building industries – essentially the same major that **ALEXANDER** pursued when he was a student at Tuskegee. **BEATRICE**, being the fiery personality and informed teacher that she was, surely was made aware of this article, and with little hesitation, made the decision to get rid of this man in her life. Less than a year after its publication, on May 26, 1944, when **CHIQUITA** was 17 and **TYREE** was 16, **BEATRICE** accompanied her children to the Cleveland County Courthouse – the same location of her marriage – and changed her minor children's names back to her maiden name – **FELDER**,[470] legally removing any trace of **ALEXANDER HULBERT** from their lives as well. One available court record reflects that at some point they officially divorced, because **BEATRICE** had provided sole care since 1930, and

---

469 Negro Chamber, Negro Year Book, 128.

470 Petition to Change Name, Attorney Benjamin Green, Case #7537, Chancery Court, Bolivar County.

because since that time, her children had been known as **FELDER** in their school records, it was logical to change their names. Five years later, on May 29, 1948, at age 63, **ALEXANDER** died of "uraemia secondary to hypertrophy," which a cystotomy could not arrest.[471] Sadly, the legacy of absent parents through death, illness, hushed adoptions, divorce, amnesia, or straight out fabrication of truth has repeated itself throughout generations in the **FELDER** and **HULBERT** families.

An interesting aside and possible connection, or just pure coincidence: the New York Find a Grave Index, 1550-2012, lists a male child, "**Robbie Hulbert**" as the son of George and Fannie **Hulbert**. He was buried in Old Chatham, Columbia County, New York, the location of Columbia University – the graduate school attended by "**UNCLE JAMES**" (**JAMES ALEXANDER HULBERT**). **UNCLE JAMES'** sister was **ROBBIE HULBERT** – "**AUNT ROBBIE**." In 1846, **Alexander Hulbert**, a white building contractor, was born and lived in Columbia, New York, before later moving to Ohio. And, finally, the combination of names – Alexander, James, Martin, and Hulbert, is a continuing practice. Confused? I sure am!

Our **FELDER** ancestors seemed to have lived relatively prosperous and upstanding lives; but not **HULBERT**. What, I still wonder, were the "sins of the father" ... and, which father?

---

[471] Ancestry.com, Tennessee Death Records, 1908-1958, Alexander Hulbert.

HULBERT **FAMILY TREE**

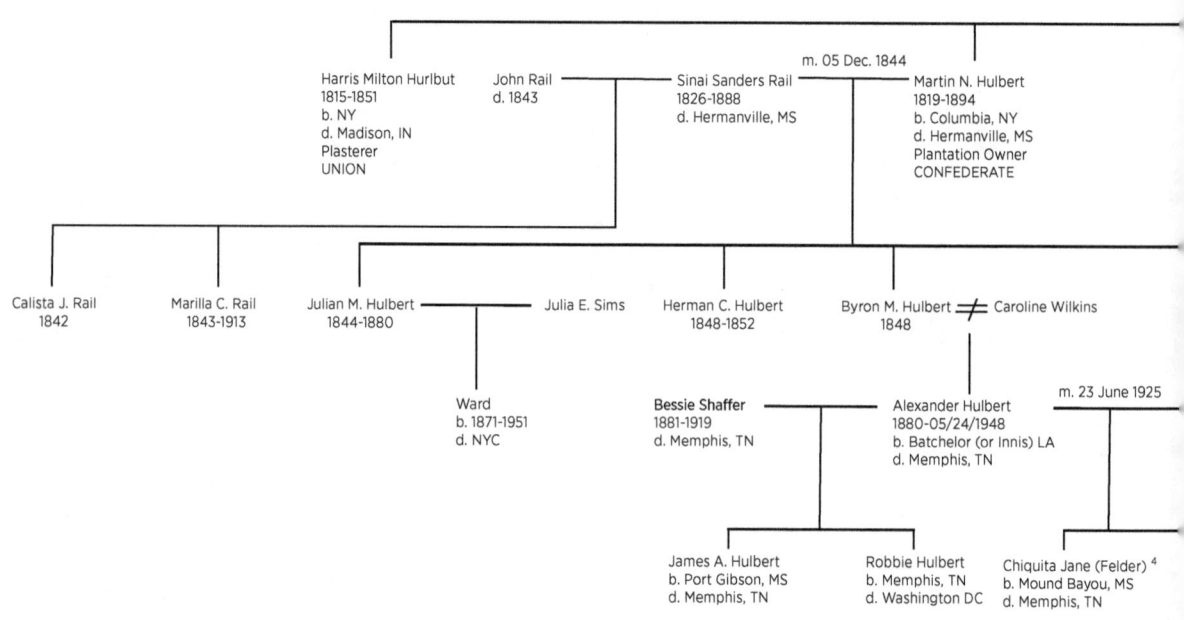

1 *Surgeon in French War* 2 *To MS w/ Lyman Company (3 slaves)* 3 *Assisted w/ BM & Julian's release* 4 *Legal name change from Hulbert 1941*

≠ *Did not marry*

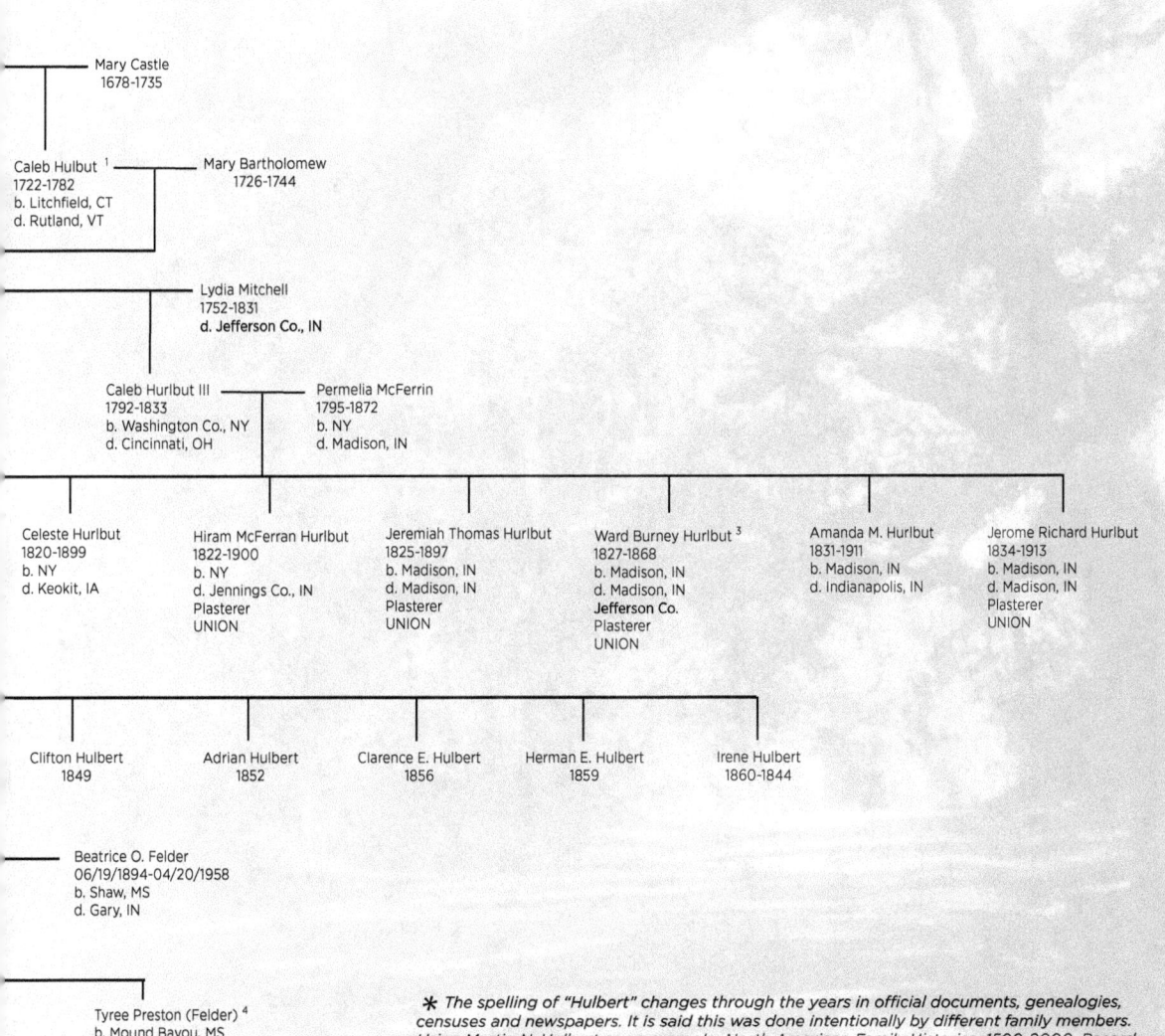

```
Mary Castle
1678-1735
│
Caleb Hulbut [1] ── Mary Bartholomew
1722-1782           1726-1744
b. Litchfield, CT
d. Rutland, VT

        Lydia Mitchell
        1752-1831
        d. Jefferson Co., IN

    Caleb Hurlbut III ── Permelia McFerrin
    1792-1833            1795-1872
    b. Washington Co., NY  b. NY
    d. Cincinnati, OH      d. Madison, IN
```

Celeste Hurlbut	Hiram McFerran Hurlbut	Jeremiah Thomas Hurlbut	Ward Burney Hurlbut [3]	Amanda M. Hurlbut	Jerome Richard Hurlbut
1820-1899	1822-1900	1825-1897	1827-1868	1831-1911	1834-1913
b. NY	b. NY	b. Madison, IN	b. Madison, IN	b. Madison, IN	b. Madison, IN
d. Keokit, IA	d. Jennings Co., IN	d. Madison, IN	d. Madison, IN	d. Indianapolis, IN	d. Madison, IN
	Plasterer	Plasterer	**Jefferson Co.**		Plasterer
	UNION	UNION	Plasterer		UNION
			UNION		

Clifton Hulbert	Adrian Hulbert	Clarence E. Hulbert	Herman E. Hulbert	Irene Hulbert
1849	1852	1856	1859	1860-1844

Beatrice O. Felder
06/19/1894-04/20/1958
b. Shaw, MS
d. Gary, IN

Tyree Preston (Felder) [4]
b. Mound Bayou, MS
d. Chester, VA

✱ *The spelling of "Hulbert" changes through the years in official documents, genealogies, censuses and newspapers. It is said this was done intentionally by different family members. Using Martin N. Hulbert as an example: North American Family Histories, 1500-2000, Record of the descendants (Hurlbut); Madison IN Republican and Banner, 1933 (Hulbert); Port Gibson Herald, 1846 (Hulbert); 1850 US Census (Hulbert); 1850 US Slave Census (Hulbert); 1860 US Census (Hurlbut); 1860 US Slave Census (Hulbert); 1860 US Slave Census (M.N. Hurlburt); 1865 Confederate Application for Presidential Pardon (Hurlburt); 1866 MS State Census (Hulbert); 1880 US Census (Hulburt); 1900 US Census – for descendants (Hurlburt)!*

© Frankie Felder, 2020

VIRGINIA

The weeping willow tree dropped its leaves in our front yard, but its branches never broke; they just bent and tossed about furiously in the changing winds, waving us onward. After the storms, the tree always stood its ground, firmly anchored by its roots; Mississippi roots transplanted to Virginia by daddy.

E. O. Felder, October 2018, Stellenbosch, South Africa

6 | PATTERNS AND LEGACIES

The meaning of our surname, **FELDER**, bore itself out in the lives of both the black and white families. They were industrious people. The white **Felders** were Methodists, Baptists, Democrats, Masons, plantation and slave "owners," and farmers. The black **FELDERS** were African Methodist Episcopalians, Baptists, Episcopalians, Republicans, Masons, ministers, and educators. Supporting each other was important in all branches of these families' trees, and although elusive marriage relationships existed in both, and families began to splinter, siblings and extended family were close-knit in both. As a result of – or in spite of – our ancestors' experiences on the Mississippi and Louisiana farms and towns of the 1800s, three prominent patterns to which they were exposed clearly influenced the values they incorporated into their lives once freed from the oversight, the confines, and the degradation of slavery: 1) gratitude to the God who brought them out of bondage (religion); 2) determination in spite of all odds to ensure opportunities for literacy for their descendants (education); and 3) freedom to be and to become (economic empowerment and property ownership). This concluding chapter discusses these patterns and provides examples of the legacies that were borne of them.

Felder's Campground

THE PATTERN: RELIGION

We went through fire and through water: but thou broughtest [sic] us out into a wealthy place.
Psalm 66:12, KJV

God's Felders/FELDERS' God

In Pike County, Mississippi, **John Felder**, the youngest of **Peter Felder's** sons, donated land and time to help establish the Methodist church in that state as a co-founder of **Felder's Campground**[472] on the outskirts of Magnolia, three miles from McComb. At the campground, started in a brush arbor that quickly expanded to a campsite, people came from miles on horseback and in carriages and camped out typically from a week to 17 days,[473] giving praise and thanksgiving for the blessings of safety from wild animals they did not consume, like the panthers and wolves, but also being thankful for the wild animals they could consume, like deer, turkeys, possums, and coons. Certainly they prayed fervently for protection from the Catawba, Iroquois, Chickasaw, Choctaw, and Natchez Native American tribes on whose land they squatted, nearly 20,000 square miles in Marion County alone.[474] Lastly, they thanked the Lord for the bountiful harvests and the prosperity they anticipated from the cultivation *[by their slaves]* of their cotton farms and plantations. Just as in South Carolina, the founding settlers of Mississippi and Louisiana went to those states to get rich and to prosper.

---

472 Luke W. Conerly, Pike County, MS, 1798-1876: *Pioneer Families and Confederate Soldiers, Reconstruction and Redemption* (Nashville, Tennessee: Brandon Printing Company, 1909), 38.

473 "Tracing the History of Area Churches," The Magnolia Gazette, October 29, 1986.

474 Conerly, *Pioneer Families and Confederate Soldiers*.

At these **Felder** camp meetings, they sang and preached and ate, and the children played. When the open-air camp constructed its first building, it was "a wooden structure without ceiling, window sash or heat ... built for monthly preaching services on both Saturday and Sunday."[475] They accommodated their chattel in a section "partitioned for the colored people, who at the time were slaves and had no organized church, and who participated in communion services following the white congregation,"[476] sitting on log pews off to the side of the long wooden benches. Slaves used fans that they wove together of pine leaves to shoo the pesky flies and mosquitoes *[of which there had to be millions in these humid woods!]* away from their "masters." Slaves served water throughout the services to the white congregation. Oddly, in 1856, "40 persons were converted, 10 or 12 cleansed from sin, and 35 whites and 18 colored members *[were]* admitted on trial."[477]

Slaves sat in benches off to the side

Dr. H. F. Johnson, President of Whitworth College (Brookhaven, Mississippi), preached **John Felder's** funeral on April 23, 1876. He said **John** was of "great worth, as a neighbor, a citizen and a Christian ... he was above reproach."[478] Nearly 100 years later, in 1965, **John** was cited by a North Carolina historian (and relative) to be a man of "integrity and godliness," chiefly responsible for influencing the **Felder** community to be one that placed the Lord first. Religion and church were the cornerstones of the **Felder** families that for one hundred years lived in Pike County, Mississippi. "True Christianity," Dr. Johnson noted, being the "greatest force for good in human life," was "preached, honored and lived out in the lives of the people of the **Felder** community." He attributed the strengths of the **Felder** community to year-round worship at **Felder's Church** at Topisaw and the summer camp meetings.[479]

In addition to the camp meetings, during the antebellum years, itinerant preachers traveled the countryside, holding service in someone's home or under a tree on someone's plantation or farm. These slave "owners'" worship and praise services where they gave thanks to the Almighty Creator modeled a social custom and tradition in the white **Felder** families that took hold among their black **Felder** slaves, although most surely for different reasons. Today in our black **FELDER** families, overall, the expectation of worship and thankfulness is foundational. Since the days of slavery, and probably also before, albeit in different form, our black **FELDER** ancestors have worshipped, prayed, praised, sang, and served.

---

475 *Felder's (Topisaw) Camp meeting*, 1977, 5.

476 *Felder's (Topisaw) Camp meeting*, 1977, 5.

477 *Felder's (Topisaw) Camp meeting*, 1977, 5.

478 Mary E. Sandel and Elias W. Sandel, *The Felder Family in South Carolina, Mississippi, Texas and Louisiana* (Roseland, Louisiana: self-published, 2000), 19.

479 Sandel and Sandel, *The Felder Family*, 12.

Aside from **John Felder's** influence in building Methodism in Mississippi, first at **Felder's Campground** and later at **Felder's Church**, at least three other men became ministers in the community who were part of the **Felder** clan. The first of these was **Rev. Charles Felder (John's** brother). He preached nearly ten years in South Carolina prior to moving west and becoming an itinerant preacher in Mississippi and Louisiana where he founded, co-founded, and/or pastored numerous Baptist churches in the state. In 1819, he became the minister at East Fork Baptist Church where he pastored for the entire 24 years of his ministry. On August 18, 1826, he co-founded and became the first pastor of the 19-member Salem Baptist Church, which grew immensely despite being destroyed twice by fire, relocating three times, and changing its name as many times. After a fire destroyed the building in 1839, the church changed its name to Magnolia Baptist when, with its membership of 150, it relocated to a plot of land southwest of Magnolia. Continued growth in membership, and another fire in 1869, necessitated relocation again, purchasing additional property and constructing a new facility. For a final time, the church changed its location and its name. First Baptist Church of Magnolia grew to accommodate 450 parishioners and consumed an entire city block in Magnolia. Part of the land on which this present-day church was erected was purchased in 1958 from **Dwight Felder**.[480] Finally, continuing to build the Baptists in Mississippi, in 1839, **Rev. Charles Felder** cofounded Liberty Baptist Church. He also pastored at Zion Hill Baptist Church.

The second minister from the community was Rev. Thomas Bond, husband of **Peter's** daughter, **Nancy Felder**. Rev. Bond was trained by, and served as assistant to, his father-in-law, **Rev. Charles Felder**. The third minister, **Rev. Albert G. Felder**, was grandson of **Rev. Charles Felder** and became an itinerant preacher in Mississippi and Louisiana towns, often preaching at Red Bluff Baptist Church in nearby Greensburg, Louisiana.

In the settling of Mississippi, plantations and landholdings were typically quite expansive; "grants" of ceded Indian land still being doled out by the government to adventurous white Americans who dared go west. **Rev. Charles Felder**, himself, received a landgrant of 80 acres on July 1, 1827, in Amite County. With individuals owning so much land, rural next-door neighbors were spread significant distances from one another, consequently, many churches were established to minimize the travel distance of church-goers. Churches often met only one Sunday a month. As such, ministers could manage pastoring several churches simultaneously, as did **Rev. Charles Felder**.

Of **Rev. Charles Felder**, the Mississippi Baptist Association said upon his death:

> He was a sound consistent [sic] and able minister of the New Testament. As a pastor he has been surpassed by none in our country, as an evangelist and revivalist, few exceeded him. His Christian deportment and soundness in the faith, connected with his indefatigable labors for the extension of the Redeemer's Kingdom, his making and preserving peace in the denomination, with all men, have embalmed his memory with undying esteem.[481]

---

480 "Tracing the History of Area Churches," McComb Enterprise-Journal, September 25, 1970, 5.

481 T. C. Schilling, *Abstract History of the Mississippi Baptist Association from Its Preliminary Organization in 1806 to the Centennial Session in 1906, Years, 1831-1849*, accessed March 8, 2008, http://baptisthistoryhomepage.com/miss.association.hist3.html.

In 1856, Ansel Prewitt, future founder of Magnolia, deeded a portion of his plantation to the relocation of Magnolia Methodist Church. Most of the Methodists then began attending there. This Methodist "charge," by 1871-72, was assigned to Pastor John Wesley Sandel (former "owner" of seven slaves) and included the Holmesville, Magnolia, Summit and Topisaw areas[482] – all communities in which the **Felder** families and **FELDER** slaves resided, and the area to which **SONA** later returned to minister. **Peter Felder**, **Isaac Felder**, **Aby Jane** (**Felder**) **Vaughn**, and Henry Sandel were all charter members of Muddy Springs Church, the church built between the inactive years of **Felder's Church** (because its services were canceled during the war) and the construction of Magnolia Methodist Church.[483] It appears that the slaves of the Sandels, Vaughns, Bonds, Prewitts, and **Felders** all attended Muddy Springs Church along with these plantation owners, as this was already the established custom at **Felder's** Campground. These families' slaves worked on contiguous and nearby plantations and farms. They worshipped and prayed together when they could. They knew each other.

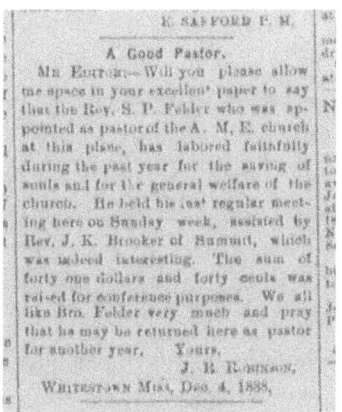

Plea to retain their "good pastor." Whitestown was a town near Magnolia.

Slavery was the Answer to Freedom. For Them.

The Founding Fathers, through their authorship of "The Three-Fifths Compromise,"[484] Article 1, Section 2, of the newly-written U.S. Constitution, supported the continuation of slavery, and shrewdly, white southern Baptist and Methodist slave-holding preachers used the Constitution and the *Bible* to sustain their advantage as "masters" over an entire race of people *[my race; my people; my ancestors]*. My ancestors were "property" to be treated according to the whims of their "owners"; "property" to be used towards their "owners'" freedom – economic freedom; freedom certainly from poverty, and in many instances, freedom even from the middle class, as the profits they earned from the work of their slaves propelled them into the elite of society. William Wills Brown, African American abolitionist lecturer and historian of the antebellum days, put it this way: "A more praying, preaching, psalm-singing people cannot be found than the slave holders of the South."[485] Yet, despite the horrors of the institution of slavery and the blatant use of Christian doctrine to sustain it, and likely because of this, by July 22, 1862, when Abraham Lincoln announced to his cabinet that he intended to free the slaves in states in rebellion against the Union, thousands of slaves had already joined, and were practicing, some denomination of Christianity. The overwhelming majority had joined the Methodist and Baptist denominations.

---

482 *The Magnolia Gazette*, December 3, 1998, 1.

483 *The Magnolia Gazette*, October 29, 1986, 1.

484 For more information, research the "Three-Fifths Clause of the U.S. Constitution," Article 1, Section 2, Ratified 1788; accessed November 15, 2014.

485 Marcella Grindler, Andrew Leiter and Jill Sexton, "Guide to Religious Content in Slave Narratives," *Documenting the American South*, accessed November 15, 2014, https://docsouth.unc.edu/neh/religiouscontent.html.

A quote from the McComb *Enterprise-Journal* stated, "Like all churches in the South at that time, slaves were members of the same church as their masters, and attended services with their masters, or owners, in the same building."[486] While this is recorded in *his*tory, it is an inaccurate and misleading statement, as all slaves were *not* accorded access to worship. But it is true that at least in the **Felder** churches in Pike and Amite counties, the slaves were able to worship before and after Emancipation, albeit under the watchful eye and religious indoctrination of their "masters" or plantation overseers. Two specific examples elucidate this point. First, although Liberty Baptist Church was organized April 14, 1838, with **Rev. Charles Felder** as its first pastor, one year later, in 1839, slaves were admitted to membership. However, eight years after the Civil War, on March 15, 1873, the then freedmen withdrew their membership and established their own church.[487] Second, when Salem Baptist Church relocated and became Magnolia Baptist Church, its burgeoning membership of 150 included "75 whites and 80 *[N]*egroes." However, just as soon as the law allowed, in 1868, "the *[N]*egroes asked permission of Salem Baptist to withdraw their membership in order to constitute an organization of their own. This request was granted, *[and they organized]* a church of their own."[488]

While these examples do confirm that some churches in Amite and Pike County were integrated during antebellum years, they do not explain why the "*[N]*egroes asked permission" very soon after Emancipation to withdraw from **Felder** churches. Possibly the information below will shed some light. **Rev. Charles Felder** was at the helm of the Mississippi Baptist Conference many times over the 24 years that he pastored in Mississippi and Louisiana. But, despite the incorporation of **Felder** slaves into the worship experience, it was not without thought of personal security and of self-interest. **Rev. Charles Felder** was the moderator in 1819 when the following instructions[489] were prepared and delivered by the leadership of the Mississippi Baptist Conference to the slave-holding "masters" regarding treatment of their slaves:

> Masters, give unto your servant that which is just and equal knowing that you also have a Master in Heaven. (Corinthians, 4:1). Wisdom and prudence on this point are necessary in as much as it requires that different treatment should be administered at different times to the same servants, *[sic]* according to his ability or disability.

And, to the slaves who had joined the churches of the Mississippi Baptist Association, including his own, the instructions they received under the leadership of **Rev. Charles Felder** regarding their condition of servitude read accordingly:

> Brethreen, under the dispensation of God you have been brought into a state of bondage, however, dark, mysterious and unpleasant those dispensations ... they are no doubt founded in wisdom and goodness. In the discharge of your duty, it is necessary that you

---

486 "Tracing Area Churches," McComb *Enterprise-Journal*, 5.

487 "History of Liberty Baptist Church," accessed November 20, 2014, http://www.libertybaptistchurch.biz/clientimages/49109/lbc%20history.pdf.

488 "Tracing Area Churches," The Magnolia Gazette, October 29, 1986.

489 Frankie Felder, *Since Brown*, plenary speech, Council of Southern Graduate Schools, Annual Conference, Biloxi, Mississippi, February 2006. Text of instructions from the *Minutes of the Mississippi Baptist Conference*, 1819, Mississippi Department of Archives and History. See photo of A.G. Felder in T. C. Shilling, The Abstract History of the Mississippi Baptist Association: From I*ts Preliminary Organization in 1806 to the Centennial Session in 1906* (New Orleans: publisher unnamed), 175; accessed June 5, 2015, http://baptisthistoryhomepage.com/miss.association.hist.html.

should be industrious, honest, faithful, submissive and humble and that you should treat your Master and all his lawful commands with much attention and respect (Ephesians 6: KJV5);… you must obey your earthly Master with fear and trembling whether they are perverse and wicked (1 Peter 2:18, WEB) or pious and gentle.

[Thank goodness the law changed and outlawed the previous "lawful commands" of the many "perverse and wicked" slave holders referenced by Peter!]

Their Freedom Compromised

Albert G. Felder enlisted as soon as he was able. He was 14 years old. Captured at the Battle of Liberty on November 17, 1864,[490] by General Albert Lee's Baton Rouge cavalry, the 17-year-old witnessed the General's freeing of the slaves in Amite County and surrounding communities, hopefully including all of our **FELDER** slave ancestors, although by the Emancipation Proclamation issued January 1, 1863, they were technically already "free." Two months following his capture, on January 31, 1865, the 13th Amendment of the Constitution officially ended slavery. Once released as a prisoner of war, he followed in the footsteps of his noted grandfather, **Rev. Charles Felder**, and became moderator of the Mississippi Baptist Conference.

Despite the close of the war and the passage of the Thirteenth Amendment, the intentional instruction of black Americans through and by the church was an ongoing disquieting issue on the minds of much of the white Southern Christian leadership. The Louisiana Baptists, who held membership in the Mississippi Baptist Association, addressed the issue of education and evangelization of the freedmen with intensity over several years. At the March 29, 1866, State Convention No. 451, the topic dominated discussion. Rev. W. E. Paxton, historian, noted:

> The altered condition of the blacks was a source of solicitude to the Convention. Some favored their immediate evangelization, the establishment of Sunday-schools among, *[sic]* and an earnest effort to improve their spiritual condition. Others were not prepared for this, and a report on the subject recommending this policy was strongly opposed. The chairman finally withdrew the report and offered the following … resolution: Resolved, that in view of the present and prospective condition of the colored population, we recommend that special attention be paid to preaching the Gospel to them.

This resolution was adopted. However, three months later, in June 1866, the subject came up again of evangelizing to the "blacks."[491] A bit of that conversation proceeded accordingly:

> Christianity and humanity both demand that we should not follow the dictates of unhallowed prejudice, but that we should calmly and in the spirit of Christianity, study the interests of the colored population. Your committee believe, unhesitatingly, that it is our duty, as Baptists, to assist them in acquiring a correct knowledge of the *Bible*, in order that their notions of human depravity, of salvation by grace, of the ordinances of the

---

490 Andrew Booth, *Records of Louisiana Confederate Soldiers and Louisiana Confederate Commands, vol. 1 and II, A-G* (Spartanburg, SC: Reprint Company, 1984), 827.

491 Rev. W. E. Paxton, full text of *A History of the Baptists of Louisiana: From the Earliest Times to the Present," 1888,* Cornell University Library (450 - History of Louisiana Baptists), accessed August 12, 2013, http://archive.org/stream/cu31924029452038/cu31924029452038_djvu.txt.

New Testament, church government, and all scriptural truths, may be correct. While we are conscious that they are not equal in intellect to our race, we feel that it is our duty to do all we can to enlighten them, to improve the standards of morals among them, believing that in all this we will be conferring a benefit upon them and upon ourselves.[492]

Discussion ensued in which several Elders commented upon the "bad morals" of the black race and the need to instruct them to prevent the bad influences upon their own children, who would indeed come in contact with them *[African Americans]* daily. Others agreed that prejudice needed to be set aside for the good of the white race and the protection of their children against these amoral people: "We must instruct them and raise them up to us or they will drag us down to them."[493] *[Which "amoral blacks" do they reference that will "drag them down," the ones that raised their crops, cleaned their homes, cooked their food, nursed their babies, and had their babies? Which "amoral blacks" did they mean?]*

Several Elders urged adoption of the amendment to instruct the freedmen, and as a Convention, to promote the establishment of "Sabbath schools" for the simple reason that Jesus said, "Go into the world and teach all" ... not just white, or red, or black. Some felt that any appearance of the Convention acting towards political ends would assist Northerners in their attempts to evangelize and instruct the Negro in accordance with *their* perspectives – certainly not consistent with the perspectives of the southern man. Some noted that Sunday schools were already being established for blacks and that "many were already teaching the Negroes." They reasoned aloud that "[t]he time had come ... to suppress prejudice."[494]

One elder questioned whether the amendment pledged the Convention and fellow pastors to educate the blacks. Bro. George said that the amendment did not pledge them to educate the blacks and shared his belief that to "teach the Negro the Scripture," they did not even need to know the alphabet, would require no funds, but just a "little Christian zeal." And heaven forbid, the Northerners see the prejudice that they held towards the blacks! ...Could the Convention afford to "show the Radicals that they were right by refusing to educate *[the Negro]*?" "No," he said. "We must interest ourselves in them. They have been our servants and our friends; they have stood by us in our sorest trials and are not responsible for our disasters. Prejudice must give way. There is no disgrace in teaching the negro. [sic] *[I]* would rejoice to see it; and would take by the hand the young man who would engage in this work."[495]

The hotly debated amendment to promote establishing Sabbath Schools passed, but conversation about this subject did not, and many conventions after this one rehashed the same discussion.

The Pattern Repeats

Clearly, *OURstory* was influenced by the religious practices the slaves observed and the policies and philosophies of the religious conventions of churches. One sees a similar pattern to the white **Felders** among our black ancestors as boys became men – at least three ministers came from this

---

492 Paxton, "History of Baptists of Louisiana."

493 Paxton, "History of Baptists of Louisiana."

494 Paxton, "History of Baptists of Louisiana."

495 Paxton, "History of Baptists of Louisiana."

plantation background who were once **FELDER** slaves: **REV. SONA FELDER**, **REV. HENRY FELDER**, and **REV. JAMES WASHINGTON**. **REV. JAMES WASHINGTON's** grandmother was "owned" by Rev. Henry Sandel, father-in-law to **John Felder**. **JAMES'** half-sister, **SARAH FELDER** – **JOSEPH's** mother – was "owned" by **Rev. Charles Felder's** son, **Dr. Charles F. Felder**. **JOSEPH**, likely the slave convert to Christianity at Shady Grove Baptist Church in Summit in 1859, was most likely "owned" by **Levi Felder**, **John Felder's** son. **JOSEPH's** older brother, **HENRY**, became a minister in Texas in the same county as **Gabriel Felder's** massive land and slave holdings. **JOSEPH's** son, **SONA**, embraced life as an African Methodist Episcopal (A.M.E.) minister and Presiding Elder. **JOSEPH's** great-grandson, **TYREE FELDER**, A.M.E. by birth, Baptist by letter, Sunday School teacher, usher, and choir member, became "Man of the Year" multiple times at Gillfield Baptist Church in Petersburg, Virginia. **JOSEPH's** great-great-grand-nephew, **TYREE BEARDEN**, is currently associate pastor and elder of The R.O.C.K., a church in Houston, Texas, and **JOSEPH's** great-great-great-grand-nephew, **N'GAI WASHINGTON**, Reggae/hip hop artist, founded Lone Soul Jah in Miramar, Florida, which is dedicated to negating the ill effects of rap lyrics on the spiritual journey of the younger generation.[496]

Daddy with Rev. Powell and me

There was also an influence on the women in the family. Among **JOSEPH's** descendants was his daughter-in-law, **WILDA**, A.M.E. North Mississippi Conference Branch President and first lady of Bethel A.M.E. Church, Mound Bayou. **JOSEPH's** granddaughter, **BEATRICE FELDER**, was music director for the State of Mississippi A.M.E. Conference and organist at Bethel A.M.E. Church, Mound Bayou; and his granddaughter, **KORRINE TYREE FELDER JACKSON**, became Sunday School superintendent and pianist at her church, St. Paul's Episcopal, in Des Moines, Iowa. **JOSEPH's** great-granddaughter, **CHIQUITA FELDER BEARDEN**, was pianist, organist, usher, and assistant church secretary at Pilgrim Rest Baptist Church in Memphis, Tennessee. Certainly, in our **FELDER** family, there were, are, and will be, many more ministers and ministries.

Freedom was the Answer to Slavery. For Us.

> *You intended to harm me, but God intended it for good to accomplish what is now being done, the saving of many lives. Genesis 50:20, KJV*

Despite the surreptitious use of religion to advance slavery, and the insincerity of many of the preachers' messages about faith, slaves converted to Christianity in overwhelming numbers when this

---

[496] "Lone Soul Jah" – New Genre Entertainment Group.

choice became available. Singing uplifted their souls. Praying clarified desire and intent. Sermons provided direction and promised hope. Praise confirmed a higher being. Forgiveness cleared the way for peaceful coexistence with former enemies.

The answer to slavery was always freedom. Freedom especially of the mind, which enabled freedom of everything else – of religion, of education, of opportunity, and of choice. The **FELDER** slaves survived their horrendous individual and collective life circumstances of servitude and bondage because they could imagine freedom in their minds. Fortunately, the underlying meaning of servitude as interpreted by white "masters" took on a different meaning to freedmen as they established new lives post-slavery; at least in **JOSEPH FELDER's** lineage. Servitude meant contributing service by choice in significant ways in the community in which one lived. It did not mean perpetual service by force to enrich the coffers of their previous white "owners."

Forgiveness, above all, resonated deeply in African Americans' consciousness. "Father, forgive them, for they know not what they do," lamented Jesus as he took his last breath on the cross. *[Uhm, I wonder if this Luke 23:34 verse was ever used in* **Felder's** *sermons! I wonder, did the similitude really escape these Southern preachers?]* Coretta Scott King (Baptist) and Nelson Mandela (Methodist) are two of the best examples of how forgiveness can change not just men's hearts, but the very soul of nations. Mrs. King once remarked, "As one whose husband and mother-in-law have died the victims of murder and assassination, I stand firmly and unequivocally opposed to the death penalty. …An evil deed is not redeemed by an evil deed of retaliation."[497] In perhaps the most powerful illustration of spiritual enlightenment and application of this essential Christian value, our African brother, Nelson Mandela, eloquently shared in his autobiography, *Long Walk to Freedom*, how forgiveness navigated each of his steps away from bondage – from 27 years of unjustified imprisonment: "As I walked out the door toward the gate that would lead to my freedom, I knew if I didn't leave my bitterness and hatred behind, I'd still be in prison."[498]

Thomas Anderson

Freedom was the answer. *To forgive. Freedom!*

Although education was available in this country, and abroad for those of means, more than 20%[499] of white southerners were illiterate in the years leading up to the Civil War and immediately afterwards. As such, the text of the *Bible* was interpreted by ministers of the Gospel – often men who had no scholarly education in religion, themselves, but who had only contributed money or land to build a church, or who had an interest in the salvation of other's souls and took it upon themselves to share the good news of the Gospel as best they could. Church was a social event and an expectation for white Americans. It was the reason that many

---

497 "Brainy Quote, Coretta Scott King Quotes," 2, accessed April 20, 2018, https://www.brainyquote.com/authors/coretta_scott_king.

498 "Fifty Inspirational Mandela Quotes That Will Change Your Life," accessed April 20, 2018, http://awakenthegreatnesswithin. com/50-inspirational-nelson-mandela-quotes-that-will-change-your-life/.

499 www.digitalhistory.uh.edu/disp_textbook2014 (accessed November 2014); website moved.

Europeans purportedly came to the New World – to have the opportunity to worship as they believed and to follow the religion of their choice.

And yet, slaves had no choice. Most, in fact, were not invited or otherwise allowed to join their "master's" churches. Most could not read the *Bible* and interpret it for themselves. By the 1800s, most were subjected to the various "black codes" that made worship, education, families, marriage, and property ownership illegal, and thus, impossible. Most were exposed to the Southern interpretation that heaven was the reward for "being a good and faithful servant," which translated in white "masters'" language to mean "good and faithful slave," with eternal obligations to the white power structure and family. It is generally noted by historians, however, that "slaves readily saw through [*this*] white gospel [*interpretation*]," and they were able to find something "in the Christian message that was comforting and communal and that offered a type of release from their oppressive bonds."[500] Certainly the coded messages of the Negro spirituals, sung in the fields, and hummed in the big houses, revealed this intuitive understanding.

In My Father's House are Many Mansions[501]

Bethel A.M.E. Church, Friars Point

Booker T. Washington, principal of Tuskegee Normal and Industrial Institute (now Tuskegee University), was of the opinion shortly after slavery that "[*t*]he need of the little country Negro churches in the South is not yet so much preachers who are trained in theological doctrines as men of wholesome moral and industrial life who will teach the people of their churches not only religion but also practical daily life."[502] He found such a man in **THOMAS ANDERSON** (father of **IRENE ANDERSON** – maternal grandmother of the **FELDER** children). Booker T. would drive through the Tuskegee community and see **THOMAS** hard at work in his field on his farm a few miles down the country road from the emerging school. Impressed by **THOMAS'** industriousness and his application on his farm of the principles of agricultural economics being taught by George Washington Carver, Booker T. also was aware that **THOMAS** was a model theology student at Tuskegee, as well. Booker T. asked his student to organize the first chapel for Tuskegee Industrial Institute. In a brush arbor, under an oak tree, **THOMAS** became the founding pastor[503] of Washington Chapel A.M.E., which continues today to hold services in Tuskegee.

Freedom was the answer. To be a visionary. Freedom!

As black churches were founded throughout the South, the lessons and examples gleaned from the *Bible* and the services rendered by the church began to sustain not just black individuals, but the

---

500 Randall M. Miller and John David Smith, editors, *Dictionary of Afro American Slavery* (New York: Greenwood Press, 1988), 417.

501 John 14:2, *Holy Bible*, KJV.

502 Booker T. Washington, *Booker T. Washington Rediscovered*, Michael Scott Biezer and Mary Beth Gasman, editors (Baltimore: Johns Hopkins University Press, 2012), 133.

503 Interview with Essie Anderson Wallace, daughter of Rev. Thomas Anderson, October 9, 2005. See also "Washington Chapel Observes its Celebration of Centennial," The Tuskegee *News*, July 4, 1996, 8.

black community as a whole as it struggled to find its bearings in a country that did not know exactly what to do with its people. Many houses of worship were built – proliferating in black rural and urban areas alike, sometimes mere yards apart from each other. They provided solace for worship and a place for schooling. For example, in the community of Crystal Springs, Mississippi, with a post-slavery predominantly black population, more than 20 churches were built in less than a seven-mile radius. Some quite tiny structures like Bethel A.M.E. Church, erected in the little river town of Friars Point, Mississippi, and once pastored by, and located in, the district charge of Presiding Elder **S. P. FELDER**, housed at inception not only the church but also a school.

Freedom was the answer. *To worship; to study; to learn. Freedom!*

But, the phrase, "in my father's house," often became synonymous in the black community with the church building itself. Borne of the desire to elevate worship from the fields to the sanctuaries, from the white "masters'" churches to their own, sparsely-populated rural communities of African Americans built tiny structures for their families and friends to come together to praise God for the many blessings of freedom. Symbols of religion (the cross, the Bible, the pulpit, the offering plates and communion cups) were often reserved for touching only by the holiest of the congregation (the minister, the deacons, the deaconesses). Urban areas emerged as blacks trekked off the plantations to the cities for better economic opportunities. Thousands can now worship together in contemporary, mammoth, literal mansions, like the 191,000 square foot sanctuary of the Potter's House, pastored by Rev. T. D. Jakes in Dallas, Texas, or the 1,000,000 square foot World Changers Church, pastored by Rev. Creflo Dollar in Norcross, Georgia. These churches accommodate 7,600 and 8,500, respectively, in their Sunday morning worship services and shepherd congregations in excess of 30,000 each once their parishioners from their satellite campuses around the country are counted.

Freedom was the answer. *To build the physical structure in which to house one's religion. Freedom. To exceed white men's expectations of possibilities. Freedom!*

In between the construction of brush arbors, tiny churches like Bethel A.M.E. Church in Friar's Point, Mississippi, and the mammoth facility in Norcross, Georgia, African Americans were gaining a deeper theological understanding, and the purposes of religion were expanding. A more critical path that the development of black churches took involved navigating the *figurative mansions* of the church – the mechanics of political strategy, literacy, and economic empowerment of an entire race of people denied every basic tenet of this country's democracy. The church became the cornerstone of the black community post-slavery. It was respectable and an expectation to belong to a church, and very few African Americans went without formally associating

Literacy

with a church and professing a belief in a superior being – essentially the Almighty God of the Christian religion to which they had been exposed on American soil. The church became the chief social organization – the glue, if you will – which exercised "influence over social relations, setting up certain regulations for behavior, passing judgments which represent[ed] community opinion, censuring and penalizing improper conduct by expulsion."[504] Just like the **Felder** churches in Pike and Amite counties in Mississippi. Just like **REV. JAMES WASHINGTON's** Mount Flowery Baptist Church in Magnolia. Just like Gillfield Baptist Church in Petersburg, Virginia.

Freedom was the answer. To define life, liberty, happiness, and a moral compass within the context of one's God. Freedom!

Style, Form and Substance

The black church quickly grew to provide to the freed black community somewhat of a parallel religious experience to that which white masters demonstrated at the camp meetings of old; many of the customs and traditions of the black church being modeled after what slaves had seen on the plantations and in the towns where church buildings were constructed, Sunday morning services were held, and funerals were officiated. And while modeling, perhaps, after white camp meetings where, *yes*, white folk also screamed and shouted when the spirit moved them, African Americans developed a unique style all their own, in the manner of preacher and congregation relating during worship, drawing on their instinctive African ancestral lineage.

Illustrative of this point, at Topisaw Campground (**Felder's Campground**) in Pike County, **Uncle Gabriel Felder** was said to have told his wife, "Shout, Fannie, shout, and I'll buy you a white jacket with a split tail,"[505] apparently the fashion statement of the day. In Tuskegee, Alabama, the pastor at Damascus Baptist Church requested, "I think somebody oughta get 'quainted wid Jesus. We gonna sing while the doors of the church be open… . Someone wid de spirit please come ter the altar and pray." Charles Johnson then writes of the "sudden sharp groans of spiritual torture, then screams of exultation. Three or four persons are expressing themselves with shouts accompanied by a variety of physical demonstrations, while most of the audience responds in low accents – referenced as "helpin' out the preacher."[506]

Freedom was the answer. To create style and form of expression.

Coming to terms with the post-slavery responsibilities of building the church and determining how the church would guide the community, the Damascus Baptist Church service provides an example of Booker T. Washington's philosophy on the need for ministers to provide practical social and moral guidance to its congregants. At the same time, however, this sociological "observation" by Charles Johnson, unfortunately sadly demonstrates a stereotypical white Southerner's perception *[hopefully of old]* that "… the Negro achieves a natural vigor of speech that few writers obtain. With a severely limited vocabulary and a child-like innocence of grammatical niceties, he resourcefully gathers all

---

504 Charles S. Johnson, *Shadow of the Plantation: A Classic Study of Rural Negro Life* (Chicago: University of Chicago Press, 1934), 150.

505 *Source Material for Mississippi History – Pike County*, Volume LVII, Part I, Chapter VI, "Ante-bellum Days" (Jackson, Mississippi: MDAH), 151.

506 Johnson, *Shadow of the Plantation*, 160.

the color of a scene and in simple words drives home his meaning with a sledge-hammer force."[507] Johnson observed the pastor preaching about behavior:

> My friends, we done sung the songs of Zion; done broke ter you the bread of life; done opened ter you de doors of de church; and done prayed these 'firmed prayers; and still there's more. You know I thinks 'bout the people in the community; how can you dance when there's a starvin' family over there? When you been dancing all Saturday night you ain't a fit subject fer the Lord. You gotta cut the dancing out.... You say you is a Christian; if you is a Christian you better show some signs. If you don't quit you're on the road to hell; talkin' 'bout you 'blige ter dance and you can't help it. The old folks talking 'bout chillen young gotta have some fun, but they just stumbling blocks in their way.... Now next month when the convention meets in Birmingham, I wants you sisters and brothers ter git around and git your pastor a seersucker suit, some socks, and some shirts. And I need shoes too. I gotta go down there and represent you, and I wnta do hit right.[508]

This excerpt is included because, in part, it provides levity to this all-serious discussion, and in part because it elucidates one of Booker T. Washington's rudimentary beliefs about a crucial need in the black community.

Freedom was the answer. *To ignite the spirit. To expect churches to guide the community's morality. Freedom!*

Service, not Servitude, Moral Reconstruction and Knowledge

Frederick Douglass, former slave who spoke and wrote with eloquence about slavery and its aftermath, had this to say in 1875 about the influence of religion on the freed slave and what he saw as the next critical evolutionary phase of freedom needed to ensure continued progress of the race in general. In contrast to the religion that taught slave to look forward to their heavenly home, Douglass suggested:

> What the emancipated man wants now is knowledge. To get this he needs money and land, something that will give him time to think and improve his mind. His poverty and destitution are his greatest obstacles to progress. Teach him how to make the best of this world, how to be useful to himself, his family, to the community and to the world of mankind. Most of our colored preachers represent the old religion borrowed from their masters, and are hardly fit for the new work of moral reconstruction needed in the South. The new times require new men and new ideas.[509]

Freedom was the answer. *To voice dissenting opinions about the needs of the newly-freed slave. Freedom!*

Rev. Walter Brooks, D. D., born a slave in Richmond, Virginia, August 30, 1851, to parents belonging to different "masters," was ultimately united with his mother and father in slavery when,

---

507 Professor Brown, *Negro Folkways*, reproduced from the Collection of Manuscript Division, Library of Congress.

508 Johnson, *Shadow of the Plantation*, 161.

509 *The American Missionary*, vol. 19, August 1875, 171.

through the aid of a white man, his father was able to purchase his mother and two of his siblings. *[One good example of a black slaveowner!]* His experience as a highly educated minister, who later taught in Petersburg and at Union Theological Seminary, led him to this conclusion about the state of religion in the black church in the early 1900s, about 50 years after slavery ended:

> It is certain that the Negro Christian is displaying commendable zeal in erecting spacious houses of worship; in acquiring school property; in giving the Gospel to the heathen in Africa, and in other parts of the world; in raising funds for the cause of education, and in providing himself with a religious literature of his own making. In the quality of his religion, we dare say, there is room for improvement. But the changes mostly needed for his highest good are intellectual, material, social, commercial and political in nature, rather than religious. The Negro Christian is as a rule as good as he knows how to be. He often errs, not knowing the scripture. He sometimes plunges headlong into the ditch of shame, because his spiritual adviser and instructor is a "blind leader of the blind." Christian schools, however, are giving us better leaders every year, and the time is hastening when the Negro Christian of America shall be respected and loved because of his intelligence, his Christian piety, his zeal for God's cause, his manly bearing, his general worth as a moral and material contributor to the well-being, both of the State and of the country which claim him as a citizen, and because of his excellent spirit and gentlemanly deportment.[510]

Freedom was the answer. *To mature as Christian educators. To imagine change. Freedom!*

Rev. Brooks' views generally reflected the philosophy of the A.M.E. Church, borne of the Methodist *General Rules or Discipline*, promulgated by Richard Allen, founder. Rev. Allen believed that elevation of the black race through religion, education, land ownership, general deportment, manner, and dress would change the broad sentiment in the country among whites and lead the race to a position of respect and humaneness. Allen, born a slave, but through industry and thrift purchased his freedom, concentrated his founding efforts on describing appropriate Christian ethical behavior, which he adopted from the white Methodist Church to which he had earlier belonged. By "prohibiting swearing, fighting, drinking, Sabbath breaking, gossiping, failing to pay debts, attending the theater, and engaging in the slave trade,"[511] Allen believed fervently that white America would come to embrace black America if they could see, *with their own eyes*, that blacks were not uncultured, ignorant, shiftless, lazy, slovenly heathens, but were instead ordered and disciplined, neat, respectable men and women who desired only to be treated

Richard Allen

---

510 Rev. Walter H. Brooks, D.D., "The Negro as a Christian," in *Multum in Parvo: an authenticated history of progressive Negroes in pleasing graphic and biographic style*, compiled by I. W. Crawford and P. H. Thompson (Jackson, Mississippi: self-published, 1912), 64.

511 Clarence Walker, "Rock in a Weary Land: The African Methodist Episcopal Church during the Civil War and Reconstruction," (PhD dissertation, Louisiana State University, Baton Rouge, 1982), 5.

as equals under the law.[512] Little did he realize that the hatred he could see *with his own eyes*, heaped upon the black race by white America, had nothing to do with these observable personal character traits that any black man could change if he chose, but instead were deeply ingrained white men's beliefs that the color of the black man's skin – an observable that he could not change – made him intellectually and morally inferior, deserving of his depressed economic, political, and educational status in America, which he – the white man – created and sustained. Intentionally.

Unfortunately, this was not just a Southern attitude. Whites in the North, while perhaps generally supporting abolition, did not believe blacks to be "equal" to them either.[513] The A.M.E. Church, from the day of its formal inception on April 9, 1816, and throughout its history, promoted self-improvement, property ownership, thriftiness, employment, ethical behavior, business ownership, civic pride, Christian worship, and any other means of "elevating the race," including education *by black teachers* to address the psychological damage done by slavery. The church banned slave-owners from membership, and although from its beginning it was open to white members, it banned whites from the pulpit.

Freedom was the answer. *Of self-education. Freedom. From calculated white Biblical interpretations of freedom for black people. Freedom. From the psychology of the likes of Willie Lynch, whose methods of slave breaking (How to Make a Slave) are simply too horrendous to print here. Freedom!*

"Onward Christian Soldiers, Marching as to War" [514]

The organizational hierarchy that Richard Allen developed in the A.M.E. Church mimicked that of the white Methodist church he worshipped in prior to walking out one Sunday morning following a racist experience in the church he attended in Philadelphia. The A.M.E. General Conference and the multiple regional and state conferences Richard Allen conceptualized, overseen by bishops and presiding elders who supervised the districts of itinerant and stationary preachers, went to work immediately to establish what would become one of the greatest denominations of Christian faith for African Americans. And while the Church's structure evolved somewhat over time (for example removing the position of presiding elder at one point prior to the Civil War but then restoring it), the strength of the Church's message – despite some who would argue that it was "unrealistic" and "naïve" or "misplaced"[515] to believe that white America would be influenced by a productive black society – essentially remained consistent and definitely had, and continues to have, its place in the history of racial healing in America. Obviously, Rev. Allen's dream of using the church to destroy American racism and prejudice never materialized. Nevertheless, this is the denomination that caught the attention of **SONA FELDER**, who at a very young age, sought the Lord's guidance in his life and heeded the call to become a Christian servant.

---

512 For more detail on Allen's philosophy, see Walker, Rock in a Weary Land, 15-45.

513 Walker, "Rock in a Weary Land," 35.

514 Written in England in 1865 by Sabine Baring-Gould but first published in America by the Methodist Episcopal Book Room. Widely used in black Baptist churches of our youth.

515 See discussion on pages 45 and 141 in Walker, "Rock in a Weary Land."

Freedom was the answer. *To dream a century before Martin Luther King, Jr., that one day blacks would be respected for the content of their character and not despised because of the color of their skin. Freedom!*

I. T. Montgomery

Early churches sprang up in communities by the efforts of many. There were the families in the area with land who typically offered to give a portion of their property on which an edifice could be constructed, as did **John Felder** in Pike County at **Felder's Campground**. Neighbors then gathered together and decided which of them would minister to their spiritual needs. Sometimes, however, a man would ride horse-back or walk miles, knocking on doors in a recently settled community to determine if there was an interest in establishing religious services. At other times, someone from a denomination was appointed to spread the Gospel into unsaved parts of the countryside. These itinerant preachers, also known as circuit riders, would often establish churches in more than one community, using either the open space shielded in the summers by the shade of the trees (a brush arbor, if intentionally designed) or the comfort of someone's home or barn, until a church structure and formal, weekly prayer meetings, or more interspersed but more lengthy camp meetings, were arranged. **Reverends Albert G. Felder** and **Charles Felder** were such itinerant preachers early on in their careers in Mississippi, traveling across state lines into Louisiana to teach and preach. **REV. S. P. FELDER**, likewise, as the appointed initiator of the A.M.E. religion in the Gulf region – in Bay St. Louis, Jordan River, Logtown, and Pearlington, Mississippi – would have rotated these towns on his schedule, traveling either on foot or on horseback and sleeping in the homes of black freedmen along the way, ministering the Gospel.

The values of the A.M.E. Church undergirded the establishment of the Mound Bayou, Mississippi, community. Isaiah T. Montgomery, founder of Mound Bayou, and a founding member of the first church in the town – Bethel A.M.E. Church – realized that the eyes of the nation would be on his town, waiting for failure. As such, it is said that Isaiah and his cousin, Benjamin Green, who later became the town's mayor, hand-picked all of the early settlers who joined the community. The personal selection of future residents continued for many years. As is a standard organizational practice in the A.M.E. discipline, preachers, exhorters, and presiding elders were transferred from one community to the next. In less than 10 years, **SONA** went from an initial assignment in the economically progressive Bay St. Louis, Pearlington, and Logtown communities in Mississippi's most southeastern county (Hancock), to a locale in one of the most rural and poverty-stricken counties (Coahoma) in the northwestern part of the state. But, his ability to draw souls to the church so garnered the attention of the founders of Mound Bayou that, somewhere around 1912, **SONA** and his family were hand-picked by Charles Banks, the president of the Bank of Mound Bayou, to live in this historic community.

Soon after its founding, the town boasted a population of 600 where "*[t]he entire church-going population worshipped together while they commonly contributed to the construction of edifices to house their independent faiths. ... So strong was the sense of community and sharing that there was no need for a jail because there was no crime.*"[516] In the immediately ensuing years of its founding, six churches were constructed in this all-black town that was less than one square mile wide. **REV. S. P. FELDER** contributed significantly for more than 30 years to the cohesion that bound these townspeople into the collective pursuit of God's best.

Freedom was the answer. To be. To become. To realize one's dreams. To define the worship experience. To expand the role of the church. Freedom!

THE LEGACY: RELIGION

Got "Up from Slavery,"[517] He Did!

As an illiterate freedman, **SONA** joined the A.M.E. Church in 1878 on probation (one year before he started night school), was licensed as an exhorter in March 1885 at the age of 22 and became licensed as a preacher in September of that same year. An exhorter was a gifted motivational speaker, persuader and guide for those tempted with sin. Rev. Charles Stanley (pastor, First Baptist Church, Atlanta, Georgia) describes exhorters as people-oriented, discipleship-oriented, growth and maturity-oriented encouragers of spiritual and personal growth in others and promoters of the acceptance of Jesus Christ and the Holy Spirit as the model for application of Christianity in one's life.[518] **S. P. FELDER** was such a man.

Rev. Dr. Sona Felder

SONA FELDER studied theology under the tutelage of T. A. (or J. A.) Wilson. Professor James Wilson served as the principal of the school at Bethel A.M.E. Church in Mound Bayou; perhaps this was his tutor, because years later, **REV. FELDER** would be appointed pastor at Bethel in Mound Bayou. Or perhaps, and more likely, **SONA** was converted under the study of Rev. T. A. Wilson of the Cross Roads A.M.E. Church (now Greater Turner A.M.E. Church) in Greensburg, Louisiana. Obviously very brilliant and extremely well-respected, he quickly rose through the A.M.E. ranks.

In 1888, Bishop R. R. Disney ordained 25-year-old **SONA** a deacon,[519] and at the tender age of 36, on December 22, 1899, **SONA FELDER** became an Elder, appointed to this post also by

---

516 Jean E. Dawson, "Mound Bayou," *Our Heritage*, vol.1, no. 3 (Winter, 1995), 24.

517 *Up from Slavery* is the title of Booker T. Washington's autobiography.

518 Rev. Charles Stanley, "The Gift of Exhortation," accessed October 10, 2013, www.intouch.org/you/article-archive/content/topic/the_gift_of_exhortation_article#.U7MHhr3D-9A.

519 Richard Wright and J. R. Hawkins, *Centennial Encyclopaedia of the African Methodist Episcopal Church*, (Philadelphia: no publisher identified, 1916), 89.

Bishop Disney, to represent Mississippi's Eighth District in the A.M.E. Church. That same year, he was appointed Presiding Elder to the Friars Point District by Bishop William Derrick. In his first year as Presiding Elder, he became "Dollar Money King" of the Eighth Episcopal District, making him "especially prominent" in the eyes of the church leadership.[520] His ascendency to leadership in the church reflected his values of commitment to task, focus, vision, and service to mankind – particularly to the African American. His own personal life experiences imbued in him a faith in that power higher than any conceived by government or man.

He was considered one of the organizing "pioneer trail blazers" of the Masonic Order, joining the T. W. Stringer Grand Lodge, which was the first Black Prince Hall Masonry in Mississippi.[521] He associated with the other Republican leadership of the A.M.E. Church, as "one of Mississippi's greatest preachers"[522]... converting more than a thousand souls by his sermons,[523] and earning him a reputation of being "one of the most progressive ministers of the State."[524] When the A.M.E. Church found itself financially strapped in the midst of The Great Depression, **REV. FELDER's** skills as an organization man were called upon. In 1933, he was one of the 14 members of the national A.M.E. General Board who wrestled with restoring the organization to solvency after the impact of The Great Depression of 1928-32, which severely stifled church members' ability to meet even the expected $1.00 annual contribution to the Church. The net effect was a staggering $42,308 deficit, necessitating the decision to cut the salaries of all general officers of the A.M.E. Church by fifty percent. At that conference, **SONA** was elected as one of the five members of the National Executive Committee and one of eight members of the National Committee on Organization.[525]

He apparently knew how to energize a congregation, the skill to which Charles Johnson alluded in his study of Damascus Church in Tuskegee. He would "stomp his feet, and the sisters would be shouting," according to Mound Bayou resident, Rev. Woodley, A.M.E. Presiding Elder who was proud to share that he was "credit*[ed]* by the A.M.E. Church as being the closest one to serve as high as **DR. FELDER**." He very proudly stated, "They *[the A.M.E. Church leadership]* said I am the only one who really walked in his footsteps. He was outstanding! Other Presiding Elders came after him, but none rose as high as he did. He ran for Bishop and he was respected." Rev. Woodley continued, "He would talk about slavery and say that the only way to be free and come from under the rawhide would be to put trust in God: 'Pray that our children would be free.'" Sometimes after a church business meeting, according to Rev. Woodley, he would start lecturing about slavery and how to be free.[526] While Rev. Woodley was a young man when **SONA** was active in Mound Bayou, he recalled his parents and other adults in the community praising **REV. FELDER** and telling stories about his ministry and style.

---

520 R. A. Adams, *Cyclopedia of African Methodism in Mississippi*, (Natchez: no publisher identified, 1902), 85.

521 *Bethel AME Church Anniversary Celebration* (1864-2014), Vicksburg, Mississippi, August 16, 2014, 1.

522 J. J. Morant, *Mississippi Minister*, 1st edition, (New York: Vantage Press, 1958), 63.

523 Wright and Hawkins, *Centennial Encyclopaedia*, 89.

524 Adams, *Cyclopedia of African Methodism*, 84.

525 "AME's Carry On Tho *[sic]* Deficit is $42,308," Baltimore *Afro American*, April 29, 1933.

526 Telephone interview with Presiding Elder Woodley, Mound Bayou, Mississippi, Sunday, October 24, 2004.

From the plantation to the pew to the pulpit, **SONA FELDER** left a legacy of faith and Christian service that emerged clearly as one of the strong guiding forces responsible for sustaining the A.M.E. Church worldwide when the economy nosedived during The Great Depression,[527] and when African American Mississippians needed leadership during the uncivil years of race relations post-Reconstruction, he raised his voice to mobilize community strength for freedom and justice. He was a distinguished member of the A.M.E. Church, often called upon to deliver "special addresses,"[528] and to provide leadership at meetings of state, regional, and national committees, boards, and conferences he attended.

As a young man in Christ, **SONA** made an indelible impression on the senior members of the A.M.E. Conference. He was extremely well respected, and various national black newspapers and A.M.E. publications extolled his contributions and his skills. Such praise is atypical amongst ministers, but it was quite typical to read the following types of comments about him, recorded in 1906 in the Baltimore *Afro American Ledger*, a national weekly newspaper of the early and mid-1900s:

> The General Conference will meet in Norfolk, and already I have my stopping place… I would not be out of order if I should mention some of the men who make up the conference, but then there are so many of them I will not do so. **REV. S. P. FELDER** is among the young men and he is coming to the front. I could just sit down and tell you about him for the next hour or more, but then that would not do.[529] (J. O. Midnight)

Or, nine years later –

> As it is now, Rev. J. J. Morant is a candidate for the episcopacy, and there is **REV. S. P. FELDER** for the same position, and it will not be possible for **FELDER** to make it and Morant, too… so the delegates will meet and decide … I do not know who it will be as both are popular men… .Coming back to the conference, I saw them elect all the delegates on one ballot, and they have 12 in this conference. **REV. S. P. FELDER** was placed at the head of his delegation. He was picked out from the rest, before they took a ballot, a motion passed authorizing the secretary to cast the unanimous vote for him for the position, and this was done. They treated Rev. Dr. H. M. Pillow in the same manner, but this **FELDER** is the choice of his conference for the episcopacy, and he may get through.[530]

But, he did not. He ran twice for Bishop; in 1920 and 1932. Although not elected Bishop, **REV. DR. S. P. FELDER** was always a man on whom the community, the church, the schools, and his family could depend. **SONA** served for many years on the Board of Finances of the A.M.E. General Conference, even representing Mississippi in 1909 as one of the members of the A.M.E. Conference Extension Board who, along with members of the A.M.E. Financial Board, visited the White House

---

527 Norfolk *Journal and Guide*, April 29, 1933, 1.

528 For example, Sona Felder is identified as a lead speaker in "Mississippi AME's End 44th Conference," *The Chicago Defender*, national edition, December 12, 1936, 23; in *The Chicago Defender*, September 18, 1937, 6; and *Pittsburgh Courier*, November 20, 1937, 19.

529 "Midnight's Musings," Baltimore Afro-American Ledger, accessed June 28, 2016, https://newspaperarchive.com/baltimore-afro-american-ledger-feb-03-1906-p-5/.

530 "The Colonel in Mississippi," Baltimore Afro-American Ledger, accessed June 28, 2016, https://newspaperarchive.com/baltimore-afro-american-ledger-dec-18-1915-p-6/.

at the invitation of President Taft. But he was not perfect. Disappointingly, he served on the church court panel of three that ruled in judgement of Bishop R. A. Grant, bishop of the A.M.E. Alabama churches, charged with impregnating the young teenage daughter of a rural Alabama preacher. She was allowed to keep and raise their baby with a $2000 allotment from the Bishop. He was allowed to keep his freedom and his position in the church, saving the church from "embarrassment."[531] The ministers, including **SONA**, had an opportunity to make a strong statement about morality, but did not.

Bishop Greene, presiding at the November 10, 1935, North Mississippi Conference, recognizing **SONA's** sustained work in the church stated, "I don't know a more dearly beloved brother than that of **BROTHER S. P. FELDER**."[532] At that conference, W. M. E. Barnes, Dr. E. Pullet, Dr. S. S. Stevens, Dr. R. A. Scott, Dr. C. G. Scrivens, Dr. D. H. Butler, Dr. P. W. Hair, and Dr. J. J. Morant all praised his work as well, and he was "elected *[Presiding Elder]* by acclamation" *[an enthusiastic, approving voice vote without taking a count]* following at least two lengthy prefaced motions.[533] He received the first doctorate in the **FELDER** family – an honorary doctorate from Campbell College.

Always at his side, supporting his ministry and engaged in her own, was his second wife, to whom he was married for forty-six years, **WILDA JANE ELLIS FELDER**. Aside from knowing that she was a very attractive woman who served in at least one leadership position, president at one point in the Women's Foreign Home Missions of the A.M.E. Church, and that she, too, was a writer, publishing a poem in May 1924 in the *Voice of Missions*, the communique of the W. H. and F. Missionary Society, little else has been found about her life. But her poem spoke of her "enemies" and her "friends," among whom she could not discern the difference. As an attractive, involved female leader, one could imagine jealousies and backstabbing amongst "friends," even those active in the church. **WILDA's** life was more affluent than most in Mound Bayou and the neighboring communities. For example, in 1930, theirs was the only home in their neighborhood that owned a radio, and the value of their home, $6000, exceeded the value of any nearby, the next highest property value being $2000.[534] **WILDA** took her last breath at 5 p.m. on April 7, 1937. At only 60 years old, she died of comatose malaria at her home in Mound Bayou.[535] Three years later, on February 1, 1940, **SONA** joined **WILDA** for an eternal rest, succumbing possibly to a stroke following a lengthy illness in Mound Bayou. **REV. DR. SONA FELDER**, my great-grandfather, left a legacy of faith and service.

Got Up Two Generations from Slavery, He Did!

The church in Mound Bayou established, monitored, and sustained the values of the community. So successful was this aspect of Mound Bayou that it received national attention at the highest possible level. President Theodore Roosevelt stopped his train for a three-minute address to the residents on October 21, 1907, and left what was probably the entire town gathered at the train station with this message:

---

531 "Bishop Grant Paying $2000 to 20 Yr.-Old Girl-Mother," accessed June 28, 2016, https://newspaperarchive.com/baltimore-afro-american-aug-22-1931-p-1/.

532 *AME Christian Recorder*, Thursday, November 28, 1935.

533 Minutes of the meeting of the North Mississippi Conference, Bishop S. L. Greene, presiding, November 10, 1935.

534 1930 U. S. Census.

535 Death Certificate, Wilda Jane Ellis Felder, Mississippi Department of Vital Statistics, Certificate #6302, April 19, 1937.

It is a great pleasure for me to see you and I have heard much of the prosperity of your town. I am glad that you have not permitted a saloon in the limits. The qualities that make a good citizen must come from within and not without. The law can give absolute equality of treatment, absolute justice before the law, to all men, big or little. It should treat them all alike. But after the law has done its part, it remains true that the fundamental factor of success in any man's life is his own character, his own capacity for work, for doing justice by his neighbors and in getting justice from them in return. I congratulate you from the evidence of prosperity that even tonight I can see from here and about what I have heard about you. There is no royal road to good citizenship or to success in life. I welcome all that I have learned about this town. I am glad to see the children here. I hope you will see them well brought up: that you will have good schooling for them and yet that you will remember that no school can entirely take the place of good home teaching. The father and mother have to do their duty to the children, for the teacher cannot wholly take their place. Teach them reading and writing but also teach them to do well industrially.[536]

The "character" of the man, of which Roosevelt spoke that night, was built by the church in this little community. Fortunately, the community's teachings strengthened the character of Mound Bayou residents, like Medgar Evers, to challenge Mississippi laws that, in fact, provided nothing near "equality of treatment" or "justice" to any black man or woman, "big or little," in the state or in the nation. *[What "law" was Roosevelt thinking about?!]*

Mound Bayou was a national model of religious, economic, and political success and sustainability until the economic crash of the Great Depression began to erode its economy. Irrespective, to understand the A.M.E. Church's influence on the town of Mound Bayou and the character of its people is to understand **TYREE PRESTON FELDER**, my father, illustrated by these few lines from a song he wrote around 1974, and later shared with me:

The Stranger

Music and lyrics by Tyree Felder

I prayed for the master; the e'er loving master; to comfort and console me.
He did not deceive me; His heart did receive me; At last my soul is set free.
Chorus:
Jesus! Jesus! I seem to hear. Jesus! Jesus! Rang loud and clear.
Jesus! Jesus! The open door; Take Jesus and be stranger no more!

---

536 "President's Advice to Negro Townspeople," *The Day* (New London, Connecticut, October 22, 1907), 1.

An ever-abiding faith in a personal God was a legacy left to us by our **FELDER** ancestors. That it has been passed down for generations, at least since **JOSEPH** joined church, is clearly evident. There is no doubt that Mound Bayou taught **DADDY**, and he did his best to model, strength of character imbued with unquestioned faith in God's authority and ability.

THE PATTERN: EDUCATION
"Blacks don't value education." Says who?

"There are many puzzling legacies of slavery. One very much unsubstantiated by any facts has been the perpetuation of the notion that African Americans 'don't value education.' Here the facts of the development of black churches and historically black colleges and universities (HBCUs) belie this myth."[537] And examples from all over the South of blacks seeking out education, learning to read, marveling at the ability to write their names for the first time, walking *hundreds* of miles, as did the two boys who walked from their homes in North Carolina – five hundred and fifty miles – to get to Tuskegee Normal and Industrial Institute[538] to have the opportunity to get an education – these, and innumerable other examples, belie this myth perpetuated by those intent on portraying a black race desirous of nothing and intellectually capable of even less.

Here is a perfect case-in-point of the perpetuation of an education myth, a "propaganda of history,"[539] as W.E.B. DuBois *[and I]* would call it, a clearly biased and antiblack, subjective, non-scholarly, data-void statement cloaked as a historical fact, written by S. G. Thigpen, reprinted in Robert G. Scharff's history of Hancock County, Mississippi:

> After the war, at the urging of northern 'do-gooders,' the Federal government sent people south to civilize "those savage southern people." The politicians also used the opportunity to brainwash and regiment the Negroes into the Republican party. This brainwashing was disguised as a program to educate the Negroes, so many of those who were sent to implement the program were school teachers. ...
>
> In spite of great efforts, the young Negroes would not go to these schools. They were definitely not hungering for knowledge, as the teachers had been led to believe. Neither did the older ones want to be uplifted. From the very first, the program was destined to fail.[540]

Clearly this was no historical analysis of truth; yet a multitude of books and journal articles still line shelves of libraries throughout the South that are written with this obviously malicious intent to generate and perpetuate a *his*tory that does not reflect accurately the condition of the black race either during or after slavery. Fortunately, it is very well documented that even before Emancipation, many slaves were being taught to read, and post-Emancipation data from those involved in the education

---

537 Felder, *Since Brown*, 4.

538 Washington, *Rediscovered*, 129.

539 Christopher Span, *From Cottonfield to Schoolhouse: African American Education in Mississippi*, 1862-1875, 2009, 8.

540 Robert G. Scharff, *Louisiana's Loss, Mississippi's Gain: A History of Hancock County, Mississippi, from the Stone Age to the Space Age*, 1999, 237.

Lessons

Booker T. Washington used education to "lift the veil of ignorance" from freedmen and steer them towards productive lives. (Gladys and me at Tuskegee University.)

of freedmen reveal that the development of schools and opportunities for education quickened exponentially as individuals and organizations whose hearts and minds supported freedom hastened to do what they could to respond to the ever growing demand for formal learning from the masses of ex-slaves – now freedmen and women.

On January 8, 1864, the *Liberator* newspaper printed a report received from a United Presbyterian Church missionary, Thomas Calahan, whose heart-wrenching description of the situation he encountered in Louisiana, brings me to tears. It is shared here in abbreviated form:

> You have no idea of the state of things here. Go out in any direction and you meet negroes on horses, negroes on mules, negroes with oxen, negroes by the wagon, cart and buggy load, negroes on foot, men, women and children; negroes in uniform, negroes in rags, negroes in frame houses, negroes living in tents, negroes living in rail pens covered with brush, and negroes living under brush piles without any rails, negroes living on the bare ground with the sky for their covering: all hopeful, almost all cheerful, every one pleading to be taught, willing to do anything for learning. They are never out of our rooms, and their cry is for "Books! Books!" and "When will school begin?" Negro women come and offer to cook and wash for us, if we will only teach them to read the Bible.... Every night hymns of praise to God and prayers for the Government that oppressed them so long, rise around on every side – prayers for the white teachers that have already come – prayers that God would send them more. These are our circumstances.[541]

---

541 Margaret E. Wagner, *The American Civil War: 365 Days*, "Thomas Calahan," (New York: Harry N. Adams and LOC), 6/9.

While this is an anecdotal report, lacking also in data and scholarly analysis, it at least was personally witnessed and experienced, lending substantially more credence to its veracity than the previous description borne of Thigpen's racist, hopeful musings. The Freedmen's Bureau records, and those of the religious organizations that came South to assist in educating the freedmen, do much to establish a believable account of the hunger and thirst for knowledge exhibited by the black race; and for those records, I am so grateful to history. They give a different and more accurate account – one that generates pride in knowing the extent to which black parents and children sought to lift the brutal mallet of intentionally-architected ignorance that slavery had forced upon them. *[How unfortunate that the white slaveholders could neither recognize nor anticipate the damage to the future competitiveness of the United States they were creating by mandating illiteracy of blacks in the South. The present state of education in the South is much the brainchild and legacy of the Southern slaveholders and their allies.]*

State of the State: Schooling in Louisiana

Until approximately 1830, the Code Noir *[Black Codes]* allowed, and even guaranteed, education of slaves in Louisiana – very basic instruction in reading and writing – as a part of their religious instruction,[542] and well before the war ended, in 1862, a philanthropist opened a free school for former slaves in New Orleans. One by one in the larger cities around the state, small schools and academies sprang up under the auspices of organizations and individuals. Immediately after the Emancipation Proclamation took effect, the enthusiasm and insistence of the freedmen to be educated even influenced the army to consider educational possibilities for them; many refusing to work without the assurance that schooling would be made available.[543] Under the State Reconstruction Constitution of 1864, all children between the ages of six and 18 were to be provided public, free education. But this is where policy and practice diverge, and we find Louisiana providing a classic example of how the implementation of policy is always dependent upon those on the ground at the local level charged with the details. State Superintendent, Robert M. Lusher, had no intent of educating freedmen's children, and he was quite specific about expressing his prejudices, issuing Circular No. 3 in June of 1866 instructing the local assessors to establish an education system that would address the needs of "every white child"… consistent with the "supremacy of the Caucasion *[sic]* race."[544] Lusher, it comes as no surprise, was born and raised in Charleston, South Carolina, and served in several critical posts during the Civil War for the Confederate State of Louisiana including Clerk of the Confederate States District Court as well as chief tax collector for the State.[545]

Thank goodness for the Federal Government and the troops stationed in the Southern states for twelve years (1865-77) following the war, which maintained some semblance of order and control in the five military districts the South had been divided into for the protection of the freedmen. In contrast to Superintendent Lusher's total disregard for the mandates of the Reconstruction Constitution,

---

542 Charles B. Roussève, *The Negro in Louisiana: Aspects of His History and His Literature*, (New Orleans: Xavier University Press, 1937), 42.

543 Barry A. Crouch, "Black Education in Civil War and Reconstruction Louisiana: George T. Ruby, the Army, and the Freedmen's Bureau," *Louisiana History*, vol. 38, no. 3 (Summer, 1997), 289-90.

544 Mohamed J. Shaik, "The Development of Public Education for Negroes in Louisiana" (PhD dissertation, University of Ottawa, 1964), 45.

545 Robert M. Lusher Papers, Inventory, MSS. 696,788, 1025, 1161, 1353, (revised, 2008), 4, accessed September 22, 2015, *www.lib.lsu.edu/special/findaid/0696m.pdf*.

U.S. RECONSTRUCTION'S FIVE MILITARY DISTRICTS

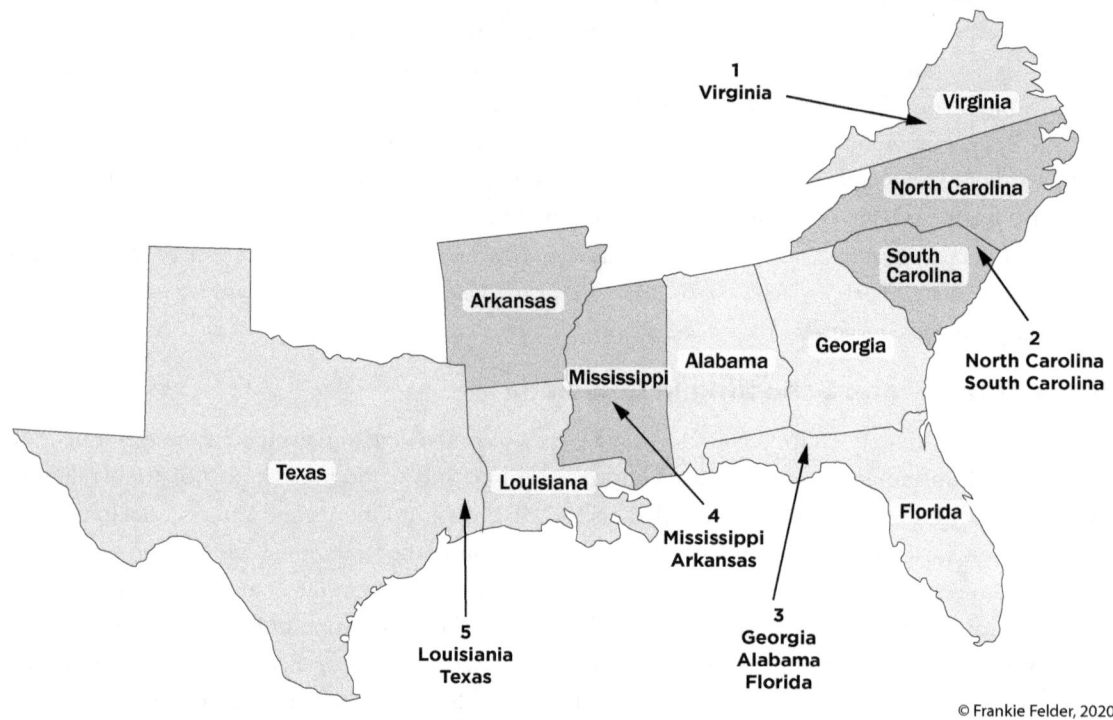

© Frankie Felder, 2020

At least 32 Freedmen's Bureau field offices were established in Mississippi, including these cities where our ancestors experienced life: Columbus, Friars Point, Greenville, Jackson, Magnolia, Natchez, and Port Gibson.

At least 15 Freedmen's Bureau field offices were established in Louisiana, including these cities where our ancestors experienced life: Baton Rouge, Bayou Sara, Clinton (Port Hudson), Hammond Station, Milliken Bend, New Orleans, and New Rhoads (Point Coupee).

General Nathaniel Banks, for example, issued General Order No. 38 on March 22, 1864. Pursuant to this order, a formal organization was created under which schools for freedmen expanded initially well beyond the few private academies that had emerged. The Order included the establishment of the Enrollment Commission, which in turn created seven schools in New Orleans in a two-month timeframe, as well as a Board of Education for the Gulf area.[546] The work of the army was commendable, noticed and praised all the way up the military chain, and into the hallowed halls of the U.S. Supreme Court, where Justice Salmon P. Chase acknowledged the progress. Even before the Freedmen's Bureau officially assumed responsibility for education of the freedmen in Louisiana, reports indicated more than 11,000 black children were attending schools taught by 162 teachers, with more than 5000 children daily in attendance.[547] However, that represented an average of 68 children per teacher! The North and the military engaged in a shared ownership of educating the freedmen,

---

546 Howard Ashley White, "Country Parish Schools," *Redeeming the People from Ignorance*, 294.

547 White, *County Parish Schools*, 294.

with the military promising to secure buildings and provide protection and transportation for teachers. The military expected the Northern societies to provide the teachers, the books, and the supplies. By July 1865, 19,000 former slaves were in attendance in more than 126 schools throughout the state of Louisiana – 4000 of whom were soldiers, and 1000 of whom were considered adult learners.[548]

For a brief while, this arrangement worked. But then, as evidenced by local activities in the communities, modern-day racism and practices of a dual educational system were beginning to take root. In Greensburg, several educational institutions existed in the early- to mid-1800s, including Daniel's Academy, the state-funded Greensburg Academy, and the Florida Classical Institute, but these institutions were not open to blacks. Mostly funded by tuition, the Floridian Academy, on October 10, 1857, placed a notice in the Greensburg *Imperial* imploring everyone to "pay your bills so we can keep [the] academy going."[549] In New Orleans, the public schools available for white kids were closed even to freeborn blacks, except in some unusual cases where "fairness of complexion"[550] provided an entrance ticket. The Army issued General Order No. 38 to assure that schools would be accessible, and so for a time, they were dotted all across the Louisiana landscape. In houses rented by the Bureau for educational purposes "nearly in every city and parish in the state," schools were established by the Freedmen's Bureau providing free tuition, books, and school supplies. The 51 public schools that had been established in Louisiana under the auspices of General Order No. 38 were augmented by approximately 60 Sunday Schools and 20 night schools,[551] which operated often in black churches. As an older teen, **SONA** began attending such a school at night, using the daylight hours to work to save money for the future.

Educational opportunities established by the Bureau did not last long, however, partly because of the enormous expense the Bureau was incurring. On December 24, 1865, just one year and nine months after the Bureau issued General Order No. 38 to establish schools, it sent out the order to "suspend [all] schools in operation effective January 31, 1866."[552] As a substitute for closing the schools, in large cities like New Orleans, Baton Rouge, and Shreveport, a tuition system was established, and patrons were required to pay $1 – $1.50 a month. This worked generally well. In the rural parishes, however, a system was established to take 5% of the pay of each laborer to pay teachers' salaries and to rent places to use as school buildings. This meant that white laborers, as well as freedmen with work contracts, were being taxed to pay for the education of the freed slaves, and the white laborers were extremely displeased. Resultantly, the regulations were soon modified to discontinue the tax for laborers who did not send their kids to school. Those who "were averse to schools" were released from the tax as well. Finally, the philosophy evolved that it was politically incorrect to "force" school on the freedmen. The Bureau reported that *"[s]chools languished [in the rural communities]* and were discontinued one by one."[553]

---

548 White, *County Parish Schools*, 295.

549 Greensburg *Imperial*, October 10, 1857.

550 White, *County Parish Schools*, 293.

551 Crouch, "Black Education in Reconstruction Louisiana," 287-308.

552 Freedmen's Bureau, *Annual Narrative Reports of Operations and Conditions, October 1866-October 1868*, National Archives Microfilm Publication, Roll 27, Target 1.

553 Freedmen's Bureau, *Annual Narrative Reports of Operations*, 1866-68.

The Bureau attempted to address this dire emerging situation by assigning a former black teacher and Freedmen's Bureau supervisor of schools in New Orleans, George Ruby, a new role to "survey and evaluate" the status of schools in the state, as well as to "observe" how much effort was being expended by the white field agents to ensure that schools were being operated for black children. Not only was this a highly unusual arrangement – a New York free-born mulatto, raised in Maine, placed in authority to evaluate the performance of white southern men – it had to be a frightening assignment for this 25-year old man, as well. Yet, he began his task. It was April 1866.

JOSEPH FELDER was about 21 years old at the time; **SONA**, his son, somewhere between the ages of three and five. In both St. Helena and Livingston parishes, post-Civil War relations between the black and white residents were generally considered "friendly" and "good" by the Freedmen's Bureau's agents in the field, who reported that in both parishes, the planters and freedmen worked essentially well together; honoring the contracts that required freedmen to be paid. At some point in time, the educational effort was augmented by the Bureau's ability to access money from the Corps d'Afrique Fund, the Sequestration Fund, and the Hospital Tax Fund to help defray expenses.

In St. Helena Parish, Ruby located buildings and convinced the Freedmen's Bureau to help pay the salary of a teacher who had formerly taught in the local schools. Because schooling would not be new to the area, he believed that he had the support of the community to revive education in the parish,[554] but he was wrong. He was unable to raise money for the schools[555] because the white residents of the parish simply refused to support the education of their newly freed slaves.

> The 'poor whites' in St. Helena Parish, 'intensely rebel in sentiment, hating all Yankees most heartily,' wrote Ruby, disliked the 'trouble of education for themselves and *[their]* children,' but they also bitterly resented the idea of schools for the freedmen. They consequently did all they dared to intimidate and frighten local blacks. In April 1866, at one of the innumerable meetings Ruby initiated, two dozen of the hostile whites entered the building armed with cudgels *[clubs]*. The 'freedmen were frightened,' Ruby stated, and many a 'stout fellow' became reluctant to attend the gathering.[556]

George Ruby made his best effort to help the Freedmen's Bureau establish a system of schools in Louisiana. But on the afternoon that he found himself being pistol whipped and thrown in Thompson's Creek in Jackson Parish by a group of hostile whites who informed him that "they would not tolerate 'any damned nigger school in that town,'"[557] only five months after he began this job, he quit. It was September 1866. He relocated to Galveston, Texas, continued to work with the Freedmen's Bureau there, and became perhaps the most influential black politician in that state.

In keeping with Livingston Parish's reputation, the "young men fell into one of three groups ... draft dodgers, desperadoes and individualist extremists ... forming guerilla bands and raid*[ing]* both Union and Confederate camps ... or *[hiding]* in the swamps, or gathering together for drinking

---

554 Crouch, "Black Education in Reconstruction Louisiana," 301.

555 Crouch, "Black Education in Reconstruction Louisiana," 267.

556 Crouch, "Black Education in Reconstruction Louisiana," 303-304.

557 Crouch, Black Education in Reconstruction Louisiana, 307.

and rabble-raising, or all of the above."[558] During the 14 Civil War skirmishes that occurred in the parish, federal troops commandeered the Denham Springs hotel but they burned it down when they left.[559] So, although the Civil War had ended, the uncivil war between the races was just beginning! It is not surprising to learn that the Livingston area was a hub of KKK activity[560] and that most of the blacks that had lived in the parish, including all the black **Felders** except one, left at the first opportunity. Even the initial period of "reconstruction" brought with it intense destruction in Louisiana as whites, angered by the presence of Federal military staffers and religious organizations establishing schools and educational opportunities for blacks in what they believed still to be *their* communities, responded by burning schools, insulting, attacking and terrifying teachers, "whipping and robbing students," and murdering freedmen. When the military was withdrawn, rural schools were discontinued because the "civil authorities would not protect the freedmen or punish the perpetrators." Planters would not allow Northern "Yankee" teachers to live in their homes, so teachers had to quit or "take room and board with the colored people."[561] St. Helena and Livingston parishes became intensely violent and intimidating communities.

"Bad dudes" in Livingston Parish

Although the situation waxed and waned depending on the prosperity of the white employers, violence became a part of everyday life. Particularly when the economy was weak, even though "planters discovered freedmen worked better when [*their*] children had advantages of education," blacks faced the escalating wrath of resentful white former slave owners and neighbors. In more lucrative economic months, black education was not viewed as so much of a threat, and education, in some form, was generally tolerated. The net effect, however, of the tensions and disregard for state policy by locals charged with administration, was that by the end of 1867, the entire contingent of state-supported schools could only accommodate approximately 5000 black children, leaving "a balance of eighty-five thousand colored children uncared for except by the Bureau."[562]

As the chart on the next page reveals, private academies continued to be developed although, according to the Freedmen's Bureau field agents, the teachers were black and could hardly read and write themselves. *[Of course, but at least they were making their best effort! The best proof yet of the value that blacks placed on education.]* The chart below also reveals some of the challenges inherent in each of the approaches used to develop schools to educate the freedmen in Louisiana; the most obvious being teacher/pupil ratio and the discontinuation of Freedman Bureau schools. Over a nine-month period, January – September 1867, the following occurred:

---

558 Kathryn McQueen Kendall, "*A Study of Placenames in Livingston Parish, Louisiana,*" (Master's thesis, University of New Orleans, December 1975), 9.
559 Louisiana loose papers, untitled, vertical file, Livingston Parish, Livingston Parish Courthouse, accessed November 2013.
560 Louisiana loose papers, untitled.
561 Crouch, "Black Education in Reconstruction Louisiana," 267.
562 Shaik, "Development of Public Education," 49.

SCHOOLS FOR FREEDMEN IN LOUISIANA, 1867[563]

	Freedmen's Bureau			5% Tax Structure			Private "Academies"		
Month	schools	teachers	pupils	schools	teachers	pupils	schools	teachers	pupils
January	104	202	1134						
February	1	1	35	14	40	1550			
March	3	6	225	29	50	2525	3	3	150
April	1	2	80	27	46	2182	2	2	42
May	1	3	99	40	57	2665	9	9	361
June	-	-	-	61	72	2642	12	13	334
July	-	-	-	66	76	2239	28	28	1074
August	-	-	-	60	64	2773	48	48	1406
September	-	-	-	66	69	3154	40	41	1581

Louisiana's 1868 Reconstruction government wrote a new constitution. In it, Article 135 more explicitly defined the duty of the state, through the General Assembly, to provide free, public schools in each parish for all children ages six through 21, "without distinction of race, color, or previous condition." The duty further defined that "[t]here shall be no separate schools or institutions of learning, established exclusively for any race by the State of Louisiana." Article 136 of this Constitution forbade any "municipal corporation" to pass any act, "rule or regulation contrary to the spirit" of Article 135.[564] This Constitution also disallowed public funds to be used to support private education and it established English as the official language of instruction in the schools. However, in 1869, former Louisiana State Superintendent Robert M. Lusher, hired by the George Peabody Fund to administer $11,000 of aid to Louisiana for education, misused the grant to "attempt to build an exclusively white school system, similar to the one he had established as State Superintendent."[565]

Captain James McCleery, US Army Superintendent of Education, in August 1870, reported that the freedmen virtually funded education entirely on their own, providing the financing for all teachers in the district except one at the cost of "fourteen thousand eight hundred and seventy five dollars, an amount that is surprising considering the obstacles they had had to encounter. They have manifested a zeal in the cause of education, a thirst after knowledge that is worthy of all praise."[566] In 1871, State Superintendent of Public Education for the Second Division, E. S. Stoddard, observed and reported to State Superintendent Thomas Conway, the following:

---

563 Statistics from Freedmen's Bureau, Annual Narrative of Reports.
564 Shaik, Development of Public Education, 51.
565 Howard Ashley White, "Country Parish Schools," *The African American Experience in Louisiana, Part B: From the Civil War to Jim Crow*, 347.
566 Freedmen's Bureau Records, M 803, Roll 23, Louisiana, Summary of the Year's Work, 15d.

The colored children, as a rule, are advancing rapidly, much more so than the white. (I refer to the rural districts.) There is a reason for this however. As a class their appreciation of education is undeniably greater than that of the whites, as proven by the facts in the case. They are more regular in attendance, will go further and sacrifice more to attend school than will the white. Many colored children in my Division have been in constant attendance, traveling to do so a distance from four to six miles, while the whites will grumble if the school is placed a half mile from their door.[567]

Our Ancestors Embrace Education

It is against this backdrop of hostility and disruption of schooling for blacks in Louisiana, in general, and in Greensburg, specifically, that **SONA** began his formal education around the age of 17. **SONA** hired a tutor, (T. A. or J. A. Wilson), who provided private instruction in religion. He later enrolled in one of the public schools' night programs. The year was likely 1878 but records have not yet been found. Although he is not enumerated on the 1880 U.S. Census, it is clear that in 1881, he was still in St. Helena Parish or somewhere relatively close by because Greensburg, the county seat for St. Helena Parish, is the location of the court records documenting execution of his 1881 marriage bond to **EMMA JENKINS**. Oddly, **SONA** was a brilliant reflection of the black community's urgent desire to become educated, although **EMMA** was illiterate and remained so.

In fact, so proud were black Americans of the education that they were receiving that even as late as 1939, virtually every black college documented and reported the numbers of their graduates, and every student's name was listed by institution in the national black newspapers. It was reported that *"[p]ractically everyone [sic] of the institutions reporting their commencement activities declared the present class to be tht [sic] largest in the history of the school."*[568]

Reporting in at the time of press of the June 10, 1939 edition of *The Chicago Defender* were Tennessee State (TN); Bethune-Cookman (FL); Shaw (NC); Virginia Union (VA); Morgan (MD); Alcorn A. & M. (MS); the residential high school, Bordentown Manual Training and Industrial School for Colored Youth (NJ); Bennett (NC); Dowington Industrial and Agricultural School (PA); Cheney Teachers College (PA); Lincoln Institute (KY); Winston-Salem (NC); and Tillotson Collegiate and Normal Institute (TX). Imagine the pride in these families to see their children's names in the article in *The Chicago Defender* – "Graduates Pour From [sic] Nation's Colleges"! Imagine the pride of freedmen and women to be able to sit in a school room and learn what had been forbidden! Imagine the pride freedmen and women felt to be able to witness their children going off to college!

Just imagine ...

State of the State: Schooling in Mississippi on a Famous Plantation

Begin by imagining on the plantation of Joseph E. ("J. E.") Davis, Benjamin Montgomery and his family experiencing life as slaves more unconventional than perhaps any other blacks living below the Mason-Dixon Line. It is ironic the freedoms allowed by this man whose brother would help bring down

---

567 Shaik, "Development of Public Education," 57. See also Louisiana Department of Education, *Annual Report of the Superintendent of Public Education, Thomas W. Conway, to the General Assembly of Louisiana, for the Year 1871*, Printed 1872, 122 (Google Book, accessed May 4, 2015).

568 "Graduates Pour From [sic] Nation's Colleges," *The Chicago Defender* (national edition), June 10, 1939, 11.

School on Milestone Plantation, Mississippi around 1939

the entire South in a war that could not be won and which would ultimately be fought over an issue (slavery) that tore, if ever so slightly, at the foundation of his own morality. In 1860, "Jeff" Davis had 113 slaves on his 1000-acre plantation ("Brierfield") in Warren, Mississippi, one-third (31) of whom were mulattos.[569] His oldest brother, Joseph, a lawyer twenty-three years Jeff's senior, allowed Jeff "use" of 1000 acres from his own 5000-acre plantation ("Hurricane").[570] Joseph "owned" 356 slaves in 1860, of which nearly one-third (106) were mulattoes.[571] When his younger brother accepted the presidency of the seceded Confederate states, Joseph was one of the richest men in the state of Mississippi.[572] *[Why so many mulattoes at Davis Bend?! A seldom mentioned tidbit of information for another book is that Jefferson's wife, Varina Howell Davis, was also mulatto. A great example of HIStory. Shape, and share, the narrative just as you wish!]*

Benjamin Montgomery and his son, Isaiah T., were respected as brilliant and industrious slaves by Joseph Davis, who experimented with establishing on his plantation a "community of cooperation" and trust among his "servants." It was said that he never called them "slaves."[573] The slave population at Hurricane became essentially a self-governing community, doling out punishment themselves after holding trials, and determining judgements, for misdeeds. However, despite Joseph's connections in and around Mississippi and across the country as a seasoned, accomplished lawyer, southern whites appreciated neither his philosophy nor the freedoms he bestowed on his slaves. It smacked in the face of their beliefs of white superiority. Teaching slaves to read suggested that, in fact, perhaps they were not as ignorant and incapable as most southern slave holders chose to believe.

Nonetheless, the plantation experiment in self-management and self-government continued and laid the foundation upon which the entire Montgomery family became literate and upon which Benjamin established on Hurricane Plantation possibly the first and only integrated school on a southern plantation during the antebellum period. Benjamin personally financed the white tutor of Joseph Davis' children and established a classroom on the property in which this teacher taught both Joseph's children and his own in the same classroom at the same time![574] One version of this story suggests that when Joseph Davis discovered that the Montgomery children were receiving a better education than his own children, he opted to have his children be taught by the same teacher as well, and thus the integrated classroom emerged. Irrespective of how this classroom arrangement evolved,

---

569 Ancestry.com, 1860 U.S. Slave Schedule.

570 *Wikipedia, The Free Encyclopedia,* "Hurricane Plantation," accessed October 18, 2014. http://en.wikipedia.org/wiki/Hurricane_Plantation.

571 Ancestry.com. 1860 U.S. Slave Schedule.

572 *Wikipedia,* "Hurricane Plantation."

573 Neil R. McMillan, "The Life and Times of Isaiah T. Montgomery," accessed October 21, 2014, http://mshistorynow.mdah.state.ms.us/articles/55/isaiah-t-montgomery-1847-1924-part-I.

574 McMillan, "Life and Times of Isaiah T. Montgomery."

it is known that all the Montgomery children became literate during slavery on the plantation of the brother of the president of the Confederacy.

Benjamin Montgomery's talents were applied at Hurricane as a "mechanic, machinist, civil engineer," and dry goods store owner, who ultimately, as a slave, established his own line of credit with wholesalers in New Orleans. He was Joseph Davis' accountant and was manager of all cotton transactions for both Hurricane and Brierfield plantations, working thus for Joseph and Jeff Davis simultaneously. His story is unparalleled and not told in American *his*tory classes. His values of industriousness and enterprise permeated the upbringing of all his children in a way that certainly he could not even have imagined. Isaiah, particularly, learned the value of education from his father (who had been tutored by his former master in Louden County, Virginia, prior to being purchased in 1850 at the age of 17 at the Natchez Slave Market by Joseph Davis).[575] When Benjamin married and fathered children, he either requested, persisted, or insisted that Joseph Davis allow his children to learn to read. Amazingly, Joseph was accommodating. Years later, Isaiah, reflecting on the education that he received at Davis Bend, documented that his parents did much of the teaching in their own home prior to him being removed, at age 10, to provide daily care for Joseph Davis. In fact, he could already read and write, but he continued, when time allowed, to sit in the classroom on the plantation. The classroom experience for him was of short duration and rudimentary, as he recalled, but sufficient:

> My duties to a considerable extent were those of a private secretary and office attendant, at night sleeping in his room and performing such services for him as a boy of my age *[10]* could render. Shortly after leaving home my regular lessons ceased but being regularly employed in one of the finest libraries for which this section was proverbial and having free access to all reading matter which came daily, weekly and monthly to the parlor and library of the Davis family, I read a great deal, but it was without method and served only to give a fair knowledge of history and current events, of language and composition by familiarity and use, which has stood me well in hand to this day, for I have never studied either.[576]

Isaiah, like his father, took advantage of the privilege they were accorded to use Joseph Davis' extensive library, which was a separate building on the plantation that had books, newspapers, and magazines in what was purportedly one of the largest personal libraries in the South. Isaiah was an avid reader, as were all the rest of his siblings. When the war came close enough to Vicksburg (only 20 miles north from the Davis Bend peninsula) in April of 1862, Joseph left for safety, taking a few of his "servants" with him and leaving the Montgomery family to function in his absence to protect and maintain his plantation. It was then that Joseph discovered that the slaves on his plantation were not happy! *[Really?! Geezz!]* He "watch*[ed]* from afar" as his whole system collapsed - slaves looted his property and left the plantation, overseers deserted, and his plantation possessions were stolen by both Union and Confederate armies.[577]

---

575 Milburn Crowe (Mound Bayou historian), "Mound Bayou: Cradle of African American Self Government in America, Preview of a Pictorial History," not dated.

576 Isaiah T. Montgomery, "Isaiah T. Montgomery Tells His Own Story: Recounts Early Life as a Slave, and Points to Path Leading Toward Success," reprinted in *The Voice*, (Mound Bayou, July 1971), 6.

577 McMillan, "Life of Isaiah T. Montgomery."

While Joseph was away from Davis Bend, as slaves were freed following Emancipation, and subsequently as towns were seized by the Union armies, Davis Bend became one of the locations where the Freedmen's Department of the Military established an experiment in slave refugee farm management. Called "General Grant's Negro Paradise," one such farm manager was Benjamin Montgomery and his family, who worked the land rent-free and operated his dry goods store, netting $2,500 profit.[578] At the close of the war, once Joseph was pardoned for his treason against the United States, his plantation was restored to his ownership. However, shortly thereafter, now essentially financially destitute, "in one of the more astonishing turnabouts in southern history" – a secret transaction – he actually sold Hurricane to Benjamin Montgomery and his family for $300,000 – "with liberal terms" that enabled Benjamin to make the mortgage over a period of 14 years."[579] But before the war's end, Benjamin purchased something of even greater value from Joseph – his wife's time – to be home with her children and to become a seamstress, sewing for whites and earning money of her own.[580] *[Herein is another example of a black slaveowner; but, oh, how joyful!]*

The decline in cotton prices ultimately forced the family to foreclose.[581] But, before Benjamin lost the plantation, the Montgomery family had become one of the most productive cotton farmers in Mississippi. The Montgomery's cotton won first place at the St. Louis Agricultural Fair in 1870, the International Exposition in Cincinnati in 1873, and the U.S. Centennial Exhibition in Philadelphia in 1876. *[That is, the Montgomery family produced the best cotton in the entire country!]* This family, blessed in unfathomable ways as slaves at Davis Bend, took full advantage of the opportunities accorded them to read and study, to self-govern and to earn, manage, save and invest money. They ultimately established a strong family unit that incorporated those values amongst others into their lives and dreams for their futures. Their daughters attended Oberlin University. They bought a third Davis plantation. Unfortunately, at only 58 years old, Benjamin died one year after they lost the plantation to foreclosure.[582] His life, however, became a model that would have a reverberating impact beyond the wildest dream he could have ever had.

Churches and Schools: A Necessary Relationship

There simply is no separation that can be made between education and the church in the black community in the early years following Emancipation. Withdrawing from white churches provided the freedom to build church-related primary and elementary schools. To "catch up," to begin to "pull yourself up by your boot straps," phrases we heard often as children in segregated neighborhoods, schools were started in the black community – primarily in and by churches, or by Christian and missionary organizations – both black and white. In addition to teaching religious tenets, they concentrated on teaching the rudimentary skills of reading, writing, and arithmetic to children and adults. Those hungry for knowledge, which seemed to be the overwhelming majority, could find it in a church – in Sunday School ("Sabbath School"), or in the day or evening school held in the

---

578 Claude F. Oubre, *Forty Acres and a Mule: The Freedmen's Bureau and Black Land Ownership* (Baton Rouge: Louisiana State University Press, 1978), 168.

579 McMillan, "Life of Isaiah T. Montgomery."

580 McMillan, "Life of Isaiah T. Montgomery."

581 McMillan, "Life of Isaiah T. Montgomery."

582 McMillan, "Life of Isaiah T. Montgomery."

church facility. The A.M.E. Church grew exponentially after the war, easily gaining favor with black Americans because of its fundamental practices and "liberation theology" based on ministering to the sociological needs as well as the spiritual needs of its congregants.[583] In one decade (1856-66), A.M.E. membership increased from 20,000 to 75,000. By the subsequent decade, the membership had risen to 200,000.[584] By 1880, the A.M.E. Church membership in the South approached 400,000. One of those 400,000 was **SONA FELDER**, who converted to this religion in 1878.

Withdrawing from white southern churches provided the freedom to establish church-related colleges. To minister to the sociological and educational needs of the black community, at least 19 colleges were established throughout the South under the auspices of the A.M.E. Church, often with the assistance of white liberals with good hearts. The first such institution, Wilberforce College, was established as the training institute to supply teachers for the myriad of A.M.E. schools that were set to soon emerge, like Paul Quinn in Dallas, Texas; Allen University in Columbia, South Carolina; Kittrell College in Kittrell, North Carolina; Edward Waters College in Jacksonville, Florida; Western University in Quindaro, Kansas; Shorter College in North Little Rock, Arkansas; Payne College in Selma, Alabama; Turner Normal College in Shelbyville, Tennessee; Payne Institute in Macon, Georgia; Lampton College in Delhi, Louisiana; Flegler High School in Marion, South Carolina; Bethel College near Montgomery, Alabama; Payne Theological Seminary in Wilberforce, Ohio; and Morris Brown College in Atlanta, Georgia – all established prior to 1900! Today, Wilberforce, Allen, Edward Waters, Shorter, Payne (Ga), and Morris Brown continue in operation, and many other historically black colleges and universities have evolved over time.

Mary Holmes Seminary

Mary Holmes Seminary was built to provide a Christian education for female children of freed slaves. Its intended purpose was to instill Christian virtues in young women and prepare them to be homemakers and "wise leaders in society and the church."[585] Admission required that students be able to furnish a "comb, hair brush, needles, thimble, pins and a teaspoon ... plus three sheets, three pillow slips, six towels and three table napkins."[586] **SUSIE P. FELDER** gathered her comb and brush and other required items and enrolled. As a teen, she was learning how to live her life as a

Mary Holmes Seminary

---

583 Afroamhistory.about.com/od/africanamericanculture/a/AMC/Church.htm, (accessed December 1, 2014).

584 www.socialwelfarehistory.com/eras/african-methodist-episcopal-a-m-e-church, (accessed December 1, 2014).

585 Pamela Foster, 21st Annual HBCU Faculty Development Network Conference, Raleigh, NC, October 16-18, 2014, Slide 30.

586 Foster, 21st Annual Faculty Conference.

Christian woman. She is enumerated in the 1900 U.S. Census as a 16-year-old African American boarding student at the seminary in Clay County.

Started by the Board of Missions for Freedmen of the Presbyterian Church,[587] this school first opened its doors in Jackson, Mississippi, but following a fire, was rebuilt in Clay County at West Point and survived until closing in 2005. **SUSIE P. FELDER** reported to the 1900 census worker that she was born in Louisiana in 1883 and that her mother and father were also born in Louisiana. The **S. P. FELDER** *Bible* records that **EMMA's** and **SONA's** first child, **SUSIE**, was born in 1881 in Louisiana. **EMMA** and **SONA** were both born in Louisiana. Clay County is the location where **WILDA ELLIS** (**SONA's** second wife) and **WILDA's** mother, **JANE**, were born and raised. There is no doubt that this **SUSIE FELDER** is a part of *OURstory*, the child of **EMMA** and **SONA**. This is the only record found to date on this young lady.

Campbell College

Another such college, established by the A.M.E. Church, was Campbell College, which got its beginnings in Vicksburg, Mississippi, in 1887, just 22 years after freedom was won. When classes began at Vicksburg and Friars Point, Campbell College became the first college founded in Mississippi by African Americans "without the aid of whites."[588] The school was intended to "meet the educational needs of the Negro youth of the twentieth century by offering them the advantages of a Christian education through its Normal, Industrial, Scientific, Collegiate, Missionary, and Theological Departments. Training in these, coupled with practical work in domestic economy, *[was intended to]* enable them to lead useful lives."[589] Isaiah T. Montgomery, who by this time had founded Mound Bayou, helped to establish Campbell College and served in the capacity of a trustee[590] as well as its second president.[591] As president, he operated in the style for which he had become known nationally, mustering people and money together almost singlehandedly.

First building, Campbell College, Vicksburg Mural

By 1925, Campbell College owned 1053 acres of land on the outskirts of Mound Bayou, and at one time the college owned a total of 1137 acres of land, more than any other A.M.E. school facility.[592] Beginning in 1898, the school oper-

---

587 http://www.aaregistry.org/historic_events/view/mary-holmes-college-founded, (accessed December 10, 2014).

588 Mississippi History Timeline, accessed February 7, 2013, http://mdah.state.ms.us/timeline/zone/1890/.

589 Charles S. Smith, *A History of the African Methodist Episcopal Church, 1856-1922, vol. II*, (Philadelphia: Philadelphia Book Concern of the A.M.E. Church, 1922), 364.

590 *Cyclopedia of African Methodism in Mississippi*, 1902, 143.

591 Crowe, Cradle of Self Government, 3.

592 Smith, H*istory of the African Methodist Episcopal Church*, 364.

ated in Jackson, but in 1925, the Board of Trustees voted to move it to Mound Bayou, the location of "a large group of the race *[whereby through]* contact with the city of Mound Bayou,"[593] it was certain that financial support would be easily obtained, given that promises had already been secured from both black and white city and county officials who requested and supported the move.[594] Bishop W. W. Beckett, then Chairman of the Board, led the campaign in 1925 to move the college to Mound Bayou, fervently of the opinion that by placing the college in the midst of the nation's largest and most self-reliant community of African Americans, the college would not only sustain itself but would grow to greatness. Beckett declared, "I believe Campbell College ought to come rapidly to the front. *[sic]* and soon rank as one of the leading institutions for the education of the colored race."[595] Apparently the timing was all wrong.

The Delta Blues

There were many reasons why African American Mississippians sang the blues aside from the fact that this genre of music was birthed in the Delta, only 30 or so miles from Mound Bayou and Cleveland. In August of 1926, one month before **CHIQUITA HULBERT** was born, a weather system stalled over the middle of the United States and began raining and raising the levels of the Mississippi River and its tributaries in eleven states. It was a serious reason to sing the blues. By the spring of 1927, the rains had become incessant and persistent, and for weeks, they did not stop. In more than 165 places, the man-made levies cracked, and water began to seep, slowly at first, then at a deluge, and later roaring ferociously into the pasture lands of the Delta. No one knew that the "Mighty Mississippi" was poised in just a few days to overflow its banks and become the worst flood disaster in U.S. history.

The Mississippi River swept into towns north and south, east and west, covering somewhere between 23,000 and 27,000 square miles (an area as large as Vermont, New Hampshire, Massachusetts, and Connecticut combined)[596] causing more than 400 million dollars in damage, killing thousands of farm animals, taking upwards of 1000 lives, and leaving tens of thousands to a million homeless in nine states from Cairo, Illinois to New Orleans, Louisiana, and including Texas, Arkansas, Missouri, Tennessee, Kansas, Oklahoma, and of course, Mississippi. When it was apparent that the crack of the levee at Mounds, Mississippi, in lower Bolivar County, was of major issue, hundreds of African Americans were corralled to the site to fill sandbags. They could feel the ground shaking under their feet and just knew the levee would

Flooding in Mound Bayou

---

593 The Baltimore *Afro-American*, June 27, 1925, A 14.

594 "Campbell College to Move to Mound Bayou," The New York *Amsterdam News*, July 8, 1925.

595 "Campbell College to Move."

596 Another description of the extent of the flooding indicated that more than 10 million acres were covered in a matter of a couple of days from this flood, see "Map, static: Comparing Floods," accessed February 7, 2013, http://www.pbs.org/wgbh/americanexperience/features/map/flood-maps/.

Cleveland flood victims awaiting food at Birdsong Camp

break – they could "feel it boiling up" – but at gunpoint, they, joined by 1500 more black men who had been rounded up, were forced to keep working through the night.[597] Yet, the river won; the levee broke and these workers were swept away. "Soon every fire whistle, church bell and mill whistle rang out to warn the county."[598]

Although on April 20, 1927, Secretary of Commerce Herbert Hoover was appointed by President Calvin Coolidge to take charge of directing the American Red Cross in general flood evacuation and relief efforts, this mostly African American share-cropping population, inexperienced in asking the government to assist them,[599] suffered greatly. In addition, and in many ways more poignant, although perhaps not unexpected, the plantation owners on whose lands they sharecropped demonstrated how their penchant for greed continued to overshadow their respect for humanity. Out came the bullwhips again. Black men were whipped on one plantation by the owner intent on saving his lands from the flood by working these men around the clock against the forces of nature – even killing one man for refusing to work a double shift after food, distributed based on race (white first/black last), left many blacks with no rations at all for their segregated relief camps. It reminded many of the residents of the city of Greenville (Washington County) of "slavery" all over again. Five weeks after the levy break, the Army Corps of Engineers recorded waves 12-feet high and water more than 100-feet deep in areas where water simply should not have been. A 65-acre lake now extends along a three-quarter mile stretch near where the levee broke on that fatal day.[600]

---

597 http://www.pbs.org/wgbh/americanexperience/features/general-article/flood-levee/, "The Mounds Levee Landing Break."
598 "The Mounds Levee Landing Break."
599 https://archive.org/details/mississippi_flood_1927, silent film, "The Mississippi River Flood of 1927," U.S. Army silent film.
600 www.pbs.org/wgbh/americanexperience/features/general-article/flood-levee/.

Residents of Cleveland, Mississippi, a mere 30 miles from Greenville and 10 miles from Mound Bayou, lined up waiting for tents and provisions at Birdsong Camp,[601] erected after the flood. **BEATRICE HULBERT** had just found out that she was pregnant for a second time with her son, **TYREE**. **CHIQUITA** was one year old. They lived in Cleveland and surely stood in line just like everyone else.

Black Tuesday, October 29, 1929, was only a few short years ahead, unbeknownst to anyone. The unforeseen worldwide economic depression sank all hopes and dreams of maintaining the farm lands that were to provide income to support the growth of Campbell College. Sixty-eight-year-old **SONA FELDER**, responsible at that time for managing the farmlands in Mound Bayou for the college, had a daunting task. Although he had been the first president of the People's Saving Bank in Shaw, an initial investor and stockholder in the Bank of Mound Bayou, had earned the title of "A.M.E. Dollar Money King" in his inaugural year as Presiding Elder, raising more than $2000 between 1897-99,[602] had built a parsonage and had raised funds sufficient to support other church activities as well,[603] **SONA's** financial genius was insufficient to combat the effects on the college of the 1927 flood and the stock market crash of the Great Depression. Individuals and businesses were impacted for more than a decade (1929-1940).

By 1932, it was doubtful that Campbell College would survive. However, to the surprise of many, on October 5th, the college opened the academic year with a faculty of fifteen "coming from the best colleges and universities throughout the country," prepared to teach the more than 100 students enrolled in courses in the bachelor curriculum including "commerce, science, music, art, education, theology, physical education and mathematics."[604] Remodeling and refurbishing improvements that year included removing tubs and installing showers, installing gas heaters in the residence halls, and improving the interiors of the president's home and the chapel.[605]

The College did survive, with sweat, tears, prayers, and commitment from the associated leadership. It apparently took four years, but between 1932 and 1936, Campbell College emerged a stronger institution from what had been described as "a school long since dead and in a much worse condition than Lazarus."[606] All local debts had been paid, enrollment had reached 350, 14 ministers were in training in the theology program, 100 high school students had matriculated, and grammar school, including for the first time a "primary cradle roll," had been added to the curriculum.[607] There was even money available to help the teachers with Santa Claus. In 1937, more than 1000 persons came to commencement to see 31 students receive their diplomas and certificates![608] In 1938, the WPA reported that Campbell College had several brick and wooden buildings, a high school department

---

601 Mississippi Department of Archives and History, 1927 Flood Photograph Collection.

602 I. W. Crawford, P. H. Thompson, Multum in Parvo, An Authenticated History of Progressive Negroes in Pleasing and Graphic Biographical Style, 2nd edition, 1912, 74. $2,000 is equivalent to $57,100 in 2012 real wealth value (measuringworth.com).

603 *The Freeman*, (Indianapolis, Indiana) July 9, 1898, vol 11, issue 28, 5.

604 "Campbell College Accomplished a Near-Miracle," *Atlanta Daily World*, October 28, 1932, 6.

605 "Campbell College Accomplished a Near-Miracle."

606 Wallace Jones, Dean of Theology, "President Scott of Campbell College is Called 'Miracle Man,'" *The Pittsburgh Courier*, January 11, 1936, 5.

607 Jones, "President Scott of Campbell College Called 'Miracle Man.'"

608 Rev. Thomas J. Brown, "Campbell College," in *The Chicago Defender* (national edition), June 12, 1937, 8.

MEMBER
GENERAL EDUCATIONAL BOARD
A. M. E. CHURCH

REV. S. P. FELDER
PRESIDING ELDER

CHAIRMAN
BOARD OF TRUSTEES
CAMPBELL COLLEGE

MOUND BAYOU, MISS.

Campbell College letterhead, ~1929

and a four-year college course leading to the Bachelor of Science Degree. **TYREE FELDER** became one of the high school department attendees.

It took 12 years from the height of the Depression – until 1944 – before the school could actually retire the mortgage, but it was an over-joyous occasion, celebrated at the Founder's Day Rally, February 8-10, 1944, where nearly 10,000 A.M.E.'s gathered from Louisiana and Mississippi to see the ground-breaking for the $150,000 administration building that would be named in honor of Bishop S. L. Greene, Eighth District Bishop who stewarded the successful comeback of the school. One hundred thousand (100,000) church workers from the Eighth Episcopal District, of which Mississippi and Louisiana were the designated states, pulled together to liquidate the mortgage and to build the "commodious Episcopal residence" in New Orleans. Once again, however, Mound Bayou would figure prominently in the Campbell College's history, as Judge Benjamin Green, Mound Bayou's Harvard Law School-educated mayor, would untangle the receivership of the lands held by the College.[609] While **SONA** did not live to see this day, his efforts during his years as Chairman of the Board of Trustees and as manager of the Campbell College farm were a part of the fund-raising, preaching, speaking, and praying that resurrected and sustained this historic institution through a challenging existence. At the 1940 A.M.E. Conference, only seven months after the death of her father, **BEATRICE FELDER** carried on in his name as he had taught her, assuming a fiduciary role in the oversight of funds for the A.M.E. Conference, responsible for the financial stability of Campbell College. She was elected conference accountant.[610]

Campbell College at Jackson MS, first building

After the unsuccessful attempt to move the college to Mound Bayou, Campbell College was merged into Jackson State University in 1965 after graduating its last class in 1964. Nonetheless, Campbell College was but one shining example of the speed by which the newly freed black race engaged in establishing schools at the highest level they could actualize, even with limited resources. Assisted by numerous other religious entities, such as the Society for the Propaganda of the Gospel, the African Missionary Society, the Freedmen's Bureau, and the Federal Commission of Enrollment, as well as many good-hearted individuals,

---

609 *The Pittsburgh Courier*, "Bishop Greene Breaks Record; Campbell College Out of Debt," January 29, 1944, 16.

610 "Miss. Conference Closes Sessions," *The Pittsburgh Courier*, November 23, 1940.

private academies and schools were established throughout the South in response to the national need to find a solution to the black underclass it had created by the miseducation and enslavement of four million people.

The impact of the speed of developing collegiate institutions and elementary and secondary level schools on the illiteracy rate of the black American population – nearly 95% during slavery – was astonishing. In 1930, the definition of illiteracy according to the U.S. Census Bureau was, "any person 10 years of age or over who is not able to read or write, either in English or in some other language." The corresponding declining illiteracy rate of black Americans from the ending of slavery in the 19th century through four decades of the 20th century is illustrated in the chart below:

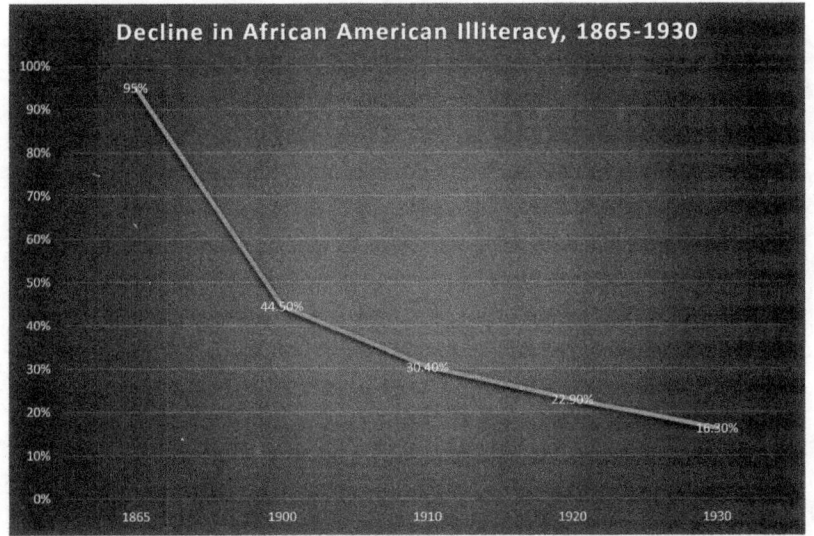

Louisiana was the state with the second highest percentage of black illiteracy in every census year, 1890 – 1920.[611] In 2003, 14% of all adult Americans were considered to be below the then current literacy standard (to read basic prose); 20% of whom were black, 39% Hispanic, and 37% white.[612] But, although the illiteracy rate showed a steady decline in the black population over the decades because of the efforts of many to educate the black race, the proponents and facilitators of education were met in nearly every Southern community with disdain, hostility, intimidation, and violence; even well into the 20th century.

Today, 150 years post-Reconstruction, issues of dual education systems, unequal resources, resentful white parents, re-segregation, the achievement gap, the dearth of black teachers in public K-12 schools, the dearth of black professors in post-secondary colleges, unfair use of standardized testing that results in exclusion of many black students from higher education opportunities, and a dearth of black administrators and boards of trustee members involved in institutional policy setting across

---

611 Bishop Reverdy Ransom, "The Decline of Illiteracy," *Year Book of Negro Churches*, 1935-36, (Wilberforce, Ohio: A.M.E. Church, 1935), 55.

612 National Center for Education Statistics, National Assessment of Adult Literacy: *A Look at the Literacy of America's Adults in the 21st Century*, "Profile of Adults with Below Basic Prose Illiteracy," 5, December 2005.

the entire education spectrum continue to persist at alarming rates throughout the country. America currently grapples with a legacy of poor schooling for African American children, which, if not corrected, will certainly have a major impact on the future potential of our ability to sustain international leadership as we trend towards a nation of majority minorities. *[HIStory repeats itself!]*

FELDER and **HULBERT** descendants must be ever grateful for the commitments made by our ancestors to education and to their intuitive understanding that slavery bound their feet and their wrists but left their minds free to wander, to imagine and to dream. It was because of their dreams that I can write this story.

THE LEGACY: EDUCATION

Got "Up from Slavery," he did!

JOSEPH FELDER, around the age of 40, acted boldly and courageously as one of the pioneer freedmen who had the audacity to help establish education for African Americans during the tumultuous years of race relations in post-Civil War Mississippi. Along with 35-year-old David Sam, a laborer, and 20-something year old Ed Christmas, he served "for a number of years" as a trustee of the Bogue Houma Ridge School for black children, which began public education for blacks in the most southeastern part of the state. Classes were held in the late 1880's, beginning somewhere around 1887 – only 22 years after Emancipation – first at the A.M.E. Church "organized and built in 'The Point,'"[613] but later these three men, all still illiterate themselves, helped to construct and maintain a school building in this all-black community "just east of the Gainesville Road"[614] outside of Logtown and Possum Walk. **JOSEPH** demonstrated the type of determination and initiative essential to designing a destiny of equal opportunity for his children, specifically, and for future generations of black children, generally; opportunities he could only dream of on the plantations and farms of his past. He took control of his life circumstances and prioritized both education and religion as guiding principles and important values for his family. He recognized the relationship between faith, self-determination, education, and economic progress. **JOSEPH FELDER** was an architect of aspirations and possibilities. That education is a highly valued commodity in the **FELDER** and **HULBERT** families is owed in good measure to the efforts of this ancestor's wisdom, vision, and mettle. Remarkable! **JOSEPH FELDER**, my great-great grandfather, born a slave.

Got "Up from Slavery," he did!

SONA FELDER served not only the local and national A.M.E. Church community, but his local hometown business community and the state of Mississippi education community, as well. His wisdom in financial affairs landed him in the seat of Chairman of the Board of Trustees of Campbell College and manager of the Campbell College farm, a property of 1000+ acres on the outskirts of Mound Bayou. An honorary Doctor of Divinity (D.D.) was bestowed on him by Campbell College

---

613 Phone interview with Ms. Andrea Pack, Branch Manager, Pearlington Library, January 2, 2014.

614 Etienne William Maxson, Etienne Maxson, *The Progress of the Races* (Washington, D.C.: Murray Brothers Printing Company, 1930), 63.

in recognition of his contributions to the objectives of education of the African American, the purposes and advancement of the A.M.E. religion, and his leadership in the A.M.E. Church's national connectional organization. Always highly spoken of and highly respected, he was proclaimed by one Mound Bayou A.M.E. resident to have been "most excellent!"[615] **REV. DR. SONA FELDER**, my great-grandfather, born a slave.

Got up from a slave mother, she did!

WILDA ELLIS FELDER taught school for two years in Shaw, Mississippi, when the A.M.E. Church sent **SONA FELDER** there for a three-year appointment. She "gave up teaching"[616] when **BEATRICE** was born but helped to instill in her children the love of learning such that for a time, both daughters would follow in this profession as well. **KORINNE** would later become a licensed practical nurse but would continue to teach piano and voice. **WILDA FELDER**, my great-grandmother, child of a slave mother, born and raised during Mississippi's surge in lynching.

Wilda Felder

Got up from a slave father, she did!

BEATRICE OTTOWIESS FELDER took education in the town of Mound Bayou by storm and opened a private "academy" – T.O.C.K. – The Opportunity Center Kindergarten – on October 19, 1932 – that is still held in high esteem by those graduates who realized that the values she taught them prepared them for lives of success. Of "**Miss B. O. Felder**," one of her alumni, recalling her influence, had this to say: "All of us, we had a label on us. You could tell her students. When we went to the school *[public school]*, everybody said you had been to **MISS FELDER's**. Even the teachers knew us."[617] **BEATRICE** completed two years at Alcorn College but her thirst for knowledge kept her always learning new skills, enabling her to be always employed and financially stable even in the Mississippi Delta during the Great Depression. Among the many positions she held in Mound Bayou, aside from proprietor of T.O.C.K., were telephone exchange operator, public school teacher (instructor of music and high school English), secretary to the town clerk, secretary-treasurer of the *Demonstrator* (local newspaper), mailing clerk of the *Advance* (local newspaper), secretary to Col. Charles Banks, and bookkeeper of the Y and MV Depot.[618] **BEATRICE FELDER**, my grandmother – a fierce-some single parent and standout educator in the Delta.

Beatrice Felder

---

615 Personal interview with Mrs. Dorothy Micou at Bonner-Campbell College, Edwards, Mississippi, 2002.

616 *S. P. Felder Family Bible.*

617 Dr. Matthew Holden, UVA Emeritus Professor of Political Science, statement in Frankie Felder, *Lessons for Life: Alumni Remember Miss B. Ottowiess Felder, Mound Bayou, Mississippi*, 116th Homecoming (Belton, SC: self-published, 2003), 11.

618 *Southern Advocate*, September 3, 1938, vol. 3, no. 47 (Mound Bayou, MS), 1.

Got up from a single parent household, he did!

TYREE PRESTON FELDER, after graduating from Campbell College in Jackson and quitting his high school job at Topps Cleaners, left Mound Bayou in 1945 on a train bound for Tuskegee Institute where he took the lessons learned from his rural, poor Mississippi upbringing to Macon County, Alabama. There he dutifully carried on with community expectations firmly implanted in his mind, knowing that it was nothing less than a family requirement to excel in his chosen academic major and in the campus organizations he joined. After earning his Bachelor of Arts degree from Tuskegee in mechanical commercial industries, and receiving a commission as First Lieutenant in the U.S. Army, he left Mississippi behind, never to return except to visit his "Little Mother Dear." Following in the footprints of his mother, grandmother, grandfather, and great-grandfather, he spent many years as an involved parent of school-age children, as the PTA (parent-teacher association) president or other officer, and as our family's homework sergeant-in-arms, ensuring a watchful eye over the education of his children (and many others in the neighborhood as well). He expected all of his children and grandchildren to earn college degrees. In 1972, at the age of 45, he earned his MBA (Master of Business Administration) degree from Virginia Commonwealth University while employed full-time as the University's first Equal Opportunity Officer. It is no surprise that in this role, he crafted for himself the responsibility to recruit from among the 1,524 VCU employees with less than a 12th grade education those individuals who would participate in one of the two literacy training centers at VCU, the first in the nation established at a university for its underemployed staff.[619] Of this work he reflected, "Our purpose is to help adults who have no other place to go; [sic] a means for upgrading themselves ... [t]he cost of living makes people recognize they're being left behind."[620] Without education, he intimated, these employees' dreams of securing better jobs were nearly impossible to realize.[621] **TYREE PRESTON FELDER**, my father; my mentor; an educator in his own rights.

Got up from slave-owning grandparents, he did!

JAMES ALEXANDER HULBERT, born to teenage parents, was a pioneer in the U.S. Information Service. He became one of the first African Americans to serve in this prestigious organization. He studied at Hampton Institute (B.S., 1932), Morehouse (A.B., 1933), and Columbia University, where he earned his master's degree in library services in 1939. He served six years as Director of Library Services in East Pakistan, Director of the American Staff of the USIS Library in Paris, and librarian at Virginia State College, Atlanta University, and Talladega College. He authored two books, *The Negro College Library* (1943) and *An Introduction to Library Service* (1971), the latter of which was widely received as an "authoritative" textbook on libraries as public service institutions.[622] It was "translated into French for use in the French-speaking countries of the world,"[623] and was used widely in colleges and universities in the United States. **JAMES ALEXANDER HULBERT**, my half-uncle.

---

619 VCU Magazine, accessed May 6, 2015, http://archive.org/stream/vcumagazine221973virg/vcumagazine221973virg_djvu.txt, 22.

620 VCU Magazine, 22.

621 VCU Magazine, 22.

622 James A. Hulbert, *An Introduction to Library Service* (New York: Exposition Press, 1971), book jacket.

623 Memorial Services program for the late Mr. James Alexander Hulbert, July 31, 1974.

Got up from slave-owning great-grandparents, she did!

MARILYN E. HULBERT followed in her father's (**JAMES ALEXANDER HULBERT**) footsteps and joined USIA (United States Information Agency) as a trainee in 1966, becoming one of the still few African Americans selected for such employment with the U.S. government. Some of her many achievements included serving as Director of the Office of African Affairs, Counselor for Public Affairs in Nairobi (Kenya), Deputy Chief of Mission in Antananarivo (Madagascar), Deputy Public Affairs Officer in Lagos (Nigeria), and Public Affairs Officer in Antananarivo and Bamako (Mali). In addition, she served as Assistant Cultural Affairs Officer and Branch Chief of the Africa Wireless File, Desk Officer for Anglophone West Africa and in the English Teaching Division. She earned her Bachelor of Arts from the American University of Beirut (Lebanon), a Master of Science in French Literature from Howard University and pursued graduate study in Applied Linguistics and Teaching English as a Second Language at Georgetown University. **MARILYN HULBERT**, my half-cousin.

THE PATTERN: ECONOMIC EMPOWERMENT AND PROPERTY OWNERSHIP

Why stagger at the difficulties confronting you? Have you not for centuries burned the miasma and hewn down forests like these at the behest of a master? Can you not do it for yourselves and your children unto successive generations, that they may worship and develop under their own vine and fig tree?[624] *Isaiah T. Montgomery*

Forty Acres and a Mule

Imagine the excitement when the word got out that the Federal government was providing "40 acres and a mule" to every freedman! The dancing, the singing, the hugging, the crying, the shouting, the praying, and the thanksgiving was nearly as much as when the word got out that President Lincoln had signed the Emancipation Proclamation on January 1, 1863, and when General Robert E. Lee met General Ulysses F. Grant at Appomattox, Virginia, on April 9, 1864, to negotiate the surrender of the Confederate states to the Union army. Finally, the war was over! Finally, all the slaves were free! Finally, dignity brought to the men, women and children who for 245 years had labored in the fields, homes, and businesses of white men and women generally with no pay, no respect for their humanness, no belief in their intelligence, little concern for their welfare, no consideration for their love of their offspring and their families, and no desire to educate them. No longer were *they* property but now they could finally begin to participate in the "American dream" and buy and sell property for themselves – land, horses, mules, farm implements, cows ... all the same kind of property that was inventoried above and below their names in the wills, conveyance records and auction documents of "masters" who would sell them right along with the other *stuff* they had accumulated over their lifetimes! But how?

---

[624] Isaiah T. Montgomery in Charles C. Stringer, Jr., "A Capstone Submitted in Partial Fulfillment of the Requirements for the Degree of Bachelor of Arts in Human Communication," Senior Capstone, California State University, Monterey Bay, May 2002), 21.

Working for daily wages in Livingston Parish, Louisiana, freedmen could earn upwards of $24 - $45 a month; although according to one record, there were not many freedmen employed. Recall that this parish had very few slaves, comparatively speaking, when the practice was legal. The freedmen's pay was relatively *[un]*substantial, as on average, working on the Livingston plantations brought in somewhere around $10/month and rations. Monthly rations[625] were provided to freedmen and typically included: 10 ounces of pork or bacon; 16 ounces of beef; 16 ounces of flour or soft bread; 12 ounces of hard bread; 16 ounces of corn meal; 10 pounds of beans, peas or hominy; 8 pounds of sugar; 2 quarts of vinegar; candles, soap, salt and pepper until such time the freedmen were able to supply themselves with sustenance from their labor. Generally, the Freedmen's Bureau found these rations to be insufficient to stave off illnesses and reported that immediately after the war, thousands of freedmen died because of ill health. When President Lincoln signed the Homestead Act into law on May 20, 1862, although the Act provided 270 million acres of free land to Americans at 160 acres per family unit or individual over a period of 124 years (the program actually did not end until 1986!),[626] the hostility of whites toward "Negroes owning land and cultivating it on their own" severely impacted the administration of the Act on behalf of freedmen.[627]

It was "unsafe" for freedmen to settle some portions of the state except in "large colonies" for fear of being killed or driven away.[628] Vigilante groups like the Jayhawkers formed, especially in numerous rural parishes, and the Black Horse Cavalry in Franklin Parish, composed of planters who blackened their faces and disguised themselves for the purpose of "whipping freedmen *[while simultaneously]* preventing them from leaving the parish, were well-known."[629] These groups not only intimidated and attacked freedmen, "*[both white and black]* civil authorities *[were]* afraid to do their duty and dare*[d]* not give the freedmen justice if they would."[630] Freedmen's Bureau agents in the field called for troops in some counties as "no one *[felt]* safe."[631] This was the situation in St. Landry Parish.

Far too many planters across Louisiana parishes refused to pay their laborers and often "on the slightest of provocation – the pretense of idleness, insolence or other trivial reason" *[after work had been done]* ... they would fire them despite signed labor contracts. In St. Helena Parish in 1866, 134 planters had employed 963 "hands"; in Livingston Parish, two planters had employed 16 "hands." The Freedmen's Bureau reported some success for some freedmen in some of the "country" *[rural]* parishes where crops were successful. Some freedmen were thrifty and saved their money; ultimately "work*[ing]* *[on]* plantations for themselves or work*[ing]* land they may have located under the Homestead Act *[of 1862]*."[632] Even then, however, when freedmen were successful in locating homestead lands, difficulties plagued them in settling there, including selecting land with so many trees it could not be cleared for farming, or building a home or settling a property that was located in

---

625 War Department, Bureau of Refugees, Freedmen and Abandoned Lands, Louisiana, Circular #8, June 1865, M1027, #26, 1865-1869.

626 www.archives.gov/legislative/features/homestead-act/.

627 War Department, Freedmen's Bureau, Circular #8.

628 War Department, Freedmen's Bureau, Circular #8.

629 War Department, Freedmen's Bureau, Circular #8.

630 War Department, Freedmen's Bureau, Circular #8.

631 War Department, Freedmen's Bureau, Circular #8.

632 War Department, Freedmen's Bureau, Circular #29, Regulations for Employer/ee, December 1865.

the prairies where there was insufficient timber or no water.[633] An additional problem was caused by the flooding of the Mississippi in this region. For example, in 1865, and again in the spring of 1866, the Mississippi flooded Louisiana land above Baton Rouge and spread "50 miles wide and 100 miles long," rendering all of this land unusable and of no benefit for either race.[634] Thus, the Homestead Act did not provide 40 acres to freedmen. It provided essentially nothing.

The process of filing a homestead in Louisiana required access to a land office, one of which, seen in this photo, was next to the courthouse in the center of the town of Greensburg. However, although the resources of all five Louisiana land offices would have been necessary to execute the Homestead Act efficiently in the state given the number of freedmen, President Johnson closed two land offices – including the Greensburg Land Office – making it impossible for anyone residing in the area to file their applications for land prior to the government-imposed deadline of January 1, 1867.[635] The incredible bureaucracy, the intentional delay tactics employed, most notably the failure of President Johnson to make timely appointments of staff to accomplish needed functions to execute the Homestead Act, made it impossible for this federal mandate to be implemented. It seemed obvious that the President was not in support of this economic development program designed to aid the freedmen.[636]

Greensburg Land Office, town square

Of the 49 homesteads located in Louisiana in 1867, **JOSEPH** apparently did not own one. The tax record in Livingston Parish listed a **JOSEPH T. FELDER** as having paid taxes in 1866. It is not clear if this was our **JOSEPH**, or if it was actually **Jesse Thomas Felder**, **David's** son; but if it was our **JOSEPH**, it meant that he was a property owner. It is evident, however, that **JOSEPH FELDER** did not tarry long in Louisiana after the war ended. Certainly seeking better opportunities and a less hostile environment, he moved to Pearlington, Mississippi. **SUSANNAH** and **SONA** must have initially stayed behind, perhaps while he went to secure a job and establish a home. Often slaves observed that "masters" would go to find or build a home with every intention of sending for their families afterwards. On many occasions, evidently fairly often, these men never returned and would simply remarry in the new location! Often it was observed that white men married four or five times, having large families with each wife. What happened to the other wives does not seem to get clearly told with the stories that have been handed down; definitely not those that have been written down! **Dr. Charles F. Felder**, for example, married four times in Amite County, Mississippi, and had children with three of the wives. In his case, the previous wives died early, and with so many

---

633 War Department, Freedmen's Bureau, Circular #29.

634 Oubre, *Forty Acres and a Mule*, 250.

635 Oubre, *Forty Acres*, 251.

636 Oubre, *Forty Acres*, 251.

children and slaves, he needed help. Most stories of white men with multiple wives, and even wives with multiple husbands, do not clearly explain why, although death during childbirth was not unusual and surely accounted for some of the multiple marriages. Women who bore these large families also married very early. **Ann O'Neal Felder**, **Charles'** first wife, married him when she was somewhere between the ages of 15 and 20.

Nonetheless, early instability of the family unit in the African American race was, expectantly, somewhat reflective of the practice of separation of the families during slave auctions: buyers purchasing the mother separating her from her children; purchasing the man/father, leaving the mother and children; purchasing part of the family (some of the children with or without one of the parents) and sending them off to distant states. Emotional survival during these forced separations required an inner strength that could only have come from faith that God would intervene somehow, somewhere, if only in heaven. The reality, however, was that many parents and their children, blood relatives, lovers, and friends, never saw each other again. So, while surprised to discover records in Pearlington, Mississippi that **JOSEPH FELDER** married **SOPHIA PARKER** in 1875 and fathered five more children ... without any family oral history that could explain the possible reasons or clarify the whereabouts of **SUSANNAH**, there is nothing to say. I can only assume that the legacies of slavery continued, and that in this, as in many instances among African American couples, the marriage practices modeled by the "masters" once again impressed upon African Americans a standard of acceptability. Perhaps more detail will emerge later. Or, could this have been what **TYREE** meant by "the sins of the father"?

Ownership of property was also modeled by the slave holders, and the slaves certainly noticed the difference in lifestyles and life choices that accompanied property ownership. In Livingston Parish, Louisiana, following the war, the **Felder** brothers (**Rufus**, **Jesse**, **Otis** and **Baxter**) held real estate, separate from their personal property, valued from $1000 to $4000. **Louisa**, their sister, who with her husband, William Gates, was once one of the largest slaveholders in Chickasaw County, had returned to Livingston with her two sons but without her husband, and owned real estate valued at $500.

Many freedmen realized the value of property ownership, economic empowerment, and their relationship to freedom; adopting astute business practices with acumen, displaying a solid understanding of the connections between work, pay, ownership, financial responsibility, and personal and economic progress. It was clear that economic prosperity required employment, that education without application was of little use, and that property ownership required frugal use and investment of money earned. Freedmen did not inherit a hand-me-down of thousands, or even hundreds, of acres of land from their fathers' or other relatives' estates. There were no estates. They were not able to exercise squatter's rights as did the **Felders** and other settlers of Mississippi who arrived between 1800 and 1815 from South Carolina, Georgia, North Carolina, and Tennessee to claim their division of the "20,000 square miles"[637] of *[Indian]* lands made available for the taking to those who would venture to settle the open western territories of the United States. They were not provided landgrants, like **Peter Felder**, who, prior to moving to Mississippi, acquired 1036 acres in Orangeburg, South

---

637 *Felders' (Topisaw) Campmeetings: Descendants of the Founders; History of Felders'* (Topisaw) Campmeetings, 3.

Carolina in the mid- to late 1780s through three state landgrants,[638] or **Rev. Charles Felder**, who was granted 80 acres in Mississippi. Virtually none participated in the great migrations west through the 1862 Homestead Act's free property opportunity except to drive the mules, oxen, and carriages transporting their "masters" to these free lands.

In the state of Mississippi, the five million acres of public land made available through the Southern Homestead Act of 1866 was equally a travesty, as Mississippi had no land office – essential to distributing the lands. Consequently, access to maps and other documents necessary for processing what could have been land claims by freedmen was an impossibility![639] No one left freedmen money except on rare occasions in unusual slave-"master" relationships where a paltry few of the four million ex-slaves were deeded property and/or inherited money after the death of their "owners," who were sometimes their lovers or fathers. They did not receive "40 acres and a mule." In fact, they did not receive one acre, most of them, or a mule. Most freedmen who acquired acreage or mules did not get them for free. They purchased them as they had purchased their relatives during antebellum times when they earned the ability; rendering them property owners in the former instance, and unfortunately, "slave-owners" themselves in the latter instance.

What freed slaves did receive after Emancipation, however, was a personal choice: a choice to attempt to succeed or to fail on their own merits. An overwhelming majority chose to succeed, scrapping by, working as share croppers on former plantations and slave-holding farms, but very often, amazingly, saving significantly from the little they earned to be able to purchase homes of their own, and at times, to leave something of monetary value to their children. Sounds like the system was finally on their side, right? But this was not so!

It was primarily through the Freedman's Savings and Trust Company (which operated on an incredibly uneven and grenade-dotted landscape in 17 states between 1865 and 1874 until it collapsed following the 1873 depression), and the advent of 55 black banks organized in 11 states between 1888 and 1908 (that had their genesis in fraternal orders like the Masons), that black Americans were able to secure loans and mortgages to open businesses and purchase homes. These banks were the backbone and most important "mobilizer" of black businesses, followed closely behind by black churches – the second most powerful influence on black finance.[640]

Mound Bayou

Isaiah T. Montgomery's town of Mound Bayou illustrates a perfect example of the application of the values of economic empowerment. Isaiah carried on as one would expect after the death of his father, Benjamin, with the work ethic and the value of economic prosperity inculcated in him and his siblings as children by the strong nuclear family he was so fortunate to experience as a child. Ten years after Benjamin's death, Isaiah founded the town of Mound Bayou in the Delta region of Mississippi. Expanding on his father's and Joseph Davis' ideas of a "community of cooperation" and

---

638 Marion C. Chandler, archivist, South Carolina State Department of Archives and History, email, July 22, 2014.

639 National Archives and Records Administration, Bureau of Refugees, Freedmen, and Abandoned Lands (Freedmen's Bureau) for Mississippi, 1865-1872, RR# 117, 1.

640 Flournoy Coles, Jr., *Black Economic Development*, (Chicago: Nelson Hall, 1975), 106.

personal respect, he and his cousin, Benjamin Green, also born at Hurricane Plantation,[641] developed Mound Bayou – "the first attempt at Negro self-government in America"[642] – into an American utopia for industrious African Americans that attracted national attention as a model to be replicated.

This little community, birthplace and childhood home of **TYREE** and **CHIQUITA**, has an *OURstory* that any African American descendant of an early settler or later resident of Mound Bayou should know. It can only make one proud of his/her ancestors who settled and built this town. Booker T. Washington once said, "that Mound Bayou was not merely a town, but at the same time in a very real sense of the word, a school. It is not only a place where a Negro may get inspiration ... but a place, also, where he has the opportunity to learn some of the fundamental duties and responsibilities of social and civic life."[643] So, despite the Great Depression that spanned the 1920's and 1930's, which impacted Mound Bayou severely – the Bank of Mound Bayou failed and then closed in 1922, the Oil Mill closed in the mid-20's, people started exiting and moving to Chicago and St. Louis for employment opportunities, cotton prices experienced a severe depression in 1926, the mighty Mississippi flooded in 1927, and a major fire destroyed businesses in the town – it comes as no surprise that in 1929, the Mound Bayou Foundation was formed to specifically secure investors to raise $1 million in capital to stimulate resettlement to the community by those who had left during the exodus to seek employment. Two years later, in 1930, a severe drought seized the Delta community, and in 1941, a year after **SONA's** death, another major fire gutted the center of town destroying nearly the entire business section. But, as Maya Angelou stubbornly proclaimed "...and *still* I rise!" And, so they did; they rebuilt. Every time, they rebuilt, and they survived!

Mound Bayou, referenced as the "Jewel of the Delta" by President Theodore Roosevelt, recovered slowly; determination and persistence being the seeds sown deeply by its founding fathers and the initial twelve families that constituted this experiment. The roots of success, anchored firmly in 1887, sprouted leadership across the 840 acres[644] that this community originally occupied in the Delta. These residents were survivors. They continued to pass on to their children, and their children's children, the values of economic empowerment, personal accountability, and community cooperation ironically acquired on Joseph Davis' Hurricane Plantation. As such, it comes as no surprise that the community at one time had five newspapers, fifteen businesses, three schools, a post office, train station, a hospital (Mount Tabor), credit unions, a bank, several private academies (including **BEATRICE FELDER's** T.O.C.K.), a Carnegie Library, cotton gins, and insurance companies. Philanthropic support came from around the country – Andrew Carnegie, for example, providing the support for the construction of the library. The influence of the seven churches within the community had such a positive impact on the Christian values and moral compasses of its residents that there was no need for either a policeman or a jail. Although a "policeman" was hired, he carried no gun. No

---

641 Crowe, Cradle of Self Government, 1.

642 *The Southern Advocate*, vol. 4, no. 30, July 10, 1937, 1.

643 Representative Benjamin Thompson, in 114th Congress, 2nd Session, April 26, 2016, Remarks Honoring Mound Bayou Public Schools, accessed August 2, 2018, https://www.congreses.gov/congressional-record/2016/4/26/extensions-of-remarks-section/article/E584-3.

644 An interesting aside, Clemson University, plantation property of John C. Calhoun, former Vice President of the United States, and Thomas Green Clemson, was exactly 840 acres. Mound Bayou, thus, can be compared to the size of a moderate antebellum size plantation or the campus of a mid-size Southern university. For more information see National Register of Historic Places, https://www.nps.gov/nr/feature/places/pdfs/13000735.pdf.

alcohol could be sold in the town, no prostitution was allowed, cohabitation of unmarried couples was against the law and punishable by an order to marry, be prosecuted, or move out of town.[645]

In Mississippi, the state that elevated the consciousness of the nation to the senselessness of racial discord, hatred, and violence, Mound Bayou served as a tiny speck of hope, a flickering light from a candle, and an "oasis in *[many]* turbulent times," for example, being probably the only place that Ms. Mamie Till could stay safely in the entire state during the 1955 lynching trial of her 12-year-old son, Emmett.[646] Money, Mississippi, the scene of that unimaginable crime, is only 44 miles southeast of Mound Bayou.

City scene in Mound Bayou circa 1922

Aerial view of Mound Bayou

THE LEGACY: ECONOMIC EMPOWERMENT AND PROPERTY OWNERSHIP

Got "Up from Slavery," he did!

S. P. FELDER rises to the apex of the **FELDER** early ancestors regarding economic empowerment and ownership of property. Quickly becoming known for his financial astuteness, math ability, and business acumen, he was a founding stockholder in the Bank of Mound Bayou, organized in 1904, making a $100 deposit in 1912, and became the first president of the People's Savings Bank in Shaw, Mississippi. He was one of nine directors of the Mound Bayou Foundation, established to secure $1 million capital during the Great Depression. He built several homes, including one at 209-211 on the Corner of Edison and Felder's Alley in Greenville, Mississippi, that had 1.5 stories

---

645 Booker T. Washington, *Rediscovered*, 129.

646 Mound Bayou, accessed April 7, 2015, Storycorps.org/mound-bayou-mississippi-the-jewel-of-the-delta/.

with six rooms downstairs and two upper rooms.[647] Until that home was completed, the family, which included **WILDA**, **KORINNE**, **DORA**, and himself, lived on Muskadine Street. He owned "one of the first cars *[a Cadillac]* in Mound Bayou."[648] Once the family moved to Mound Bayou, they were initially provided three lots and assistance "in getting started" with their first house – a seven room house with a "large hall downstairs and two rooms upstairs." That house unfortunately burned down.

Got up from a slave parent and the era of the Great Depression, she did!

BEATRICE FELDER followed right behind her father, owning property in addition to owning her own business, the private academy, T.O.C.K. (The Opportunity Center Kindergarten). Although she died intestate, her properties went to her two children, **TYREE** and **CHIQUITA**, who disposed of it as they deemed fit – the decision being made to sell it all. On February 13, 1922, 25-year-old **BEATRICE** paid $100.00 cash and purchased from Ida and John Revels the property at Lot #2 in Block 14 in the Banks and Francis Addition of Mound Bayou.[649] Upon her death, her property located in the 2nd judicial district of Bolivar County, was sold to Tommy Hearon for $4350.00 *[$34,558]*[650]: N1/2 of the Northeast Quarter (NE1/4) of Southwest Quarter (SW1/4) of Section 28, Township 24 North, Range 5 W; and a 20-acre farm track – Lots 3, 4 and 5 of Block 10, Lot 2 of Block 14, Lots 1 and 2 of Block 15, and Lots 9 and 10 of Block 16 – all located in the Banks and Francis Addition of Mound Bayou – were sold to George Moore with the permission of her sole heirs at law, **TYREE** and **CHIQUITA**. Lots 1 and 2 in block 15 were purchased for the sum of $80.00 by **MRS. OTTOWIESS HULBERT** of Cleveland, Mississippi, from Mrs. W. E. Roberson, on October 4, 1932.[651] Lots 4 and 5, in Block 10 were purchased by **MRS. W. J. FELDER (WILDA)** for the sum of $100, cash, from the Hazlehurst Lumber Company on October 15, 1915[652] although they seemed to have been initially purchased for the sum of $325 by **S. P.** and **W. J. FELDER** on July 27, 1911, sold to them by Charles Banks and John W. Francis.[653] On November 1, 1948, Lots 3, 4, 5, and 10, belonging to "daughter and heir in law of **W. J. FELDER**," **KORINNE T. JACKSON**, were quit claimed for the sum of $1.00 and "other DOLLARS" to **B. O. FELDER**, with **E. P. JACKSON** ("Uncle Jack") relinquishing his "right of dower in and to" the property. $1.10 Rev stamps were "affixed and cancelled" on this document.[654] On January 16, 1930, Lots 9 and 10 and the buildings situated on these lots, of Block 16, were purchased from Katie Robinson of New Orleans by **CHIQUITA JANE** and **TYREE PRESTON FELDER**.[655] At the date of purchase, **CHIQUITA** was four years old and **TYREE** was three! Finally, she owned property in Greenville, Mississippi, which was sold at her

---

647 S. P. *Felder Family Bible*, notation by Wilda Felder.

648 Interview with Rev. Woodley, AME Presiding Elder, Mound Bayou, Mississippi, June 13, 2003.

649 Abstracts of Titles, Deed No. 1812, M-3, 601, Chancery Court, QCD, Cleveland, Mississippi.

650 Inflation calculator, 2012 value.

651 Abstracts of Titles, M 84, Chancery Court, QCD, Cleveland, Mississippi, 196. T.O.C.K. was opened on October 19, 1932, so this was Beatrice's home as well as the facility in which she operated her school until she moved it to the Bethel A.M.E. Church basement.

652 Abstracts of Titles, Land Deed Record No. 2535, E-12, QCD, Bolivar County, Chancery Court, QCD, Cleveland, Mississippi, 366.

653 Abstracts of Titles, E-8, Deed No. 3036, Bolivar County, Chancery Court, QCD, Cleveland, Mississippi, 326.

654 Abstracts of Titles, M 38, Bolivar County, Chancery Court, QCD, Cleveland, Mississippi, 489.

655 Abstracts of Titles, M 22, Bolivar County, Chancery Court, QCD, Cleveland, Mississippi, 351.

death for $900.00. Despite the Great Depression, loss of her parents within three years of each other, and shortly thereafter, divorce from her husband who left her to raise two children as a single parent, **BEATRICE** lived a productive and awe-inspiring life, influencing family, friends, and townspeople. Her estate of farm land, vacant lots, multiple homes, cash, and postal savings certificates valued at more than $3000 in 1958, enabled her to teach by example that thrift, industriousness, and a will-get-it-done-at-all-costs attitude is proof that life is what you make it.

Got up with a family legacy of survival, determination, and vision, he did!

TYREE FELDER built and owned homes throughout his lifetime, and steadily moved up from a new 720-square-foot, four-room, one-bath home on North Carolina Avenue (built in 1953), to which he built a barbeque pit and planted a garden in the back yard; to the 1157-square-foot, three-bedroom, 1.5-bath home with attached carport and barbeque pit (844 Augusta Avenue), that he built in 1959. At this home, Daddy planted a garden in the back yard and the weeping willow tree rooting from Mississippi in the front yard. It was at his last house that he planted a garden, wrote music and contemplated his life. Planting and tending a garden, which he did so well, was a legacy he inherited from his mother *[although this one did not seem to get passed down to his children!]* Even during the depression, he witnessed his mother feeding others in Mound Bayou because her garden flourished with pear and mulberry trees, onions, peppers, asparagus, nuts, and more.[656] **TYREE** did the same at each of his homes, growing corn, greens, watermelon, cantaloupe, tomatoes, string beans, cabbage, squash, and more – always sending visitors away with plates, bags, and containers of fresh vegetables or cooked concoctions he made himself, and never not having food to feed his family.

216 North Carolina Avenue

Home Daddy built

Daddy in his garden

---

656 Frankie Felder, *Lessons for Life: Alumni Remember Miss B. Ottowiess Felder*. Students from Miss Felder's school, TOCK, spoke affectionately of picking and eating fruits and vegetables from her garden in her yard.

Got up from his "slave-owning" grandfather, he did!

ALEXANDER HULBERT, general contractor, built homes and owned several properties. In 1930, amid the Great Depression, his home on Mississippi Boulevard was valued at $8000 *[$109,985 in 2012 dollars]* with only one other home on the street valued higher. According to the Memphis black Chamber of Commerce, he built "modern and palatial homes in the East end of Memphis" over the many years that he worked as a builder, with more than 300 homes credited to his efforts. "Among the biggest and most costly structures he has to his credit are an Eight Apartment *[sic]* flat on Harbert Avenue, costing approximately $35,000 *[$573,985]* and a $25,000 *[$409,989]* home on Trezevant."[657] **ALEXANDER** owned several homes in Memphis, and, at least in this regard, was an inspiring role model for his children – *all* of them.

Got up from parents who lived through the depression, she did!

GLADYS LOIS FELDER WASHINGTON followed the examples of the legacies left in our family, and early in her life, began to own property. The oldest of **TYREE FELDER's** daughters, she was also the first to purchase a home. At age 27, she and her husband, **LLOYD**, bought a three-bedroom, Tudor Cape English-style home in Queens, New York, with a finished basement and detached one-car garage, all perfect for their family of three little ones and a Great Dane! *[Well, maybe not for the Great Dane that they finally gave to someone with a large yard!]* Eight years later, they moved to Florida and bought a four-bedroom, two-bath 1950 square-foot home with an enclosed Florida sunroom, a screened-in patio that provided an inviting view of the property, which included several papaya, banana, and mango trees *[and cows in the neighboring back pasture!]*. Finally, on their third move, the family purchased a custom-built 4025 square-foot, six-bedroom, four-bath home with a three-car garage and covered patio and pool, setting a standard for all of us siblings.[658] **GLADYS**, my first-born sister.

My sister's home in Florida

---

657 Memphis Negro Chamber of Commerce, *Negro Yearbook and Directory of Memphis and Shelby County*, 1943, 37.

658 Text by Gladys Washington, October 2014.

RECALLING
OURstory

OURstory
IN LOUISIANA

- Where the discovery of the first bit of documentation about our ancestors initiated this book;
- a place that introduced our family to slavery;
- the location of the national cemetery of our Civil War hero;
- where our roots spread and we never knew.

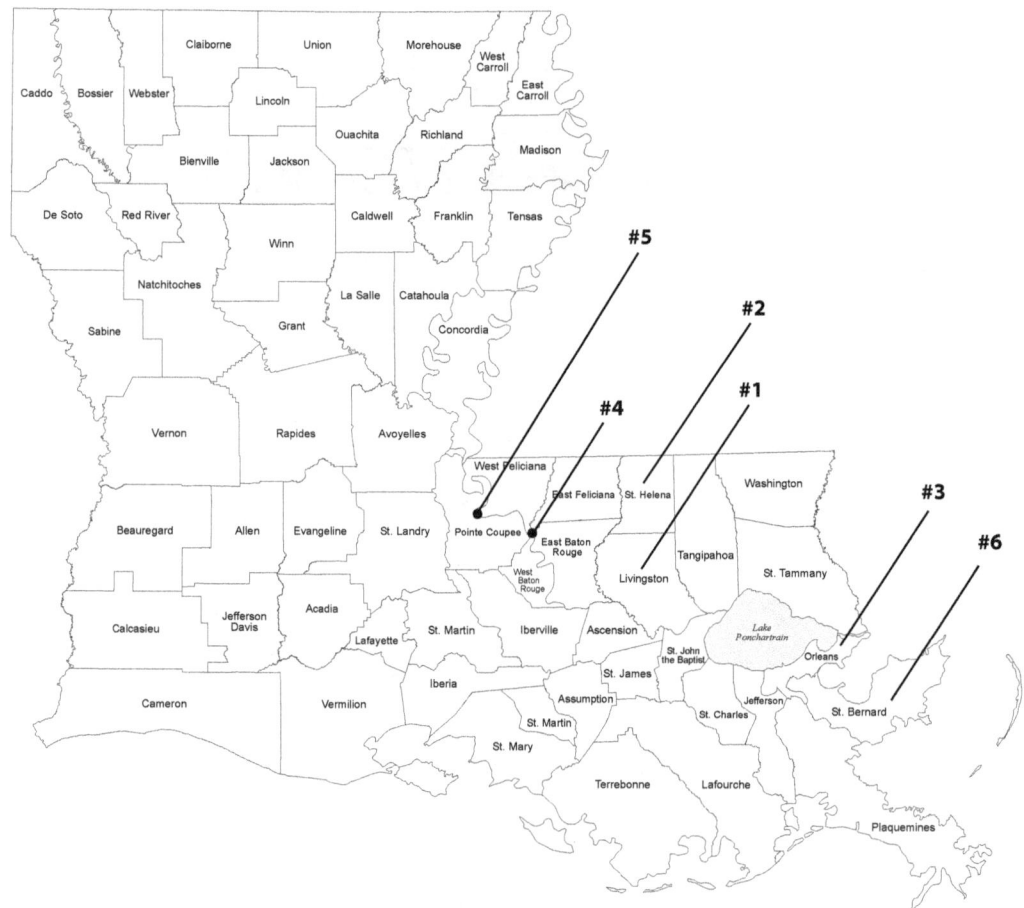

1. St Helena Parish (Gates LA; later Livingston Parish)
2. Greensburg
3. New Orleans
4. Port Hudson (East Baton Rouge Parish)
5. Batchelor/Innis
6. St. Bernard Parish

© Frankie Felder, 2020

FRANKIE FELDER

WHAT HAPPENED HERE?

St. Helena Parish (1830 – 1881)

Gates
David Felder moved from Mississippi to Gates to become first Felder in Louisiana, 1830

Greensburg
Dr. William Riley Felder lived, with slaves (Joseph possibly the five-year-old), 1850
Dr. William Riley Felder died, August 20, 1853; first Felder to own slaves in Greensburg
St. Helena Rifles formed in Greensburg and left for Civil War, 1861
Sona P. Felder born, ~1861-63
Joseph Felder and Susanna Lewis married, January 28, 1869
Peter Jenkins and Millie Coffee married; parents of Emma Jenkins, 1869
Sona Felder and Emma Jenkins married, February 17, 1881
Susan P. Felder born November 24, 1881

Livingston Parish (1840 – 1865)

St. Helena divided; southern part becomes Livingston Parish, 1840
David Felder "owned" slaves; lived here until death, 1842
Slaves not included in inventory of David Felder's property

Orleans Parish (1860 – current)

B. M. Hulbert enlisted in Confederate army, April 23, 1864
Sgt. Isaac Felder and Margaret married, May 12, 1867; Old Baptist Church, Cypress Street
Sgt. Isaac Felder makes deposit into Freedmen's Bureau Bank of New Orleans, May 31, 1872
Sgt. Isaac Felder died, April 5, 1909; Margaret died, May 5, 1926; relatives continue to live here

East Baton Rouge Parish (1863 – 1866)

Port Hudson
Sgt. Isaac Felder fought in Civil War, 1863-1865; honorably discharged October 22, 1866

Pointe Coupée Parish (1881 – 1900)

Batchelor or Innis
Alexander Hulbert born, ~November 25, 1881 (or 1878), and lived here

St. Bernard Parish (1909 -)

Chalmette National Cemetery
Sgt. Isaac Felder buried here, April 1909

OURstory
IN MISSISSIPPI

- A place we always feared;
- where our father grew up in the all-Black Delta town of Mound Bayou;
- where our grandmother lived until illness required us to get her to a Chicago hospital, where she died;
- where ancestors are buried in unmarked graves;
- where our roots are deeper than we ever knew.

1. Summit
2. Liberty
3. Natchez
4. Port Gibson
5. Columbus
6. Magnolia
7. Vicksburg
8. Logtown/Possum Walk
9. Osyka
10. Hermanville
11. Shaw
12. Jackson
13. Friars Point
14. West Point
15. Waveland/Biloxi
16. Mound Bayou
17. Greenville
18. Cleveland
19. Bayou Pierre (stream in Claiborne County)

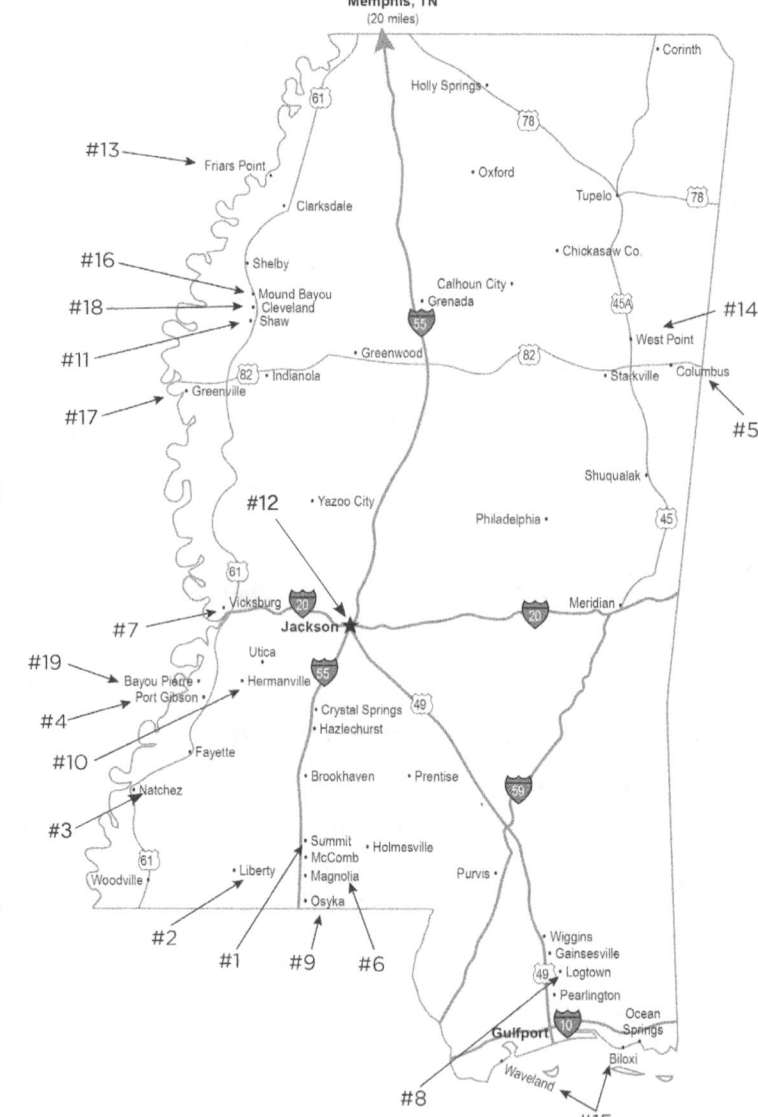

© Frankie Felder, 2020

WHAT HAPPENED HERE?

Bayou Pierre
William Hurlburt arrived in Mississippi, brought slaves here in 1773

Summit
Peter Felder moved to the Vaughn House from Orangeburg, South Carolina, 1810
Joseph, Levi Felder's slave, joined Shady Grove Baptist Church, 1859

Liberty (1819 – 1870s)
Rev. Charles Felder pastored East Fork Baptist Church, 1819; his and others' slaves joined
Rev. Charles Felder established Liberty Baptist Church, 1839; his and others' slaves joined
Dr. Charles F. Felder's house located between Liberty and Magnolia, 1840s-
Freedmen withdrew from Felder's churches; established their own churches, 1868

Natchez (1840 – 1909)
Possible auction/purchase site of Keziah Ellis (grandmother of Wilda Ellis); possibly a slave from Tidewater region of Virginia who walked to Mississippi via Slave Trail of Tears
Benjamin Montgomery (father of I.T. Montgomery-founder of Mound Bayou) purchased at Natchez Slave Market by Joseph Davis (Confederate president Jeff Davis' brother), 1837
Sonny Felder (Joseph Felder's father) lived and worked, 1870s
B. M. Hulbert died; date unknown (after 1900)

Port Gibson/Claiborne County (1843 – 1888)
Martin Nathaniel Hulbert and Sinai Sanders Rail married, December 5, 1843
B. M. Hulbert born, August 1848
Location of Dunbarton Plantation of Martin Nathaniel Hulbert, 1840s-1860s
Mundy escaped Martin Hulbert's plantation, November 1850! Unfortunately captured.
Martin N. Hulbert and son, Julian, enlisted in Confederate army, 1862
Bessie Shaffer (Alexander Hulbert's first wife) born, 1881
Sinai Hulbert died and buried, May 15, 1888

Columbus (1850s – 1880s)
Jane Ellis born, January 2, 1852
Wilda Ellis born, May 3, 1876; married Rev. S. P. Felder at First Baptist Church, 1894

Magnolia (1830s – 1865)
"Aunt Chloe," sister of Joseph, Isaac, Henry, Katie and Alice, was the cook at Prewitt Plantation

Vicksburg (1863 – 1887)

Julian Hulbert captured by Union forces during Vicksburg surrender, 1863
Campbell College began, 1887

Logtown/Possum Walk/Pearlington (1871 – 1887)

Isaac Felder and family lived, 1871-72
Joseph Felder served as trustee for school he helped build for freed slaves, 1870s
Joseph Felder married Sophia Parker, April 5, 1875; John, Simon, Nathaniel, Adeline, and Daniel born here
Rev. S. P. Felder started A.M.E. Church in region (Jordan River, Logtown, Bay St. Louis), 1885-87

Osyka (1866 – 1880s)

Martha Felder (Joseph Felder's grandmother), hoe hand on Dr. Charles F. Felder's plantation, moved near here to work for Sam Newman, ~1866
Christopher Columbus Felder (son of Dr. Charles F. Felder) moved here, ~1866
David and Eva Vaughn moved here, 1878

Hermanville (1800s –)

Sanders family lived and died here, 1800s
John Rail (Sinai's first husband) died, 1840
Julian Hulbert raised his family; died and was buried, October 1880
Martin Nathaniel Hulbert lived here after Sinai passed; died here, October 1894
Black Hulberts still live here

Whitestown (1888-89)

Rev. S. P. Felder pastored the A.M.E. Church, 1888

Shaw (1891 – 1894)

Wilda Felder taught school, 1892-1894
Beatrice Felder born, 1897
Sona Felder first president of Peoples Saving Bank

Jackson (1898 – 1944)

Campbell College relocated here, 1898
Rev. S. P. Felder received honorary doctorate degree from Campbell College
Tyree Felder graduated from high school at Campbell College, 1944

Friars Point (1887 – 1900)

Campbell College held classes, 1887
Rev. S. P. Felder appointed Presiding Elder, 1899; pastored Bethel A.M.E. Church
Robbie Hulbert Thompson, husband, Autry Thompson, and son, Autry Jr., lived nearby, ~1899

West Point (1900)

Susie P. Felder (daughter of S. P. and Emma Felder) studied at Mary Holmes Seminary, 1900

Greenville (1900 – 1912)

Korinne Tyree Felder born, 1900
James Hulbert born, 1906
Rev. S. P. Felder built a house here at 209-211 Edison and Felder's Alley, 1910

Waveland/Biloxi (1905 –)

Clarence Hulbert (B.M. Hulbert's brother) moved here, 1905; died in Biloxi, 1923
Kathleen Casper (Martin and Sinai Hulbert's great-great granddaughter) lived; died here, 2015
Hulbert relatives still live here

Mound Bayou (1912 – 1957)

Rev. S. P. Felder and Wilda moved their family here, 1912; place of residence until 1957
Chiquita Hulbert born, September 11, 1926
Tyree Felder born, October 6, 1927
Beatrice O. Hulbert purchased land, October 4, 1932; opened her school (T.O.C.K. – The Opportunity Center Kindergarten), October 19, 1932
Wilda (1937) and Rev. S. P. Felder (1940) buried in Mound Bayou City Cemetery, unmarked graves
Beatrice took ill; transported to Chicago by Tyree for surgery where she died, 1957

Cleveland (1925 – 1944)

B. O. Felder and Alex Hulbert married here, 1925
Beatrice O. Hulbert and children's home located here, 1925-32
Birdsong Camp established during Great Flood, 1927
Name change – from Hulbert back to Felder – at courthouse, 1944

Legacy

a gift by inheritance ... values passed down from one generation to the next ... heritage ... birthright ... accomplishments, actions, service to be replicated ... traditions ... perspectives of the ancestors ... spirits of protection and guidance ...

OURstory
PROFILE IN COURAGE
Sergeant Isaac Felder

Marquett Milton
Representing Sgt. Isaac Felder and all the brave men of the United States Colored Troops
African American Civil War Museum in Washington, DC

The battles at Port Hudson and Milliken's Bend, Louisiana were a critical turning point in the Civil War. A turning point in military strategists' minds, both Union and Confederate – turning slaves into soldiers. A turning point in slaves' minds – turning victims into invincible fighters for freedom.

ISAAC FELDER liberated his mind and then himself when he walked off the Carter's plantation and into the Corps d' Afrique's recruitment office in Baton Rouge on October 23, 1863, to join a unit headed to Port Hudson just months after the news broke that blacks fought for freedom at Milliken's Bend with bravery unmatched in any battle of the war. At most 22 years old, he left behind his young wife, **MARGARET**, whom he had married, likely "jumping the broom," around 1859 in a plantation ceremony, fortunately witnessed by

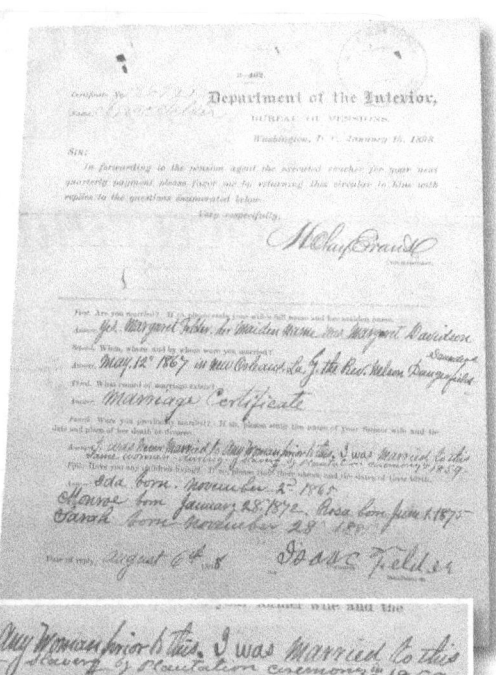

Bureau of Pensions documentation showing plantation wedding

other slaves who later would be able to come to their defense, vouching for their long-standing, monogamous marriage and their integrity. He promised to return as soon as possible. His intent in enlisting was to liberate his wife, as well as his mother, **SARAH**, and her siblings, his cousin, **PRISCILLA**, and his many other relatives and friends who could not, or would not, take the bold and dangerous step to take up arms against their "masters." Two years earlier, Carter men from local plantations put their grey uniforms on, gathered their arms, and vowed to fight to the end to keep **ISAAC** and all his kin enslaved.

For three gruesome years, **ISAAC** applied his God-given intellect and his plantation-acquired skills in the engineering and infantry units of the 81st, 89th, and 93rd regiments of the United States Colored Troops (USCT). Serving with excellence as an engineer, he moved up in rank from corporal to sergeant as he worked alongside his comrades in providing garrison duty at Port Hudson, extending his military service beyond Lee's surrender and Lincoln's assassination. As did most soldiers in this war, however, **ISAAC** fought more than mortal enemies; he also fought unfair treatment and disease. **CORPORAL FELDER** was "reduced in rank" to private by Major O. N. Blackington on September 27, 1865, for reasons unstated in the military documentation but was reinstated to corporal on December 1, 1865, by Colonel Gaskell.[659] Eighteen hundred sixty-six proved to be an extremely difficult year. Hospitalized on several occasions, by God's grace he defeated small pox, fevers, boils, and cholera, and mustered out

---

[659] Widow's Certificate No. 693663, Isaac Felder, Sergeant, Company B, 81st USCI, Louisiana; Case Files of Approved Pension Applications of Veterans Who Survived in the Army ("Civil War and Later Survivors' Certificates"), 1861-1934; Records of the Department of Veterans Affairs, Record Group 15; National Archives Building, Washington, DC.

of military service physically whole and honorably discharged on October 22, 1866.[660]

ISAAC's enlistment in Company H of the 9th Infantry Regiment speaks volumes for his intellect and skills and suggests that his work while enslaved involved technical knowhow. Short in stature – standing only 5'6-1/2" (not atypical of soldiers in that period) – but tall in intellect, he was one of only a few **Felder** soldiers, black or white, Union or Confederate, who mustered out of service with a rank higher than that of a private. Further, he enlisted as an engineer.

On August 13, 1864, **CORPORAL FELDER** was transferred from the 89th Regiment to Company B of the 93rd Regiment, comprised of its predecessor, the USCI (United States Colored Infantry) and the 25th Regiment Infantry. This Regiment served duty at New Iberia and Brashear City from April 1864 until June 23, 1865, at which time it, too, was dissolved. For much of that time, however, **ISAAC** was infirmed, so it is unclear if he, too, served in these locations. **CORPORAL FELDER** was later mustered into Company B of the 81st Regiment (USCI), which was originally organized April 4, 1864, from the 9th Corps d' Afrique Infantry and consolidated several times subsequently including being attached in 1864 to the Engineer Brigade. This Regiment served garrison and post duty at Port Hudson. When the Regiment was dissolved and its soldiers mustered out of Company B in 1866, **ISAAC** left with his comrades and returned to the plantation proudly displaying a three-stripe insignia on his sleeve identifying him as the first documented military sergeant in our family.

Sergeant

ISAAC was born around August 1844 in Pike County, Mississippi, to **SARAH** and **SONNY FELDER**. It is known that **SARAH** was "owned" by **Dr. Charles F. Felder** and that she bore 12 children. **ISAAC** stated in numerous testimonies that he grew up in Louisiana, indicating that he was either sold away or hired out as a young boy to a slaveowner in Louisiana. It is not certain on which Carter plantation he was enslaved, as to date no "owner's" first name surfaces in any of **ISAAC's** records. However, there were only a few Carter plantations/farms in all of Louisiana. Given the closeness of the **Felder** families and their friends from South Carolina, it is likely that the Carter plantation where he slaved was either in St. Helena (with Louisiana Carter and husband mentioned in the departure ceremony of the St. Helena Rifles when they went off to war from Greensburg), or one of the Carters in East Feliciana (only 20 miles from Port Hudson where **ISAAC** served while enlisted). Another possibility is the plantation in Rapides Parish where **Maria Felder** (sister of the South Carolina **Felder** brothers in Pike and Amite MS) and her husband Isaac Carter lived. When one narrows these choices down based on the ages of the male slaves living on these plantations/farms in 1860, the most likely Carter farm appears to be in St. Helena Parish where a Leonard farm also existed. **MARGARET** was enslaved on a Leonard farm. Absent adequate documentation, suffice it to say that **ISAAC** was never too far from the rest of his relatives who remained in Pike and Amite counties in Mississippi. Nor was he ever too far from **MARGARET**.

---

660 Records of the Adjutant General's Office, Entry 534: (92 U.S.C.T. Ashton, David to 96 U.S.C.T. Young, Silas), Box 3708; H.M. Done 1991. National Archives, Washington, D.C.

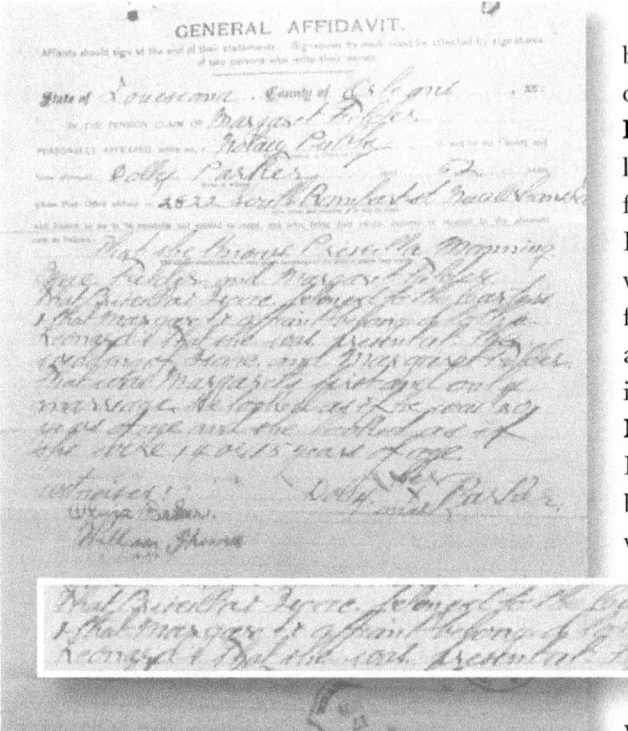

Affidavit naming slave holders

After the war, **ISAAC** probably went back to the Carter plantation one more time, certainly to see his kinsmen from bondage. **ISAAC** was a man of his word who was in love with **MARGARET**, and she waited in faith that he would return, as he promised. He did return but only briefly. This time when he left the Leonard plantation, he left for good with his one-year-old baby girl, **IDA**, and her mother, **MARGARET**. This family walked away together from Greensburg; **MARGARET** no longer beholden to the Leonard family, and **ISAAC** no longer beholden to the Carter family. The war was over, the union was preserved, and they were free! Their kinsmen from bondage were free! Their parents and siblings were free! Imagine their feelings as they made their way to Logtown, Mississippi, where **ISAAC** went to work as an engineer on a steamer and **MARGARET** gave birth to and cared for their growing family. Just imagine . . .

In a formal and now legal wedding ceremony held on May 12, 1867, at the Old Baptist Church in New Orleans on Cypress and Howard streets, they began their journey, surrounding themselves with a family of many children, relatives, and friends from their years of bondage. Sadly, all of their 11 children did not survive to adulthood, but those who did remained close by their parents. While residing in Logtown, in addition to their children, grandchildren, cousins, sons- and daughters-in-law lived in their home. It was also here that he and his brother, **JOSEPH**, reunited, and where **SONA**, his nephew *[JOSEPH's son]*, was soon to come and initiate the A.M.E. religion in this region of the state. Later, when **ISAAC** relocated to New Orleans, numerous relatives and former plantation friends formed a close-knit community there as well.

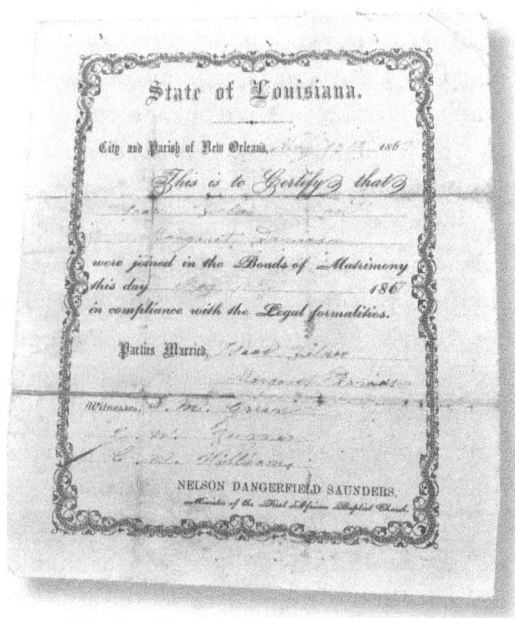

Marriage Certificate of Isaac and Margaret

ISAAC purchased property in New Orleans after the war but struggled with paying taxes on his 31-foot by 100-foot lot facing Thalia Street. On October 21, 1876, his property was slated to be auctioned by the state collector. The amount unpaid since 1873 totaled $5.80.[661] Unpaid or late taxes plagued **ISAAC** over numerous years, as his property on Thalia Street showed delinquencies on several occasions. Whether he resolved these specific issues or not is unclear because his house address does change on Thalia Street, but this was the street on which he and his family remained the rest of their lives. According to court records,[662] he was once fined $5.00 for failure to properly repair screens surrounding two cisterns in his yard. But, despite obvious economic challenges at home, **ISAAC** participated actively in his church, First African Baptist, continuing the legacy of fiscal oversight – a pattern evident across generations in the **FELDER** family – having been elected in 1887 as one of seven trustees of the church.

Twenty-five years after the war, serious health problems emerged – chronic conjunctivitis and asthma – impeding **ISAAC's** ability to continue to earn a steady income performing manual labor as an engineer and later as a mechanic. Often, he simply could not get out of bed, laboring just to breathe. Struggling with painful, bloodshot and feverish eyes, significantly impairing his vision, life was becoming exceedingly difficult. He was hospitalized at Charity Hospital and soon afterwards **MARGARET** began to work as a nurse to help provide for the family. **ISAAC** applied to the Bureau of Pensions for a disability pension, which was approved on November 4, 1890. However, from that time until his death nineteen years later, the disability was questioned by the Bureau. As the review process unfolded, relatives, friends, physicians, and employers who had known him anywhere from 25- to 40-plus years were required to provide notarized testimony of his integrity and his disability. His medical records during and after his war service were ordered, scrutinized, and challenged as documentation of his health. The continuous requests for more and more documentation, necessitating lawyers and notaries to submit voluminous paperwork over many years, stressed this obviously already ill man who was at the same time attempting to provide care for two daughters suffering from typhoid pneumonia. Four children had already died, possibly victims of the 1878 yellow fever epidemic in the South, which originated in and ravaged New Orleans, taking the lives of approximately 20,000 people.

ISAAC's documentation ultimately was rejected by the Department of Insurance of the Pension Bureau. His disability pension, which commenced on November 4, 1890, was deemed invalid. But, to add insult to injury, in the June 8, 1891 documentation prepared by the War Department Record of Pension Division (which had access to his entire military file), the commanding officer recorded **ISAAC's** military service as a private in one unit, placed blank marks in the spaces for his additional service as if it never even occurred, and failed to acknowledge that **ISAAC** joined the military as a corporal and was discharged as a sergeant. While he appealed, his pension was ordered to be reduced from $12/month to $8/month beginning March 1, 1895, apparently with intentions to discontinue it altogether as soon as the anticipated unsuccessful appeal had concluded. However, with only 30 days to respond, his highly influential and well-connected African attorney, Oscar Pilman, launched a

---

661 New Orleans *Republican*, October 11, 1876. $5.80 in equivalency is $128.00 (*measuringworth.com*).

662 New Orleans *Times-Picayune*, August 2, 1907.

successful appeal on his behalf. Fortunately, the testimony of friends from bondage on the plantations where **ISAAC** and **MARGARET** were enslaved, and the notarized affidavits of neighbors, physicians, co-workers, and employers in New Orleans, where he worked as a mechanic and machinist and served in his church and community, vouched for this couple's identity and character and rescued **ISAAC** from this abyss of disgrace and disrespect. The Bureau's medical chief's determination of a reduction was reversed, he retained his monthly rate, and his disability was finally permanently established.

ISAAC never recovered good health, although he died not of ailments that established his disability but of acute indigestion. Once he passed, **MARGARET** received a widow's pension of $12/month beginning May 18, 1909. **MARGARET's** ability to advocate for herself following **ISAAC's** death was learned from years of observing and participating in the legal processes enacted on her husband's behalf by their attorney, Oscar Pilman. Pilman, as early as 1868, began participating in the affairs of state in Louisiana and was revered as competent and credible. Among other positions, he served as assistant secretary of the Algiers Radical Republican Club, Louisiana State Assessor, Justice of the Peace, and President of the Police Jury. In 1916, by writing to the Bureau of Pensions regarding the bill in Congress passed to increase soldiers' pensions, **MARGARET** secured an increase of her pension benefit to $20/month on September 8, 1918, and before her death, May 5, 1926, her benefit had risen to $30.00 a month. The legacy of self-advocacy continued in **ISAAC's** family as **MONROE**, his only living son, wrote the Pension Bureau following the death of his mother and asked if he, too, would be eligible for benefits given that he was ill. Unfortunately, because he had passed the age of 16 prior to his father's death, **MONROE** was ineligible for benefits.

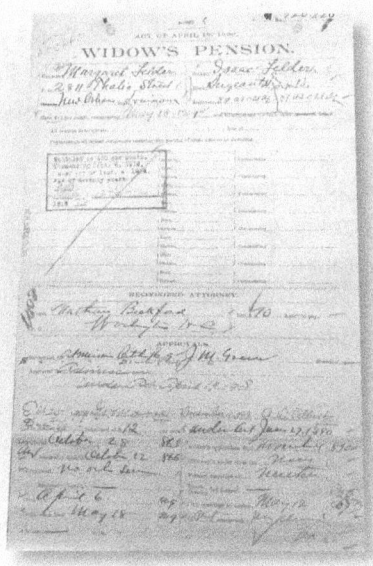

Widow's Pension

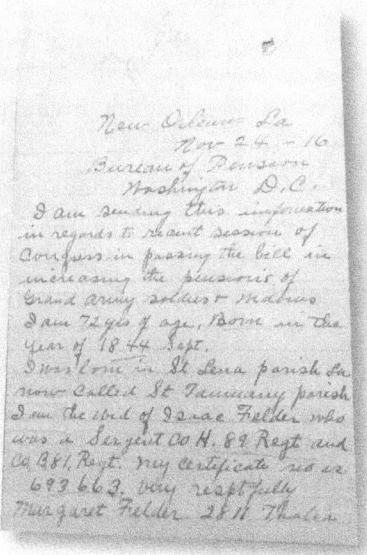

Letter from Margaret to Bureau of Pensions

Chalmette National Cemetery

Isaac Felder's tombstone

On April 5, 1909,[663] **ISAAC** laid down his burdens at Chalmette National Cemetery[664] in New Orleans. This cemetery was established in 1864 as a final resting place for Civil War veterans. Annually, New Orleans holds a Memorial Day program on-site honoring the soldiers who gave their lives to save the union and to free the slaves. **ISAAC** served every year from 1893 to 1901 as a member of the Executive Committee that planned and executed those memorial celebration programs. He is immortalized, as well as all African American soldiers of the Civil War, in Washington, DC, at the African American Civil War Museum.

Got up from slavery, he did – with courage, bravery, determination, and always with service! My great-great-grand-uncle.

Isaac Felder's name engraved on the USCT monument

---

663 Records differ (April 5th or 6th, 1909) per Margaret's statement, the military documentation, and the undertaker's statement recorded at the Board of Health.

664 Gravesite 12549, Section 53.

Chalmette National Cemetery

ISAAC FELDER'S **FAMILY TREE**

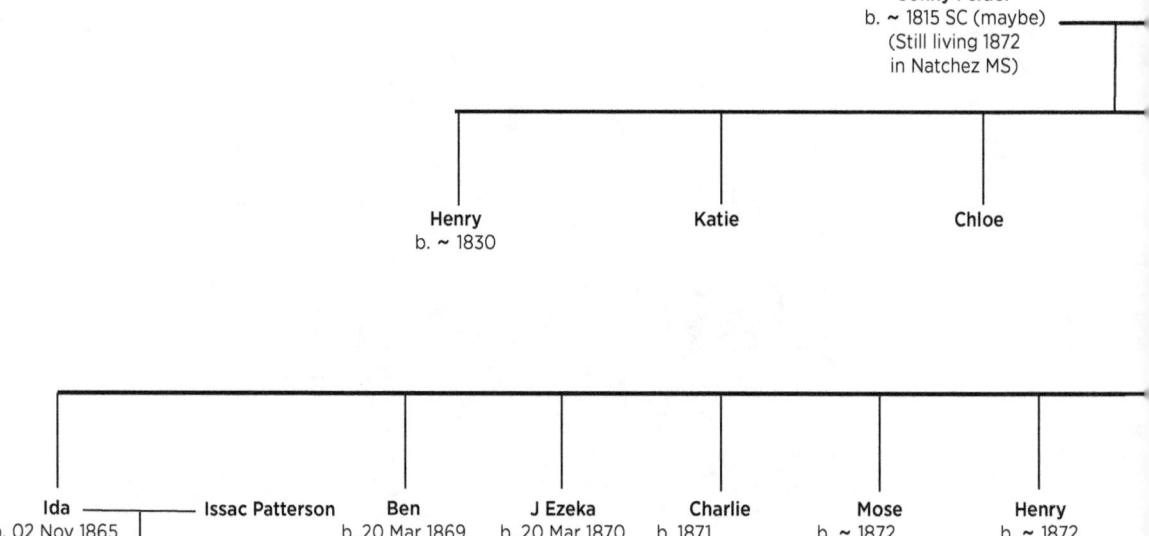

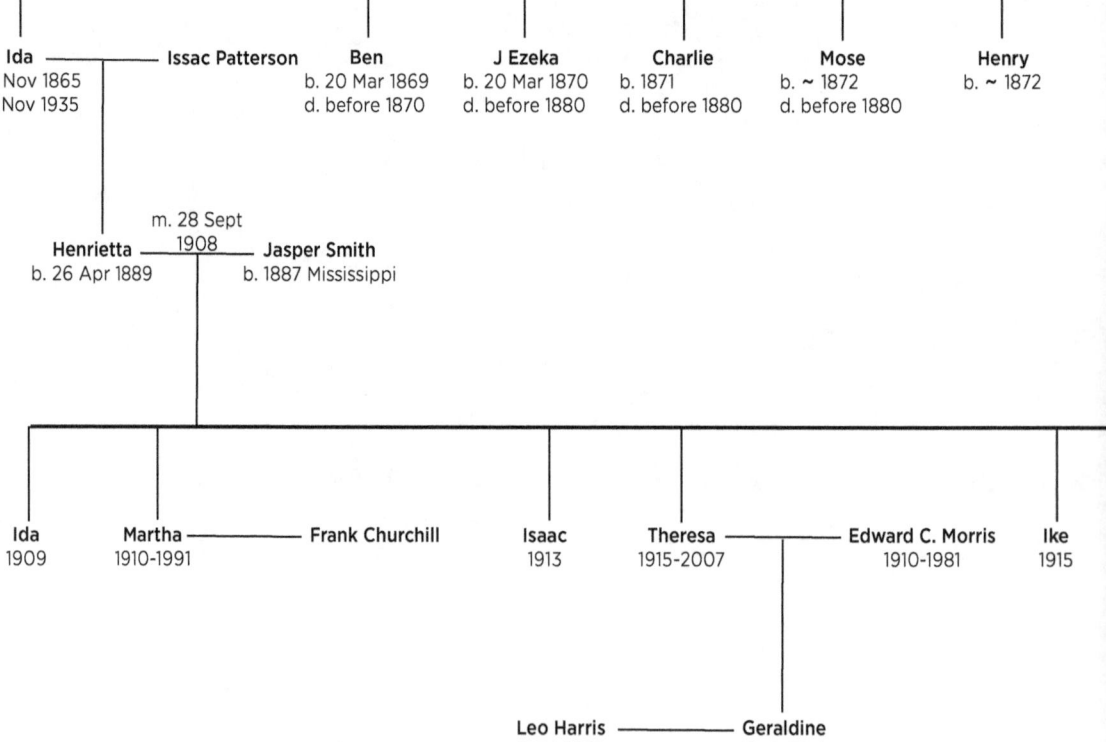

Data reflects best information gleaned from all relevant censuses, 1870-1840.
Dates are often inconsistent from one census to the next.
b = birth   d = death   m = marriage   ~ = around

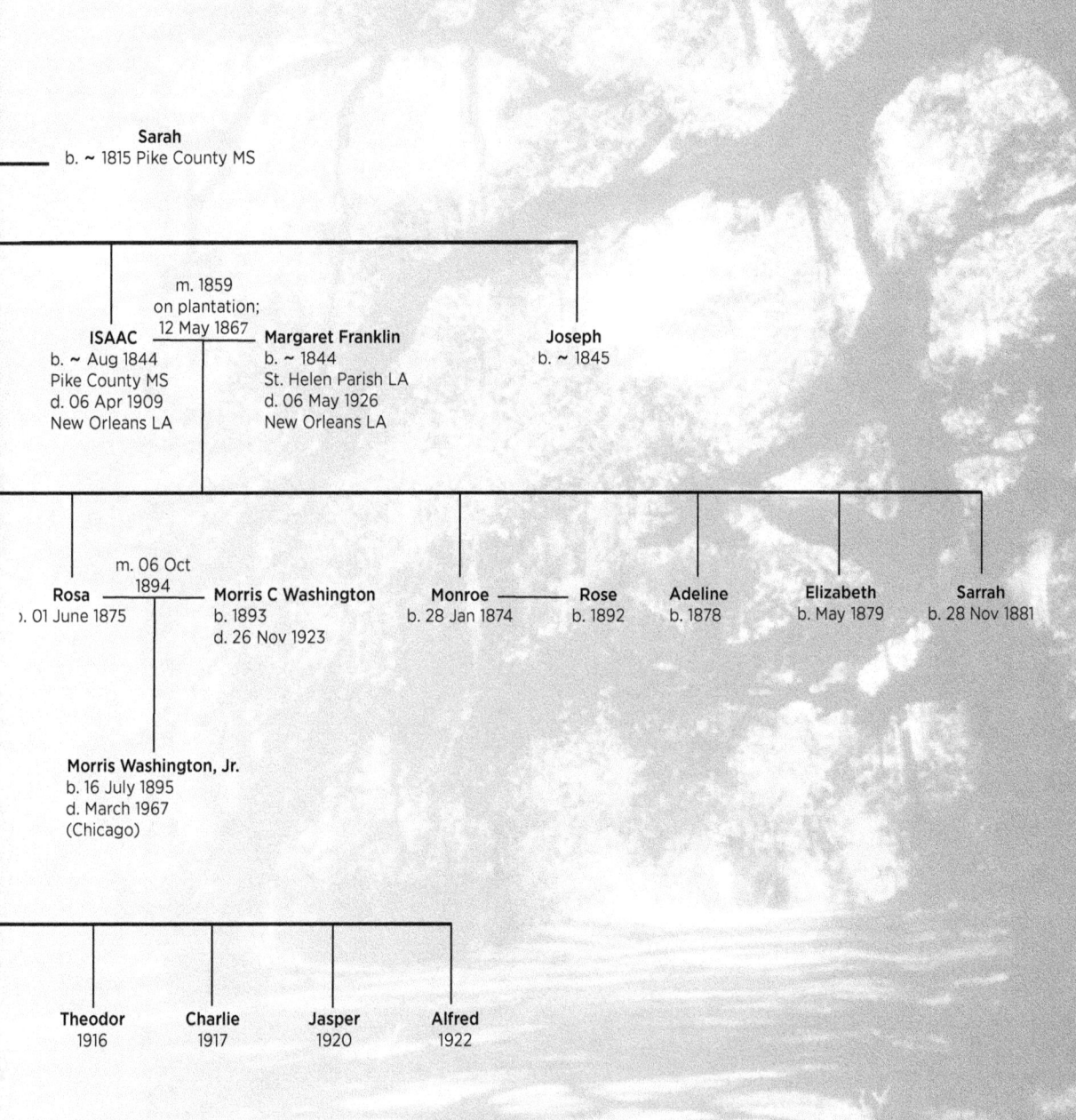

Sarah
b. ~ 1815 Pike County MS

ISAAC
b. ~ Aug 1844
Pike County MS
d. 06 Apr 1909
New Orleans LA

m. 1859
on plantation;
12 May 1867

Margaret Franklin
b. ~ 1844
St. Helen Parish LA
d. 06 May 1926
New Orleans LA

Joseph
b. ~ 1845

Rosa
b. 01 June 1875

m. 06 Oct 1894

Morris C Washington
b. 1893
d. 26 Nov 1923

Monroe
b. 28 Jan 1874

Rose
b. 1892

Adeline
b. 1878

Elizabeth
b. May 1879

Sarrah
b. 28 Nov 1881

Morris Washington, Jr.
b. 16 July 1895
d. March 1967
(Chicago)

Theodor
1916

Charlie
1917

Jasper
1920

Alfred
1922

CONCLUSION

There really is no such thing as a conclusion to a family research project such as this; there really is only a beginning. Eighteen years is not enough time to answer all the questions that arise from answering some of the questions that arise. I am not quitting – but I am stopping. More research will require more family members to go from here in whatever direction they so desire, if at all, to uncover more treasures of family heritage or to correct any errors in that which is included here. Certainly there are errors; so many records are inconsistent from year to year – spellings of names, dates of life events (births, deaths, marriages), relationships on censuses, repetition of names from generation to generation, and so on.

However, as I bring closure to this work, I do so with a somewhat lightened heart. Headed to Mississippi in April 2018 for what I thought would be my last research trip *[it was not!]*, on a stopover in Atlanta, my husband's cousin remarked to us that Mississippi was one state in this country that she was never comfortable enough to visit. Neither was I until I began going there in the beginning stages of this research in 2002. I was stunned when an older white gentleman held open the door of the Mississippi State Archives for me and pleasantly greeted me, "Good morning!" I was equally as stunned when, years later, I stopped at a cotton museum near Indianola and had a thoroughly delightful and informative "tour" conducted by the elderly white man who sat inside each day, patiently waiting for curious passersby to become patrons.

Despite the obvious desire of many Southerners to resurrect Confederate bodies from the ashes of the Civil War and return America to a mirage of southern perfection – void of the truths of miscegenation and other legal and illegal liaisons between the races – the actual *H-I-S-T-O-R-Y* of our interwoven American family continues to surface anyway, changing our understanding of our past and providing some guidance for our futures. The Confederate flag finally got removed by then Governor Nikki Haley from the statehouse grounds shortly after the Emanuel A.M.E. Church massacre in South Carolina in 2014. On May 19, 2018, Meghan Markle, an African American of mixed parentage, married into what the world would consider one of the "purest" families of the Caucasian race – the British royal family – although the Queen finally shared openly some of her family history; she, too, is of mixed ancestry.

Mississippi is changing. As I draw closure to this research, Magnolia, Mississippi, has elected an African American mayor. The Vaughn House on West Railroad Street in Magnolia, once the center of plantation life that included some of my **FELDER** ancestors, was recently purchased by a young black entrepreneur who intends to turn it into a bed and breakfast. A few blocks further on West Railroad, my husband and I enjoyed a wonderful lunch at Porters – and listened to the young, impassioned, black co-proprietor tell us the history of the Pullman Porters and the reason he and his business partner honored these historically black railroad employees by naming their newly-opened restaurant after the porters' contributions to the railroad industry and the expansion of the black middle class. I did not share at that time that my paternal great-great-great-grandfather, **SONNY FELDER**, was likely a Pullman Porter in Mississippi, and that my great-great-great-aunt, **CHLOE FELDER**, was the cook on the expansive plantation that consumed virtually all of Magnolia, including the property on which his restaurant now stood, where his mother now serves as head chef, and where the Vaughn House is located!

This research has enabled me to unearth the origins of our **FELDER** name, along with some of its frayed branches and scattered leaves, as well as our **HULBERT** tangled and shameful roots, all signified by our weeping willow tree, grown from a clipping from Mound Bayou, Mississippi, that Daddy unwittingly, but providentially, planted in our yard in Petersburg, Virginia after his mother passed in 1957. In the arduous process of conducting this research, I have discovered that ours is a story of slavery and bravery; property rights and civil rights; patterns of destruction and patterns of instruction; Jim Crowism and activism; Biblical misappropriation and prayerful supplication. I have stumbled upon a long-held belief in God in our ancestors' Christian values; stalwartness and proactivity in their determination to be educated; secrets in the courthouses; Confederates in our basements; mistruths in the censuses; hints to our heritage through my DNA; and differences in opinions amongst relatives as to the importance of knowing our past and telling *OURstory*.

This book reflects merely a tiny piece of *OURstory*, but it is a beginning. *OURstory*, as I have framed this narrative, has been my attempt, using my family, to show the interconnectedness of *OURstory*, *HIS*tory, H-I-S-T-O-R-Y, and the current state of blacks in this country who descended from that cruel and most "peculiar institution" of American-style human bondage – slavery. The interconnected lives, the truths and the lies, the silence of records in the attic, and the overblown bios of pioneers, are all a part of *OURstory* and they are a part of *HIS*tory. But *HIS*tory absent *OURstory* is not H-I-S-T-O-R-Y. *OURstory* is not separate from American history. It is not ancillary. It is a thoroughly enmeshed, integrated journey of the people, *all of the people*, who have made this country what it is today.

Unraveling details of *OURstory* has angered me, but it has also empowered me. My anger stems mostly from the hours and years searching for even a name to call my ancestors – *just a name* written somewhere! A *tidbit* of information! *Anything!* This information was intentionally chained up and stowed away just like our forefathers were chained up and stowed on those ships leaving the African shores. Extremely, painfully frustrating! But my empowerment emanates from the realization that our race as a people rose up from unfathomable economic, political, and educational circumstances, and with a very deep and abiding faith – some Christian, some remnants from Africa – began the march to freedom for us. They initiated our march to freedom. For this, we must be both knowledgeable and eternally grateful. I do not ascribe to the epigraph of the Amite County Historical and Genealogical Society, "Without a past there is no future." Our obscure past will not obfuscate our future.

OURstory continues to unfold. It includes so much that happened before and since I was born that laid a pathway for me, individually, and for us, collectively, as a family and as a country. There are endless examples of stories we should know and teach. *OURstory* began with the millions of slaves who were captured or sold into slavery from their African countries by African kings and tribesmen who participated in the European exchange of black bodies for liquor, guns, trinkets and trash. Most of those who survived the journey experienced life on the plantations and farms in the South, but many also lived in captivity in the North. It includes Louisiana's free people of color – those born free and those who purchased their freedom by coartación – some of whom owned slaves. Included also are the white Americans who participated in every way to sustain slavery and those who helped to eradicate it. *OURstory* is about the slaves who escaped and fought in the Civil War alongside free-born blacks and northern and southern whites who knew that the chains had to be broken.

OURstory evolved to the many educational institutions that emerged and called themselves colleges even while teaching the alphabet to illiterate freedmen in the 1870s. Schools like Tuskegee Normal and Industrial Institute, which in 1881 was established by a negotiated promise from two incumbent white legislators to secure funding for a school for blacks in exchange for community black businessman/former slave, and **MOTLEY** relative, Lewis Adams' delivery of the Tuskegee black vote for them. The affirmative vote of the Alabama legislature, signature of the governor on the bill introduced by these two re-elected legislators, and the visionary administration of a freed slave (Booker T. Washington), opened doors for us. Our relatives **ALEXANDER HULBERT**, **TYREE FELDER**, and **AYSE WASHINGTON** walked through those doors.

OURstory includes the 5,401 Rosenwald Schools built across the South in the 1920s by the hands of black parents and the philanthropy of Julius Rosenwald, son of Jewish German immigrants, which provided education for more than a third of black children living in rural communities in 15 states, primarily in the South. These schools in turn produced many of the teachers of our segregated southern neighborhood schools. Maya Angelou and Rep. John Lewis walked through those doors. Rosenwald fellowships for graduate students created opportunities for the genius of James Baldwin, Marian Anderson, and Maya Angelou, among many others including our uncle, **JAMES ALEXANDER HULBERT**, to emerge as pioneers in their crafts and professions.

The mental stress, humiliation, isolation, and personal sacrifices of Lloyd Gaines (*Gaines vs Canada*, 1938 - University of Missouri), George McLauren (*McLauren vs Oklahoma State Regents*, 1950) and Heman Sweatt (*Sweatt vs Painter*, 1950 – University of Texas) opened doors for us. These cases, argued before the U.S. Supreme Court, finally desegregated law and graduate schools and virtually ensured the passage of *Brown vs Board of Education* in 1954. The "Little Rock Nine" who enrolled in Central High School in Arkansas with the protection of the federal national guard – these and thousands of other unsung child heroes opened educational doors. It is how I graduated from John Yeates High School in 1968 and enrolled in Virginia Commonwealth University my sophomore year, becoming one of the first group of black students at both of those schools. *OURstory* includes Harvey Gannt being the first black student at Clemson University, and Clemson University being the first white college in the South to desegregate in 1963 without riots and bloodshed. But even with the desegregation progress made between the 1950s and 1970s in higher education, as late as 1996, the *Hopwood vs University of Texas* law school case regarding race and the law school's admissions practices once again raised challenges to educational opportunity. In 2003, *Grutter vs Bollinger* (University of Michigan), successfully argued before the U. S. Supreme Court, overturned the *Hopwood* case, allowing consideration of race and historical underrepresentation to be used as relevant components of admissions decisions. *OURstory* in educational equity and opportunity continues to unfold.

It was President Truman's 1948 executive order desegregating the U.S. military that laid the path for General Gary Cooper to become the first black Marine to lead a rifle company in combat (in Viet Nam) in 1966, and for General Colin Powell to become Chairman of the Joint Chiefs of Staff in 1989.

The hundreds of demonstrators, both black and white, who risked their lives marching across the Edmund Pettus Bridge in Alabama in 1965 to demand voting rights for African Americans opened the doors for Rev. Jesse Jackson to become a serious contender for President of the United States in 1984 and 1988, which paved the way for Barack Obama to be elected as the first African American United States President twenty years later (2008), which paved the way for Kamala Harris to become the first African/Asian American female Vice President of the United States.

The racism and sexism experienced by the brilliant "hidden figures," Katherine Johnson, Mary Jackson, Dorothy Vaughan, and the many other black female mathematicians at NASA in the 1950s, opened doors for Dr. Mae Jemison to become America's first African American female astronaut in this white-male-dominated career. Generals Benjamin Davis (Tuskegee Airmen) and Chappie James (first four-star general of the U.S. Air Force) opened doors for black astronauts Guion Bluford, Ronald McNair and Charles Bolden, and for Frederick D. Gregory to become the first African American astronaut to pilot and command a shuttle mission, and later serve as the first African American acting administrator of NASA. Major General Bolden served as NASA's administrator from 2009-2017.

Bill Spiller's challenge to the PGA all-white policies in 1952 opened doors for Tiger Woods to become the 2nd highest ranked PGA winner in the history of the game. Jack Johnson, the first African American heavyweight boxing champion of the world (1908) fought racism to open doors for Muhammad Ali. Jackie Robinson (#42), endured racism as the first African American major league baseball player. Hired in 1947, he opened doors for all-time greats like Hank Aaron and Willie Mays.

America is reeling today, mostly *en masse* – people of all races, ethnicities and ages – saying "enough is enough" to racism and to the contradictions perpetuated in our *HIS*torical narratives. Confederate symbols of *HIS*tory are being toppled across America as the general public becomes more knowledgeable about the H-I-S-T-O-R-Y of race relations in this country. Revelations amplify the resemblance between police brutality in the streets and corporate policies in the board rooms when race is the topic, steeped in the same veiled resentment concerning *all* Americans' expectations and demands for equal and fair opportunities. *OURstory* continues to evolve as we continue to become the "first" in so many fields historically closed to our participation.

Deeply rooted under those beautiful cypress, magnolia, weeping willow, and palmetto trees blanketing the South is the undeniable truth that we are all one humanity, like it or not. "We, the people." The reckoning that many Americans are making since the merciless murder in plain sight of George Floyd, and the creation of Black Lives Matter Plaza in the heart of the capitol aptly convey that the struggle continues. They represent the thousands of unsung heroes who have pried open doors for us. Our road has indeed been stony, but with prayer, concerted effort, determination, education, and persistence, we continue to move ahead, each generation contributing its essentialness and value to the shifting landscape.

On our last ride through Mississippi, my husband and I decided to spend the night in McComb, another small town with ties to the **FELDER** story, a few miles north of Magnolia on Interstate 55. There we happened upon a very well-dressed mixed group of teens (black, white, male, female) gathering outside a restaurant. My husband reasoned it could not be prom night – it was Tuesday. So, once we exited the restaurant (we had finished our dinner as they were getting ready to begin theirs), I approached one of the handsome young boys and asked what special occasion they were celebrating. This unplanned encounter led to our introduction to the director of the Jubilee Performing Arts Center who promptly offered for us to hear his choir sing! Assembling all the choir members together (even those who had already gone inside for their meal), the choir performed for us right outside the entrance of Golden Corral! No better conclusion to our trip, or to this manuscript, could I have anticipated than the song they sang . . . "My Soul's Been Anchored in the Lord!" My final thought: I praise God from whom all my blessings have flowed! My soul's been anchored in the Lord, and now I know why.

OURSTORY

Apryl and Lincoln

OURstory: Unchained and Liberated from HIStory creates a more inclusive narrative of the **Felders/FELDERS** of South Carolina, Mississippi, Louisiana and Texas. I am hopeful that it also shines a light on the unbreakable, unshakable, unmistakable link to our indestructible ancestors. We ARE because they WERE!

I AM BECAUSE THEY WERE

Whatever it is that I am, is not of me alone.
It's that long journey from some unknown blood-soaked motherland
And the survival lessons the ancestors' lives have shown
That bring me to opportunities bought with shattered hands.

I'll not hang my head in feigned shame; the shame cannot be mine.
Whether man, woman or child — they withstood each captor's bout.
Tho' skin whipped raw, and bleeding, then brutally soaked in brine,
Their resolve never faltered; those attacks they meant to flout.

They laid down a firm foundation to prosper and to grow
To use our God-given talents to learn, and build, and till,
To add now to this our nation, this is the least I owe.
With humble appreciation, their steps I'll vow to fill.

This truth, for sure, I won't deny when all is said and done
Today I am that vision the ancestral slaves did spur.
May their pride, their toils, and their ransom be ignored by none.
I owe a debt I'll always pay; I am because they were.

— GLADYS LOIS FELDER WASHINGTON
October 2020

APPENDIX A

Ancestry.com DNA Test Results

In 2013, I submitted a saliva sample to Ancestry.com DNA project to initiate the tracing of our family to its home origin. In 2018, Ancestry.com updated the analysis based on more testers. As of 2020, the distribution of my genetic communities and ethnicity estimates have changed again, but to eliminate confusion, suffice it to say that the majority of the analysis is reasonably the same, with the major exceptions identified above with percentages in square brackets. It is clear that while this method provides some useful information about our family's ethnicity, a much larger sample is needed to be more precise.

Nonetheless, the following reflects the results obtained: left percentage – 2018 update; right percentage in parenthesis – 2013 initial result; square bracket July 2020 percentage:

60% African
 1% Nigeria (28%); [33%]
 4% Ivory Coast/Ghana (14%); [2%]
 29% Cameroon (7%)
 24% Benin/Togo (2%); [16%]
2% *African Trace Regions*:
 0% Senegal (5%); [7%]
 1% Mali (3%); [7%]
 % South-Central Hunter Gatherers (1%)

38% European
 23% Great Britain (16%); [10%]
 8% Ireland (7%)
 Scotland [9%]
7% *European Trace Regions (15%):*
 0% Iberian Peninsula (5%); [0%]
 0% Europe-West (4%)
 6% Europe-Jewish (4%); [7%]
 1% Scandinavia (2%)
 France (1%)

2% American (1%)
 2% Native American
 0%/100% West Asia-Near East (1%/100)
 Haiti/Dominican Republic [1%]

APPENDIX B

LAND OFFICE RECORDS OF SELECT MISSISSIPPI FELDER PROPERTY HOLDERS 1831 - 1861[665]

Property Owner	Mississippi Land Office	Acres	Date(s) of Issue
Charles F Felder	Washington	679.73	10 Nov 1840 – 1 Oct 1860
Daniel Felder	Mt. Salua; Augusta	160.06	1 Sept 1831 – 5 Jan 1841
David F Felder	Washington	999.78	1 Dec 1849 – 30 Nov 1859
Gabriel Felder	Washington; Jackson; Columbus	880.26	10 May 1826 – 19 Jan 1835
Gabriel N Felder	Washington	80	1 Feb 1859
Hansford D Felder	Washington	40	1 Sept 1851
Isaac Felder	Washington	200.02	1 Sept 1851 – 15 Nov 1853
James W Felder	Washington	800	9 Sept 1835 – 1 Oct 1860
John Felder	Washington	400	1 Sept 1834 – 1 Feb 1859
Levi D Felder	Washington	320	1 Feb 1859
Nathaniel Felder	Jackson	40.19	1 Jan 1850
Peter Felder (Jr)	Washington	680	10 Nov 1840 – 1 Dec 1849
Rufus H Felder	Jackson	160.08	1 Jan 1850
Wyatt Felder	Washington	557.89	10 Nov 1840 – 22 Jan 1861
Elson A Felder[666]	Washington	118.6	1 Feb 1859
TOTAL PROPERTY		**6,116.61**	

665 Extracted from land office records, Chancery Clerk, Liberty and Magnolia, Mississippi.

666 I am completely unaware of this person but am counting him in the Felder property owners, assuming, absent further investigation, that he is a relative of these Felders.

LAND OFFICE RECORDS OF SELECT LOUISIANA FELDER PROPERTY HOLDERS 1854-1860[667]

Property Owner	Louisiana Land Office	Acres	Dates of Issue
David Felder	St Helena	157.86	2 Sept 1839 – 10 July 1854
Jesse T Felder	Greensburg	61.8	1 June 1860
Otis H Felder	Greensburg	198.48	1 June 1860
TOTAL PROPERTY		**418.14**	

---

667 Extracted from land office records, Chancery Clerk, Livingston Parish, Louisiana.

APPENDIX C

NUMBER AND SIZE OF FARMS/PLANTATIONS, 1860[668]
SELECT COUNTY DATA FOR LOUISIANA AND MISSISSIPPI

Louisiana

SIZE	Number of farms/plantations with designated acreage/parish		
ACRES	Livingston	St Helena	Pointe Coupée
3-9	2	7	29
10-19	115	36	55
20-49	124	124	121
50-99	36 – A	83	93
100-499	19 – B	139	163
500-999	1	7	43
1000+	0	0	9
TOTAL	297	396	513

A = JESSIE FELDER (61.8 ACRES)
B = OTIS FELDER (198.48 ACRES); DAVID FELDER (157.86 ACRES)

Mississippi

SIZE	Number of farms/plantations with designated acreage/parish			
ACRES	Amite	Claiborne	Lowndes	Pike
3-9	4	5	1	22
10-19	20	9	7	43
20-49	115	31	106	234 – A
50-99	135 – B	28	134	183
100-499	268 – C	135	257	197 – D
500-999	41 – E	73	112	10 – F
1000+	6	24[669]	17	0
TOTAL	589	305	634	689

A = HANSFORD D. FELDER (40 ACRES)
B = GABRIEL N. FELDER (80 ACRES)
C = ISAAC FELDER (200.02 ACRES)
D = LEVI D. FELDER (320 ACRES); JOHN (400 ACRES)
E = CHARLES F. FELDER (679.73 ACRES); JAMES W. FELDER (800 ACRES); GABRIEL (880.26 ACRES)
F = WYATT FELDER (557.89 ACRES); DAVID F. FELDER (999.78 ACRES)

---

668 http://mapserver.lib.virginia.edu/php/county.php.

669 Martin N. Hulbert owned more than 1,700 acres of land in Claiborne County.

APPENDIX D

PROPERTY OWNERSHIP OF MARTIN N. HULBURT/HULBERT

Year	Owner	Division of Section	Section/ Township/ Range	Acres	Cost
10/18/1877	Julia E. Hurlburt (wife of Julian Hulbert)	E ½ of SE ¼ and E ½ of E ½ of NE ¼	8/11/5E	120	$30
		E ½ part	17/11/5E	9 ½	
1/3-4/1876	Seized by State of Mississippi	Both parcels above for failure to pay taxes due			
9/3/1866	B. M. and J. M. Hulbert (sold by Martin, Sinai, and Robert Sanders – Sinai's brother) to Julian and Byron M. Hulbert	Lot No. 2 - 64 acres; SE ¼ of SE ¼ of section 5 - 40 acres; E ½ of section 8 - 320 acres; Lot No. 1 section 9 - 65 acres; Lot No. 2 section 9 - 60 acres: a north end strip from section No. 17 at the public road; Lot No. 1 - 58 acres north of the public road - 20 acres in section 16; all tracts immediately north of public road from Jasper Richmond's house north past Martin's house to D. Shelby's in Copiah County - also range 5E in Claiborne County with adjoining lots or parcels in the Copiah County: Lot No. 4 section 9 - 111 and ¾ acres; the north part of Lot. No. 3 section 16 - 50 acres in same township and range - about 730 acres		730.75	$1662
11/7/1865	Sinai Hulburt (deed of trust) from M. N. Hulburt to secure indebtedness of $21,200 borrowed from her prior to marriage and for the use and profits arising from her negroes *[sic]* in Claiborne and Copiah counties	"Dunbarton Plantation" including all plus mules, horses, cattle, sheep, hogs, wagons, carriages, work oxen, milch cows, household and kitchen furniture, and 3000 bushels of corn	4, 5, 8, 9, 16, 17, 18, 20 in Claiborne; 9, 16 in Copiah/11/5E	1772.75	

6/1/1857	M. N. Hulbert (deed of trust); served as security for Lemuel Baldwin to Thomas Garrison; if note not paid, Hulbert to retrieve property with 30-day notice				$1200 plus 10% interest due in eight months
1/12/1856	M. N. Hulbert	SW ¼	17/11/5E	138	$900
5/8/1851	M. N. Hulbert purchased all lands formerly belonging to estate of Robert Patton	Property in Claiborne County and in Copiah County			$3000; $1000 down and two notes of $1000 each
___/1848	M. N. Hulbert (tax lien sale of property of Robert Patton for taxes not paid 1847)	Lot No. 1	9/11/5E	64	$23.24
"	M. N. Hulbert	Lot No. 1	16/11/5E	114	
"		NE ¼	17/11/5E	161	
"		Part of NW ¼	17/11/5E	120	
"		Part of SW ¼	17/11/5E	23	
"		SE ¼	18/11/5E	160	
"		NW ¼ of NE ¼	20/11/5E	40	
"		SE ¼	8/11/5E	159	
7/9/1847	M. N. Hulbert (tax lien auction sale; property of James J. Patton for taxes not paid 1846)	W ½ of the SW ¼	8/11/5E	79	$5.45

APPENDIX E

NUMBER OF FELDERS IN THE UNITED STATES BY CENSUS YEAR
UNITED STATES CENSUSES (1790 – 1940)

Census Year	Number	General Locations and number of Felders
1790	7	6 – SC; 1 – MA
1800	6	5 – SC; 1 – PA
1810	7	6 – SC; 1- PA
1820	19	SC; MS
1830	28	18 – SC; 4 – MS 1 – LA; 3 – NY; 1 – AL; 1 – IA
1840	40	SC – 21; MS – 11; LA – 1; AL – 3; TN – 1; GA – 2;
1850[670]	303	SC – 157; MS – 71; LA – 10; TX – 2; scattered in states above plus NJ; PA; MO
1860	402	SC – 140; TX – 61; MS – 53; LA – 28; scattered in states above plus CA; FL; IL; KY; NY; OH; WI
1870[671]	1737	SC – 499; TX – 360; MS – 157; LA – 56; scattered in states above plus MN; MD; MO; MI; AR; IN
1880	2349	SC – 983; TX – 401; MS – 176; LA – 67; scattered in states above plus: NC; VA; WV; Dakota territory
1890[672]	N/A	NA
1900	3493	SC – 1311; TX – 497; MS – 273; LA – 109; scattered in states above plus Washington DC; NE; NM; OK; ND; MO; AZ territory
1910	4125	SC – 1439; TX – 538; MS – 339; A – 167; scattered in states above plus CT; SD; ND; MA; OR; KS; ME; MT; WA; AK territory
1920	4535	SC – 1578; TX – 623; MS – 313; LA – 14; scattered in states above plus NH; RI; NV; CO
1930	5344	SC – 1651; TX – 611; MS – 362; LA – 156; scattered in states above plus ME; VT
1940	4888	SC – 1488; TX – 607; MS – 259; LA – 157; scattered in states above. Wyoming (admitted 1890) is the only state having no Felder residents, 1790-1940. Hawaii not admitted until 1959.

---

670 Censuses prior to 1850 listed only the head of free white "families." In 1850 the census reports identify each individual in the family, thus the appearance of a substantial increase, however the number does not reflect "families." Native Americans are excluded, 1790-1840. The 1860 Census enumerated Native Americans not on reservations. The 1900 Census enumerates reservation and general population citizens.

671 Beginning in 1870, all citizens in the U.S., including minorities and women, are counted individually.

672 Nearly the entire 1890 U.S. census was destroyed in a fire at the Library of Congress; data is not available.

APPENDIX F
The Significance of April

Unbeknownst to me until conducting this research, the month of April figures prominently in *OURstory*, so much so that I developed this appendix. No better example emerges from *OURstory* than this of the patterns encompassed in the continuation of our ancestors' legacies.

At age 35, **BEATRICE FELDER** opened a private school during the height of the Great Depression in the all-black town of Mound Bayou, Mississippi. Her school, The Opportunity Center Kindergarten (T.O.C.K.), operated under her mantra, "Yours for Negro Education." She died on April 20th. At age 36, **APRYL FELDER**, **BEATRICE's** great-granddaughter, became a Fellow of the 4.0 Schools. Unbeknownst to her, she has followed in her grandmother's footsteps. **APRYL** has conceptualized and is currently building the Atlanta Free School in Georgia with a focus on democratic, self-directed education for historically marginalized students of color. Her mantra – "Educate to liberate." She was born on April 20th.

Knowing *OURstory* provides confidence to use our wings to soar like eagles!

So much important happened in April.

April 2, 1759	Peter Felder born in Orangeburgh, SC
April 30, 1812	Louisiana statehood established
April 26, 1843	John Rail's will recorded in Probate Court Will Book, Port Gibson
April 25, 1851	Dr. William R. Felder purchased land and building in Greensburg, Louisiana, for his medical office; possible first slave "owner" of JOSEPH FELDER (great-great-grandfather)
April 24, 1853	Eva Prewitt born in Magnolia, Mississippi
April 2, 1861 (or '63)	SONA FELDER (great-grandfather) born in Greensburg, Louisiana
April 12, 1861	Civil War started by SC's attack at Fort Sumter
April 28, 1861	St. Helena Riles left for war from Greensburg, Louisiana
April 1862	Joseph Davis left his slaves (Benjamin Montgomery and family) in charge of the Davis Bend plantations (Hurricane and Brierfield) while he hid in safety
April 16, 1862	Confederate Conscription Act requires three years of service
April 25, 1862	New Orleans seized by federal troops
April 23, 1864	Byron M HULBERT (great-grandfather) enlisted in Civil War as a Confederate private
April 2, 1865	Jeff Davis fled Richmond to avoid capture
April 3, 1865	Capital of the Confederacy (Richmond) captured

April 9, 1865	Civil War ended by Lee's surrender at Appomattox, Virginia
April 15, 1865	President Lincoln assassinated
April - 1866	George Ruby began work in Louisiana with Freedmen's Bureau
April 5, 1875	JOSEPH FELDER and Sophia Parker married in Hancock County, Mississippi
April 23, 1876	John Felder (founder of Methodism in Mississippi) funeralized
April 2, 1899	JANE ELLIS DIRD (great-great-grandmother) died
April 24, 1900	Levi Darius Felder died; possible second slave owner of JOSEPH
April 6, 1909	SGT. ISAAC FELDER died
April 20, 1920	CLARA ELLIS WHITFIELD ROSS died in Memphis, Tennessee
April 20, 1927	President Calvin Coolidge appointed Herbert Hoover to direct the Red Cross relief effort in the 1927 Mississippi flood
April 7, 1937	WILDA FELDER (great-grandmother) died in Mound Bayou, Mississippi
April 28, 1948	BEATRICE FELDER signed Certificate of Consent for TYREE to marry FRANKIE ROBERTA MOTLEY in Tuskegee, Alabama
April 20, 1958	BEATRICE FELDER (maternal grandmother) died in Gary, Indiana
April 30, 2003	TYREE P. FELDER died
April 30, 2021	*OURstory Unchained and Liberated from HIStory* was shipped from Versa Press to South Carolina where it all began.

APPENDIX G

Birth and Death Chart of Select Family Members

SURNAME (RACE)	FIRST	DOB; DOD	POB	AGE	RELATIONSHIP and NOTES	BURIAL PLACE
Anderson (B/I)	Callie Jackson	10 Dec 1875; 7 Dec 1967	Brantley AL	91	Mother of Irene Anderson; great-grandmother of author	St. John A.M.E. Church Cemetery, Tuskegee AL
Anderson (M)	Carrie	~1830; U	Upson GA	U	Mother of Thomas Anderson; married Clabe Anderson from Giles, Virginia; moved to Hinds County, MS; 2nd great-grandmother of author	U
Anderson (M)	Irene Anderson [Mattey] [Motley]	14 Feb 1909; 15 Jul 1993	Tuskegee AL	83	Mother of Frankie Roberta Motley; maternal grandmother of author	Oakridge Cemetery, Ormond Beach FL
Anderson (M)	Thomas	13 Dec 1862; 9 June 1934	Upson GA	72	Father of Irene Anderson; great-grandfather of author	St. John A.M.E. Church Cemetery, Tuskegee AL
Bearden (W)	Charles Mitchell	Dec 1874; 1938	MO	64	Father of Thomas Oscar Bearden Sr; married Samantha Alica Burris	Piney Grove Baptist Church Cemetery, Prentiss MS
Bearden (B)	Chiquita Jane [Hulbert] Felder	11 Sept 1926; 28 Jan 1995	Mound Bayou MS	69	Sister of Tyree P. Felder; aunt of author	West TN State Veterans Cemetery, Memphis TN
Bearden (B)	Everlean Wallace	21 Sept 1889; 1970	MS	81	Mother of Oscar Bearden Jr	
Bearden Jr (M)	Thomas Oscar	22 Jul 1922; 22 Apr 1995	MS	62	Husband of Chiquita Bearden; uncle of author	West TN State Veterans Cemetery, Memphis TN
Bearden Sr (W)	Thomas Oscar	11 Feb 1894; 23 Ju 1967	Prentiss MS	73	Father of Oscar Bearden Jr	Piney Grove Baptist Church Cemetery, Prentiss MS

Chapman (W)	Irene Hulbert Eddins	23 Dec 1856; 3 Jan 1944	Port Gibson MS	87	Sister of B. M. Hulbert; great-great-aunt of author; died from cerebral accident	Memorial Park, Memphis TN
Ellis (B)	Keziah	1830; U	VA	U	Mother of Jane Ellis; 3rd great-grandmother of author	Columbus MS
Ellis (B)	Kezziah	1810; U	VA	U	Mother of Keziah Ellis; 4th great-grandmother of author	Maybe TN
Ellis (B)	Mary Jane	1852; 2 Apr 1899	MS	47	Mother of Wilda Ellis Felder; 2nd great-grandmother of author	Columbus MS
Felder (B)	Adeline Salena	1 Jan 1894; 14 Mar 1957	Pearlington MS	63	Daughter of Sophia and Joseph Felder; death from cerebral hemorrhage and hypertension	Orange City Cemetery, Houston TX
Felder (B)	Beatrice Ottowiess [Hulbert]	19 Jun 1897; 20 Apr 1958	Shaw MS	61	Mother of Tyree and Chiquita (Bearden) Felder; paternal grandmother of author; death from pulmonary infarction; colon cancer	Oak Hill Cemetery, Gary IN
Felder (B)	Chloe	U; U	Pike County MS	U	Sister of Isaac, Joseph, Alia, Katie, and Henry Felder; cook at Prewitt Plantation; great-great-grand aunt of author	U
Felder (B)	Daniel	Feb 1888; U	Logtown MS	U	Son of Joseph and Sophia Felder; mill laborer at age 12	U
Felder (M)	Emma Jenkins	~1866; U	Greensburg LA	U	1st wife of S. P. Felder	U
Felder (B)	Ezekiel	20 Mar 1870; 7 Jan 1889	New Orleans LA	19	Son of Isaac and Margaret Felder; great-grand-uncle of author	New Orleans LA
Felder (B)	Frankie Roberta Motley	7 Feb 1928; 9 July 1961	Tuskegee AL	33	Mother of author; death from coronary thrombosis	City Point Military Cemetery, Hopewell VA

Felder (B)	Henry	~1830; U	Pike County MS	U	Brother of Isaac and Joseph Felder	Chapel Hill TX
Felder (B)	Isaac	Aug 1844; 6 Apr 1909	Pike County MS	64	Brother of Joseph and Henry Felder; uncle of S. P. Felder; 1st Sgt. In Felder family; Civil War Veteran (USCT great-great-grand-uncle of author	Chalmette National Cemetery, Chalmette LA
Felder (B)	John Wesley	8 May 1882; 12 Feb 1969	Logtown MS	87	Son of Joseph and Sophia P. Felder; half-brother of S. P. Felder; death from acute pneumonia and atherosclerosis	Memorial Park Cemetery, Oroville CA
Felder (B)	Joseph	~1845; U	U	U	Father of S. P. Felder; 2nd great-grandfather of author	U
Felder (B)	Katie	U; U	Pike County MS	U	Sister of Isaac, Joseph, and Henry Felder	U
Felder (B)	Margaret Franklin	Sept 1844; 6 May 1926	U	85	Wife of Sgt. Isaac Felder; married 1861; great-great-grand aunt of author	New Orleans LA
Felder (B)	Martha	U; U	U	~112	Mother of Sarah Felder; 4th great-grandmother of author	Maybe Pike County, MS
Felder (B)	Nathaniel	18 Jan 1886; 7 Sept 1968	Westonia MS	82	Son of Joseph and Sophia P. Felder; half-brother of S. P. Felder	San Francisco CA
Felder (B)	Sarah	U; U	U	U	Mother of Isaac, Henry, Joseph, Katie, and Chloe Felder; 3rd great-grandmother of author	Maybe Amite County, MS
Felder (B)	Simon	3 Feb 1890; 23 Jan 1971	Logtown MS	80	Son of Joseph and Sophia Felder; half-brother of S. P. Felder; married Alfreda Henderson 4/20/1916; death from cancer of left mandible, chest and spine	Hollywood Cemetery, Orange, TX

Felder (B)	Sona P.	1 Jul 1861 or 2 Apr 1863 or 1 July 1863; 1 Feb 1940	Greensburg LA	~79	Father of Beatrice and Korrine Felder; grandfather of Tyree and Chiquita (Bearden) Felder; great-grandfather of author	Mound Bayou Cemetery (unmarked), MS
Felder (B)	Sonny	~1810; U	Maybe SC	U	Father of Isaac, Joseph, Henry, Chloe, and Katie; 3rd great-grandfather of author	Maybe Natchez, MS
Felder (B)	Susan	Nov 1881; U	Greensburg LA	U	Daughter of Emma Jenkins and S. P. Felder	U
Felder (B)	Susannah Lewis	U; U	U	U	1st wife of Joseph Felder; mother of S. P. Felder; 2nd great-grandmother of author	U
Felder (B)	Tyree Preston	6 Oct 1927; 30 Apr 2003	Mound Bayou MS	75	Father of Frankie Felder; death from lung cancer	City Point Military Cemetery, Hopewell VA
Felder (M)	Wilda Juanita/ Jane Ellis	3 May 1876; 7 Apr 1937	Columbus MS	60	Mother of Beatrice and Korrine Felder; wife of S. P. Felder; grandmother of Tyree and Chiquita (Bearden) Felder; great-grandmother of Frankie Felder; death from comatose malaria	Mound Bayou Cemetery MS
Hulbert (W)	Adrian	11 Oct 1852; 7 Nov 1867	Port Gibson MS	15	Brother of B. M. Hulbert; uncle of Alexander Hulbert; married Maria Moore	U
Hulbert (M)	Albert Alexander (Alex)	May 1880/81/83/85; 24 May 1948	Innis or Batchelor LA	~68	Paternal grandfather of author; death from uraennia/hypertrophy [sic]; likely uraemia	New Park Cemetery, Memphis TN
Hulbert (M)	Bessie Shaffer	1881; 1919	Port Gibson MS	38	Mother of James and Robbie Hulbert; 1st wife of Alexander Hulbert	Memphis TN

Hulbert (W)	Byron M. ("B. M.")	9 Aug 1848; 1901	Port Gibson MS	53	Father of Albert Alexander Hulbert; married Maria Moore after brother's death (Adrian); great-grandfather of author	Natchez MS
Hulbert (W)	Clara Alberta	1873; 1936	U	63	Daughter of Julian and Julia Hulbert	U
Hulbert (W)	Clifton	1855; U	Port Gibson MS	U	Brother of B. M. Hulbert; uncle of Alexander Hulbert	U
Hulbert (W)	Herman C.	20 Jan 1848; 8 Aug 1852	Port Gibson MS	4	Brother of B. M. Hulbert; uncle of Alexander Hulbert	Wintergreen Cemetery, Port Gibson MS
Hulbert (M)	James Alexander	16 Mar 1906; 28 Jul 1974	Greenville MS	68	Half-brother of Tyree and Chiquita Felder	Elmwood Cemetery, Memphis TN
Hulbert (W)	Julia Eliza Simms	1848; 29 Ju 1932	Hermanville MS	84	Wife of Julian M. Hulbert	Jefferson County MS
Hulbert (W)	Julian M.	10 Sept 1845; 18 Oct 1880	Port Gibson MS	35	Brother of B. M. Hulbert; uncle of Alexander Hulbert	Hermanville MS
Hulbert (W)	Martha Sheffield	~1819; 25 Dec 1842	Port Gibson MS	23	1st wife of Martin N. Hulbert; married Jan 1842	U
Hulbert (W)	Martin Nathaniel	~1810/14/19; Oct 1894	Columbia, NY	79	Slave-owning great-grandfather of Tyree and Chiquita [Hulbert]; 2nd great-grandfather of author	Hurlburt Cemetery, Claiborne County (Trim property) MS
Hulbert (W)	Parmelia McFerrin	21 Sept 1795; 31 Mar 1872	U	77	Mother of Martin N. Hulbert; 3rd great-grandmother of author	IN
Hulbert (W)	Sinai Sanders Rail	4 May 1823; 14 May 1888	Hermanville MS	65	Mother of B. M. Hulbert; great-grandmother of Tyree and Chiquita [Hulbert]; 2nd great-grandmother of author	Hurlburt Cemetery, Claiborne County Line (Trim property) MS
Hulbert (W)	Ward Martin	18 Jul 1871; 1951	Hermanville MS	80	Nephew of B. M. Hulbert; son of Julien and Julia Hulbert	New York City NY
Hurlburt (W)	Joseph	1646; 1732	Great Britain	86	3rd great-grandfather of Martin Hulbert	U

Hurlburt (W)	Thomas	U; U	Scotland or Great Britain	U	First Hurlburt in America (~1635); arrived Boston, then to Saybrook and Wethersfield CT	U
Hurlbut (W)	Benoni	~1741; 28 Sept 1791	Litchfield CT	50	Uncle of Martin N. Hulbert; moved from PA to Whitehall NY to Ohio; "honest/worthy"; death from Indian ambush; shot and scalped; widow and kids moved to Athens County, OH afterwards	Belprie OH
Hurlbut (W)	Caleb Alexander	1722; 1782	Litchfield CT	60	Great-great-grandfather of Martin N. Hulbert; 5th great-grandfather of author; surgeon in French War	Rutland VT
Hurlbut (W)	William	U; U	Litchfield CT	U	Possibly the first Hurlbut in Mississippi (with Lyman Company)	U
Hurlbut III (W)	Caleb Alexander	1792; 21 Apr 1833	Washington/ New York County NY	41	Father of Martin N. Hulbert; married Permelia McFerrin ~1815; 3rd great-grandfather of author	Cincinnati OH
Hurlbut Jr (W)	Benoni William	U; U	OH	U	Son of Benoni; possibly the landowning taxpayer in MS in 1834 and 1840 who later moved to Ohio; Martin N. Hulbert's great-uncle	U
Hurlbut Jr (W)	Caleb	Aug 1753; Sept 1824	Litchfield CT	71	Grandfather of Martin N. Hulbert; married Lydia Mitchell in Skeensboro, now Whitehall, NY; 4th great-grandfather of author	Cana Memorial Cemetery, Paris Crossing, Jennings County IN
Hurlburt Jr (W)	Joseph	1677; 21 Jun 1729	Great Britain	42	Great-great-grandfather of Martin N. Hulbert	Litchfield CT

Jackson (B/I)	Frank	1853; U	Pike AL	U	Callie Anderson's father; 2nd great-grandfather of author	U
Jackson (B/I)	Irie	1854; U	Pike AL	U	Callie Anderson's mother; 2nd great-grandmother of Frankie Felder	U
Jackson (B)	Korrine Tyree Felder	27 Jul 1900; 23 Mar 1979	Greenville MS	78	"Auntie K"; daughter of S. P. and Wilda Ellis Felder; aunt of Tyree Felder and Chiquita Bearden; death from stroke; arteriosclerosis	Broadlawn Memorial, Des Moines IA
McFerrin (W)	Lydia Hurlbut	U; U	Washington County NY	U	Sister of Caleb Hurlbut III; married John McFerrin in Washington County, NY; likely parents of Permelia McFerrin	U
Mitchell (W)	Lydia	~1752; Nov 1831	U	79	Wife of Caleb Jr; grandmother of Martin N. Hulbert; 4th great-grandmother of author	Jefferson County IN
Motley (M)	Augustus	~1825/30; U	Kershaw SC	U	Father of Robert L. Motley; 2nd great-grandfather of author	Cross Keys AL
Motley (M)	Augustus G.	~Aug 1889; U	Tuskegee AL	U	Brother of Frank A. Motley; grand uncle of author	Montgomery AL
Motley (M)	Frank Alphonso	6 Aug 1902; 17 Sept 1977	Tuskegee AL	74	Father of Frankie R. Motley; maternal grandfather of author; death from colon cancer	Ashdale Cemetery, Tuskegee AL
Motley (M)	Ida E. Huffman	~1872; 21 Dec 1950	U	~78	Mother of Frank A. Motley; wife of Robert L. Motley; great-grandmother of author	Ashdale Cemetery, Tuskegee AL
Motley (W)	John	~1784; U	Kershaw SC	U	Likely father of Augustus Motley	AL
Motley (W/M)	Missouri Thrower	~1840; 10 Dec 1929	AL	~89	Wife of Augustus Motley; 2nd great-grandmother of author	Coffee County AL

Motley (B)	Thomas Alphonso	14 Mar 1929; 17 Dec 2003	Tuskegee AL	74	Brother of Frankie R. Felder; uncle of author	Birmingham AL
Motley Sr (M)	Robert Lincoln	~1868; Nov 1941	AL	~73	Father of Frank A. Motley; great-grandfather of author	Tuskegee AL
O'Neal (A)	Adam	U; U	U	U	Husband of Dianah O'Neal; 5th great-grandfather of author	Maybe Amite County MS
O'Neal (A)	Dianah	U; U	U	U	Wife of Adam O'Neal; 5th great-grandmother of author	Maybe Amite County MS
Rail (W)	Calista (or Celista)	3 Oct 1842; 21 Jan 1911	Claiborne County MS	69	Daughter of Sinai Sanders and 1st husband, John Rail; married ___ Carter	Higbee Cemetery, Higbee, MO
Rail (W)	John	25 Dec 1783; 23 Mar 1843	Claiborne County MS	56	1st husband of Sinai Sanders	Torrey Cemetery, Hermanville MS
Rail (W)	Marilla Christina	2 Oct 1841; 20 Jan 1930	Claiborne County MS	89	Daughter of Sinai Sanders and 1st husband, John Rail; married James Wiley	U
Richardson (B)	Adline Felder	1 Jan 1894; 14 Mar 1957	Pearlington MS	63	Daughter of Joseph and Sophia Felder; died from cerebral hemorrhage due to hypertension	U
Richardson (M)	Alice	1 Sept 1897; 29 Mar 1986	Pearlington MS	88	Joseph and Sophia Felder's granddaughter	Houston TX
Richardson (M)	Edna	16 Aug 1901; 17 Dec 1985	Pearlington MS	84	Joseph and Sophia Felder's granddaughter married	U
Richardson (M)	Fred	~1862; 6 Jan 1936	AL	88	Husband of Adeline Felder; owned restaurant in Hancock County, MS	Pearlington Cemetery, Pearlington MS
Richardson (M)	Ophelia	~1908; Apr 1999	Pearlington MS	91	Joseph and Sophia Felder's granddaughter	Houston TX
Rouse (B)	Edward	~1857; U	MS	U	2nd husband of Sophia Parker Felder	U
Rouse (B)	Sophia Parker Felder	~1862; U	Pike County MS	U	Stepmother of S. P. Felder; 2nd wife of Joseph Felder	U

Sanders (W)	Ann Carolyn Gibson Baker	9 Sept 1784; Aug 1859	SC	75	Mother of Sinai Sanders Hulbert; 3rd great-grandmother of author; maternal family (Sutton) English royals	Hermanville MS
Sanders (W)	Pothana	2 Sept 1825; 16 Dec 1900	Hermanville MS	75	Sister of Sinai Sanders Hulbert	Cooper Place, Claiborne County MS
Sanders (W)	Robert Baker	14 Oct 1828; 28 Jan 1891	Claiborne County MS	62	Brother of Sinai Sanders Hulbert; had 14 children w/Martha Lupo	Claiborne County MS
Sanders III (W)	Robert T.	10 May 1770; Jul 1844	NC	73	Father of Sinai Sanders Hulbert; 3rd great-grandfather of author	Hermanville MS
Thompson (M)	Robbie Lou Hulbert	7 Jan 1908; 17 Ju 1989	Memphis TN	81	Daughter of Alexander and Bessie Hulbert	Harmony Memorial Park, Landover MD
Washington (B)	James Wilfred	July 1854/59; 1945	Pike County MS	85	Son of Martha Felder and William R. Washington; founded Mount Flowery Baptist Church; provided Mississippi slave narrative	Greenwood Cemetery, McComb MS
Whitfield (M)	Clara Willie Ellis	25 Aug 1897; 20 Apr 1920	Columbus MS	23	Sister of Wilda Ellis	U
Wilkins (C)	Caroline	Mar 1832; U	U	U	Mother of Alexander Hulbert; lived in Louisiana; great-grandmother of author	U

Race: (A) – African; (B) – black; (B/I) – black/Indian; (C) – Chinese; (M) – mulatto; (W) – white

Key: DOB – date of birth; DOD – date of death; U – unknown; POB – place of birth

NOTES: [ ] denotes divorce; DOB (date of birth) is often incorrect by several years, as various records conflict.

PHOTO/ILLUSTRATION CREDITS

All photographs taken, illustrations created, and documents provided by Frankie O. Felder except as noted below:

Amite County MS Courthouse, 105

Ancestry.com public photos, 18

Ancestry.com African American Photo Collection, 108, 196

Ancestry.com, Fold3 Military Records, 141 both, 153 all

Asya Blue, interior and cover design

Campbell College Bulletin (1909), 204 bottom

Samuel D. Cargile, 235

Robert Carter, cover art

Century Magazine, 132

Chronicling America, Liberty Advocate, 104

Cleveland MS Courthouse, 159

Wikimedia Commons, 7, 199

Frankie Roberta Felder, xviii, 1 top, 201

Tyree P. Felder, 1 bottom, 186

Hancock County Historical Society, 94, 95, 97 both, 99

Joseph Jones, 3

Library of Congress, 26, 29, 37, 38, 39 top, 41 both, 43, 45, 47, 49, 50, 56, 59, 63, 68 both, 72, 73, 96, 102, 120, 127, 128, 176, 179, 181, 188, 227 all Civil War soldiers

National Archives, 50 top and middle, 64 both, 65, 66, 228, 230 both, 232 both

Magnolia Gazette, 86, 169

McComb Enterprise, 89

Mississippi Department of Archives and History, 202, 215 both

Madison Republican and Banner, 148 top left,

Port Gibson MS Courthouse, 143, 151

Port Gibson Herald, 156

Port Gibson Reveille, 144

George Sells, 193
   Courtesy of George Sells

South Carolina Department of Archives and History, 15

South Carolina Gazette, 12

South Caroliniana Library, 28
   Courtesy of the South Caroliniana Library, USC, Columbia, S.C.; Henry Felder Papers

Southern Advocate, 207

St. Helena Parish LA Courthouse, 76 both, 93

St. Helena Echo, 82

Tasha Washington, 188

Gladys Washington, 173

Lloyd Washington, 218

Elaine Wickens, 2

Note:
Newspaper articles can be searched on microfilm, newspapers.com, newspaperarchive.com and Chronicling America. Every attempt was made to identify the copyright holder of all photographs to secure use permission. Please notify the author of any corrections to be made to include in future reprints of this book.

ABOUT THE AUTHOR

Frankie Ottowiess Felder, Ed.D. is a change agent, a listener, a writer, a speaker, a doer. A possibility thinker. A believer in the goodness of mankind. A graduate educator who encourages excellence in elementary children as readily as doctoral students. A mentor to assistant professors as well as seasoned, full professors on matters pertaining to diversity. A Harvard-educated, African American Southerner who lived and worked among Confederate symbols and stories throughout her years as a child and young professional in Petersburg and Richmond, Virginia. Dr. Felder was recognized by the Council of Southern Graduate Schools as an outstanding contributor to graduate deans' growth and understanding of the history and present conditions of race and equity in higher education. *OURstory Unchained and Liberated from HIStory* is written from her perspective as the first African American dean hired at Clemson University in its then 98-year history, the first in the FELDER family to earn a doctorate, the first FELDER to live on the African continent (South Africa for nearly two years), and now the first FELDER to dig into the family's history. She enjoys her home in South Carolina as a wife, mother, grandmother, sister, friend, and emeritus associate professor.

INDEX

Note: There are some instances where the same name refers to two different people. In these cases, names in all capital letters are black relatives, while lower-case names refer to white non-relatives.

Aaron, Hank, 242
Act Reorganizing the American Customs System in Support of British Trade, 19
Adams, Lewis, 241
Adams, Samuel, 19
African American Civil War Museum, iii, 227, 233
African Methodist Episcopal (A.M.E.) Church, xvi, 2, 28–29, 92, 93, 97, 98, 126, 173, 179–186, 199, 200, 206–207, 239
Aguiar family, 132
Alcorn College/University, xiii, 119
Alexander, Henry, 101
Allen, Henry, 69
Allen, Richard, 179–180
Allen University, 199
American Revolution, 18–24
Ancestry.com DNA test results, 247
Anderson, Irene, 175, 259
Anderson, Marian, 241
Anderson, Thomas, 174, 175, 259
Andrews, Elisha, 83
Angelou, Maya, 214, 241
Archdale, John, 17
"Aunt Chloe." *See* Felder, Chloe

Baldwin, James, 241
Banks, Charles, 181, 207, 216
Banks, Nathaniel P., 63, 65–66, 190
Barbados, 24–28
Batchelor family, 136–137
Bates, William, 105

Battle of Port Gibson, 140
Bayou Pierre, Mississippi, 133, 223
Bearden, Chiquita Felder (Chiquita Jane Felder; Chiquita Hulbert), 110, 115, 127, 150, 160, 173, 203, 214, 216
Bearden, Gwendolyn, 115
Bearden, Tyree Curtis (Rev.), 173
Bearden family, 128
Berkeley, William, 14
Bethel A.M.E. Church (Friars Point), 175, 176
Bethel A.M.E. Church (Mound Bayou), 173, 181, 185–186
Bethel College, 199
Big Mount Zion A.M.E. Church, 98
Bill of Rights (American), 20, 37
Biloxi, Mississippi, 154, 225
Birdsong Camp, 202, 203, 225
Black Horse Cavalry, 210
Black Lives Matter Plaza, 242
Blackington, O.N., 228
Blind Tom, 71–72
Blue Goose, 95
blues music, 201
Bluford, Guion (Dr.), 242
Bogue Houma Ridge School, 206
Bolden, Charles (Maj. Gen.), 242
Boling, Samuel P., 119
Bond, Thomas (Rev.), 82, 84, 168
Bond family, xix
Boston Massacre, 19
Boston Tea Party, 19
Bridgers, Elias, 143
Brooks, Anna, 99
Brooks, Walter (Rev.), 178–179

Brown, James, 3
Brown, John, 61
Brown, William Wills, 169
Brown v. Board of Education, 241
Bruce, Blanche, 119–120
Bryant, Carolyn, 125
Bryant, Roy, 125

Cailloux, Andre (Capt.), 64–65
Calahan, Thomas, 188
Calhoun, Ezekiel, 143
Calhoun, John C., 40–41, 52
camp meetings, 166–167
Camp Moore (Louisiana), 48, 49–50
Campbell College, 185, 200–201, 203–204
Canada, 19
Cardozo, Francis Lewis, 119
Cargile, Samuel (Dr.), ii
Carnegie, Andrew, 214
Carre, Henry, 96
Carre, W.W., 96
Carrington, Ida, 98
Carter, Isaac, 79, 229
Carter, Louisiana, 47
Carter, Robert, iii
Carter, Heather, iii
Castro, Jordan Tyree, xvii, 115
Castro, Julien, xvii
Chalmette National Cemetery, 221, 233–234
Charles I (King of England), 7
Charles II (King of England), 7, 14
Chase, Salmon P., 190
Chesterfield, Virginia, 71
Chinn, Wilson, 29

271

Christmas, Ed, 206
City Point, Virginia, 50
City Point National Cemetery, 260, 262
Civil Rights Movement, 2, 128
Civil War
    Battle of Grand Gulf, 142
    Battle of Liberty, 171
    Battle of Milliken's Bend, 66–67, 71, 228
    Battle of Port Gibson, 140
    Battle of Port Hudson, 61–66, 71, 140, 149
    Battle of Vicksburg, 69
    controlling the Mississippi, 62–67
    and disease, 49–50, 83
    First Louisiana Native Guards, 64
    hospitals, 49–50
    Hulbert family in, 139–144
    Louisiana's participation in, 35, 45–50
    in Port Gibson, 140, 142, 148–149
    Port Hudson campaign, 62–65, 71
    roots of, 40–41
    secession of southern states, 41
    slaves' participation in, 56–60, 62–73
    Third Louisiana Native Guards, 64
    timeline of secession, 42
Claiborne County (Mississippi), 136, 142, 143, 146, 149–151, 156
Cleburne, Patrick, 69
Clemson University, i, vii, viii, x, 40, 53, 241
Cleveland, Mississippi, 122, 123, 159, 160, 201, 202–203, 216, 225
Cobb, Howell (Maj. Gen.), 70
Coercive Acts, 19
Coffee, Emma. *See* Felder, Emma Coffee Jenkins

Coffee, Mildred "Millie" (Jenkins), 92–93
Colleton, John, 14
Columbus, Mississippi, 118, 119, 122, 125–127, 223
Conerly family, 85
Conkling, James C., 67
Conscription Act, 139
Continental Association, 20
Coolidge, Calvin, 202
Cooper, Gary (Gen.), 242
Cope, David, 114
Cope, George, 114
Corps d'Afrique, 192, 228
Costello, Brian, 131, 138
Creole culture, 134–135, 138
Creoles of Color, 135–136
Crosby, Emilye, 157
Cross Roads A.M.E. Church (Greenburg, LA), 182
Currency Act, 19

Damascus Baptist Church (Tuskegee), 177
Dana, Charles A., 67
Daniell, Smith, 148–149
Daniel's Academy, 191
Davenport, D.D.D., 155
Davenport, Laura L., 155
Davidson, John Wynn (Gen.), 50
Davidson, T.G., 78
Davis, Benjamin (Gen.), 242
Davis, Charles, 106
Davis, Jefferson, 69–70, 71, 140, 196–197
Davis, Joseph E. ("J.E."), 62, 195–198, 213, 214
Davis, Samuel B. (Maj.), 54
Declaration of Independence, 21–22
Declaration of Rights, 20
Declaratory Act, 19
Derrick, William (Bishop), 183
Disney, R.R. (Bishop), 182
Dollar, Creflo (Rev.), 176
Doubleday, Abner (Gen.), 72
Douglas, Stephen, 37

Douglass, Frederick, 178
Drayton, William, 23
DuBois, W. E. B., xx, 187
Dunbarton Plantation, 152
Dungan, J.W., 155
Dungan, Mary L., 155
Dunn, Joseph, 106
Dunning, Oscar J., 119

East Baton Rouge Parish, 35, 37, 221
economic empowerment
    the legacy, 215–218
    the pattern, 209–215
Edgar, Walter (Dr.), 14, 17
education
    the legacy, 206–209
    the pattern, 187–206
    and religion, 198–206
Edward Waters College, 199
Ellis, Cassir, 118
Ellis, Cassy, 118
Ellis, Cinda, 119
Ellis, Clara (Whitfield), 119
Ellis, Dora, 118, 216
Ellis, Hanny, 119
Ellis, James, 119
Ellis, Jane, 118–119, 128, 200
Ellis, Joseph, 118, 119
Ellis, Keziah, 118–119, 128
Ellis, Kezziah, 118–119
Ellis, Letetia, 118
Ellis, Lewis, 118
Ellis, Matilda, 118, 119
Ellis, Stephen, 119
Ellis, Thomas, 119
Ellis, Wilda Jane (Wilda Jane Felder), 99, 100, 118–119, 120, 122, 125, 128, 173, 185, 200, 207, 216
Ellis family, 118
Ellis Island of African Americans, 26
Emancipation Proclamation, 31, 39, 52, 57–58, 60, 171, 209
Emanuel A.M.E. Church, 2, 28, 239

Everett family, xix
Evergreen Plantation, 133–134
Evers, Charles, 157–158
Evers, Medgar, xiii, 127, 158

FELDER
　origin of surname, 4-5
　in U.S. Census, 255
Felder, Abraham, xviii, 22, 23
Felder, Aby Jane (Vaughn), xviii, 79, 86–88, 169
Felder, A.D., 79
Felder, Ada V., 100–101
Felder, Adeline, 98, 99, 101
Felder, A.F., 116
Felder, Albert G. (Rev.), 79, 92, 102, 168, 171, 181
Felder, Alia/Alice, 96, 110
Felder, Ann (Everette), 103
Felder, Ann O'Neal, xix, 109, 111, 212
Felder, Annie, 101
Felder, Apryl, xiv, 244, 257
Felder, Baxter, 101
Felder, Bertha Beatrice Ottowiess, xv–xvi, 99, 110, 114, 125, 150, 159–160, 173, 203, 204, 207, 216–217
Felder, Bernhardt, 8, 16
Felder, Catherine, 51, 53, 91
Felder, C.B., 116
Felder, Charles Sr. (Rev.), xviii, 79, 82, 84, 85, 103, 168, 170, 171, 173, 181, 213
　slaves "owned" by, 102–104
Felder, Charles F. (Dr.), xix, 55, 79, 85, 91, 92, 102, 103, 111, 116, 211, 229
　slaves "owned" by, 106–110, 229
Felder, Charlie, 97
Felder, Chiquita Jane (Chiquita Felder Bearden; Chiquita Hulbert), 110, 115, 127, 150, 160, 173, 203, 214, 216
Felder, Chloe ("Aunt Chloe"), 87, 89, 96, 110, 223, 240
Felder, Christopher Columbus, 85, 91, 111, 116
Felder, Daniel, 79
Felder, DANIEL, 98, 99, 101
Felder, David. *See* Felder, Henry "David"
Felder, David F., 85, 91, 116
Felder, David Watson, 82–83
Felder, Deborah (Schorlemmer) "Debbie," ii
Felder, "Dik," 99
Felder, Dwight, 168
Felder, Eleanor (Brabham), 103
Felder, Elizabeth (Everette), 103
Felder, Emma Coffee Jenkins, 92–93, 98, 115, 125, 195, 200
Felder, Eva (Grob), 8
Felder, F., 116
Felder, Fannie, 177
Felder, F.J., 116
Felder, Frank, 53, 91
Felder, Frankie Ottowiess (Dr.), xvii, 3, 173, 188
　family tree, xxvi–xxvii
Felder, Frankie Roberta (Motley), xxiv, 1–2
Felder, Frederick, 22, 23
Felder, Frozene, 93, 126
Felder, F.W., 116
Felder, Gabriel, xviii, 53, 54–55, 79, 91, 100, 105, 106, 110, 116, 177
　slaves "owned" by, 104–105
Felder, George, 81
Felder, Gladys. *See* Washington, Gladys Lois Felder
Felder, G.W., 91
Felder, Hans Heinrich, xviii, 7, 11–12, 15–16, 31
　family tree of descendants, 33
Felder, Hansford D., 85, 91
Felder, H.D., 116
Felder, Henry "David," xvii, 35, 51, 79–82, 84–85, 96
Felder, Henry Jr., 22, 23, 28, 30
Felder, Henry Sr. (Capt.), xviii, 16, 18, 20–23, 24, 28, 52
Felder, HENRY (Rev.), 96, 97, 110, 173
Felder, Ida, 97, 98
Felder, Isaac, 79, 93, 169
Felder, ISAAC (Sgt.), iii, v, 68, 93, 95–97, 99, 100, 110, 115, 116, 126, 169
　Civil War service, 227–233
　family tree, 236–237
　Freedmen's Bureau record, 95–96
Felder, J. Ezekiel, 97
Felder, J. Hamilton (Capt.), 23
Felder, Jacob, 22, 23, 79
Felder, JACOB, 93, 100, 126
Felder, James W., 79, 80, 85, 91, 103, 109, 110, 116
Felder, Jane McMorris, 79–80, 85, 91, 96
Felder, Jesse G., 116
Felder, Jesse Thomas, 51, 79–81, 91, 211, 212
Felder, Jesse Young, 53
Felder, Johannes Heinrich (John Henry) "Henry." *See* Felder, Henry Sr. (Capt.)
Felder, John, xviii, 8, 22, 23, 79, 85, 91, 116, 166–167, 173, 181
Felder, JOHN, 98. 99, 100, 101
Felder, John L. (Dr.), 30
Felder, John Myers, 28, 30, 31, 52–53, 91, 106
Felder, Joseph (Joe; Josuf), xiv–xv, 37, 39–40, 48, 58–59, 75–76, 83–85, 92, 96–97, 99, 100, 110, 115, 116, 173, 174, 192, 206, 211, 212, 230
Felder, Josephine, 100
Felder, Julia, 99–100
Felder, Katie, 96–97, 110
Felder, Kessiah (Rawls), 79
Felder, Korrine Tyree (Jackson), 99, 115, 125, 173, 207, 216
Felder, Lenora, 110
Felder, Levi Darius, 85, 88–89, 173
　slaves "owned" by, 106

Felder, Louisa (Gates), 79–80, 212
Felder, Lucy, 99, 100
Felder, Maggie M., 100
Felder, Malinda (Barron), 103
Felder, Margaret, 96, 229–232
Felder, Maria (Carter), 79, 229
Felder, Martha, 100, 107, 111, 115
Felder, Mary (Dickerson), 79
Felder, Miers, 51–52, 53
Felder, Monroe, 232
Felder, Nancy (Bond), 168
Felder, Nancy (Winborn), 79
Felder, NATHANIEL, 98, 99, 100–101
Felder, Nathaniel F., 105–106
Felder, Otis Henry, 51, 79–81, 82, 91, 100, 101, 212
Felder, Peter, xviii, 22–24, 28, 31, 35, 51, 52, 79, 82, 84–85, 85, 93, 169, 212
Felder, Peter Jr., 79, 88
Felder, Rachel (Hartzog), 79
Felder, Rebecca (Bond), 103
Felder, Robert Henry, 88–89, 116
Felder, Rufus King, 51–52, 53
Felder, Rufus Knight, 79–81, 85, 91, 101, 212
Felder, Samuel, 22, 23, 28, 30, 52
Felder, Samuel Sr., xviii
Felder, SARAH, 110, 115, 116, 173, 228, 229
Felder, Sarah (Wigley), 103
Felder, Sarah Lea, 82
Felder, Simon, 91, 116
Felder, SIMON, 98, 99, 101
Felder, Sona Paul "Sonny" (S.P.) (Rev.), xiv, 38, 76–77, 81, 89, 92, 93, 96, 97–98, 99, 100, 110, 115, 116, 119, 125, 159, 160, 169, 173, 176, 180, 181, 192, 199, 200, 206–207, 211, 216, 229, 230, 240
  economic empowerment of, 215–216
  education of, 195
  family tree, 112–113
  and the Great Depression, 203
  involvement with education, 191–192, 195, 199, 203–204, 206–207
  involvement with religion, 169, 173, 176, 180–185
  as pastor, 182–185
  as Presiding Elder, 182–185
  run for Bishop, 184
Felder, Sophia Rouse (Parker), 99–99, 101, 212
Felder, Susannah (Lewis), 38–40, 59, 75–76, 92, 211, 212
Felder, Susie P., 93, 115, 199–200
Felder, Tyree Preston, xviii, 1, 99, 110, 115, 127, 150, 160, 173, 186–187, 203, 204, 208, 212, 214, 216, 217, 241
Felder, Ursula Zuber, 8, 11, 15–16
Felder, Vickie, 2
Felder, Wilda Jane (Ellis), 99, 100, 118–119, 120, 122, 125, 128, 173, 185, 200, 207, 216
Felder, William Riley (Dr.), 37, 79, 82–84, 85, 92, 96, 102–103
  slaves "owned" by, 104–105
Felder, Willie, 99–100
FELDER family
  birth and death chart of select family members, 259–267
  family tree, xxvi–xxvii
  significant happenings in April, 257–258
Felder family, xix, 89, 128
  and the Confederacy, 51–53
  in Greensburg, Louisiana, 82–84
  in Louisiana, 85, 89–90, 100
  in Mississippi, 84–85, 89–90, 115–116, 166–167
  as planters, 31, 79
  property holders in Louisiana, 250
  property holders in Mississippi (1831–1861), 249
  slaves "owned" by, 35, 79–81, 84–85, 89–91
  in South Carolina, 52
  in Texas, 52, 89–90, 100, 116
  transfer of slaves across states, 54
Felder-Richmond home, 109–110
Felder's Campground, 166, 167, 168, 169, 177, 181
Felder's Church, 167, 168, 169
Felderville A.M.E. Church, 23
Finding Your Roots (PBS documentary), xx
First African Baptist Church (New Orleans), 231
First Continental Congress, 19–21
First Louisiana Native Guards, 64
Fledger High School, 199
flooding, 201–202, 211
Florida Classical Institute, 191
Floridian Academy, 191
Flowery Mount Baptist Church, 107, 177
Floyd, George, 242
Foley, Clara Elizabeth, 100
Ford, Mary Jane, 128
Fort Hill Plantation, 40–41
Francis, John W., 216
Franklin, John Hope, xx
Freedman's Savings and Trust Company, 213
Freedmen's Bureau
  and education in Louisiana, 190–192
  in Louisiana, 210
  records, 189
Friars Point, Mississippi, 175–176, 183, 200, 224
Fuqua, James (Col.), 47

Gadsden, Christopher, 19–20
Gaines, Lloyd, 241
Gaines v. Canada, 241
Gannt, Harvey, 241
Gates, Henry Louis "Skip" (Dr.), xx
Gates, Louisa (Felder), 79, 101
Gates, Louisiana, 35, 79
Gates, William Jefferson, 80, 101, 212

Geissendanner, John (nephew), 12
Geissendanner, John (Rev.; uncle), 12
Gierson, Benjamin (Gen.), 48
Gillfield Baptist Church, 2, 173, 177
Gourdin, John, 114
Grand Gulf, Battle of, 142
Grant, Ulysses S. (Gen.), 67, 70, 139–140, 142, 149, 157, 209
Gray, Charles, 94
Greater Mount Zion A.M.E. Church, 98
Greater Turner A.M.E. Church (Greensburg, LA), 182
Green, Benjamin, 181, 204, 214
Greene, Catherine, 43
Greensburg, Louisiana, i, ii, xiii, xiv, xv, 37, 38, 39–40, 45, 77, 81–84, 85, 92–93, 96, 98, 102, 104–105, 117, 168, 182, 191, 195, 211, 229, 230
   Civil War in, 46–49, 57, 62, 73, 75
   Felder family in, 82–84
   fighting in and around, 48–49
Greensburg Academy, 191
Greenville, Mississippi, xxi, 99–100, 119, 122, 202, 215, 216, 225
Gregory, Frederick D., 242
Grutter v. Bollinger, 241
Guthrie, Woody, 18

Halbart, D.M., 138
Haley, Alex, xiii, xx
Haley, Nikki, 239
Hall, Gwendolyn Midlo, 131
Harris, Kamala, 242
Hartzog, George, 79
Harvard University, xv, 3
Hayes, Rutherford B., 157
Hearon, Tommy, 216
Heath, Robert, 7
Hemings, Sally, 21
Hermanville, Mississippi, 48, 154, 155, 224
Heyward, Nathaniel, 21

Heyward, Thomas Jr., 21
Hicks, Michell, xx
Holliday, Billy, 124
Holloway, Joseph (Dr.), 61
Homestead Act (1862), 52, 210–211
Hoover, Herbert, 202
Hopwood v. University of Texas, 241
Hospital Tax Fund, 192
Hudson, Berkley, 126
Hulbert, Adrian, 146–147
Hulbert, Albert Alexander ("Alex"), 158–160
   marriage certificate, 159–161
Hulbert, Albert (father), 137
Hulbert, Albert (son), 137
Hulbert, Alexander, 35, 127, 136, 137, 138, 139, 147, 154, 218, 241
Hulbert, Beatrice Ottowiess. *See* Felder, Bertha Beatrice Ottowiess
Hulbert, Benoni, 142, 147
Hulbert, Byron (B.M.), 136, 137–140, 142, 146, 152, 154–155
Hulbert, Caleb, 147, 148
Hulbert, Caroline, 137
Hulbert, Chiquita (Chiquita Felder Bearden; Chiquita Hulbert), 110, 115, 127, 150, 160,
Hulbert, Clarence Everett, 146, 147, 154
Hulbert, Clarence Jr., 154
Hulbert, Clifton, 146
Hulbert, Henry, 137
Hulbert, Herman C., 146, 154
Hulbert, Hiram, 142
Hulbert, Irene, 146
Hulbert, James Alexander, 127, 147, 159, 160–161, 208, 241
Hulbert, Jeremiah, 142
Hulbert, Julia ([E]Liza Sims), 152
Hulbert, Julian M., 139, 146, 152, 154, 155
   parole oath, 141
   prison roll card, 141

Hulbert, Marilyn E., 209
Hulbert, Martin Nathaniel (Hulbert/Hurlbert/Hurlburt), 136, 139–144, 146–150
   application for special pardon, 152–153
   children of, 154–155
   court order to sell property, 144
   deed of trust, 151
   financial difficulties, 151–153
   proof of family relations, 148
   property ownership of, 253–254
   slaves "owned" by, 140, 145–146, 152, 156
Hulbert, Nancy, 154
Hulbert, Permelia, 148
Hulbert, Peter, 137
Hulbert, Richard, 142
Hulbert, Robbie (Thompson), 127, 159, 160–161
Hulbert, Ronnie, 157–158
Hulbert, Sinai/Senai. *See* Rail, Sinai (Sanders) (Hulbert)
Hulbert, Ward Martin, 142, 154
Hulbert family, 132–133
   birth and death chart of select family members, 259–267
   in the Civil War, 139–144
   family tree, 162–163
   See also Hulbut family; Hurlburt family; Hurlbut family
The Hulbert Genealogy, 133
Hulbert plantation, 149, 150
Hulbert/Hurlburt, M.N. *See* Hulbert, Martin Nathaniel (Hulbert/Hurlbert/Hurlburt),
Hulbut family. *See* Hulbert family; Hurlburt family
Hume, Mary (Rail), 143
Hurger, Eddie, 101
Hurlbert, Martin. *See* Hulbert, Martin Nathaniel (Hulbert/

Hurlbert/Hurlburt),
Hurlburd, William, 133
Hurlburt, John C., 147
Hurlburt, Kathleen, 142, 147
Hurlburt, William, 133
Hurlburt family. *See also* Hulbert family
Hurlbut, Henry Higgins, 133
Hurlbut, Thomas, 132–133, 158
Hurlbut family. *See* Hurlburt family
Hurricane Plantation, 196–198, 214

"I Am Because They Were" (Gladys Washington), 245
indentured servants, 12, 14–15
Indianola (Union warship), 62
Indians. *See* Native Americans
Innis, James, 136
Innis family, 136–137

Jackson, E.P., 216
Jackson, Jesse (Rev.), 242
Jackson, Korrine Tyree Felder, 99, 115, 125, 173, 207, 216
Jackson, Mary, 242
Jackson, Mississippi, 109, 122, 142, 200–201, 204, 208, 224
Jackson State University, 204
Jakes, T.D. (Rev.), 176
James, Chappie (Gen.), 242
Jamestown, Virginia, 11, 118
Jayhawkers, 210
Jefferson, Thomas, 21–22
Jemison, Mae (Dr.), 242
Jenkins, Emma Coffee (Felder), 92–93, 98, 115, 125, 195, 200
Jenkins, John, 93
Jenkins, Mary, 93
Jenkins, Peter, 92–93
Jenkins, Ripley, 93
Jenkins, Sarah, 93
Jenkins, William, 93
Johnson, Brother (Rev.), 97
Johnson, Charles, 177–178, 183
Johnson, H.F. (Dr.), 167
Johnson, Jack, 242

Johnson, Katherine, 242
Johnson, Samuel, 22
Johnston, Joseph (Gen.), 140
Jordan, Winthrop, 26
Jubilee Performing Arts Center, 243

Kenner, Duncan, 70
King, Coretta Scott, 174
King, Martin Luther Jr. (Rev.), 2, 128
Kitrell College, 199
Ku Klux Klan, 2, 121, 126, 128, 193

Lampton College, 199
landgrants, 7, 12, 14–15, 23, 26, 79, 133, 140, 168, 212–213
Lawry, Sarah, 104
Lea family, xix, 89
Lee, Albert L. (Gen.), 48, 72–73, 171
Lee, G.A., 119
Lee, Robert E. (Gen.), 61, 70, 71, 209
Leonard, Elijah, 133
Lewis, John (Rep.), 241
Lewis, Sona Paul, 38, 76–77, 92. *See also* Felder, Sona Paul
Lewis, Susannah, (Felder) 38–40, 59, 75–76, 92, 211
Liberty, Battle of, 171
Liberty, Mississippi, 82, 85, 102, 105, 106–107, 109, 223
Liberty Baptist Church, 168, 170
Lincoln, Abraham, 37, 41, 47, 52, 57–58, 67, 71, 169, 209, 210, 244
literacy, decline in (1865–1930), 205
Little, Thomas, 26
Little Rock Nine, 241
Livingston Parish, iii, 35, 51, 55, 77–82, 85, 90, 93, 96, 98, 100, 101, 192–193, 211, 212, 221
Logtown, Mississippi, 94–99, 116,

154, 181, 206, 224, 230
Lone Soul Jah, 173
Long, Thomas (Pvt.), 67
Louisiana, 35–40
    battle at Milliken's Bend, 66–67, 71
    black illiteracy in, 205
    Camp Moore, 48, 49–50
    in the Civil War, 45–50
    Creole culture in, 134–135, 138
    East Baton Rouge Parish, 35, 37, 221
    farms/plantations, 251
    Felder family in, 79–80, 85, 89–90, 100
    Felder property holders in (1854–1866), 250
    First Louisiana Native Guards, 64
    freed slaves in, 58–59
    Greensburg, 46–49
    Greensburg courthouse, 39
    Livingston Parish, iii, 35, 51, 55, 77–82, 85, 90, 93, 96, 98, 100, 101, 192–193, 211, 212, 221
    Magnolia, 87–89
    Orleans Parish, 35, 37, 58, 221
    OURstory in, 220–221
    Pointe Coupeé Parish, 131, 133–135, 136, 138
    Port Hudson campaign, 62–65, 71
    Reconstruction in, 189–195
    schooling in, 189–195
    schools for Freedmen (1867), 194
    secession of, 41–42
    slaves and slavery in, 42–43, 45, 131–132
    St. Bernard Parish, 35, 37, 58, 221
    St. Helena Parish, xiv, 35, 37, 40, 45, 47–49, 57, 58, 68, 75–77, 79–81, 93, 98, 102, 104, 192, 193, 195,

210, 221, 229
Third Louisiana Native
Guards, 64
U.S. Census (1860), 78
Lusher, Robert M., 189, 194
Lyman, Phineas, 133
Lyman, Thaddeus, 133
Lynch, Thomas, 19–20, 21
lynchings, 121–123
   in Mississippi, 126–127

Magnolia, Mississippi, 85, 87–89,
   93, 107, 109, 166, 168–169,
   177, 223, 239
Magnolia Baptist Church, 168,
   170
Magnolia Methodist Church, 169
Malone, Ann P., 39
Mandela, Nelson, 174
March on Washington (1963), 124,
   128
Markle, Meghan, 239
Mary Holmes Seminary, 199–200
Masonic Order, 183
Massachusetts, 19
Maxson, Etienne (father), 94–95
Maxson, Etienne W. (son), 94
Mays, Willie, 242
McCleery, James, 194
McDonald, Bonus/Lewis (Clark),
   114
McDowell, Thomas, 105
McGinnis, George F. (Gen.), 140
McLauren, George, 241
McLauren v. Oklahoma State Regents,
   241
McMurchy, J.B., 155
McNair, Ronald (Dr.), 242
Meeropol, Abel, 124
Methodist church, 166, 179–180
Middleton, Arthur, 21
Middleton, Edward, 26
Middleton, Henry, 19–20
Middleton, William, 26
Migliazzo, Arlin, 8
Milam, J.W., 125
Milliken's Bend, Battle of, 66–67,

71, 228
Milton, Marquett, 227
Mississippi
   Bayou Pierre, 133, 223
   Biloxi, 154, 225
   changes in, 239–240
   Claiborne County, 136, 142,
      143, 146, 149–151, 156
   Cleveland, 122, 123, 159, 160,
      201, 202–203, 216, 225
   Columbus, 118, 119, 122,
      125–127, 223
   during Reconstruction,
      119–122, 124
   farms/plantations, 251
   Felder family in, 84–85, 89–90,
      115–116, 166–167
   Felder property holders in
      (1831–1861), 249
   Friars Point, 175–176, 183,
      200, 224
   Greenville, xxi, 99–100, 119,
      122, 202, 215, 216, 225
   Hermanville, 48, 154, 155, 224
   Jackson, 109, 122, 142,
      200–201, 204, 208, 224
   Liberty, 82, 85, 102, 105,
      106–107, 109, 223
   Logtown, 94–99, 116, 154,
      181, 206, 224, 230
   lynchings in, 121–123,
      126–127
   Magnolia, 85, 87–89, 93, 107,
      109, 166, 168–169, 177,
      223, 239
   Natchez, 118, 121, 124, 133,
      149, 155, 156–157, 166,
      223
   Osyka, 73, 88, 109, 111, 224
   OURstory in, 222–225
   Pearlington, 95, 98, 99, 101,
      116, 154, 181, 211, 212,
      224
   Possum Walk, 94–98, 116,
      206, 224
   Reconstruction in, 156
   schooling on a plantation,

195–198
   secession of, 41–42
   Shaw, 122, 203, 207, 215, 224
   Summit, 85–86, 89, 169, 173,
      223
   Vicksburg, 56–57, 68, 71, 109,
      139, 140–142, 149, 197,
      200, 224
   Waveland, 154, 225
   West Point, 200, 225
   Whitestown, 169, 224
   See also Mound Bayou,
      Mississippi; Port Gibson,
      Mississippi
Mississippi Baptist Association,
   168, 170, 171
Mississippi Baptist Conference,
   170, 171
Monday, Jane, 101
Montgomery, Benjamin, 195–198,
   213
Montgomery, Isaiah T., 62, 181,
   196–197, 200, 209, 213
Montgomery family, 198
Morris Brown College, 199
Motley, Frank Alphonso, 2
Motley, Frankie Roberta (Felder),
   xxiv, 1–2
Motley, Ida Huffman, 98
Mound Bayou, Mississippi, x,
   1, 93, 99–100, 119, 173,
   181–183, 185–187, 200–201,
   203, 204, 206, 207, 213–217,
   225
   Bethel A.M.E. Church
      (Mound Bayou), 181,
      185–186
Mount Flowery Baptist Church
   (Magnolia), 107, 177
Muddy Springs Church, 169
Muhammad Ali, 242
Multum in Parvo, i

NAACP (National Association for
   the Advancement of Colored
   People), 127, 158
Natchez, Mississippi, 118, 121,

124, 133, 149, 155, 156–157, 166, 223
Native Americans, 10, 12, 16–18
Negro Yearbook and Directory of Memphis and Shelby County, 138
Newmans, Sam, 109, 111
Newsome, Bree, 2

Oakland College, 150
Obama, Barack, 242
Oberlin University, 198
Old Baptist Church (New Orleans), 230
O'Neal, Abner, 109
O'Neal, Ann (Felder), xix, 109, 111, 212
O'Neal family, xix, 89
O'Neil, Abner, 107
O'Neil, Adam, 107
O'Neil, Dinah, 107
Orleans Parish, 35, 37, 58, 221
Osyka, Mississippi, 73, 88, 109, 111, 224

Paul Quinn College, 199
Paxton, W.E., 171
Payne College (Alabama), 199
Payne Institute (Georgia), 199
Payne Theological Seminary (Ohio), 199
Pearlington, Mississippi, 95, 98, 99, 101, 116, 154, 181, 211, 212, 224
Pemberton, John, 140
Percy, Hugh, 8, 11, 15
Percy, William Alexander, xxi
Petersburg, Virginia, xiv, 1, 2, 70, 71, 98, 128, 160, 173, 177, 179, 240
Peyton, Phillip, 20
Pickens, Francis W., 41
Pilgrim Rest Baptist Church, 173
Pilman, Oscar, 231
Pinchback, P.B.S., 119, 138
Pinckney, Charles, 21
Pointe Coupeé Parish, 35, 72, 136, 138, 221

Port Gibson, Mississippi, 223
  Battle of, 140
  Civil War in, 140, 142, 148–149
  Hulbert family in, 136, 146, 147–149, 150, 152, 154–158, 223
  library, xiii–xiv, xv
  mural in town square, 157
  racial violence in, 121, 122, 127–128, 158
Port Hudson, Battle of, 61–66, 71, 228
Porter, David (ADM), 62
Possum Walk, Mississippi, 94–98, 116, 206, 224
Potter's House, 176
Powell, Colin (Gen.), 242
Powell, Grady (Rev.), 173
Power, Ellen, 62
Prewitt, Ansel H., 87, 87–89, 90, 109, 169
Prewitt, Elisha, 87
Prewitt, Julia, 87
Prewitt, Lucinda (Barron), 87, 88
Prewitt, Naomi Eveline "Eva" (Vaughn), 88
Prewitt family, 85, 89
Prewitt Plantation, 86–87
Pritchard, Jack, 28
Proclamation of 1763, 18
Progress of the Races, ii
property ownership
  the legacy, 215–218
  the pattern, 209–215
Prosser, Gabriel, 61–62
Pulliam, Andrew, 105
Purry, Jean Pierre, 8–12, 15–16, 24, 26

Quarles, Benjamin, xx
Quartering Act, 19
Quebec Act, 19
Quinn, Peter A., 109
Quinn family, 85

Raborn family, xix

Rail, Calista/Celesta, 144, 146, 152
Rail, Christina Marilla, 143, 144, 146, 152
Rail, John, 143–144, 146, 149
  will of, 143
Rail, Sinai (Sanders) (Hulbert), 142–144, 146, 149, 152, 154–155
Rawls, Jabus, 79
Reconstruction
  five military districts, 190
  in Louisiana, 189–195
  in Mississippi, 156–157
Red Bluff Baptist Church, 92, 102, 168
Reese, J. (Rev.), 76
religion
  and education, 198–206
  the legacy, 182–187
  the pattern, 166–182
  Sunday school, 171–172
Reshaping of the Plantation Society, 151
Revels, Hiram R., 119–120, 150
Revels, Ida, 216
Revels, John, 216
Revolutionary War. *See* American Revolution
Richards, Amable Peltier, 47, 62, 71
Richardson, Alice, 98, 101
Richardson, Edna, 98
Richardson, Ophelia, 98
Richmond, Virginia, 2, 3, 51, 61, 70, 71, 101, 109, 110, 178
Robinson, Jackie, 242
Robinson, Katie, 216
Roosevelt, Theodore, 185–186, 214
Roots: The Saga of an American Family (Haley), xiii, xx
Rosenwald, Julius, 241
Rosenwald Schools, 241
Ross, Alma, 119
Ross, Lee Roy/Leroy, 119
Rouse, Eddie W., 98–99, 99

Rouse, Sophia. *See* Felder, Sophia Rouse (Parker)
Ruby, George, 192
Rutledge, Edward, 19–20
Rutledge, John, 19–20, 21

Salem Baptist Church, 168, 170
Salley, Alexander, 12
Sam, David, 206
Sams, Lillian, 97
Sams, Robert Neville (Rev.), 97–98
Sandel, Henry, 169, 173
Sandel, John Wesley, 169
Sandel, Mary, 89
Sandel family, xix, 85, 89
Sanders, Robert, 152, 155
Scott, Dred, 37, 120
Second Continental Congress, 21
Second Provincial Congress, 20–21
Seddon, James, 69, 70
Sells, George, 77, 78
Sequestration Fund, 192
serfs, 15
Shady Grove Baptist Church, 92
Shaffer, Bessie (Hulbert), 127, 159
Shaw, Mississippi, 122, 203, 207, 215, 224
Shaw College (Rust College), 127
Sheffield, Martha (Hulbert), 143
Sheffield, Richard, 143
Shorter College, 199
Simmons, Chiquita Ottowiess, 115
slaveholders
    from Barbados, 24–28
    Felder family, 30–31, 32, 79–81, 84–85, 102–111, 116
    in Louisiana, 78
    richest slaveholding families (1860), 44
    by state (1860 census), 30
    on the Supreme Court, 37
    treatment of slaves by, 28–30
slaves
    in the 1860 slave census, 32
    arming to fight in the war, 56–57
    auctioning of, 39–40
    Civil War participation, 56–60, 62–73
    in the Confederate army, 69–73
    and the Continental Association, 20
    countries of origin, 26, 27
    as "freehold property," 28
    freeing of. *See* Emancipation Proclamation
    "ideal" characteristics, 27
    in Louisiana, 42–43, 45, 131–132
    "owned" by Felder family, xix, 5, 23–24, 35, 79–81, 89–91, 102–111
    "owned" by Hulbert/Hurlbert family, 140, 142–146, 152, 156
    "owned" by signers of the Constitution, 21
    rebellions and insurrections, 61–62, 135
    runaway, 12, 106, 156
    slave codes (South Carolina), 26–29
    in South Carolina, 9–11, 21, 24–32
    in St. Helena parish, 47–48
    by state (1860 census), 30
    treatment of, 11, 28–32, 37–38, 39, 40, 42, 53–54, 71, 72, 85, 89
    value of, 103–104
slaves (referenced by name)
    Adaline, 106
    Adam, 107
    Adam O'Neil, 107
    Alia/Alice, 96
    Anderson, 103
    Andre Cailloux (Capt.), 64–65
    Barbara, 108
    Ben (bequeathed by Dr. Charles Felder), 103
    Ben (hired out by Gabriel Felder), 105
    Benjamin Montgomery, 195–198, 213
    Billy, 106
    Blind Tom, 72
    Bob, 106
    Bonus McDonald, 114
    Booker T. Washington, 117, 175, 178, 188, 241
    Cassy Ellis, 118
    Celia, 107
    Charlie, 107
    Chloe, 87, 89, 96, 110, 223, 240
    David Cope, 114
    Delia, 107
    Denmark Vesey, 28–29, 61
    Dick, 40
    Dinah, 107
    Doctor, 40
    Dora Ellis, 118, 216
    Dred Scott, 37, 120
    Easter, 103
    Edmund, 106
    Elizabeth, 106
    Emma Coffee, 92–93, 98, 115, 125, 195, 200
    Farry, 40
    Flora, 106
    Frances, 40
    Frank, 107
    Fry, 23
    Gabriel Prosser, 61–62
    George, 107
    Guster, 103
    Hannah, 103
    Harriett, (sent to Choctaw Nation by Nathaniel Felder) 105
    Harriett (sister of James Washington), 107
    Henry, 96
    Ida, 230
    Isaac. *See* Felder, ISAAC (Sgt.)
    Isaac (in Liberty, Mississippi), 106
    Isaiah T. Montgomery, 62, 181,

196–197, 200, 209, 213
Jack, 103
Jacob, 103
James, 111
James W. Washington (Rev.), 106, 107–110, 111, 115, 173, 177
Jane Ellis, 118–119, 128, 200
John, 103
Joseph, 106
Joseph Ellis, 118, 119
Joseph Felder. *See* Felder, Joseph (Joe; Josuf)
Judy, 40
Katie, 96
Keziah, 118–119, 128
Kezziah, 118–119
Little Jim, 106
Letetia Ellis, 118
Lewis Ellis, 118
Lucretia, 106
Lydia, 106
Manny, 83
Margaret, 96
Maria (sold by Peter Felder), 28
Maria/Mariah (daughter of Easter), 104
Mariah, 103
Martha, 107
Mary (sister of Emma Coffee Jenkins), 93
Mary (bequeathed by Rev. Charles Felder), 103
Mary (sent to the Choctaw Nation by Nathaniel Felder), 105
Mary (sister of James Washington), 107
Matilda, 107
Matilda Ellis, 118, 119
Milly/Mildred, 92
Molley, 40
Mose, 106
Mundy, 156
Nancy, 40
Nat Turner, 61

Peter, 105
Peter Jenkins, 92–93
Phill, 106
Prince, 106
Priscilla, 228
Rachael, 106
Rhody, 40
Ripley, 93
Rogena, 106
Rose, 103
Russell, 103
Sally Hemings, 21
Sam (on plantation of Catherine Greene), 43
Sam (hired out by Gabriel Felder), 105
Sam (bought/sold by Gabriel Felder), 106
Sarah (sister of Emma Coffee Jenkins), 93
Sarah (sister of James Washington), 107
Sonny, 96
Sona Lewis. *See* Felder, Sona Paul "Sonny" (S.P.) (Rev.)
Sophy, 106
Stacia, 103
Stephen Ellis, 119
Susannah (Felder) Lewis, 38–40, 59, 75–76, 92, 211
Tamarind, 106
Thomas Long (Pvt.), 67
Tom, 106
Vilet, 40
Wilfred, 107
William, 103
William Raiborn Washington, 107
Willie, 107
Wilson Chinn, 29
Slave Insurrections in the United States, An Overview, 61
Smith, D.H., 122
Smith, Joseph, 22
Smith, Phebe (Hurlbut), 147
South Carolina
  arrival of slaves in, 26–27

borders of, 13–14
classes of nobility, 14–15
Clemson University, i, vii, viii, x, 40, 53, 241
evolution of slave culture in, 24–26
Felder family in, 52
government of, 13–16
impact of the slave code, 27–28
indigenous people in, 16–18
map, 13
population (Blacks vs. Whites), 25
secession of, 40–42
settlement of, 7–12
Southern by the Grace of God, 4
Southern Christian Leadership Conference (SCLC), 128
Southern Homestead Act (1866), 213
Spears, Elaine G., 117
Spiller, Bill, 242
St. Bernard Parish, 35, 37, 58, 221
St. Helena Parish, xiv, 35, 37, 40, 45, 47–49, 57, 58, 68, 75–77, 79–81, 93, 98, 102, 104, 192, 193, 195, 210, 221, 229
St. Helena Rifles, 46–47, 48, 62, 71, 92
St. Paul Methodist Episcopal Church, 97
St. Paul's Episcopal Church, 173
Stamp Act, 19
Stanley, Charles (Rev.), 182
Stoddard, E.S., 194–195
"Strange Fruit," 124
Streets, David, 115
Suffolk, Virginia, 2, 13, 118
Sugar Act, 18–19
Sullivan's Island, 26
Summit, Mississippi, 85–86, 89, 169, 173, 223
Sweatt, Heman, 241
Sweatt v. Painter, 241

Tannehill, George, 143

Taylor, J. B., 47
Taylor, Joe Gray, 63
Texas, Felder family in, 52, 89–90, 100, 116
Thigpen, S.G., 187
Third Louisiana Native Guards, 64
Thomas, Lorenzo (Gen.), 66
Thompson, Autry, 159
Thompson, Autry Jr., 159
Thurmond, Strom, 2
Till, Emmett, 125, 215
Till, Mamie, 125, 215
T.O.C.K. (The Opportunity Center Kindergarten), 207, 214, 216
Topisaw Campground. *See* Felder's Campground
Tougaloo College, 160
Townshend Act, 19
Truman, Harry, 242
Turner, Mary, 124
Turner, Nat, 61
Turner Chapel A.M.E. Church, 92, 98
Turner Normal College, 199
Tuskegee Institute (Tuskegee University), 158, 175, 187, 208, 241

United States Colored Troops, iii, 68, 227, 228
United States Constitution, 21–22, 37, 169
 amendments to, iii, 120, 171
U.S. Census (1880), 5
U.S. Slave Census (1850), 5

Valley, Winfield, 99
Vaughan, Dorothy, 242
Vaughn, David, 88
Vaughn, Elisha, 85–86
Vaughn, Helen, 89
Vaughn, Josiah, 79, 86, 88
Vaughn family, xix, 86–87, 89
Vaughn House, 86, 239, 240
Vaughn/Vaughan, Wilma, 89

Vesey, Denmark, 28–29, 61
Vicksburg, Battle of, 69
Vicksburg, Mississippi, 56–57, 68, 71, 109, 139, 140–142, 149, 197, 200, 224
Virginia
 Chesterfield, 71
 City Point, 50
 City Point National Cemetery, 260, 262
 Jamestown, 11, 118
 Petersburg, xiv, 1, 2, 70, 71, 98, 128, 160, 173, 177, 179, 240
 Richmond, 2, 3, 51, 61, 70, 71, 101, 109, 110, 178
 Suffolk, 2, 13, 118
 Wakefield, 118
 Waverly, 118
Virginia Commonwealth University (VCU), xvi, 3, 208, 241
Virginia State College, 160

Wakefield, Virginia, 118
Walker, Wyatt Tee (Rev.), 2, 128
Walters, John Esq., 12
Ward, Joshua J., 30
Washington, Ayse (Dr.), 241
Washington, Booker T., 117, 175, 178, 188, 241
Washington, George, 21
Washington, Gladys Lois Felder, xviii, 98, 188, 218
 "I Am Because They Were," 245
Washington, James W. (Rev.), 106, 107–110, 111, 115, 173, 177
Washington, Lloyd, 218
Washington, N'Gai Canute Tyree, 115, 173
Washington, William Raiborn, 107
Washington Chapel A.M.E. Church (Tuskegee), 175
Waveland, Mississippi, 154, 225
Waverly, Virginia, 118

Wayne, Michael, 151
Wells, Ida B., 127, 128
West Point, Mississippi, 200, 225
Weston, Henry, 96
Whilkins, Hanier, 138
White Over Black (Jordan), 26
Whitestown, Mississippi, 169, 224
Whitfield, Clara Willie (Ross), 119
Whitfield, Cleo Louise, 119
Whitfield, Emmett Valley (Vallei Emmit), 110, 119
Whitfield, Maymie Lou, 119
Whitfield, Vantee Genia, 119
Whitney, Eli, 43
Whitworth College, 167
Wigley, Sarah (Felder), 103
Wilberforce College, 199
Wilkens (Wilkins), Caroline (Hulbert), 136, 137
Wilkins, Albert Alex, 137
Wilkins, Eliska, 137
Wilkins, Frederick, 137
Wilkins, J. de, 138–139
Wilkins, John D., 138–139
William, James, 160
Williams, James A., 46
Williams, M.C., 47
Wilson, T.A. (J.A.), 182, 195
Winborn, David, 79
Windsor House, 148–149
Winston, Lottie, 100
Winston, Mike, 100
Womack, Henry, 78
Wood, Peter, 26
Woodley, (Rev.), 183
Woods, Tiger, 242
World Changers Church, 176
Wright, Catherine, 82
Wright, Isaac H., 82
Wright, Richard, 124
Wurtzer, Henry, 16

Yanney, Allen, 114
Yeamans, John, 26
Young, Charles B., 89

Zion Hill Baptist Church, 168

www.ingramcontent.com/pod-product-compliance
Lightning Source LLC
Chambersburg PA
CBHW081506080526
44589CB00017B/2660